AMBROISE

THE CRUSADE OF
RICHARD LION-HEART

NUMBER XXXIV OF THE

RECORDS OF CIVILIZATION

SOURCES AND STUDIES

AUSTIN P. EVANS, *Editor*

THE SO-CALLED CRUSADER FOUNTAIN
IN JERUSALEM

THE CRUSADE OF
RICHARD LION-HEART

By AMBROISE

TRANSLATED FROM THE OLD FRENCH BY
MERTON JEROME HUBERT
PROFESSOR OF ROMANCE LANGUAGES
THE UNIVERSITY OF CINCINNATI

WITH NOTES AND DOCUMENTATION BY
JOHN L. LA MONTE
HENRY C. LEA ASSOCIATE PROFESSOR OF HISTORY
THE UNIVERSITY OF PENNSYLVANIA

OCTAGON BOOKS

A DIVISION OF FARRAR, STRAUS AND GIROUX

New York   1976

Reprinted 1976
by special arrangement with Columbia University Press

OCTAGON BOOKS
A DIVISION OF FARRAR, STRAUS & GIROUX, INC.
19 Union Square West
New York, N.Y. 10003

Library of Congress Cataloging in Publication Data

Ambroise, fl. ca. 1196.
   The crusade of Richard Lion-Heart.

   (Records of civilization—sources and studies; no. 34.)
   "Based on the text of the Estoire [de la guerre sainte] edited by
Gaston Paris in the Collections des documents inédits sur l'his-
toire de France in 1897."—Pref.

   Reprint of the ed. published by Columbia University Press, New
York.

   Bibliography: p.
   Includes index.
   1. Crusades—Third, 1189-1192. 2. Great Britain—History—
Richard I, 1189-1199. I. Title. II. Series.

D163.A3A52 1976   940.1'8   75-46598
ISBN 0-374-94009-6

Manufactured by Braun-Brumfield, Inc.
Ann Arbor, Michigan
Printed in the United States of America

DEDICATED TO OUR WIVES

DOROTHY SMITH HUBERT

KATHERINE RICHARDSON LA MONTE

who, like medieval chatelaines, have waited
and hoped the while their husbands preoccupied
themselves with the business of the crusade
and who find in the completion of the affair
cause for rejoicing

RECORDS OF CIVILIZATION

SOURCES AND STUDIES

EDITED UNDER THE AUSPICES OF THE
DEPARTMENT OF HISTORY, COLUMBIA UNIVERSITY

PREFACE

When this translation of Ambroise was begun there was no English translation of his work; indeed the first draft of the whole work had been completed before the publication of Professor E. N. Stone's prose translation of the poem. The existence of the prose translation removes some of the motive which urged us to this work, but we feel that the metrical version offers so much more than any prose can do that we do not apologize for bringing into the world another volume of Ambroise. The story of Richard's crusade is a good tale well told, and much of the charm of the original lies in the verse in which it was composed. This we have endeavored to retain. Ambroise was not one of the world's great poets, and there are times when his verse drags and descends into the worst doggerel. This also we have tried to capture, and the reader will find, if he takes the time to compare our text with the original, that the style and rhyme of our translation reflect in detail the characteristics of the Old French poem. Our purpose throughout has been to render as faithfully as possible the words, rhymes, and meanings of the author. We have at no time attempted to improve his style, even when such improvement might perhaps have made him more palatable to the reader. We have not attempted to fill in the occasional lacunae in the French text, except in a few rare cases where the context or the parallel Latin account made obvious the contents of the missing lines. Passages thus supplied are enclosed in brackets. The one liberty which we have allowed ourselves (and from which we derived no inconsiderable pleasure at times) is the series of paragraph heads which we interpolated into the text to break the steady and seemingly unending flow of couplets. The notes aim to explain Ambroise's references, and, on occasion, to discount somewhat his obvious prejudices.

This translation is based on the text of the *Estoire* edited by Gaston Paris in the *Collection des documents inédits sur l'histoire de France* in 1897. Much use has also been made of the notes with which Paris accompanied his text, although in some places we have come to quite different conclusions from those of the eminent French savant. The Latin version of the work, the *Itinerarium*, and the notes of Bishop William Stubbs to his edition of that work have also been utilized extensively.

In rendering thanks for assistance given us during the preparation of our volume, acknowledgment must first be given to the generosity of the Committee of the Charles Phelps Taft Memorial Fund for financial assistance, which enabled, in part, the publication of the volume. To the authorities of the University of Cincinnati thanks are given for the sabbatical leave which enabled us to do part of the work in the then congenial atmosphere of Paris. For further assistance in the aforesaid matter of leave the authors thank respectively the Charles Phelps Taft and the John Simon Guggenheim Memorial funds. Professor Austin P. Evans has been most considerate of our problems and has preserved his patience and his unfailing sense of humor throughout the intricacies of our versification, our apparent determination never to spell the same name twice the same way, and our insistence upon genealogical details in the notes; for his suggestions, his coöperation, and above all his infinite patience we express our utmost gratitude. Professor Sidney Painter, of the Johns Hopkins University, read the notes and gave us material aid in identifying many of the persons mentioned; his suggestions were most helpful and contributed much to our notes. We are indebted to Dr. Hilda Buttenwieser and Dr. Laurence Chenoweth, of the University of Cincinnati, for valuable advice in matters of philology and medicine. The maps are based on those published in T. E. Lawrence, *Crusaders' Castles*, which have been used with the kind permission of Harry Pirie-Gordon and A. W. Lawrence. Permission to copy the illustrations was generously granted by the National Geographic Society, the Harvard University Press, G. P. Putnam's Sons, and the Librairie Orientaliste Paul Geuthner.

Without the able and cheerful assistance of Miss Genevieve Elbaum, who typed and retyped the manuscript, assisted in research and as amanuensis, this book could hardly have been completed. If there is any uniformity in the spelling of proper names it is primarily due to her efforts, as the authors did their best to keep them as confused as possible. Mr. Peter Topping, Mr. Alfred Klein, and Mrs. Margaret Stahl also helped in reading and preparing portions of the manuscript for publication. Finally, to our wives, who have been served Ambroise in their homes, at cafés, at parties, and long into the night over a period of years, and to whom the translation is dedicated, we express our appreciation and sympathy.

We must admit that we have thoroughly enjoyed the preparation of this translation. It is our hope that those who may read the work will derive therefrom some modicum of the pleasure that we have had in writing it.

MERTON JEROME HUBERT
JOHN L. LA MONTE

May 15, 1941

CONTENTS

INTRODUCTION   3

THE CRUSADE OF RICHARD LION-HEART   31

APPENDICES   451

BIBLIOGRAPHY   457

INDEX   463

ILLUSTRATIONS AND MAPS

THE SO-CALLED CRUSADER FOUNTAIN IN
JERUSALEM   *Frontispiece*
By permission of Maynard Owen Williams

MAP TO ILLUSTRATE RICHARD'S ROUTE
FROM MARSEILLES TO ACRE   76

CASTLE AND HARBOR OF CERINES   104
From Philip de Novare, *The Wars of Frederick II against the Ibelins in
Syria and Cyprus*, translated by John L. LaMonte, with verse translation
of the poems by Merton Jerome Hubert, New York, Columbia University
Press, 1936, p. 150

FAMAGUSTA IN 1933   104
By permission of the National Geographic Society

MEDIEVAL ACRE, AFTER THE PLAN OF
MARINO SANUDO   195

ACRE IN 1686   202
From Camille Enlart, *Les Monuments des croisés dans le royaume de
Jérusalem*, Paris, 1926, Atlas, Vol. I, Plate 51

ACRE IN 1933   202
By permission of the National Geographic Society

REGION OF RICHARD'S CAMPAIGNS IN PALESTINE 237
Adapted from Pirie-Gordon's map in T. E. Lawrence, *Crusaders' Castles*

The headpieces of the chapters are from medieval manuscripts and windows. The figures on pages 74, 119, 158, 193, 280, and 326 are from
P. Paris, *Guillaume de Tyr* (Paris, Firmin Didot, 1880); pages 398 and
428, from Joinville, *Vie de St. Louis* (Paris, Firmin Didot, 1874); the
seal of Richard on page 31 and the cuts on the title page and on page 365
are republished from T. A. Archer, *Crusade of Richard I* (New York and
London, 1889), by permission of G. P. Putnam's Sons; the cut from the
window of St. Denis on page 235 is republished from C. W. David,
Robert Curthose (Cambridge, Mass., 1920), by permission of the Harvard
University Press.

INTRODUCTION

INTRODUCTION

THE POEM here presented has unusual value both for the historian
and for the student of medieval literature. Of all the accounts of the
Crusade of Richard written down by those who lived through it, the
Estoire de la guerre sainte of Ambroise and the *Itinerarium regis
Ricardi* provide the most complete and circumstantial narratives that
we now possess. They furnish, indeed, the major part of our factual
knowledge of that ill-fated expedition. The evidence of an eyewitness
is always precious, doubly so in the case of medieval events, for which
only meager records were kept or have survived. On the face of it, the
Estoire de la guerre sainte is the work of such an eyewitness, and many
scholars have taken it at its face value. As will be set forth later in this
Introduction, the present editors consider it to be a second-hand version, based directly on the account of one who had seen the events he
described. We have reason to believe, however, that the existing text
follows the original with so large a degree of exactitude and was written at so short an interval after the end of the crusade as to possess
an evidential value only slightly inferior to that of a first-hand account.

IMPORTANCE OF THE POEM

As a piece of literary craftsmanship, the poem stands almost unique,
occupying a transitional position between the fiction of the heroic
chansons de geste and the prose narratives of men such as Villehardouin
and Joinville. Whatever we may think of the theories of the origin of
the epic set forth by the late Joseph Bédier and those who have followed in his footsteps, we may fairly assume that the medieval man
accepted as fact the tales of Charlemagne and William of Orange and
Doon of Mayence which furnish the matter for the *chansons de geste*.
The poets usually took pains to cite their authorities and to surround
their fictions with something like an air of verisimilitude. Nevertheless, they told of events that were presumed to have occurred three or
four hundred years before they were born: they were, in substance,
ancient history.

In the *Estoire*, on the other hand, we have a writer who told, in metrical form, a tale of happenings that were fresh in the minds of the living men who heard or read his words. For those who had no Latin, here was a great chapter of contemporary history. Here was a war correspondent, who told in the vernacular the very latest episodes in the struggle to throttle Islam and keep western Europe safe for Christianity. He wrote in verse, because he was a jongleur, trained in the art of writing, and verse was the natural and traditional way of telling a story meant to be read aloud. He told more than the march of armies, the succession of rulers, and the quarrels of dynasties. He told something of how ordinary men lived and felt, ate, drank, and slept. After him came Villehardouin and Joinville, aristocrats and soldiers, who told their stories in prose because they were men of action unskilled in writing poetry. With them history in the vulgar tongue came into being. Whereas before there had existed, on the one hand, the Latin chronicle giving the bare bones of political and military events, and on the other the *chanson de geste*, with its mass of tradition, legend, propaganda, and fancy, we now have the beginnings of historiography in the modern sense of the term.

SOURCE OF THE POEM AND ITS RELATION TO THE *Itinerarium Ricardi*

The *Estoire de la guerre sainte* was first brought to light when Gaston Paris published his edition of the text, with elaborate critical material, in 1897. For centuries it had lain unnoticed or unrecognized in the Vatican Library,[1] while historians of the crusades accepted as authoritative the Latin prose chronicle, the *Itinerarium regis Ricardi,* which gives a parallel, but not quite identical, account of the events that both record. After a study of the two works Gaston Paris presented in his Introduction certain conclusions concerning the author of the poem and the originality of his work, which have been partially confirmed and partially refuted by later research.

The author of the poem names himself Ambroise at various points in his narrative.[2] Gaston Paris concludes that this Ambroise was present in person at most of the events of the third crusade which he relates

---

[1] For an account of early references to the MS see Gaston Paris's Introduction, pp. ii–vi.

[2] Lines 728, 2401, 3226, 3734, 4560, *et al.*

and that his account must be accepted as that of an eyewitness except for that portion of the story which deals with the siege of Acre prior to the arrival of Richard of England and Philip of France upon the scene. The poet specifically disclaims any personal knowledge of this particular sequence of events, which he nevertheless relates on the authority of another in a long interpolated section of the poem (lines 2387–4568). This section contains the material of Book I of the *Itinerarium*.[3]

The great French scholar, basing his argument on various bits of internal evidence which further investigation has corrected in detail, but not in substance, deduced the following facts: Ambroise was neither knight, man-at-arms, nor priest. Well-read in the French poetry of his day, to which he refers at many points,[4] he knew little or nothing of Latin literature. He was in all probability a jongleur or professional poet. He was of Norman origin, and the frequency of his allusions to otherwise unknown personages from the region surrounding Evreux justifies the assumption that he was himself a native of that region.[5] The Vatican manuscript, the only one known to have been preserved, appears to have been written in England about the end of the thirteenth century,[6] and while its definitely Anglo-Norman characteristics do not prove conclusively that the original was composed in that tongue, no evidence has been adduced to the contrary.

Thus far Gaston Paris's reasoning may be accepted with confidence.

[3] The excursus on the earlier history of Jerusalem and the earlier stages of the siege of Acre were derived according to Ambroise's own statement from some earlier existent book. What this was we cannot say. The first book of the *Itinerarium* was derived from the Latin Continuator of William of Tyre if we can credit the very convincing argument of Marianne Salloch (*Die lateinische Fortsetzung Wilhelms von Tyrus*, diss. Greifswald, 1934). But, as Miss Salloch points out, the parts of the *Itinerarium* which are derived from this source are precisely those in which it does not resemble the *Estoire*. The narrative history of the *Itinerarium* follows the Latin Continuator, but the chapters dealing with the incidents of the siege (*Itinerarium*, Bk. I, chs. xlvii–lx, 97–115) and those cursing the Marquis for his desertion of the army and the sufferings of the pilgrims (chs. lxvi–lxxxi, 124–37), while not found in the Latin Continuator, are identical with the parallel passages in the *Estoire*. It is evident that the *Estoire* did not depend on the Latin Continuator, but that both the *Estoire* and the *Itinerarium* did derive these passages from some other still unknown source, which must have been an eyewitness account of the siege.
[4] See lines 516, 1388, 4665, 8479–93, *et al.*
[5] See J. H. Round in *English Historical Review*, XVIII (1903), 475–81.
[6] Gaston Paris, Introduction, p. vi.

His conclusions regarding the originality of the poem and its relation to the *Itinerarium Ricardi* rest, however, upon assumptions that are more convenient than convincing. Briefly, the situation is that we are confronted with two texts, a Latin prose chronicle and an Old French narrative poem, which present, with one exception, accounts of the third crusade so closely parallel in word and phrase that a relation of some sort between them is obvious and incontravertible. The exception consists of the excursus in the *Estoire* previously referred to, containing the account of the siege of Acre before the arrival of the kings of England and France. Of this excursus we need here note only that while the parallelism of the two works is less striking than elsewhere, a relation is nevertheless perfectly apparent.

Before the discovery and publication of the *Estoire de la guerre sainte*, the *Itinerarium Ricardi* had been accepted as the original work of one Richard, a canon, who personally took part in the crusade and wrote at the request or under the direction of the prior of Holy Trinity in London. This in spite of the fact that the *De expugnatione Terrae Sanctae per Saladinum libellus*, one of the few pieces of evidence available, states beyond any possibility of misunderstanding that the work was translated from the French.[7] Stubbs, editor of the standard edition of the *Itinerarium*,[8] writing in 1864, affirms categorically: "It is impossible that the work should be a translation."[9] He marshals an array of arguments to demonstrate that the author of the *Libellus* must have been mistaken or deluded, conceding at the most that if any translating took place it would have been merely a putting into formal Latin of rough notes in the vulgar tongue made during the course of the campaign.[10]

Gaston Paris, rescuing from oblivion the long-buried poem of Ambroise, concluded that here was the work from which the English cleric had translated the *Itinerarium, ex gallica lingua.* Dismissing or refuting in detail Stubbs's arguments—which are indeed something less

[7] "Quorum seriem itineris et quae in itinere gesserunt, seu ex qua occasione rex Phillippus repatriavit, si quis plenius nosse desiderat, legat librum quem dominus prior Sanctae Trinitatis Londoniis *ex Gallica lingua in Latinam tam eleganti quam veraci stilo transferri fecit.*" *Libellus* in Stevenson *Radulphi de Coggeshall,* p. 257.

[8] *Chronicles and Memorials of the Reign of Richard I.* Vol. I, *Itinerarium Peregrinorum et gesta Regis Ricardi.* Edited . . . by William Stubbs (London, 1864). For convenience this work will be referred to as the *Itinerarium.*

[9] *Ibid.*, p. lviii.   [10] *Ibid.*, p. lxiv.

than objective in nature—he asserted that in any case a further discussion of them had become futile now that we have discovered the original French work which Richard of Holy Trinity had put into Latin.[11] Richard, he declared, was a downright plagiarist, who set forth deliberately to delude posterity into believing that he had shared the hardships and the glory of the crusade and was an eyewitness of the events he described.

He argues substantially as follows. First, the Latin text contains numerous traces of rhyming words, of which some are found in various equivalent couplets of Ambroise's poem, and others, particularly certain pairs of proper names, must have been in portions of the poem that have been lost through the carelessness of copyists. Second, the Latin text of Richard presents certain errors or inconsistencies which are explicable only on the theory that Richard misunderstood the French text on which he worked and, in one case, was so unfamiliar with Old French epic literature that he was led into a ludicrous mistake concerning Agoland, one of the well-known characters of that literature. Most important of all, perhaps, asserts Gaston Paris, the words and phrases of Richard's text that have no equivalent in the French poem, reveal themselves on examination to be purely rhetorical ornamentation. They add nothing of fact to the narrative, being in substance the kind of florid exhibition of literary skill and erudition with which the medieval clerk loved to bedazzle his readers. It is inconceivable, affirms the critic, that a poet should translate this sort of fancywork into the simple and direct narrative verse that we find in the *Estoire*. On the other hand, it is not merely logical, but a matter of frequent occurrence, that a learned Latinist should embellish the bare simplicity of a composition in the vulgar tongue with such literary flowers as he considered necessary to give it dignity.

In dismissing thus summarily the portions of Richard's text that have no equivalent in the *Estoire*, Gaston Paris either neglects or explains away in unsatisfactory fashion a variety of evidence which his own comparison of the two works places before the reader's eye. Richard does, in point of fact, supply numerous bits of information that can by no stretch of the imagination be termed rhetorical ornament. Such are—to choose only a few among many—the detailed itinerary of King

[11] Introduction, pp. lix ff.

Richard from Tours to Vézelay and from Vézelay to Lyons (Bk. II, chs. viii and x), the interview between King Richard and Tancred in Sicily (Bk. II, ch. xxii), a quarrel between Pisans and Genoese (Bk. II, ch. xxv), details concerning the geography of Crete (Bk. II, ch. xxvii), the names of the three bishops present at the king's marriage (Bk. II, ch. xxxv), an account of a trip made by the king to inspect the fortifications of Gaza and the Daron (Bk. V, ch. xix), and a large number of precise dates. This list might be greatly lengthened.

Gaston Paris accounts for the presence of this additional material in the *Itinerarium* by asserting that it was either (1) derived from some official itinerary of King Richard, (2) added by the author of the Latin work from his own personal information or other sources not specified, or (3) originally present in the French poem, but omitted or lost by copyists who transmitted the text to posterity. While it is true that in some cases these explanations lie within the realm of possibility, it is equally true that they rest on conjecture rather than proof.

Mention should also be made of the fact that Ambroise includes some material for which the *Itinerarium* has no equivalent. We may mention, for instance, details concerning the messengers sent by Tancred to King Richard and the names of the churchmen who arranged terms of peace between the two rulers (lines 1007 ff.), a mention of the lofty ancestry of Guy de Lusignan (lines 1722 ff.), an urgent invitation from King Philip to King Richard (lines 1879–1906), and various others.

Kate Norgate, writing in 1910, subjected the problem to further analysis.[12] While Gaston Paris had fixed on 1196 as the probable date for the composition of the French poem, Miss Norgate brought forth evidence that it should be dated between September, 1203, and November, 1207. Her proof, based on Ambroise's references in present and past tense to various personages of the crusade, may not carry conviction to those who are familiar with the laxity of tense usage in Old French. Nevertheless she makes a fairly convincing case. After studying in similar fashion the *Itinerarium*, which has come down to us in three manuscripts, she concludes:

The *Itinerarium* in the earliest of the three forms now extant was not completed till after 6 April 1199, and the conclusion in manuscript C was added

---

[12] *English Historical Review*, XXV (1910), 523 ff. This article is based on notes made by T. E. Archer, but it embodies Miss Norgate's conclusions.

probably not earlier than 1202. But one passage in lib. i was written *before September 1192;* [13] and it is chronologically possible that the whole work, except the conclusion as it stands in manuscript C, may have been written before that date.[14]

Certain passages inconsistent with this conclusion, she notes, may have been inserted later. In fine, there is no reason for rejecting her statement that "the *Estoire* and the *Itinerarium* were composed within a short distance of time the one from the other," but that the chronological evidences "are insufficient to decide which of the two works *in its original form,* is the earlier."

After refuting Gaston Paris's dismissal of Richard of Holy Trinity as a shameless plagiarist, Miss Norgate then goes on to elaborate—but, to our way of thinking, not to prove—a theory according to which both Richard and Ambroise took part in the crusade and were in fact friends and fellow men-of-letters.[15] While Miss Norgate has made valuable contributions to the solution of the problem, the body of evidence she has gathered seems insufficient to justify an inference which may best be expressed in her own words:

A Norman poet, Ambrose by name, and an English clerk who is supposed to have been Richard "de Templo," canon of Holy Trinity in London, went through the crusade together as comrades and friends. While it was in progress "Richard" took notes—whether in French or Latin—of the experiences which befell one or both of them in particular, and the host in general; and also of what information he could collect about the siege of Acre down to the time of their arrival there. He worked up a portion of these notes into fairly complete literary form before the close of the crusade. In after years he worked out the whole of them into the form in which his book has come down to us. But meanwhile, probably, before doing this— possibly while both men were still in the Holy-Land—he had lent the rough draft of his work to his Norman friend, to serve as the basis of another record of the crusade, which the latter writer intended to compose in the form of an historical *chanson.* So far as the substance of the narrative was concerned, Ambrose had only to translate his comrade's notes, perhaps from Latin into French, perhaps only from prose into verse, making such

---

[13] Italics hers. [14] *Op. cit.,* p. 526.

[15] As Dorothy Bovée (*The Sources of the Third Crusade*) has pointed out, it is extraordinary, if such a relationship existed between the two writers, that neither one so much as mentions the name of the other.

additions, omissions, and alterations as might be suggested to him by his own judgment and his own independent memory of the events recorded, and, for the introductory history, of what he too had picked up from those who had been earlier on the scene of action. On the other hand, Richard's work would also receive additions and alterations from its author when he came to revise it for publication. But it evidently never received a final revision from him; and thus certain imperfections and confusions—such as the blunder about Agoland, the confusion about Garnier of Naplouse, and that about the ransom of William de Préaux—which were no doubt in his original notes, jotted down "in the camp," amid "the din of war which left him no leisure to think quietly"—remained uncorrected and were repeated by scribe after scribe from one copy to another.

The more carefully one scrutinizes these two works, the more clearly one perceives two things: first, the poem of Ambroise cannot be a translation from the *Itinerarium*; second, the *Itinerarium* cannot be a translation from Ambroise. Yet the two books are obviously and undeniably related in some fashion. The present editors reached the conclusion that both works had their origin in a common source, now lost, and were delighted to find that Mr. J. G. Edwards, in a scholarly and penetrating study, had propounded the same theory.[16] He had also presented a certain amount of evidence to support a conjecture that the unidentified author of the lost original wrote in French, and probably in prose; we believe that the first of these conjectures is a likely one, but that the second rests on evidence that is rather tenuous.

For a complete statement of Mr. Edwards's position we refer the reader to his essay, of which we venture to include here only a summary of certain outstanding portions. One of the critical points, for instance, consists of the two references to Agoland, the Saracen king who appears in the Old French *chanson de geste* named Aspremont. The *Estoire* refers to the city of Messina as:

> E bien et bel assise vile,
> Car el siet el chief de Sezille,
> Desus le Far, encontre Rise
> Que Agoland prist par s'emprise.[17]

---

[16] "The *Itinerarium regis Ricardi* and the *Estoire de la Guerre Sainte*," in *Historical Essays in Honor of James Tait* (Manchester, 1933), pp. 59–77.

[17] Lines 513–18.

This indicates an accurate knowledge of the contents of the Aspremont, that is, Agoland *seized Reggio by force.* The parallel passage of the *Itinerarium* speaks of Messina as "situ amoena et plurimum commodo, in confinio Siciliae et Risae quae illi famoso Agolando dicitur olim fuisse pro servitio suo collata." [18] This can mean only that the writer considered Reggio to have been bestowed on Agoland as a fief in reward for services rendered and therefore believed Agoland to have been a Christian baron. According to Gaston Paris this meant that the author of the *Itinerarium* misunderstood and mistranslated the *Estoire de la guerre sainte.* According to Miss Norgate the priest who wrote the *Itinerarium,* unversed in secular literature, picked up on the spot and misinterpreted some fragment of legend transmitted by word of mouth, whereas Ambroise, seeing the error in his friend's notes, quietly and discreetly corrected it in his text.

The difficulty with both these explanations emerges when they are studied in the light of the second reference to Agoland. In Book V, chapter xxi, Richard of Holy Trinity writes of "the most powerful Agoland, who, with a great force of Saracens almost invincible to men without the aid of God, had reached Reggio, a city of Calabria." [19]

It is perfectly obvious that the writer of these words here accurately represents as a Saracen the same Agoland to whom he had previously referred in terms applicable only to a Christian. But he did not get the information from the *Estoire,* whose lines, incorrectly described by Gaston Paris as more explicit than the previous passage, contain no suggestion whatsoever of the Moslem origin of Agoland. They read as follows:

> E quant il mena l'ost par Rome
> Quant Agolant par grant emprise
> Fu par mer arivé a Rise
> En Calabre la riche terre.[20]

In other words, the priest who wrote the first passage misstated a fact which he then correctly stated in the second passage. He did not

[18] Bk. II, ch. xi.

[19] "Illi potentissimo Agolando, Roma transiens . . . qui cum manu validissima, et nisi Deo opitulante, hominibus pene invincibili, Saracenorum, applicuerat apud Rysam civitatem Calabriae."

[20] Lines 8490–93.

get that fact from Ambroise. Mr. Edwards's cogently argued conclusion can hardly be improved:

A further conclusion follows. Taken together, these passages about Agoland do much more than prove a negative. As the writer of the *Itinerarium* does not realize in one place that Agoland was a Saracen, and yet in a later passage correctly describes him as a Saracen, he must have been prompted in the later passage. Yet he was not prompted by the *Estoire*. Consequently he must have been prompted by something else. Gaston Paris was therefore following a sound instinct when he remarked upon the "contradiction" implicit between these two passages. How is this "contradiction" to be explained? How is it possible that a writer should both know and not know the same fact? The most natural explanation in this case seems to be the one which normally accounts for the same phenomenon in other writers. One is driven to the conclusion that the compiler of the *Itinerarium* was not an original author, but was reproducing an original author whose allusions, if they happened not to be clear in themselves, he did not always understand. It was presumably by this original author that the writer of the *Itinerarium* was prompted when he correctly described Agoland, in his second reference, as a leader of the Saracens.[21]

A similar confusion on the part of the author of the *Itinerarium* appears in the references to Garnier de Naplouse. At one point (p. 267) he clearly considers that Garnier de Naplouse and the Master of the Hospital were two separate and distinct persons. A little later (p. 371) he refers to Garnier de Naplouse as Master of the Hospital. Thus, observes Mr. Edwards, he seems both to know and not to know the same fact. Obviously, too, such inadvertencies as these and others pointed out by Mr. Edwards are hardly compatible with the hypothesis that Richard of Holy Trinity worked out his book on the basis of rough notes made during the course of the campaign.

A matter to which Miss Norgate gives much careful attention, but which Mr. Edwards passes over lightly, is the considerable number of passages in the *Estoire de la guerre sainte* where the poet refers to an unidentified written source for his material, using phrases such as "si dist l'estoire," "ço dist li livres," "si com testemoine la letre" and the like. Miss Norgate considers the frequency of such phrases as corroborative evidence of her theory that Ambroise was translating

---

[21] Edwards, *op. cit.*, p. 63.

from the *Itinerarium*.[22] On this point, three observations should be made. First, as she has herself noted, such formulae are the common stock in trade of the medieval jongleurs, who attempted thereby to lend some kind of authenticity to their most fantastic tales—"I saw it written down, it must be true." Their frequency, not very remarkable after all in a poem of more than twelve thousand lines, in no way proves that Ambroise was translating from the Latin. Secondly, it is obvious that the *Estoire* was written to be recited aloud rather than read. The poet addresses himself at intervals, not to his *readers*, but to his *hearers*, and minstrels reciting to an audience were particularly given to the habit of quoting written authority. It is worthy of note that in the prologue to the *Itinerarium* [23] Richard of Holy Trinity twice refers, not to a *lector*, but to an *auditor*; a fact which, Mr. Edwards conjectures, may be explained by the theory that the words in question represent an echo of something that appeared in the prologue of the original French work which Richard was translating. Thirdly, and perhaps most important, the presence of such phrases as "ço dist li livres" is entirely compatible with the hypothesis which we believe to be the true one, that is, that both works derive from a common original.

In the opinion of the present translators, certain other factors lend additional probability to this hypothesis. First, while the main body of the narrative runs along in parallel and almost identical fashion in the two works, each writer omits a number of specific facts which the other includes. We have already mentioned some of these facts; it has not seemed desirable to overburden this Introduction with a complete list of them. The *Itinerarium* is particularly rich in exact dates which the *Estoire* fails to mention.[24] No doubt the poet found, as did the present translator, that dates fit awkwardly into verse. In any case, we suggest that each writer omitted details in the common source which he considered unessential and that the author of the *Estoire* in particular omitted facts that were hard to rhyme.

In the second place, disregarding the excursus of lines 2387–4568, there are numerous points where the two writers actually *differ* in their statement of facts. Leaving out those which seem either incon-

---

[22] She has noted twenty-eight of them; *op. cit.*, p. 538.

[23] Page 4. Miss Bovée has noted another such reference: "audientibus iis etiam qui interfuerant, audenter protestamur."—pp. 439–40.

[24] See Edwards's appendix, p. 75.

sequential or easily explicable by a slight corruption of the manuscript, there remain such matters as the following. The *Estoire* states that after the collapse of the Rhone bridge at Lyons the army crossed in small boats (*bargetes*); the *Itinerarium* declares that a bridge of boats was built.[25] In recounting the terms of the treaty made with King Tancred of Sicily, each writer includes certain provisions of the pact which the other passes over in silence.[26] The same observation is true of the agreement made between Guy de Lusignan and Conrad de Montferrat.[27] It is not unreasonable to deduce that in these two cases each writer chose those of the terms of peace which he thought most important. Here an omission constitutes a difference, for obvious reasons. Where the *Estoire* names as Gilebert Taleboz a knight whom the Latin calls Gerardus Taleboz, we suggest that the divergence arose from differing interpretations of an abbreviation in the original text.[28] The same cause may have led both writers astray in the matter of the duke of Burgundy's Christian name, which they record as Henricus and Henri, whereas it actually was Hugh.[29] The author of the *Itinerarium* has clearly misread either an abbreviation or a French word when he gives "medium autumnum" for a date which the *Estoire* correctly states as mid-August ("mi aust").[30] Mr. Edwards has commented effectively upon this latter passage, as well as upon the curious line where the pilgrims in their visit to Jerusalem are said by the Latin writer to have rested "juxta montem," where the French text has "dejoste un mur" [31] (beside a wall). These matters are insignificant at first glance, but, as Mr. Edwards points out, their very insignificance gives them interest. They are so inconsequential that one cannot conceive of them as representing a correction of one writer by the other; one can easily conceive of them, however, as representing varying interpretations of an identical basic text. Miss Dorothy Bovée has called attention to another textual variation that points in the same direction, though she has not drawn from it what seems to us the obvious infer-

---

[25] *Estoire*, lines 450 ff.; *Itinerarium*, p. 152.
[26] *Estoire*, lines 998 ff.; *Itinerarium*, p. 169.
[27] *Estoire*, lines 5041 ff.; *Itinerarium*, p. 235.
[28] *Estoire*, line 4719; *Itinerarium*, p. 217.
[29] *Estoire*, line 10653; *Itinerarium*, p. 395.
[30] *Estoire*, line 5570; *Itinerarium*, p. 244.
[31] *Estoire*, line 11969; *Itinerarium*, p. 434.

ence: the *Itinerarium* describes the lance of a powerful Saracen emir as being "duabus nostris grossiorem" (heavier than two of ours); the *Estoire* states that "que dous groisseurs n'aveit en France" (in all France there are not to be found two lances that are heavier).[32] In these passages, it will be noted, both the Latin and the French are so crystal-clear that it is impossible to imagine their misinterpretation by anybody who knew enough to translate either one. But if both worked from an original that was less lucid, the divergence at once becomes understandable.

In discussing the references to Agoland and to Garnier de Naplouse we pointed out that the author of the *Itinerarium* was led into errors of fact. Several other such errors appear in his narrative. He relates, for instance, an interview between King Richard and Tancred that took place at Catania, which he says is located midway between Messina and Palermo.[33] No one familiar with the geography of Sicily could make such a blunder. The three cities lie on the coast—Catania almost due south from Messina, Palermo almost due west from Messina. The *Estoire* makes no mention of such an interview.

Even more striking perhaps are the passages in which Richard of Holy Trinity at three separate points refers to Saladin's withdrawal to Daron—which he locates in the mountains—and to his activities there.[34] As a glance at the map will reveal, Daron lies, not among the hills, but on the seacoast, many miles away from the scene of activities indicated by everything in the context. Ambroise correctly locates the action in each of these three cases at Toron of the Knights.[35] The learned editor of the *Itinerarium*, writing of course before the discovery of the *Estoire*, found himself perplexed by the obvious inconsistency in the Latin text and explained it in words which suggest that he was not too well satisfied with his own explanation.[36]

Of the remaining differences between the two narratives, we include

---

[32] Bovée: *op. cit.*, p. 74; *Estoire*, line 6026; *Itinerarium*, pp. 256–57.

[33] "Eadem autem civitas Catinensium medio spatio sita est inter Messanam et Palermam." *Itinerarium*, p. 171. Miss Bovée has noted this error: *op. cit.*, p. 68.

[34] Pages 298, 301, 303. [35] Lines 7462, 7551, 7613.

[36] "It is possible and very probable, that our author in this passage has confounded Daron and Netroun, (*le darun* and *le toron*) the position among the mountains not answering well to the former place. It is of course impossible to be exact in these points, as, in the case of so large and encumbered armies as both the contending hosts were, there might be miles between the rear and the van."—*Op. cit.*, p. 298n.

here three which seem not to have attracted Mr. Edwards's attention. The Earl of Leicester took part in a skirmish in which he was hard pressed by the Saracens, who hemmed him in on every side. Ambroise uses the phrase: "Qui l'avoient entr'els noié," in which the figurative sense of the verb *noyer* is made obvious by the accompanying "entr'els." [37] The Latin writer apparently took the drowning to be literal, though the combatants had obviously gone well past the only stream mentioned in the context, for he renders the idea in words that admit of no other interpretation: "In ipso flumine propemodum in turba submergerent." [38]

At a point shortly after the episode just mentioned the Christian leaders deliberate on the wisdom of attacking Jerusalem; the Templars, Hospitalers, and Pulani, who had most accurate knowledge of local conditions, advised against such attack, for reasons which both writers set forth in some detail. At the end of the argument, the Latin text makes the amazing assertion that their counsel was not heeded: "Sed adhuc consilium eorum non omnino exauditur," although everything in the remainder of his narrative shows clearly that the advice was not merely heeded but also followed.[39] The *Estoire* contains no such statement, which we believe to be founded, like others, upon a misinterpretation of an original text.

In the accounts of King Richard's illness provided by the two writers we note the curious fact that while the canon of Holy Trinity attempts a diagnosis of the *cause* of the malady—in terms little more illuminating to us than they would have been to the patient—the French jongleur contents himself with recording the *symptoms*, of which the Latin work makes no mention whatsoever. The two texts read as follows:

Gravissimam incurrit aegritudinem, quae vulgo Arnoldia vocatur, ex ignotae regionis constitutione, cum eius naturali complexione minus concordante.[40]

---

[37] *Estoire*, line 7518. The word "noyé" recurs with the same meaning in lines 10014–15:

> "Car cil de la nostre partie
> Esteient si entr'els noié"

Here the Latin correctly renders: "nostri . . . inter hostes prae multitudine eorum quasi absconderentur."—p. 374.

[38] *Itinerarium*, p. 300.

[39] *Itinerarium*, p. 306. See our note to line 7716, *infra*, p. 301.

[40] *Itinerarium*, p. 214.

Mais le reis Richarz iert malades
E aveit boche e levres fades
D'une emferté que Deu maudie
Qu'en apele leonardie.[41]

It seems to us probable that the original account mentioned both the symptoms and the supposed causes of the illness, while the authors of our surviving texts recorded what each one thought most pertinent.

We cannot conclude this study of the differences between the *Estoire de la guerre sainte* and the *Itinerarium* without inviting the reader's attention to the frequent cases involving numerals. There are about a score of such cases. In eleven of them the two works give different numbers; in the remainder one text gives a number, while the other does not. Sometimes one gives a larger figure; sometimes the other. Sometimes the difference is slight, as in the case of King Richard's fleet, which Ambroise credits with one hundred and seven ships, whereas the Latin says one hundred and eight.[42] Sometimes it is enormous: where Ambroise affirms that three thousand crusaders died of illness and famine at Acre during the siege and afterward, Richard of Holy Trinity puts the casualties from this source at three hundred thousand.[43] Some of the divergences are explicable on the theory that the writers, or one of them, misread or misinterpreted Roman numerals in the hypothetical original; in other cases it is hard to see how this can have been possible. The present translators find themselves obliged to fall back on the explanation that one writer or the other chose at various points to exaggerate or to minimize, for reasons of his own. While this explanation is not illuminating, it is as reasonable as any.

Of the evidence adduced by Mr. Edwards and by ourselves in support of the theory that the two works in question derive from a common basic form of the narrative, we believe that although no single item of testimony would suffice in itself to verify the hypothesis, the very considerable number of clues all pointing in the same direction does encourage a strong presumption. To put the matter from a slightly different point of view, we consider demonstrably untenable the theory that the *Estoire de la guerre sainte* was either the source of the *Itine-*

---

[41] *Estoire*, lines 4605 ff. See our note on these lines, *infra*, p. 196.

[42] *Ibid.*, line 311; *Itinerarium*, p. 440.

[43] *Estoire*, line 12245; *Itinerarium*, p. 440.

rarium, as Gaston Paris would have it, or derived from the *Itinerarium* as Miss Norgate believes. No one could maintain for a moment that the two are independent. By a process of elimination we conclude that our theory provides the only possible explanation of the facts.

The nature of the lost original must remain a matter for conjecture. Mr. Edwards finds reason to believe that it was written in French and probably in prose. His reasons are good enough to suggest such a conclusion, but hardly adequate to prove it. In the main, we incline to agree with him, and we would add to what he has said the interesting and suggestive fact that of the large number of proper names appearing in the Latin text of the *Itinerarium* a noteworthy proportion are written in the French form rather than in the Latin form which they would naturally have taken had the original been composed in that tongue. If the basic text was indeed an Old French prose history, it was a landmark in literature, the first piece of historical prose writing in the French language, antedating by a considerable period the familiar narrative of Villehardouin.

LITERARY QUALITIES OF THE POEM

If we are correct in postulating a lost original, probably in French prose, from which the existing text of the poem derives, one deduction is inescapable: the writer of the *Estoire de la guerre sainte* followed his model very closely. The amazingly close parallelism of the *Estoire* and the *Itinerarium* permits of no other conclusion. Consequently any estimate of the literary merit of the poet whose work we actually possess must apply in large measure to the man from whom he drew his material. Since we cannot evaluate a work which we do not possess, we must content ourselves with a consideration of the poem that has survived. Whether it was the author of the manuscript in the Vatican or his predecessor who bore the name Ambroise is beyond our power to determine, but for purposes of convenience we have used that name in our commentary as referring to the man who first wrote the story. While our observations on style and content are founded on a study of the present text, we make the reservation that they may more accurately describe the shadowy figure whose labor furnished the matter for that text.

Gaston Paris has presented excellent reasons for believing that the poet was not noble, priest or soldier, but in all probability a professional poet or jongleur attached to the army of King Richard. Further research has fortified the hypothesis that he came from the Evreux district in Normandy, upon whose knights and men-at-arms he lavishes particular praise for their valor and steadfastness. It is precisely because Ambroise was one of the "lesser folk" of the host that he was able to give us so precious an account, not merely of events, but of the mental and spiritual background of events. He pictures the soul of the crusader, with all its curious mélange of confusion and lucidity. Seldom does he reach greater heights of eloquence than in his descriptions of the joy of the host at some battle won or at the prospect of reaching Jerusalem, or than in his pictures of the despair that beset the pilgrims when they found themselves forced to turn back from the Holy City. Accepting the reasons given by Richard for refusing to advance on Jerusalem and criticizing those who disagreed with his royal master, he nevertheless lamented the decision that closed to the pilgrims the road to the Sepulchre.

He was not privy to the councils of the leaders of the crusade, though at times he recounts their deliberations with all the assurance of one who had participated in them. This, however, will not greatly impress anyone who knows how in any army the vaguest and falsest rumors take on authoritative precision as they spread among the rank and file. The long exhortation of the priest to Richard to remember his past fame and glories undoubtedly grew out of awed stories circulated in the camp about the temerity of the man who dared thus address the Lion Heart. Furthermore, Ambroise tells what went on in the inner circles of Saladin's councils of war with exactly the same confidence that marks his descriptions of what the Christian generals said and thought; the orations which he attributes to the Saracen emirs are, of course, nothing but the imagination and wishful thinking of the crusaders, who pictured their enemies as saying the things which, in the opinion of the Christian army, they ought to have thought and said.

Ambroise never refers to himself as participating personally in a battle. He does, however, affirm that he marched among the second group of pilgrims who visited the Holy Places of Jerusalem after the truce with Saladin, and he tells of the emotion that came over him as he trod in the footsteps of the Saviour. At this climactic or anticlimactic moment of the crusade he speaks with the sincerity and directness of one who had witnessed the event. But this same sincerity, this same tone of the eyewitness, runs throughout most of the work and gives the reader a strong conviction that he is listening to one who knew whereof he spoke.

For all its tone of earnestness, the poet's work is nevertheless very uneven in quality. For pages he will amble tranquilly along, guided by the *musa pedestris*, presenting his array of fact in matter-of-fact manner, with no tinge of enthusiasm, emotion, or poetic fire. He speaks simply and directly, to be sure, but not with the stark majesty that makes the *Chanson de Roland* so magnificent. He gives us, in rhyming couplets, a straightforward chronicle of events—no more and no less. His flow of imagery is sparse, seldom going beyond the commonplace of the medieval trouvère. In a battle arrows and spears fill the air like a heavy snowfall in winter, the victors pursue the vanquished like the wolf pursuing the hapless flock of sheep—these clichés and others of the same banality mark the limits of our poet's command of figurative language.

His accounts of battle scenes appear particularly tedious to the modern reader, though the poet evidently reveled in them with that peculiar sadistic joy that the medieval writer seems to derive from the moving accident on flood and field. One ought in all fairness to note that while one fight seems very like another, with the streaming flags and shining armor, the clouds of arrows and impetuous charges, the mighty blows and the heaps of corpses, the poet does nevertheless manage to give a lucid and presumably accurate narrative of the tactics, the disposition of troops, and the varying tides of fortune. These passages do not lack vividness, nor are they without value for the military historian, who can determine the facts with a little effort. What they do lack is a sense of perspective. A minor skirmish in which a few score men participate on each side takes on in Ambroise's narrative all the grandiose proportions of the battle of Arsur or the recapture of Jaffa. The frequency with which such skirmishes appear in the story robs them of most of their dramatic quality.

Ambroise was not an especially observant traveler. His descriptions of the topography, climate, and architecture of what was to him a new and exotic country seem comparatively meager. He mentions some of the Holy Places visited in Jerusalem, he tells the legendary stories about the walls and towers of Ascalon, he introduces here and there incidental details taken from popular legends or the *chansons de geste*, but in this respect he cannot compare with Robert de Clari, who avidly accumulated information about the wonderful things he saw in Constantinople. The summer heat and dust, the venomous insects and the heavy rains, all these are mentioned by Ambroise, to be sure, but only incidentally, only as the background against which the human drama of the crusade was being played. One feels that in themselves they held slight interest for the chronicler, though it may be that they are simply dwarfed by the surpassing magnitude of the spiritual adventure which meant so much to him.

The poet can however be dramatic and colorful on occasion. Woven into the fabric of his tale are sections of swift and skillful verse, purple patches that glow with the fire of faith or of indignation. Such are, for instance, his account of the collapse of the Rhone bridge, the surrender and humiliation of Isaac of Cyprus, the heroism of Jacques d'Avesnes, the assassination of Conrad of Montferrat, and the rhythmic invective hurled at Conrad for his aloofness from what Ambroise believed to be the cause of righteousness. His description of the pilgrims' march through France on their way to the seacoast and of their reception by the populace has astonishing vigor and pathos.

Layman though he was, few clerics could outdo him in his passionate devotion to the cause of Christendom—a devotion that has all the prejudice of the simply pious soul. He shares, naturally enough, the common medieval view that the paynim suffer from the basic wrongness and wickedness of the unbaptized, a view which the *Chanson de Roland* expresses in the ingenuous formula: "Christians are right, paynim are wrong." Whatever the Saracens do is evil, except in those circumstances—unhappily too numerous—where God chooses them as instruments whereby to punish the corruption of Christianity that has strayed from the paths of virtue. But for all that, the poet cannot suppress his unwilling admiration for their skill at arms and for the chivalry of Saladin. If such a man had only been a Christian, he laments, if he had not been a worshiper of false gods, what a man he would have been!

THE HISTORICAL VALUE OF AMBROISE

Having already given our reasons for judging that the *Itinerarium* and the *Estoire* were both based on a common lost original, we shall take the liberty in this section to consider the two as a single work and to attempt an estimate of the historical value of the original, which we have arbitrarily and for convenience called Ambroise. We have shown throughout our notes the variants and divergencies between the *Estoire* and the *Itinerarium*, and they may be summarized by stating that while the *Itinerarium* is in general more precise as to chronology and more inclusive as to proper names, there are several incidents which are given in greater detail by the *Estoire*. But as historical documents they have much the same validity, and we shall here essay to evaluate their narrative in comparison with other independent sources.

Ambroise, as we have already pointed out, cannot be called the best single source for the entire third crusade, but it is certainly the best source for the crusade of Richard. The events in Syria which led up to the crusade are treated very broadly and not too accurately by the *Estoire*, while the *Itinerarium*, which follows the Latin Continuator of William of Tyre, is more detailed, but not much more reliable. For a complete account of the crusade probably the best single source would be the *Eracles*, the Old French Continuator of William.[44] Ambroise virtually omits the expedition of Frederick Barbarossa; more attention is given it in the *Itinerarium*, where several chapters are derived from the Latin Continuator, than in the *Estoire*, but both are quite brief. Further, Ambroise's account of the crusade of Philip Augustus is incidental to the crusade of Richard; his knowledge of Cyprus, apart from the details of its conquest, seems very slight. But Ambroise does give the best account of the campaigns in Palestine, of the fighting at Messina and in Cyprus, and of the incidents in the camp before Acre.

It is not our purpose here to analyze in detail the history of Ambroise, but a very brief comparison of his work with the other major sources of the crusade adds to our appreciation of the historical significance of our chronicle. The other chief occidental accounts are those of the *Eracles*, the *Gesta*-Hoveden (which are virtually the same), Diceto, Devizes, and Rigord; while for the siege of Acre and the

---

[44] For titles and editions of authors cited here, see our Bibliography.

events before the arrival of Richard supplementary information may be found in the accounts of Haymarus and the *Libellus*. Of the oriental sources by far the most important is Beha ed Din, but Ibn al Athir, Abu Chamah, Ibn Kallikan, and Abulfaraj Bar Hebraeus all supply details. For the background of Syrian history the *Libellus* and the *Eracles* are the most informative; Ambroise appears at his worst in this connection. But Ambroise admits frankly that what he tells of these matters he knows only from the writings of others and that he has no personal knowledge thereof. The discoloration of his account by his personal prejudices will be discussed below, but it must be stated here that Ambroise is not the source to which one should turn for information on the internal history of the kingdom of Jerusalem.

Neither is Ambroise the best authority for the history of Richard in France and in England before the crusade. Diceto, Devizes, and the *Gesta*-Hoveden all provide many more details on the doings in the West, and all are better sources both for the preparations for the crusade and for the events in France and England during Richard's absence. But for the march of the crusaders and the war in Sicily, Ambroise is of the first importance. Here he writes about what he himself saw. In no other account is the narrative so vivid and lively. Hoveden is much more full and exact as to chronology, but his story lacks the freshness and spirit of Ambroise's. Hoveden wrote from sources which enabled him to quote treaties, ordinances, and the decisions of councils with a knowledge which Ambroise lacked, but, though Hoveden is the more exact, Ambroise is by far the more vivid. The forest may not be seen as clearly, but the trees are much more distinct and have greener foliage.

For the conquest of Cyprus Ambroise gives us by far the most detailed account. Here again the facts recorded are actions in which Ambroise himself may have participated, or which, at least, he saw taking place around him. He does not know the regulations Richard established for the administration of the island, which Hoveden gives, but he tells more stirringly of the fighting and the capture of Isaac.

For the scenes at the siege of Acre, Ambroise again depended upon others for information. Here we have clearly camp gossip—incidents retold from tent to tent. Ambroise's chronology is most defective in this part; there is little sequence in the order of battles, but the heroism of individuals, the suffering of the host, the alternate joy and despair of the pilgrims are told vividly and dramatically. After Richard's arrival the chronology improves, and Ambroise's account of the end of the siege equals any other.

True, he omits any considerable discussion of many details which we know from other sources. He was concerned solely with reciting the *gestes* of Richard, and irrelevant events, distracting from this single purpose, are subordinated even more in the *Estoire* than in the *Itinerarium*. Philip's voyage home, which receives so much attention in Hoveden, is omitted altogether. Ambroise is telling the deeds of the Lion Heart; he does not bother with the lesser acts of smaller folk. The *Eracles*, the *Libellus*, and Haymarus give more connected accounts of the siege; Ambroise by far the most personal.

It is in his story of the campaigns of Richard in Palestine that Ambroise is unique and unexcelled. Only in Beha ed Din, who like Ambroise concerns himself only with the deeds of his hero, can one find an equally good account of these campaigns. The details of the marches and battles, the heroic struggles, the joys and agonies of the pilgrims as fortune smiled or frowned upon them, are recorded by Ambroise colorfully, vividly, and sympathetically. The negotiations for truces were not known, and so remain largely unmentioned unless they became so noticeable that the whole camp speculated on them. Ambroise was merely one of the mass of pilgrims who followed where their lord led them, unknowing why and only able to speculate about the motives which prompted the decisions made. He explains such decisions with naïve simplicity: treason, bad faith, selfishness, were for him more acceptable motives than those reasons of state and strategy which prompted the leaders.

We have already observed that Ambroise colors his entire narrative with a strong personal bias. He writes as the avowed partisan of Richard and of all Richard's friends and protégés. This is especially noticeable in his treatment of Guy de Lusignan and Conrad de Montferrat. It is so strong as to render almost wholly false his account of the history of Jerusalem before the beginning of the siege of Acre. Ambroise gained his information of these events entirely at second hand and apparently entirely from partisans of Guy. He never understood the psychology or the problems of the Syrian Franks. Ambroise expressed perfectly the attitude of the western crusader as opposed to that of the Syrian colonists. To him all Saracens were "pagan cattle," and he reveled, almost sadistically, in descriptions of their slaughter and discomfiture. Even though he mentioned instances of the generosity and chivalry of Saladin and Saphadin, he spoke of them most unflatteringly and piously invoked God's curse against the whole Moslem breed. He did not record miracles, nor did he recount tales of the intervention of saints in behalf of the Christian army as did some of the chroniclers of the first crusade; but he did see in the sufferings of the Christians the evidences of God's wrath at the unworthy actions of the people; and the tribulations of Jerusalem were to him the direct result of the impiety of her inhabitants.

In contrast to Ambroise we must consider the accounts of Ernoul and of the *Eracles*, both written by Frankish settlers in Syria. They represent the "colonial" as distinguished from the "crusader" viewpoint, and they disagree with Ambroise in their whole interpretation of the events which led up to the crusade. While to them the Saracens were the enemy, there can be found in them none of that hatred which inspired the western writers. They wrote of the Saracens as an Englishman of that time would have written of the French or as a modern Englishman would write of the Italians: enemy neighbors with vices surely enough, but also with some virtues. The fortunes of war were observed more dispassionately by the eastern Christians; we do not find them reveling in the number of Saracens slain as did Ambroise.

These Syrian Franks knew personally the situation in the East; they judged events from the political viewpoint, and the good of their kingdom more than the zeal for the Cross governed their judgments. To these men, who knew and understood the issues involved, Raymond of Tripoli and Conrad de Montferrat were the heroes of the story, not the villains; it was to Ambroise, prejudiced and ill informed, that they appeared as base traitors and wicked scoundrels. When one considers the unanimity with which all the greater barons of Frankish Syria, men who had the greatest stake in the land, supported Raymond and Conrad; when one studies the record of the court party under Guy and Renaud de Châtillon; when one forgets religious prejudice and considers only political exigency, he cannot but realize that Raymond and Conrad represented and led the party which comprised the ablest, soundest, most far-seeing elements in the kingdom of Jerusalem. Ambroise cursed Conrad for his diversion of supplies from the camp before Acre to his city of Tyre; he did not in the least appreciate the fact that the defense of Tyre must have been the first consideration of the native Franks, in whose opinions the siege of Acre was a venture in which they could have but little hope of success, while the preservation of Tyre was the essential cornerstone in the defense of the kingdom. Ambroise forgot, or did not know, that in Tyre were the refugees from all the cities of the kingdom taken by Saladin; he ignored the fact that it was on the rock of Conrad's resistance at Tyre that the wave of Moslem conquest was broken; he condemned as treason in Conrad the negotiations with Saladin for the preservation of part of the kingdom as a vassal state—yet he had no criticism for Richard when the king subsequently offered almost identical terms to the sultan after he had come to realize the impossibility of a complete reconquest. Guy de Lusignan had amply demonstrated political and military incompetence; the lords of Syria had no confidence in him and refused to accept his leadership, trusting rather to Conrad, whose prowess had been ably evidenced at Tyre. But it never occurred to Ambroise that the Franco-Syrian lords were anything other than traitors and false when they supported the party opposed to Richard, or that Philip Augustus could have shown greater political acumen in supporting the marquis than did Richard in assisting Guy. The history of Richard's reign, as evidenced by his treatment of John and by some of his appointments, reveals the inability of the king to judge character or competence. Ambroise never suspected this, nor did he seem to feel any inconsistency either in his own statements or in his hero's policy when he finally accepted Conrad as king of Jerusalem. The villain suddenly became the ally of the hero and was recognized by all as the best man for the position to which he aspired; the false marquis became overnight the favored candidate for the throne. This change of front, which Richard accepted as he grew to learn the needs of the country and the impossibility of further supporting the incompetent and unpopular Lusignan, Ambroise recorded without a word of explanation.

It must be remembered that throughout the history of the crusaders' states there were many indications that the native Franks were able to get along better with their Saracen neighbors than they were with their Christian allies from the West. When Conrad offered vassalage to Saladin, he thought of ending the war which was ruining the country without offering chance of success. He recognized that honorable vassalage was preferable to a ruined kingdom devastated by years of fruitless warfare. Richard himself finally accepted this point of view; certainly Conrad's offers were not more treasonable than Richard's suggestion that the kingdom of Jerusalem be reconstructed as a vassal state, its king to perform homage to Saladin and provide troops for his army, especially when we remember Richard's proposal that his sister marry Saphadin and that the kingdom be given to them jointly.

Richard was not a fool. During the campaigns in Palestine he learned much: he discovered the impossibility of a complete reconquest of the kingdom; he came to realize that the baronial party knew what it was about when it preferred Conrad; and he grew to appreciate the possibility of honorable agreements between men of different faiths. Richard developed the colonial attitude; himself chivalrous and a master of the art of war, he was able to recognize these qualities in his great antagonist. Ambroise never learned these things; but he accepted the decisions of his king blindly and without question.

In our notes we have endeavored to indicate these prejudices of our author and to correct the narrative from facts derived from the eastern sources.

With all its prejudice and partisanship, with all its piety and bloodthirstiness, with all its epic redundancy and exaggeration, the account of Ambroise remains nevertheless finer than any other account of the crusade of Richard and also one of the most significant documents extant in revealing the mind and spirit of the crusaders—those men who threw themselves heart and soul into futile and disastrous warfare, enduring hardship and discouragement for the sake of a religious and chivalric ideal. But the *Estoire* is more than that; it is the epic, the saga, of the *gestes* of one of Christendom's most romantic and colorful figures.

THE CRUSADE OF
RICHARD LION-HEART

CHAPTER I

Who has a lengthy tale to tell   1
Must needs watch carefully and well,
Lest he begin by taking on
A task that he cannot make done.
So let him to his task attend
That he may bring it to good end;
Thus, that my burden be not too
Heavy, I start without ado.
My care I fain would dedicate
To matter worthy to relate,   10
Which tells the troubles dolorous
That rightfully afflicted us
In Syria, but yesteryear,
Where our rank folly cost us dear,
Which God could not do otherwise
Than make us sorely realize:
He made us feel it certainly
In France, likewise in Normandy,
As well as through all Christendom,
Where much or little it had come.   20
In little time he made us feel
It, by that cross at which all kneel

And which was then by pagan hand
Transported to another land
Than that where it was wont to lie,
Where God deigned to be born and die . . .
Of Holy Temple and Hospital
Whence many a sorrow did befall,
And of the Tomb where God was placed
And of which sin has dispossessed   30
Us. No! Say not that it was sin,
But God, Who willed once more to win
His people whom His blood had bought,
But who in service nothing wrought.
Disaster of such dreadful weight
Brought woe to people small and great
Throughout the world, and lord and hind
Scarce knew where comfort they might find.
Then stilled was joy of word or tongue,
Stilled was the dancing, hushed the song   40
And hushed the joy and hushed the mirth
Of Christian folk throughout the earth,
Until the Pope of Rome, through whom
God has saved many men from doom
(He was the eighth called Gregory,[1]
So it is told in history),
Proclaimed a grace of sovereign might
For God and in the devil's spite:
That he should have all sins forgiven
Who would attack those foes of heaven   50
Who had despoiled in very sooth
The great and noble King of Truth;
And for this, many a count and king
And other men past numbering
Took on, to follow God's command,
The cross and sought the Holy Land.
To take the cross there was no dearth
Of men of noblest rank and birth.

[1] Alberto di Morra, of Ferrara, ruled as Pope Gregory VIII for one month and
seventeen days in October–December, 1187.

RICHARD TAKES THE CROSS

The valiant count of Poitiers,
Richard,[2] would brook no least delay;   60
Hearing of God's need and God's loss,
For love of God he took the cross.
First of the noble men was he
From our lands on this side the sea.
Then in God's service took his post
The king,[3] and gave great pains and cost.
And none to sell his heritage
Delayed the holy pilgrimage;
Each man, the aged like the youth,
Was wont to show his heart's own truth,   70
Was wont his sorrow to proclaim,
And to take vengeance for the shame
That on the Lord God had been wrought,
On God, who had done wrong in naught.
Because His land had been laid waste,
His people so distraught by haste
That they were mazed and ill-advised;
And thus no one should be surprised
If then they suffered a defeat.
For, though brave men of the élite,   80
It was God's will that they should die,
And others win His victory.
So these, while they have died in flesh,
In paradise now live afresh.
And so live all who meet their end
O'erseas, their Lord God to defend.

HOSTILITY OF HENRY II AND PHILIP

Between France and Normandy
There was a war of ancestry,
Cruel and terrible and strong
And full of wickedness and wrong.   90

[2] Richard had been made duke of Aquitaine in 1187.
[3] Henry II, king of England, 1154–89.

'Twas Philip [4] who this war did bring
And Henry who was England's king,
He of the lineage so fair,
Wise, worthy, prudent, debonair,
Good father of that youthful king [5]
Who did such mighty tourneying,
Father of Richard, the well-skilled,
With wisdom and good judgment filled,
And of Geoffrey of Brittany,[6]
A youth of worth and dignity,   100
Father of John, Lackland by name,
From whom great war and trouble came.
The king who had such family
And knew himself so rich to be
Could very well a war sustain,
If one to war on him were fain;
Had he done as they did exhort,
As if to people of such sort . . .
The two kings then were in discord
And none could bring them to accord,   110
Until God led them to the truce
That had such very worthy use.

THE CONFERENCE AT GISORS

It was between Gisors and Trie,[7]
In a fair meadow broad and free.

[4] Philip II Augustus, king of France, 1179–1223.

[5] Henry, "the young king," was crowned during his father's lifetime, but died in 1183.

[6] Geoffrey of Brittany (1158–86) was the third son of Henry II and Eleanor. He was betrothed to Constance, daughter of Conon of Brittany, and was recognized by Conon as his heir in 1166, although the marriage did not take place until 1181. Geoffrey joined his brothers, Henry and Richard, in some of their rebellions against their father, but was more often opposed to Richard than with him. His son Arthur was the claimant to the English throne against John in 1199 (Dictionary of National Biography, XXI, 136).

[7] The conference held on the border of France and Normandy, between Gisors and Trie, occurred on January 21, 1188 (Gesta, II, 29). The chief matters of agenda were the interminable question of the possession of Gisors, a constant bone of contention between the Capetians and the Plantagenets, and the discussion of the marriage of

And there was spoken many a word;
Wisdom and folly both were heard.
And some for peace did greatly yearn,
Others for peace had no concern.
And there were men of many a kind
Who sought peace, but no peace could find,   120
Save that God's will did work upon
Them all, the Holy Cross to don.
And at this parley there were told
Many quarrels new and old:
Much of pride and haughtiness;
Many griefs that sought redress—
Much they sought and little found.
Meanwhile the sun shone brightly round.
From Tyre an archbishop there came,[8]
For sense and wisdom known to fame,   130
Sent by the Syrians, who knew
His judgment to be sound and true.
We saw him valiantly essay
To lead these kings in the right way;
God strove their quarrels to dispel,
And wise and learned men as well,
So that both kings their strife did cease,
Took cross, and kissed the kiss of peace.
They kissed in tears, and then did raise
Their voices, giving God their praise,   140
Because they felt great joyfulness
And were aware of the distress
Of God and how He needed aid.

Richard with Alice of France, the sister of Philip. The arrival of the Tyrian archbishop and the preaching of the crusade diverted the attention of the conference to
that issue, and nothing was accomplished in regard to the real purpose of the meeting
(Norgate, *Richard*, p. 72).

   [8] The archbishop of Tyre who was present at this conference was Joscius, archbishop
1186–1200 and chancellor of Jerusalem 1192–1200. As he appears on documents of
the year 1186 with the title of archbishop of Tyre (Röhricht, *Regesta*, doc. 653), there
can be no doubt that he had succeeded William, the famous historian, before this date.
G. Paris (p. lxviii) incorrectly identifies this archbishop as William.

Then had you seen how knights obeyed
The call and took the cross in haste!
Of fear they seemed to know no taste.
So that round the archbishops drew
And round the abbots and bishops too
A crowd so bent on enterprise
(So help me God, with my own eyes   150
I saw) midst heat so violent
(Greater was never felt nor sent),
That many people lost their breath
And well nigh stifled unto death.[9]

HENRY DIES WITH HIS VOW UNFULFILLED

For joy of the agreement made
And of the peace and the crusade
All went the Holy Cross to take,
For no one could the cause forsake
Or spurn the great remission
Of sin.[10] Yet blame must be upon   160
The sloth which led them to delay
Departure. Satan found a way
To bring back to the kings such strife
As could not be dispelled while life
Remained to one, but did abide
Till death rushed on him, and he died.
'Twas Henry, England's aged king,
Who had made plans for visiting
The Holy Tomb at God's command,

[9] This heat in January was not due to extraordinary climatic conditions, but to the internal heat of the multitude swept off their feet by wild enthusiasm. The *Itinerarium* (p. 141) says: "Tantus itaque factus est eadem die crucem accipientium concursus, ut turba sese comprimens, prae intolerabili aestus fervore pene deficeret, aestus quippe erat." One is inclined to wonder if there was not in the original Latin a play on the words *aestus* and *aestas* which has been lost in copying.

[10] Plenary indulgences were granted those who went on the crusades, while excommunication attended those who withdrew from them after having once taken the vow. The standard exposition of the privileges of the crusaders is to be found in E. Bridrey, *La Condition juridique des croisés*.

But was prevented by death's hand.[11]   170
Ambrose, who wrote this book, avers
That man is wise and never errs
Who keeps his vow, that solemn word
That he has sworn to God, his Lord.
Now of their sire, the king, bereft,
Only the brothers twain are left.[12]
And Richard was the elder's name,
The count of Poitiers, great in fame.
The younger John Lackland in truth
Was called: he was an untried youth.   180

RICHARD'S CORONATION

To Richard, then, was handed down,
As reason doth decree, the crown,
Also the wealth, the treasury,
The lands, the oaths of fealty.
First to take cross, so without fail,
As we have told ye in our tale,
To God he gave his laboring,
And so prepared for journeying,
And sailed across to England's shore;
And before many days were o'er   190
At London he received the crown.[13]
I saw gifts given in that town,
Great gifts, and food was served in such
Profusion that none knew how much.

[11] The *Itinerarium* (pp. 141–42) gives the date, octave of Sts. Peter and Paul (July 6) 1189, and adds that he was buried in Fontevrault.

[12] Geoffrey had died August 18, 1186, leaving only a baby, Arthur, to represent him.

[13] The *Itinerarium* (pp. 142–43) gives many details at this point which are omitted by our text. Richard crossed to England on St. Giles day (September 1), and was crowned king (on Sunday, September 3) by Baldwin, archbishop of Canterbury, in the presence of the queen mother Eleanor, Count John, and others. At the time of the coronation there occurred throughout England massacres of the Jews, who had been protected by Henry. These massacres of the Jews are given considerable attention in the other English chroniclers such as Richard of Devizes, Ralph of Diceto, Roger of Hoveden, the *Gesta*, and Ralph of Coggeshall. The *Itinerarium* also gives a long description and eulogy of Richard (pp. 143–44).

Ne'er in my life have I observed
A court more courteously served.
I saw rich vessels and rich plate
Served in a mighty hall of state;
And tables laden down so well
'Twas more than any man can tell.   200
But why relate at greater length;
Ye all know well this might and strength
And what great court he can maintain
Who over England's realm doth reign.
Great, rich, and splendid was the feast;
It lasted three full days at least.
The king gave many a rich award,
And to his barons he restored
The fiefs due to their lineage,
And he increased their heritage.[14]   210

RICHARD'S PREPARATIONS FOR THE CRUSADE

And then, when all the court was through,
Each one to his estate withdrew—
Each one into his own domain—
Though long he could not there remain,
Because the king had said the word.
His order by each man was heard,
That they prepare their enterprise
By borrowing or otherwise,
Because he wished to start his fleet
And all things needful, fit, and meet,   220

[14] Although Richard inaugurated his reign with a general amnesty to all malefactors and with an emptying of the prisons (William of Newburgh, I, 293), the restoration of estates to those who had opposed him politically was not without its compensation in the reliefs which he exacted from all his vassals. Richard strained every possible means of raising money for the crusade and sold fiefs, offices, and even domain lands to purchasers with ready cash which he could turn toward the expenses of his crusade. It was in this endeavor that he sold to the king of Scots his freedom from the homage which he had paid Henry II, and Richard of Devizes (p. 388), who devotes considerable attention to Richard's financial preparations, reports that he said he would have sold London itself could he but find a buyer. A full account of Richard's first acts as king and his attempts to raise money is given in Norgate, *Richard* (pp. 91-111).

So that upon an early day
His pilgrimage might take its way.
For night and day his heart did yearn
Toward those who waited his return
In Normandy and in Anjou,
In Gascony and in Poitou,
In Berri and in Burgundy,[15]
Whence many joined the company.
In each of England's churches and
In all the others of his land   230
He placed, where none had been appointed,
Bishop or archbishop anointed.[16]
He would not wait for winter's snow,
But had his ships prepared to go,
Placed therein his rich treasury,
Whose use he knew right perfectly.
Upon the seacoast, little space
He dwelt, before God sent the grace
Of a fair wind that straightway bore
Him over to the Norman shore.   240
And this may truly be believed:
With mighty joy he was received
As soon as he had come in sight.
Swiftly he had all things made right
For marching, and to Lions sent,[17]
Arranging feast and merriment.
The day of the Nativity,   Dec. 25, 1189
When God took on humanity,
The king at Lions held his feast;

---

[15] This Burgundy is obviously an error for Brittany, as G. Paris points out.

[16] The *Itinerarium* (p. 145), Ralph of Diceto (II, 69), and Richard of Devizes (p. 386) name the bishops: Geoffrey de Lucy to Winchester; Richard FitzNeal to London; Hubert Walter to Salisbury; William Longchamp, the chancellor, to Ely. Richard's half-brother Geoffrey was transferred from the chancellorship to the archbishopric of York. With the exception of York, all these sees were sold at a good price. (Norgate, *Richard*, pp. 103–4.)

[17] Lions-la-Forêt (Eure). G. Paris corrects in his notes (p. 551) the error made in the marginalia of his text. The *Gesta* (II, 104) says Richard spent Christmas at Bures, which is near Bayeux.

But singing songs of deeds soon ceased.   250
At once he had a letter writ,
Chose messenger sure, swift, and fit,
And gave this messenger command
To place it in the French king's hand
And promptly to assure the king
All was prepared for traveling.
And thus arrangements they did make
To meet, if I make no mistake.
So they assembled before Dreux,
Seven leagues distant from Evreux.[18]   260
And while the two kings made parley,
Speaking of journey, route and way,
Unto the king of France, behold,
There came a messenger, who told
Ill tidings. Coming with bowed head,
He told him that the queen was dead.[19]
And for this very mournful word
And other sorry tidings heard—
The king of Apulia's death [20]
(Which grieved us and still sorroweth)—   270
The host was so discomfortèd
That almost was abandonèd
The road that men to Syria trod.
But 'twas not so, by grace of God.
Only was set a later date,
Saint John's day, which all celebrate.   June 24, 1190

[18] The *Itinerarium* (p. 146) gives the date 1190, dominical letter *G*, but omits the seven leagues from Evreux.

[19] Isabelle of Hainault, daughter of Baldwin V of Hainault, the first wife of Philip Augustus, died March 15, 1190 (Rigord, I, 97).

[20] William II, "The Good," king of Sicily, the husband of Richard's sister Joanna, died November 16/18, 1189. He had been most active in the support of the Holy Land and had sent a fleet to assist it during Saladin's conquest of the country. When he died he left the kingdom to his aunt Constance, the wife of the emperor, Henry VI. In their absence from the country, the throne was seized by Tancred of Lecce, an illegitimate grandson of Roger II, who was supported by a large body of the Sicilian baronage. (F. Chalandon, *Histoire de la domination normande en Italie*, Vol. II.)

RICHARD AND PHILIP ARRANGE TO MEET AT VÉZELAY

When roses were with fragrance filled
The time was ready when God willed
That pilgrims' courage be awoke,
That they be joined by other folk,   280
And that each one of them prepare
For that which God would have them bear,
Ready to suffer pain and dearth
And on Saint John's day to set forth.[21]
After eight days, without delay,   July 2, 1190
The assembly met at Vézelay.
The king then Paris did forsake
And of Saint Denis leave did take.
Many a chosen knight and lord
Had not yet girded on his sword,   290
While great part of the French array
Already were upon their way.
And then the duke of Burgundy [22]
Set out to join the company.
The count of Flanders [23] tarried not,
But his contingent promptly brought.
Ye might have seen then many a band
Of men arrive from every hand.
And some in sadness did convey
Them grieving on their grieving way,   300
And made such sorrow for their sake
Their hearts were very near to break.

[21] The *Gesta* (II, 105) and Ralph of Diceto (II, 74) give this date of June 24 as the date for the meeting at Vézelay. The *Itinerarium* (p. 146) says that they met on the octave of St. John's day, as does our text. Roger of Hoveden (II, 37) says that the kings left Vézelay on the octave, after being there two days. Rigord (p. 99) on the other hand does not have Philip arrive until July 4.

[22] Hugh III, duke of Burgundy, 1162–92. He died at Acre in July, 1192, after commanding the French troops on the crusade after the departure of Philip.

[23] Philip of Alsace, count of Flanders, 1168–91. He was the grandson of Foulques of Anjou and had previously made an expedition to Jerusalem in 1177. At that time he had been offered the regency of the kingdom, but had refused (William of Tyre, pp. 1027–35). He died at the siege of Acre on June 1, 1191.

RICHARD SENDS HIS FLEET AHEAD

Richard the king was then at Tours
With harness, arms, and garniture.
Such swarm of men within the wall
There was, it scarce could hold them all.
He sent an order to the sea
His fleet to summon speedily,
And bade his navy to set sail
Upon their voyage without fail.   310
An hundred seven ships were counted,[24]
When they had all been launched and mounted,
Without the ones that later came
(The course they followed was the same).
Waters of danger and alarm
And straits—all pass them without harm.
They pass through Africa's dread narrows,
Where the sea ever beats and harrows;
Never a one did come to grief,
Nor wreck nor crash upon a reef.   320
They sailed, by grace of God in heaven,
Until they reached Messina's haven.
King Richard and his lords did start
And quitted Tours with joyful heart.
Then came forth many a goodly knight
And crossbowmen well tried in fight.
Ah, had ye seen the host come forth!
It set a-tremble all the earth.
Folk all about were dolorous
For their lords brave and valorous.   330
Damsels and dames were weeping there,

[24] This fleet stopped at Lisbon to assist in the Christian reconquest of Portugal.
After leaving Portugal it went to Marseilles, but finding that Richard had already
departed, went on to meet him at Messina. It was commanded by Robert de Sablé,
Richard de Camville, and William de Fortz of Oleron (Roger of Hoveden, III, 42).
The *Itinerarium* (p. 147) says it numbered 108 ships; Roger of Hoveden (III, 46)
says that when it left Lisbon it numbered 106 ships; Richard of Devizes (p. 394) says
100 *naves* and 14 *buccae*. A detailed itinerary of the fleet is given in Roger of Hoveden
(III, 42–51) and the *Gesta* (II, 116–22).

Both old and youthful, foul and fair;
Their hearts are nigh to break with woe
For kin and lover who must go.
Convoy was ne'er more pitiful,
Nor men on their return more full
Of sorrow; many tears were shed
And many pious vows were said.
The convoy then returned at last;
The pilgrims on their road made haste.   340
So on the king's appointed date,
Neither too early nor too late,
The host that God had stole away
From Satan met at Vézelay.[25]
Stole? Nay, He took them clear and fair;
'Twas for His sake they gathered there.

THE MEETING AT VÉZELAY

At Vézelay, mid mountains high,
God sheltered His own company,
And in the vales were many who
For Him had made their way thereto;   350
In vineyard and on hillside slope
Slept many a mother's son and hope.
The day was warm, serene the night;
And here were gathered in a plight
With God such band of gentle birth
As never had been seen on earth.
Those gathered here did for His sake
Their lands and families forsake,
Forswore forever or as gage
Did pledge their precious heritage,   360
Disseized themselves of land and sod,
That they might buy the love of God.

[25] The *Itinerarium* (pp. 149–50) gives the route of the march from Tours to Vézelay via Azay-le-Rideau, Montrichard, Celles, La Chapelle, D'Anguillon and Donzay.
See Note 21 above for the date of this meeting.

None could be better bargaining
Than for the love of Heaven's King.

RICHARD AND PHILIP AGREE TO DIVISION OF CONQUESTS

At Vézelay the two kings both
Did swear each other solemn oath
That, come whatever fate might bring,
Each king should trust the other king,
And of whate'er they might have won
They would make just division.   370
Another solemn oath they swore:
Who to Messina came before
The other, by some chance of fate,
Should there the other king await.
Thus, bound by oaths of solemn worth,
From Vézelay they sallied forth.
The two kings rode along ahead,
And of their journey much they said:
They gave honor and compliment
To each other everywhere they went.   380
The host moved on in such accord,
Of wrath there was no sign nor word;
They did each other courtesy
That should not unrecounted be.

THE MARCH OF THE PILGRIMS

As on their road they bravely trod,
Ye might have seen, so help me God,
Youths and maids and wives and vassals,
Bringing pitchers, cups and vessels,
And basins filled up to the brims
With water for the parched pilgrims;   390
Holding the basins in their hands,
They drew nigh to the marching bands
And said: "Oh God of Majesty,
Whence come these folk? What can this be?
These youths, where were they born and got?

Gaze on their faces flushed and hot!
Think on the sadness of their mothers,
Their parents, and their sons and brothers,
Their friends and all who do belong
To those that make this mighty throng!"   400
To God they did the host commend,
And wept to see it onward wend
Its way, and prayed wholeheartedly
To God, and asked Him piously
In His service the host to lead
And homeward bring as met His need.
They came, by God's grace sure and true—
Much did He, and much may He do—
With great delight and happiness
And without anger or distress,   410
Mocking or scorn, or strife or moan,
Straight to Lyons upon the Rhone.[26]

ARRIVAL AT LYONS

At Lyons then the army paused
Where the Rhone's water swelled and tossed.
The two kings there did make delay
For those who still were on their way.
Such marvel never yet had been,
Never such swarm of men was seen:
An hundred thousand men, 'tis known,
Most of whom slept within the town.   420
The kings took quarters in a spot
Neither in town nor garden-plot:
Beyond the Rhone's wave they disposed
Their tents to wait upon the host,
And it was needful they attend,
For many still did onward wend
Their way; they waited until thither

[26] The *Itinerarium* (p. 151) gives the route from Vézelay to Lyons: Corbigny, Moulins-Engilbert, Mont-Escot, Toulon (Saône et Loire), le Bois-Sainte-Marie, Beaujeu and Villefranche (Rhone).

The host had come and drawn together.
When they had made delay so long
That they were certain all the throng   430
Had gathered at the rendezvous,
Their hearts were filled with joy anew.
On a new spot they pitched their tents
So fair and rich in ornaments;
Hemmed by the host, upon the sand
They pitched them, all along the strand.

THEY PART COMPANY

Forth the two kings together came
So long as their paths were the same;
Then each betook him to his port
With great joy and with great disport.   440
Philip, the king of France, had made
Erstwhile arrangement for the aid
In shipping of the Genoese,
Most skilled in matters such as these;
While Richard, who led England's host,
Skirted the sea, along the coast,
And reached Marseilles following [27]
God's will, Who guides each righteous thing.

THE CROSSING OF THE RHONE

When the host learned the kings were gone
Ahead, some rose before the dawn;   450
Others when morning's light had shown
The road, for they must cross the Rhone.
Those who arose e'er break of day
Suffered no sort of disarray:
They crossed the bridge, by happy chance,
Without mishap or hinderance.
But those who in the morning passed
Crowded the bridge so thick and fast

---

[27] The *Itinerarium* (p. 153) gives the route from Lyons to Marseilles: Auberive, La Motte-de-Galure, Romans, Valence, Loriol, Paleys, St-Paul-en-Provence, Montdragon, Orange, Sorgues, Bonpas near Avignon, Senas, Salon, and Martigue.

Misfortune did them overtake.[28]
For one span of the bridge did break   460
Because of the waters treacherous,
Swollen so high and perilous.
For weight of men more than an hundred
O'ertaxed the pine arch till it sundered;
The arch fell and they tumbled in,
And there were shouting, groans, and din.
Each one, distraught by the great fall,
Thought he had lost his very all,
Brother or son or kin or friend.
But God did now His succor lend;   470
Though many fell, yet of all those
There were but two their lives did lose—
I mean but two discovered were,
To be more certain none would dare,
The water there so fiercely surges
That little which falls in emerges.
If these be dead in the world's sight,
They stand before God clean and bright:
'Twas on His path they set their feet;
They shall have mercy, as is meet.   480
The bridge's span was broke and shattered,
The pilgrims all distraught and scattered,
Not knowing whither they should go,
Whether upstream or down below.
They found no workman to repair
The bridge; there was no crossing there,
And on the Rhone no ship at all,
Nor boat nor barge, or great or small.
So they could neither follow nor
Join those who crossed the stream before.   490
Since they can find no other plan,
They seek the best device they can:
In tiny skiff-boats, frail and light,

[28] The *Itinerarium* (p. 152) does not mention those who went over the bridge early and in safety; it says only that the great number of the pilgrims broke the bridge.

Where men are pressed together tight,
They cross, in peril of their lives.
Thus must he do who for God strives.[29]

AND SAIL FOR MESSINA

Three days the ferrying went on
And there was great confusion.
Then wise and foolish went apace
To seek for their embarking place.   500
To Marseilles, nearest port at hand
There went a marvelous great band; [30]
Many brave Christians, in like sort,
Journeyed to the Venetians' port.
So many sought the Genoese
One could not count or number these;
And to Barlette and Brindisi,
Inspiring many a history.
And to Messina went a band
To wait till the two kings should land.   510

WHERE THEY ARE ILL MET BY KING AND PEOPLE

Messina is a citadel
Which hath been writ of oft and well;
It is a fine and fair-set town
In Sicily, and looketh down
Upon the Lighthouse,[31] where one sees
Reggio, which Agoland [32] did seize.
The town held good things numerous;

[29] The *Itinerarium* (p. 152) says that Richard had a bridge made of boats; "citato opera ex cymbis fortiter colligatis pontem, qualem suggerebat imminens necessitas, fecit praeparari."

[30] For the itinerary from Marseilles to Messina as given by Roger of Hoveden see Appendix B.

[31] The "Far de Messine," or Pharos of Messina, derived its name from the famous lighthouse which stood there in antiquity. The name passed from the lighthouse to the strait, and the *Estoire*, the *Itinerarium* (p. 153), Richard of Devizes (p. 396), *Gesta* (II, 138), and Roger of Hoveden (III, 66–67) all refer to the "Faro" as a body of water. The *Gesta* and Roger of Hoveden call it ancient Scylla and Charybdis.

[32] Agoland, a character in the *Chanson d'Aspremont* was a Saracen ruler who captured Reggio. See Introduction, pp. 10–12.

Its people we found villainous.
The king was called Tancred; [33] 'tis told
He had great store of purest gold,   520
By his ancestors saved and gained,
Who had since Robert Guiscard [34] reigned.
Then in Palermo lived a dame
Who long had dwelt there in good fame;
She was King William's wedded wife,
Queen of the realm during his life.[35]
But he, valiant and debonair,
Died, and 'twas pity, without heir.
The queen was sister of the king
Of England, who took means to bring   530
Her rights of dower back to her,
And Tancred did not dare demur,
Though he had taken in his power
Both the queen's person and her dower.[36]
Ye who have sense and memory,
Ye have heard well the history
Of how our ships [37] traversed the main
And sailed along the coast of Spain.
Unto Messina came the fleet—
Such marvel ne'er my eyes did greet—   540

[33] Tancred of Lecce, king of Sicily, 1189–94. See above, note 20.

[34] Robert Guiscard, the famous Norman conqueror of southern Italy, who founded the dynasty of the Hautevilles. He died in 1085, having made himself duke of Apulia.

[35] Joanna Plantagenet (1165–99), sister of Richard, had married William II in 1177. She accompanied Richard on the crusade and, after her return to France, married, in 1196, Raymond VI of Toulouse. It was Joanna who figured in Richard's negotiations with Saladin as a possible wife for Saphadin (*Dictionary of National Biography*, XXIX, 386).

[36] See note 55, for an enumeration of the goods claimed by Richard.

[37] The text has *énèques* which are called *esnecca* in the *Itinerarium*. T. A. Archer (*Crusade of Richard*, p. 12) says that they must have been a kind of transport, a statement borne out by the references in our text and the *Itinerarium*. Archer (*ibid.*, pp. 371–72) later defines them as "a special vessel reserved for royal use" and says that Richard's *esnecca* normally lay at Southampton and was commanded by one Alan Trenchemer. The fact that payments for these ships are found mentioned in the pipe rolls does not make of them, as Archer would seem to think, something in the nature of royal yachts, though it may indicate that they were ships owned by the crown, not leased or obtained through service due.

There to await the ordering
Of Richard, who was England's king.
There folk of divers lineaments,
With banners, streamers, flags, and tents,
Were quartered all along the strand,
For entrance to the town was banned.
Close to the ships they had contrived
To stay until the kings arrived;
For townsfolk, rabble, and the scum
Of the city—bastard Greeks were some,   550
And some of them Saracen-born—
Did heap upon our pilgrims scorn.
Fingers to eyes, they mocked at us,[38]
Calling us dogs malodorous.
They did us foulness every day:
Sometimes our pilgrims they did slay,
And their corpses in the privies threw.
And this was proven to be true.

UNCOURTLY ARRIVAL OF THE KING OF FRANCE

My lords, 'tis use and custom known
That when a prince of lofty crown,   560
Such as the king of France, whose worth
Is common talk o'er all the earth,
Or as the king of England, who
Is honorèd the whole world through,
Enters a town, whate'er it be,
Or such a land as Sicily,
He should come in like mighty lord,
To win all men's commending word;
For 'tis a true word, I esteem,
"As I see thee, thy worth I deem."   570
For this, I say, when came each king,
There was a mighty gathering.
Into Messina first was come
The French king, who was made welcome

[38] Evidently an allusion to the "evil eye."

By many who approached his place
Of landing, but saw not his face;
For he had but one ship, no more.[39]
He saw great crowd upon the shore,
And to avoid and circumvent
The mob, straight to the palace went.[40]   580

THE REGAL ARRIVAL OF THE KING OF ENGLAND

But when King Richard did arrive,[41]
There was vast throng did surge and strive
To see him disembark; old, young,
Wise men and gay were in the throng
That never yet the king had viewed.
To see him the whole multitude
Was eager, for his bravery.
And he came in such majesty
That all the sea around was filled
With galleys, where were seamen skilled   590
And men-at-arms, bold, dashing, gleaming,
With pennants and rich banners streaming.
When the king's ship approached the bank,
His barons and his knights of rank
Met him and led his steeds of war,
Which transport-ships had brought before.
He mounted, with his retinue,
And those who saw said that a true
And mighty king was such an one,
Well fit to hold dominion.   600

[39] Philip's fleet was never as large as Richard's, and we know from Roger of Hoveden (III, 39–40) and the *Gesta* (II, 113) that he had asked Richard for five galleys when the English king was at Portofino and that Richard had offered him three which he refused. Ibn al Athir (p. 41) says of Philip's arrival at Acre that: "He was not accompanied by as great a number of troops as the Christians had expected, having only six great ships." The same author reported Richard's fleet at Acre as twenty-five great galleys (p. 43).

[40] Roger of Hoveden (III, 54) says that he was most honorably received by Margarit, the admiral, and Jourdain du Pin, and was escorted to the palace of the king in Messina, where he was to lodge.

[41] Richard arrived at Messina September 23, 1190 (*Gesta*, II, 125; Roger of Hoveden, III, 55; Ralph of Diceto, II, 84).

But Greeks and Longobards [42] complain,
Because a foreign sovereign
Into their city made entrance
With such great pomp and circumstance.

THE MALICIOUS LONGOBARDS

When the kings came, the folk from Greece
Did nothing to disturb the peace;
The Longobards raised loud alarm
And menaced our pilgrims with harm,
Threatening to destroy or seize
Their tents and other properties.   610
They worried for their women's sake,
With whom the pilgrim-people spake—
So doing more to try them sore
Than for intention to do more.
The Longobards and populace [43]
Did always loathe and hate our race,
For by their fathers it was said
That our forbears had vanquishèd
Their own.[44] Their hate was furious,
And so they sought to famish us . . .   620
Not that we might profit thereby,
They had their towers raised on high,
And had their moats dug deeper still.
All this did but increase the ill,
What with the threats and rivalries,
The which on every hand did rise.

[42] Longobards are not Lombards, although there is often confusion; the inhabitants of southern Italy were called Longobards from the old Byzantine theme of Longobardia, which they inhabited. G. Paris explains the matter in some detail in *Romania*, XIX, 100 ff.

[43] Our translation agrees here with G. Paris in accepting the *commune* to mean "populace," not "municipal corporation." In the translation of the *Itinerarium* published in the "Bohn Library" the latter meaning is taken, and the author has given a note on this evidence of the development of self-governing communes in Sicily at this time. As nothing in either the French or the Latin texts indicates that this meaning is especially needed here, we have accepted the simpler meaning of the phrase.

[44] This line is used to show the Norman birth of the author and is noticed by all the editors and commentators.

FOMENT DISSENSION

One day into the host there came
A woman—Emma was her name
And she had bread for sale, 'tis said—
And seeing fresh and warm the bread,   630
A pilgrim made essay to buy,
And she did spurn disdainfully
The price he proffered. He was like
The woman in his wrath to strike,
And she was angry and confused.
Behold the tumult now unloosed.[45]
The townsfolk were enraged o'ermuch;
They seized the pilgrim in their clutch,
Tore out his hair, and flogged and beat him,
And very sorely did mistreat him.   640
King Richard heard the clamor: peace
He ordered and of strife surcease.
He quieted the disarray
And forced his men to keep away.
But the devil, who doth by his nature
Hate peace above all other creature,
Kindled the strife afresh next morn,
And by dissension all was torn.

RIOTING BREAKS OUT ANEW

Then the two kings together went,
Meseemeth, to a parliament;   650
The great of Sicily, magnate
And noble, judge and magistrate,
Spoke of the ways of making peace,
And while they spoke thus, at their ease,
And while the two kings said fair words
Of how to end these sore discords,
Came news and information
That our men had been set upon.

[45] According to Roger of Hoveden (III, 56–57) and Ralph of Diceto (II, 85) the quarrel broke out on October 3 and the city was taken by Richard on October 4.

Twice were the sorry tidings brought
That much of damage had been wrought;   660
And the third messenger who came
Said to the king: "Such peace is shame,
That people of this country may
The king of England's people slay
Within the city and without."
And it was true, beyond a doubt,
The Longobards left the gathering,
Having most falsely told each king
They meant to quiet and disperse
The strife. They went to make it worse.   670
Jourdain du Pin [46] and Margarit [47]
(All evils smite them, as is fit!)

[46] Jourdain du Pin was the commandant of Messina under Tancred (Chalandon, *Domination normande*, II, 438).

[47] G. Paris (p. 553) says in identifying Margarit: "Il ne faut sans doute pas le confondre avec le célèbre Margarit, amiral de Guillaume le Bon de Sicile, qui secourut efficacement la Syrie en 1188." However, texts other than that of Ambroise make it clear that it was the admiral who received Richard at Messina. Roger of Hoveden (III, 57) and Richard of Devizes (p. 399) both distinctly call him the admiral. Pio Rajna (*Romania*, XIV, 418 ff.) points out that the great admiral was generally called Margaritone to distinguish him from other persons of the same name which was a common one in Sicily at the time. This, however, does not preclude the use of the shorter form Margarit on occasion. Chalandon indexes this governor of Messina separately from the admiral, but gives no reason. Archer (*Richard*, p. 31) identifies him as the admiral, and we see no reason to support the conclusion of Paris and Chalandon that he was not the famous sailor. Margarit of Brindisi, count of Malta and Cephalonia, was the commander of the Sicilian navy under King William the Good and married the sister of that monarch. He was considered the greatest admiral of his time and was especially conspicuous in the eastern waters. In 1185 he conquered Corfu and the Ionian Islands; in 1188 he brought succor to Tripoli, Laodicea, and other Christian ports attacked by Saladin; it was with his assistance that Isaac Comnenus, his brother-in-law, made himself despot of Cyprus and repulsed the attempts of the Angeli to bring him to subjection. There is no mention of him in the east in 1190, so he may very well have been at Messina at that date. He was in Italy in 1192 when he defeated the Pisans off Naples. Chalandon reports that he was taken prisoner by Henry VI and sent to Germany. This is the last mention of him in Chalandon or in the *Enciclopedia italiana*, but Archer (p. 31) adds that he later made his peace with Henry and was made duke of Durazzo in 1194. Certainly at that date he was succeeded in his lordship of the Ionian Islands by his son-in-law and the Orsini. Archer further reports his death in Rome in 1200. (Chalandon, *passim*; Archer, p. 31; *Enciclopedia italiana*; Mas Latrie, *Trésor de chronologie*, p. 2219.)

These two the quarrel did begin;
They were its source and origin.[48]
There did the king of England stand,
And the king of France was close at hand,
And he who did the tale recount.
The king of England then did mount
His horse and ride to quell the fray;
But even as he rode away   680
Those of the town said villainies
To him, insults and calumnies.
The king took arms, and gave command
That on the sea and on the land
They be assailed; the whole world o'er
There was no mightier warrior.

IN WHICH THE FRENCH TAKE NO PART

Great was the stir and turmoil, great
The strife, the town in parlous state.
The French sought their king anxiously
In the king of England's hostelry,   690
For the city was in such uproar
They never thought to find him more.
Then to the palace he returned
Where he before dwelt and sojourned.
The Longobards then hastened up,
And clasped him by his left stirrup,
Gave gifts and promises to pay,
Gave him the honors of the day,
Begged his protection and his aid
Within the town, and freely made   700
Themselves subjects of his domain.

[48] The description of this trouble is clearer in Roger of Hoveden (III, 57) and Richard of Devizes (p. 399). Philip and Richard were holding a conference with representatives of Tancred, among whom were Margarit the admiral, Jourdain du Pin, the archbishops of Monreale, Pisa, and Messina. A riot broke out outside, and du Pin and Margarit went out, presumably to stop it. Instead they incited the mob to further violence and stirred up the people against the English. After peace had been concluded between Richard and Tancred, Margarit and du Pin fled from Messina and Richard sacked their houses. (Roger of Hoveden, III, 66.)

And so, with effort, cost, and pain,
Persuaded him to take up arms.
One worthy of belief affirms
That he gave the Sicilians more
Of aid than he the English bore.
The tempest once again released,
The turmoil through the host increased.
The French within the city were
At ease and free from grief and care.   710
The Longobards trusted them indeed,
Though the host gave but little heed.
Now were the gates shut fast and close;
The townsfolk, armed and bellicose,
Mounted the ramparts to defend
Them; but they needs must soon descend.
And those who from the city sallied
And in a deadly onslaught rallied
Where my lord Hugh le Brun [49] did dwell,
Were fighting hand to hand, pell-mell,   720
When England's king arrived. A score
Of men he had with him, no more,
I think, when he first joined the fray.
Seeing him, the Longobards straightway
Their threatening abandonèd
And turned upon their heels and fled.
The bold king followed close and pressed
Upon them. Ambrose doth attest
That when they saw him come, ye might
Have thought them sheep who take to flight   730
When menaced by the wolf's fierce maw.
Like oxen who on yoke do draw,

---

[49] Hugh le Brun, IX lord of Lusignan, and count of La Marche, eldest son of Hugh VIII of Lusignan, also called le Brun, and elder brother of Geoffrey, Aymeri, and Guy de Lusignan. Archer (p. 32) confuses Hugh IX with his father. It was Hugh VIII who went to Syria in 1163 and was captured by Nureddin (William of Tyre, pp. 894–97, 1063). Hugh IX became count of La Marche in 1199 by seizing the fief in the confusion at the death of Richard. In 1218 he again took the cross and died at Damietta in 1219 (Mas Latrie, *Trésor*, p. 1631).

These men toward the postern hied
Which opens on Palermo's side,
Where he assailed them, and I know
Not how many of them laid low.
The host was roused, and all took horse,
Since they had been assailed in force
By Longobards most outrageous
And angry Greeks perfidious.   740

BUT THE ENGLISH ATTACK VALIANTLY BY LAND

But ours were men of tried renown,
Who had invested many a town:
They were Normans and Poitevins,
Gascons, Manceaux, and Angevins,
While of those who from England came
Were more than one could tell or name.
So they attack them, bold and stout,
When on the wall they spy them out.
And all around the town they ride,
Until they make their way inside.   750
The townsfolk shoot, and missiles throw,
And do great harm to those below.
With shafts, from bow and cross-bow shot,
Which they had ready, fierce they fought,
Hurled stones and rocks down from the wall,
And did our men great harm withal.
Arrows and bolts flew thick as rain,
Doing our pilgrims hurt and pain.
Three of our knights were struck with mortal
Wounds, as they entered through a portal.   760
And Peter Tireproie [50] was one
Whose body they cast dead upon
The road. Maheu de Sauçoi, too,

---

[50] Peter Tireproie, Maheu de Sauçoi, and Ralph de Rovroi are not known beyond this reference to their death. Rovrai was in Normandy near Neufchâtel, and an Osbert de Rovrai and a John de Rovrai appear in the *Guillaume le Maréchal* (ll. 7616, 19153, and Meyer's note, III, 90). G. Paris (pp. xi–xii) says that Maheu came from LaManche and Ralph from the Eure.

Whose corpse on the same spot they threw.
And Ralph de Rovroi's corpse was found
('Tis proven truth) there on the ground.
For them was grief and requiem;
God grant salvation unto them!
Had the Longobards been brave and loyal,
Ill would have fared the soldiers royal;   770
But their rank folly did but make
Us eager swift revenge to take.
Those who the town defended then
Were more than fifty thousand men,
On walls and in the towers concealed,
Guarded by target and by shield.
There had ye seen fierce combat waged
By many mighty men enraged.

AND BY SEA TO CAPTURE THE CITY

The galleys toward the palace drew,
Intending to assail anew.   780
But on the shore, where they had planned
To attack, the king of France took stand,
And would not let the galleys in
The port, which thus they could not win.
But from the shore they shot and slew
Two seamen—a foul thing to do.
But on the landward side the king
Of England fierce assault did bring,
Smote the Longobards with attack
So deadly that he drove them back.   790
His men—'twas a fair spectacle—
Surmounted every obstacle
And clove the portal-bolts in twain.[51]
Many were captured, many slain.
And headlong through the streets some went,
Who of their rashness did repent;
For from the houses' upper floors

[51] The *Itinerarium* (p. 162) says that they could not cut the gates, so entered by a postern and, once inside, broke down the gate and let the army in.

Rained missiles on the warriors.
And yet, for all they strove and fought,
They could not stand 'gainst this onslaught.   800
Whoever 'twas brought up the rear,
The king was of the first to dare
Make entrance in the town, and then
There followed him ten thousand men.
Then had ye heard our men outcry

. . .

And storm and slash with fearsome shout,
And wound and smite and lay about.
They had seized Messina long before
A priest had said his matins o'er;   810
Many had perished in the city
If the king had not taken pity.
And ye may know of surety
That much was lost of property
When they successfully attacked
The town. It speedily was sacked;
Their galleys were destroyed and burned,
Which were not poor or to be spurned.
And there were women taken, fair
And excellent and debonair.   820
I could not find the truth out wholly,
But whether sense it were or folly,
Before our own host was aware,
The French had seen flung to the air
Atop the walls our flags and banners
At many points, in many manners.
Which in the French king did create
Envy that time will ne'er abate.
And herewith was the warring born
Whereby was Normandy sore torn.[52]   830

[52] This, of course, refers to the war which broke out in Normandy after Philip's return from the crusade. The fighting continued throughout the reign of Richard and was resumed after his death in the struggle between Philip and John, which ended only with the complete conquest of Normandy by the French.

PHILIP RESENTS RICHARD'S TRIUMPH

> The king, when he had seized the town
> And on the walls his standards flown,
> Had message from the king of France,
> Envious words of arrogance,
> That he and his were grieved and mazed
> Because the standards had been raised.
> Let them be lowered, he directed,
> And on the city walls erected
> French banners in their stead forsooth.[53]
> And further he sent word, in truth,   840
> That by his acts Richard did plain
> Disservice to his suzerain,
> And so he took him sore to task.
> My lords, your judgment now I ask:
> Who has more right to fly his flags,
> The one who stands aside and lags,
> Unwilling the attack to share,
> Or he who doth essay and dare?
> King Richard heard the message sent,
> And did not deign long argument   850
> To make with Philip, who was thus
> Stirred into wrath tempestuous.
> Nevertheless, was said and heard
> Many a cutting shameful word.
> But in a book it is not fit
> That every folly should be writ.

RICHARD SENDS ENVOYS TO TANCRED

> Great men and great clerks then did plead
> And argue, till they had agreed
> On peace upon such terms and manners
> That each king might erect his banners   860
> On tower and on battlement.[54]

[53] Philip was here claiming his share of everything which should be captured or acquired by either king while on the crusade; see above, p. 44.

[54] Roger of Hoveden (III, 58–60) gives the text of the accord reached between

And they arranged that word be sent
Straight to the king of Sicily
Of the outrage and contumely
That had to them and theirs been shown
By this community and town.
King Richard's legates should explain
On his behalf and make it plain
That he, by right of lawful power,
Required of him his sister's dower,   870
And such a share of the great treasure
As she might claim in legal measure,
And all that law and justice might
Award the lady as her right.[55]
The messengers were promptly named:
Right noble men, renowned and famed,
Of very lofty parentage
And lordship and high lineage
And very great capacity,
Departed on this embassy.   880
Among this deputation
The duke of Burgundy was one,
And Robert de Sablé,[56] likewise,

Richard and Philip on October 8, 1190. The treaty does not mention any partition of
conquests; it concerns itself chiefly with the disposition of the property of crusaders
who died en route, with regulations about gambling in the camp (it was permitted
only to the leaders) and the rules governing the sale of commodities to the crusaders.

[55] Roger of Hoveden (III, 61) and Richard of Devizes (pp. 395–96) enumerate
the goods and properties claimed by Richard as the dower of Joanna, and as the goods
bequeathed by King William to King Henry whose heir Richard was. Joanna's dower
consisted of the county of Mont Saint Angelo with all its appurtenances and a gilded
chair which belonged to her as queen of Sicily. As heir of Henry, Richard claimed the
legacy left his father by William which consisted of: a golden table, a large silk tent,
24 golden cups and 24 golden plates, 60,000 measures each of wheat, barley, and
wine, and a hundred armed galleys with provisions for the crews for two years. Tancred had given Joanna a million *terrini* in quittance of her dower claims; his further
concessions were made in compensation for the legacy made to King Henry.

[56] Robert de Sablé, an important Angevin baron, was one of the commanders of
Richard's fleet (Roger of Hoveden, III, 42). He would seem to be the same man
who entered the Temple and became Master 1191–96, although Archer (*Richard*,
p. 9) thinks they were not the same.

Brave, noble, skilled in courtesies;
And mayhap many another came
Of whom I do not know the name.
These noblemen then took to horse
And on the road made rapid course
Toward Palermo, there to bring
And tell their message to the king.[57]   890

WHO REPLIES WITH FAIR WORDS

King Tancred, who was very wise,
Gave hearing to the deputies.
With much adventure had been filled
His life; he was good clerk and skilled
To write. He knew what had been done.
No long deliberation
He made; he did not pause or stay,
But made reply without delay
Unto the king of England's men,
That to his country's regimen,   900
The customs of King William, and
The lords and barons of his land
This quarrel he would now submit,
And do what seemed to all most fit.
And if Messina's burgesses
Had done unseemly vilenesses
To harm the kings and to offend,
They should be held to make amend.
And when the messengers sent by
King Richard had heard this reply,   910
Some among them declared, indeed,
That the king should not thuswise plead,
And much they spoke in remonstrance.

[57] The *Itinerarium* (p. 166) has here a paragraph telling how Philip was jealous and demanded a share in the plunder of Messina. Richard, angered, made preparations to depart, but Philip forced a reconciliation and they renewed their agreement to share equally. This is the same quarrel which Ambroise narrates earlier and which was settled by the treaty of October 8. The *Itinerarium* would seem to have placed it out of its proper order.

But on the messengers of France
Were very goodly cups bestowed.
The others then their patience bode.[58]

PHILIP'S PERFIDY

Now shall ye hear the great discord,
Recorded then and afterward,
The which the king of France did do.
For he, 'twould seem, sent message to   920
King Tancred very secretly
(I know not what he hoped thereby)
To do what seemed good in his sight
And that he should defend his right;
That he of France would never make
War upon him for England's sake;
That he to Tancred aid did swear.
If this was so, ill did it fare.
History doth not guarantee
That he contrived such villainy,   930
But true or not, people averred
As truth that he had sent such word.[59]
Those who had got no cups retraced
Their footsteps in the greatest haste;
Their message held in mind and learned,
Back to Messina they returned.

MATEGRIFON IS RICHARD'S ANSWER

King Richard then was occupied
In building, with great joy and pride,

[58] The *Itinerarium* (p. 167) says that Tancred gave gold cups to the French envoys, but not so much as an egg to the envoys of Richard.

[59] The *Gesta* (II, 159-61), Roger of Hoveden (III, 98-100), and Richard of Devizes (p. 403) have a long account of plot and counterplot. Richard and Tancred had an interview at Catania at which Tancred showed Richard letters from Philip plotting against the English monarch. Richard was furious; but Philip flatly denied the authorship of the letters, and an agreement was finally reached between them through the agency of the count of Flanders. Philip agreed to free Richard of his obligation to marry Alice of France, and surrendered to him the lordship of Gisors in return for the payment by Richard of 2,000 marks of silver each year for five years.

Mategrifon, a strong château,
Which filled the Greeks with jealous woe.   940
To him the messengers then brought
Report of that which they had sought
Of Tancred and of what he had
Replied to the demands they made:
To wit, the law would be his guide
And what his barons should decide.
To this replied Richard the king,
And stayed not in his answering:
He would not plead in such a court,
But to his own means would resort.   950
When there was noised abroad the news
That there would be nor peace nor truce,
The fear of war became most grave,
For the support the French king gave
The Longobards, who, shrewd and sly,
Had made of this king their ally.

WHEREUPON TANCRED OFFERS CONCESSIONS

Now to the host came none or little
Of any kind of food or victual.
Had not the ships and God been there,
They would have had but meager fare;   960
But in the vessels of the fleet
Was store of wine and corn and meat.
The town by night was guarded well,
And the host posted sentinel
And guard. The kings were reft apart
Through envy, which doth all dispart.
'Twas not a fair or worthy thing.
People of rank strove hard to bring
Them peace and make the strife subside;
So to the palace they would ride   970
At Mategrifon, and then back
Return along the selfsame track.
For all they tried, and tried again,

Their every effort was in vain,
As the book maketh clear and plain

. . .

Before the king of Sicily,
Who knew the town's wrongs thoroughly,
Took two knights—one of them the son
Of his chancellor,[60] and the other one,   980
Meseemeth, was his constable,[61]
A brave man and reliable—
And to the king of England sent
Them, bearing word that his intent
Was not for war in any way,
But if King Richard would take pay
His claims and grievances to cease,
Most willingly would he make peace
And from his treasure pay a score
Of thousand golden ounces o'er.   990
And if of marriage he were moved
To speak, and if his lords approved,
That his own daughter, a princess
Unwed, of worth and loveliness,[62]
He'd give to Arthur of Bretaine; [63]
And that he might this end attain

[60] Roger of Hoveden (III, 62) calls him Richard, the son of Walter the chancellor. But Chalandon (*Domination normande*, II, 440) corrects to Richard, the son of the chancellor Mathew d'Ajello. This Richard was one of Tancred's intimates and appears frequently as one of the king's envoys or councilors (*ibid.*: II, *passim*).

[61] The identity of this constable is not known. William de San Severino was constable in 1186 (Chalandon, II, 689), but whether he continued in that office until 1190 we cannot say.

[62] Tancred had three daughters, Sybelle, Alvira, and Constance (Chalandon, II, 475). Alvira later married Gautier III of Brienne and carried to her husband the title of Lecce. Which daughter was here referred to is not known. The text of the treaty as given in Roger of Hoveden (III, 63) does not specify, saying only that he will give his daughter.

[63] Arthur of Brittany was the son of Geoffrey of Brittany and was Richard's nephew. He was born March 29, 1187, so was still quite young at this time. He is the prince who opposed John after the death of Richard and was probably murdered by John in 1203. (*Dictionary of National Biography*, II, 129.)

Gave solemn pledge to pay a score
Of thousand golden ounces more.
But these, he said, must be repaid
If Arthur did not wed the maid.   1,000
And likewise the king's sister he
Would send to him most readily.

WHICH RICHARD ACCEPTS

King Richard, hearing this, did not
Spend time in counsel or long thought,
But straightway other legates sent
To make sound peace and permanent.[64]
To the archbishop of Monreale [65]
And him of Reggio, faithful ally,[66]
The bishop of Evreux, hight John,[67]
On whom was wrong and damage done,   1,010
The king his mission did depute;

[64] The text of this treaty is given by Roger of Hoveden (III, 61–64), *Gesta* (II, 133–35). A letter from Richard to Pope Clement telling of the negotiation of the treaty and stating its provisions is also given by Roger of Hoveden (III, 65–67) and *Gesta* (II, 136–38). Richard acknowledged the receipt of the 20,000 gold pieces and promised that he would grant Tancred's daughter a dower out of the lands of Arthur. He declared that if he did not have heirs of his own body Arthur should be his heir and that Arthur's wife should have the dower of an English queen. A full and perpetual peace was sworn by the two kings, with terms of alliance and mutual assistance. The treaty was guaranteed by the Roman Church and by an imposing list of nobles. As these guarantors were the chief barons of the crusading host, it seems worth while to publish their names: Walter, archbishop of Rouen; Gerard, archbishop of Auch; John, bishop of Evreux; Bernard, bishop of Bayonne; Jordan des Homez, constable of Séez; William de Courcy; Richard Camville; Gerard Talbot; Robert de Sablé; Guy de Craon; Guarin Fitz-Gerold; Bertrand de Verdun; William, chamberlain of Tancarville; Robert de Newburgh; Hugh Bardolf; Wigain de Cherbourg; Gilbert de Vascueil; Hugh le Brun; John de Préaux; Amaury de Montfort; Andrew de Chauvigny; William de Fortz of Oléron; Geoffrey Rançon; Aymeri Torel.

[65] William, archbishop of Monreale, is mentioned in the treaty as one of the negotiators on the part of Tancred (Roger of Hoveden, III, 62). He was archbishop of Monreale 1183–90, was suggested by Richard for the see of Canterbury, and died at the siege of Acre, 1190 (Roger of Hoveden, III, 57n; *Gesta*, II, 148).

[66] William, archbishop of Reggio, is also mentioned as one of the negotiators in the text of the treaty. The other negotiators were Richard, archbishop of Messina, and Richard, the son of the chancellor.

[67] John, bishop of Evreux, 1180–92; he died at Jaffa (Gams, *Series episcoporum*, p. 550; G. Paris, p. 550). He was one of the guarantors of the treaty.

They knew the issue in dispute.
And other worthies went with these.
'Twas peace they sought; they brought back peace.
And caused to be brought back the gold
And wealth of which but now I told.
When they returned from their employ,
The peace filled every man with joy.
So now the charts were duly read
And verified and copièd;   1,020
And so the peace they sought and swore,
Whence folk were reassured once more.
The gold was weighed and proven right,[68]
Which gave the king no small delight.
He greatly wished it, for he meant
That in God's service it be spent.[69]
His sister back to him was brought,
And dear was her deliverance bought.
The king willed that without delay
Whate'er his men had snatched away   1,030
From burgess or from citadel
Should be restored. It stood him well.
To his confessor each must state
(Lest he be excommunicate)
How he restored all. 'Twas the wise
Archbishop of Rouen's [70] advice.

[68] The treaty acknowledges receipt of 20,000 ounces of gold (Roger of Hoveden, III, 63); Rigord (p. 106) says that Tancred paid the 40,000 ounces at this time.

[69] The *Eracles* (p. 155) says that Richard persuaded Joanna to contribute her dower to the crusade and promised her in return that he would endow her anew and find her a good husband when he came back from the crusade. William of Newburgh (I, 347) says Joanna sold her dower to Tancred that she might accompany Richard.

[70] Walter of Coutances, archbishop of Rouen 1184–1207, was one of Richard's trusted advisors. He had been a chancery clerk under Henry II and had risen to be bishop of Lincoln and archbishop of Rouen. Richard sent him back to England from Sicily to act as his representative during his absence and to straighten out the difficulties which had arisen between the chancellor, whom he had left as regent, and the barons. Walter ruled England as chief justiciar during Richard's absence and was responsible for raising much of the king's ransom. During the term of payment of the ransom he went to Germany as a hostage for the payment. (*Dictionary of National Biography*, XII, 351–54.) Richard of Devizes (p. 404) calls him "as clergy generally

AND PEACE IS RESTORED

Now was the town in fair array
Without or quarrel or affray,
And whosoever ventured to
Make strife, they promptly hanged or slew.   1,040
The host had justice true and fair;
Blessed be his soul who set it there!
The roads were traveled as before,
And there was goodly food once more,
Both food for man and food for beast.
And so it was the trouble ceased.
The townsfolk, calmed, did cheerfully
Give pilgrims hospitality.
The two kings left off strife,[71] though true
It is that oft it flared anew   1,050
At later times. The gold with care
They did divide, to each his share.[72]

RICHARD'S GENEROSITY

The knights who all the summer long
Had been there, said that it was wrong
To linger. They made loud laments
Because it cost them much expense.
And the complaints went here and there
Until they reached King Richard's ear;
Who promised so much to provide
That each one would be satisfied.   1,060
Richard, who knows not avarice,

---

are, pusillanimous and cowardly," and says that he cooked up excuses to return from the crusade, which Richard accepted, as they were accompanied by hard cash.

[71] Ralph of Diceto (p. 86) here says that Richard secured his release from his promise to marry Alice of France for a payment of £10,000.

[72] The *Itinerarium* (pp. 169–70) says that Richard gave Philip half of the money he received from Tancred and half of Joanna's dower. Rigord (p. 106) says that as it was Philip who interceded for Richard and brought about the conclusion of the peace, Richard gave him a third of the sums paid him by Tancred; but he should have given him the half. The *Itinerarium* (pp. 170–71) here inserts a chapter omitted by the *Estoire* telling of Richard's interview with Tancred at Catania (see above, p. 15).

Then gave them gifts of such rich price—
Bowls made of silver, cups of gold
In lapfuls, all that they could hold,
According to their several ranks—
That his largesse won praise and thanks
From great, from middling, and from small.
His gifts were so seignorial
That, though unmounted, each pilgrim
Received a hundred sous from him.   1,070
And he bestowed gifts of great cost
On dames and maidens who had lost
Their Syrian lands and furthermore
Had been cast forth from Syria's shore.
And with like lavish gifts the king
Of France did please his following.[73]
Now is the host all happiness
For the great honor and largesse
And for the warfare that has ceased.
Now there was held the mighty feast: 1,080
The day of the Nativity   Dec. 25, 1190
King Richard, of a verity,
Had cried about that one and all
Should hold with him their festival,
And led, by effort and by word,
The king of France to share his board.

CHRISTMAS FESTIVITIES

They held this solemn festival
At Mategrifon, in the hall
That England's king had built by might
For all the citizens' despite.   1,090
I saw the feasting and the fare,
But saw no soilèd napkin there,
No hanap and no bowl of wood.

[73] Rigord (pp. 106–7) gives the specific grants made by Philip: to the duke of Burgundy, 1,000 marks; to the count of Nevers, 600 marks; to William des Barres, 400 marks; to G. de Mello, 400 ounces of gold; to the bishop of Chartres, to Mathew de Montmorency, and to Dreux de Mello, 300 ounces of gold each.

But I saw vessels rich and good
With chiseled carvings fair inlaid
And molded images displayed,
So set with precious gems and bright
That they gave pleasure to the sight.
And I saw service that was done
So well that it pleased everyone.   1,100
It was a fine and noble fête—
As was fit and appropriate.
I never saw, together, rich
And splendid presents like those which,
Meseems, King Richard did bestow
And generously give unto
The French king and his retinue
In plate of gold and silver too.[74]

PHILIP SAILS FOR ACRE

The time now came to cross the sea;
Brave men made ready prudently.   1,110
From Our Lady's day in September   Sept. 8, 1190
Till end of Lent,[75] if I remember,   Mar. 1191
Hard by Messina had sojourned
The host, who very greatly yearned
To be at Acre, the task to share
With those who to lay siege did dare
Where there was much of grief and woe,
More than was given us to know.
Travail and hardship most severe
And pain they bore in that half-year.   1,120
Now when they all were well reposed
And for their voyage God had disposed
All things, 'twas of a verity
The king of France who took to sea

[74] The *Itinerarium* (p. 174) here inserts the story of an attack on Richard's fleet and its guards which is omitted by the *Estoire*.

[75] Lady's Day is September 8. The *Itinerarium* (p. 174) says St. Michael's Day—Sept. 29—which is nearer the correct date.

And with his men, shortly before
Palm Sunday came, he quit the shore.[76]   April 7, 1191

ADVENT OF BERENGARIA

King Richard cannot move from there,
For still unready is his gear,
The ships and galleys that he needs
For transport of his battle steeds,   1,130
His armor and supplies as well
With which to smite the infidel.
So longer time he needs must take
And better preparation make.
The French king he accompanied,
Then sailed along the Beacon's side
His galley and to Reggio went,
Whence he received a message sent,
Saying his mother had come there,[77]
Accompanying his bride, a fair   1,140
And worthy damsel, true and good,
Of very gentle womanhood,
Faithful, and clean of wrong or shame,
And Berengaria was her name.[78]
Her father, ruler of Navarre,

[76] Palm Sunday was April 7 in 1191. This agrees with other dates. The *Itinerarium* (p. 175) says Saturday after the Annunciation, which was March 30. The *Gesta* (II, 161) and Roger of Hoveden (III, 100) say the 3 Kalends of April—March 30, Ralph of Diceto (p. 91) says 4 Kalends, but a variant reading in the note says 3. The *Estoire* here is a bit more vague than the other accounts, but the general date agrees.

[77] Eleanor of Aquitaine, daughter and heiress of William X of Aquitaine, divorced wife of Louis VII of France, and widow of Henry II, mother of Richard. She arrived at Messina the same day that Philip left—3 Kalends of April (*Gesta*, II, 161). The *Eracles* (p. 158) says that she was determined that Richard should not marry Alice of France, and so brought with her Berengaria. (*Dictionary of National Biography*, XVII, 175-78.)

[78] Berengaria of Navarre, daughter of Sancho VI of Navarre, wife of Richard 1191-99, dowager queen of England 1199-c. 1230. After the death of Richard she held Le Mans as her dower. Her sister Blanche married Thibaut III of Champagne and brought the title of Navarre into the house of Champagne. (*Dictionary of National Biography*, IV, 325.) Richard of Devizes (p. 402) calls her "puella prudentiore quam pulchra."

Had given her into the care
Of Richard's mother, who did guide
Her safely to King Richard's side.
Later she was called queen; most dear
The king did love her and revere;   1,150
Since he was count of Poitiers,
His wish had wished for her alway.
He had his mother taken to
Messina with her retinue
Of maids; each to the other told
His pleasure and did naught withhold.
He kept with him the maiden whom
He loved, and sent his mother home
To rule his land in place of him,
So that naught might his honor dim.   1,160
Walter, archbishop of Rouen,
A wise man, he relied upon
With her to keep o'er England guard,
Where much he warred and labored hard.
And with them, in their company,
Went Gilbert of Vascueil; [79] 'twas he
Who let Gisors be taken away
From us. The king did not delay
Thenceforth his galleys to prepare—
To load and stock his ships with care.   1,170
He made all ready for the start,
Delayed no longer to depart.
To sea his barons he sent forth; [80]
Likewise his bride,[81] of goodly worth,

[79] Gilbert de Vascueil was a Norman knight, one of the guarantors of Richard's treaty with Tancred. G. Paris (p. xii) identifies him as from the Eure. His surrender of Gisors to the French in April, 1193, was said by the *Itinerarium* (p. 176) to have been treason. (Powicke, *Loss of Normandy*, pp. 144–45.) The *Itinerarium* here gives the route of Eleanor's return to Normandy. Landon, *Itinerary* (pp. 59, 192), gives records of his accounts showing loans from Roman bankers to get the queen home.

[80] The *Itinerarium* (p. 176) notes that the fleet was placed under the command of Robert of Turnham.

[81] Richard of Devizes (p. 422) says that Berengaria "forte adhuc virgo" was in the first ship with Joanna.

And many noble knights beside
Went with his sister and his bride,
In one great dromond, so that they
Might cheer each other on the way.

RICHARD LEAVES MESSINA

And first of all he sent them on
To sail toward the rising sun.   1,180
The vessels of the swifter sort
Remained a longer time in port
And waited for the king to eat,
Then in array sailed forth the fleet
Of ships and vessels marvelous.
'Twas in a week most dolorous
That the fleet left Messina's port
To bring God glory and support.
'Twas Wednesday of the Holy Week [82]   April 10, 1191
When God knew pain and travail bleak   1,190
That we, for our part, sufferèd
From vigils and from fear and dread.
Messina, though, where skirt the coast
So many ships, may take proud boast
That never upon any day
Did so rich fleet thence sail away.

[82] The *Itinerarium* (p. 177) says "17 days after the departure of the king of France, on the Wednesday after Palm Sunday." The Wednesday after Palm Sunday was April 10, which agrees with Roger of Hoveden (III, 105) who says "4th day before Coenam" and with Ralph of Diceto (II, 86) who says "4 Ides April." The *Itinerarium* is wrong in its statement of 17 days after the departure of Philip.

CHAPTER II

A STORM AT SEA

The fleet, in order, forth did stand
Toward the woe-stricken Holy Land;
Sped past the Beacon steadily
Towards Acre into the open sea.   1,200
To join the transport we made sail,
But then we saw the fair wind fail
So that the king would fain turn back.
That night we had to stop, for lack
Of wind, no matter what befell,
Betwixt Kalabre and Montgibel.[1]
And then on Maundy Thursday day   April 11, 1191
He Who had ta'en the wind away,
He Who can give as well as take,
Did willing restitution make   1,210
And lent it to us all day long.
But it was weak, and so the strong
And rich armada needs must pause.
The day of worshiping the Cross   April 12
A wind contrary smote us there
Upon the left, hard by Viaires.[2]
The sea was deeply stirred and troubled,

[1] G. Paris identifies Montgibel as Mount Etna.
[2] Paris suggests that this is probably Cape Spartivento.

And the strong blast its strength redoubled,
And the waves bent beneath its force,
So we did naught but lose our course.   1,220
And we had fear and we did sicken,
In mouth and heart and head sore stricken.
But though we suffered much distress,
We suffered it with willingness.
And it was justly we sustained
It, for the sake of Him Who deigned
This day the Passion to endure
That our redemption might be sure.
Strong was the gale that drove us wide
Until the fall of eventide.   1,230
And then we had a gentle wind,
Most favorable, fair, and kind.

THE VOYAGE TO RHODES

King Richard did a noble thing;
His heart to good was swift to spring.
It was his custom every night
Upon his ship to set a light,
A lantern kindled that did show
A very clear and brilliant glow
And burned all night till break of day
To show the other ships their way.   1,240
With him good mariners he had,
Stout folk and well skilled in their trade;
All drew toward the king's bright light,
And hardly took from it their sight,
And if somewhat the vessels strayed,
Nobly the king his own ship stayed.
This fleet of mighty ships and men
He guided, as the mother hen
Doth guide toward the feed her brood.[3]

[3] Richard of Devizes (pp. 422–23) gives the arrangement of the fleet. It was divided into eight sections: 3 ships in the first, 13 in the second, 14 in the third, 20 in the fourth, 30 in the fifth, 40 in the sixth, 60 in the seventh, while the eighth was made up of Richard's galleys of which there were 39. The lines were so spaced that a

Lyons

Genoa
Portofino
Portovenere
Marseilles
Pisa
Isle Gorgona
Baratto
Piombino
Talamone
Porto Ercole
CORSICA
Civita Vecchia
Ostia · Rome
Nettuno · Astura
Naples
Amalfi
SARDINIA
Salerno
Capri
Cape Licosa
Scalea
S. Euphemia
Messina
Palermo
Cefalu
Reggio
SICILY
Mileto
Catania
Syracuse

Venice

ADRIATIC SEA

Brindisi

MEDITERRAN

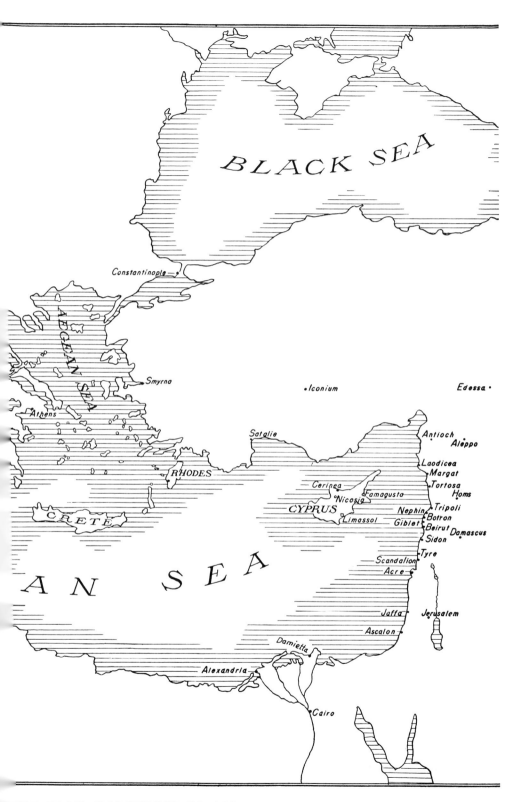

BLACK SEA

Constantinople

AEGEAN SEA

Smyrna

Iconium

Edessa •

Athens

Satalie

Antioch

Aleppo

RHODES

Laodicea

Margat

Tortosa

Homs

Cerinea

CYPRUS

Nicosia

Famagusta

Tripoli

Nephin

Botron

Limassol

Giblet

Beirut

Damascus

CRETE

Sidon

Tyre

Scandalion

Acre

SEA

Jaffa

Jerusalem

Ascalon

Damietta

Alexandria

Cairo

ꓕTE FROM MARSEILLES TO ACRE

Such was his native knightlihood.   1,250
And all that night we sailed on, free
From mishap and from misery.
And Easter eve, which was the morrow,   April 13
God led us without grief or sorrow
And that night too, without delay,
And so the whole of Easter day.   April 14
The fleet three full days onward sped,
And never sail was lowerèd.
The king himself led on the fleet.
Wednesday we came in sight of Crete.[4]   April 17
The king of England landward bore   1,261
To skirt the isle, close to the shore.
There he and the fleet with him stayed.
But five and twenty vessels strayed
That night, and drifted far from us,
Whereat the king was furious
And by distress and anger torn.
The sails were hoisted on the morn.
We sailed for Rhodes—'twas on Thursday—   April 18
Another isle not far away.   1,270
The wind was strong, the waves were high,
And swift as doth the swallow fly
So speeds the ship with bending mast.
God led us marvelously fast.
Along the coast of Rhodes we sailed
With seamanship that never failed.
A sign that He with joy did look
Upon the way His people took.
And so we went—'tis truth I tell—
Swiftly until the black night fell.   1,280
The morrow morn we came upon
A strait, whereat we did take down
Our canvas, and had rest from woes,

---

trumpet could be heard from one line to the next, and the ships within the line were
close enough that a man's voice could be heard from one ship to the next.

  [4] The *Itinerarium* (p. 179) gives here a description of Crete; a tall hill on the
island, called the Camel, was said to be just half way between Messina and Acre.

And there till Sunday did repose.[5]   April 21
And into Rhodes we came at morn,
The city where was Herod born.[6]

THEY TARRY IN RHODES AND PROCEED TO SATALIE

Rhodes was a very mighty town
And ancient; its antique renown
Was nigh to rival Rome's, although
'Tis hard the truth complete to know.   1,290
So many dwellings are defaced
And wrecked, and walls and towers laid waste,
So many churches have survived,
So many folk here dwelt and lived
So many years, so many ages,
Throughout such diverse seignorages,
That no man could enumerate
Without annoyance very great.
Its nobleness and magnitude
Have fallen through decrepitude;   1,300
Nevertheless there still dwelt there
People who sold us provender;
And since it happened that the king
Was ill and somewhat suffering,
'Twas meet that we in Rhodes sojourn.
He strove to seek out and to learn
Whither his missing ships had gone.
His galleys he did wait upon
Which followed him close to the land,
And he enquired and made demand   1,310
About the tyrant king who reigned
O'er Cyprus's isle and who detained
The pilgrims there. Ten days we spent
In Rhodes, and then, when forth we went,

[5] The *Itinerarium* (p. 179) says that they rested until Monday.

[6] This reference to Herod is not found in the *Itinerarium* and would seem to be put in for the sake of the rhyme. Herod came of an Idumaean family and is supposed by some to have come from Ascalon. We cannot find any other reference to his coming from Rhodes.

It was on the first day of May [7]   May 1, 1191
That the fleet set out upon its way
From Rhodes, with all sails hoisted free,
Straight toward the Gulf of Satalie,
Which is a pass to dread and fear;
There is no worse one anywhere.   1,320
Four seas do battle there head-on,
And each torments the other one.
And as we made to penetrate
The gulf, a wind most obdurate
Drove us back, till at evening
We were at our point of entering.
The wind then veered, which changes often,
And courteously its ways did soften;
Then from the rear it buffeted
Us so that we were filled with dread,   1,330
Because the gulf in which we were
Gave us exceedingly to fear.

WHEN A SHIP BRINGS NEWS FROM SYRIA

The king's ship 'twas that led the way
As was the custom every day.
The king the mighty sea did view
And saw a bark that thither drew
And that from Syria returned;
And since for news he greatly yearned
He came nigh to it to demand
The tidings from the Holy Land.   1,340
They told him that the king of France
Had landed safe without mischance
At Acre and waited for him there

---

[7] The *Estoire's* chronology is entirely consistent here; they reached Rhodes on Sunday, April 21, and left on May 1. This was just ten days according to the medieval method of reckoning, which counted the day of arrival as one of the days spent there. Ralph of Diceto (II, 91) gives a different chronology; he says that they arrived at Rhodes on April 20 and stayed there five days, then sailed five days to Limassol, which would bring them to Cyprus on April 30.

And each day labored to prepare
Engines wherewith the town to take.[8]
King Richard thought himself to make
A different plan within his mind.
Now is the bark left far behind;
Now with the gale the king did strive
Till God allowed him to arrive   1,350
Before Cyprus, close to the land
That God delivered to his hand.
He found his sister and his bride
Were there, and all their men beside.[9]

THE TRAITOROUS TYRANT OF CYPRUS

Hark ye, my lords; what sufferings
And what great misadventurings,
What turmoils and what storms and wracks,
What hindrances and what attacks,
What strong desires and what great woes,
What mishaps and what mighty blows,   1,360
This land of Syria endured
Before her succor was assured!
Exceeding was the pity for
Losing the German emperor,[10]
Who thither went so splendidly,
Only to die so suddenly.
The Holy Land was sorely tried
When Henry, king of England, died—
Henry the good, who was so wise

---

[8] The *Itinerarium* (p. 181) gives details of Philip's activities, his war machines, and their destruction by the Turks. The *Eracles* (p. 157) says that Philip could easily have taken Acre, but that he preferred to wait for Richard that they might share the victory.

[9] The *Itinerarium* (p. 182) says that the queens had arrived in the ship from Lyons and had anchored in the sea outside Limassol harbor.

[10] Frederick Barbarossa, Holy Roman emperor 1152–90, was the first of the European monarchs to set out on the third crusade. He was drowned while crossing the Saleph river in Cilicia, June 10, 1190. The *Estoire* tells almost nothing at all of the crusade of Frederick.

And had such wealthy properties,   1,370
Which would have served to hold entire
The land and save the town of Tyre.[11]
'Twas source of further suffering
When William died, the goodly king
Who oftentimes had brought it aid.[12]
When he died, great lament was made.
Great mishaps had the kingdom had
From griefs like these and fortunes bad;
But none had caused it such distress
And turmoil and unhappiness   1,380
As those that it from Cyprus bore—
A rich isle close to Syria's shore,
Which sent it much of aid erstwhile,
But now naught more came from that isle.
For now a tyrant therein dwelt [13]
Who in all vice and foulness dealt,
In treason and corruption
Worse than Judas or Ganelon.
All Christian folk he had forsaken
And Saladin for friend had taken.   1,390
And it was told of them as fact
That they had sealed their friendship's pact

[11] The *Itinerarium* (p. 182) says that Tyre was saved by his money; as it was certainly saved, this construction in Ambroise makes no sense.

[12] In 1188 a Sicilian fleet under Margarit had brought succor to Tripoli, Laodicea, Margat, and other Syrian towns attacked by Saladin. The Sicilian participation in the third crusade has never received adequate attention at the hands of scholars. (Chalandon, *Domination normande*, II, 416–17.)

[13] Isaac Comnenus had seized the governance of Cyprus with the assistance of Margarit, his brother-in-law. He declared himself emperor of the island and refused subjection to the emperor at Constantinople. Probably the best account of his career in English is to be found in J. Hackett, *Orthodox Church of Cyprus*, pp. 55–58. The *Itinerarium* (p. 183) mentions his regular custom of plundering and holding for ransom or enslaving all shipwrecked mariners. Neophytus (quoted in C. D. Cobham, *Excerpta Cypri*, p. 12) says of him: "He ruled over it [Cyprus] for seven years, and not only utterly despoiled the land, and perpetually harassed the lives of its rich men, but every day he hounded and oppressed its nobles, so that all lived in distress and sought how by any means they might protect themselves against him." Isaac's tyranny and the disaffection of the Cypriots explain Richard's easy conquest of the island.

By drinking one another's blood.
'Twas proved that this was no falsehood.[14]
Imperial though his state or royal,
It rightly should be termed destroyal.[15]
Himself he did destroy and wreck:
He ceased not, without let or check,
The powers of evil to invoke,
And to plague God's good Christian folk.   1,400

ATTEMPTS TO CAPTURE THE QUEENS

Of Richard's vessels that were scattered,
Three here were cast ashore and shattered.[16]
Those who escaped the shipwreck and
Through dangers made their way to land
He had them give up arms, then made
Them to be captured and betrayed,
Because unto them he assured
A safety that brief space endured.[17]
For he, who truth and honor lacked,
Caused them forthwith to be attacked.   1,410
But they defended, firm and bold,
And dear indeed their fury sold,
Each of the three having one bow
Of which the base Greeks did not know.
There was Rodin de Herdecourt,[18]

---

[14] The alliance of Saladin with Isaac Comnenus is attested by other later western writers, but the touching detail mentioned here is not found save in the *Estoire* and the *Itinerarium*.

[15] The *Estoire* here plays on the words "empereur" and "empireur."

[16] The *Itinerarium* (p. 184) gives the date: vigil of St. Mark the Evangelist, i. e., April 24.

[17] The *Itinerarium* (pp. 185–86) gives a much more complete and clear account. Roger Malus Catulus, the king's signet bearer, was drowned, but the royal signet was recovered from his corpse. The men from the ships were met by Greeks, who disarmed them and confined them in a fort. Stephen of Turnham sent them supplies from the ships, but the Greeks confiscated them. The men in the fort, fearing that the Greeks meant to kill them, determined to fight and came out of the fort and engaged in battle.

[18] J. H. Round (*E.H.R.*, XVIII, 479–80) agrees with Paris (p. xii) in identifying him as from Herdecourt or Haedecourt in the Eure.

The king's man, member of his court,
Who on a weary mare did mount
And quickly cut their number's count.
William du Bois Normand [19] as well,
Skilled archer, did his shafts propel,   1,420
Smote them in front and in the rear.
No engine could inspire more fear.[20]
So, in full view they made their way
To where the ships in harbor lay
Wherein the queen was thither brought.[21]
There was a mighty battle fought.
The prisoners fought valiantly.

RICHARD ARRIVES TO THWART HIM

When the king learned this treachery—
He had stopped in the port—and when
He learned the sore stress of his men   1,430
And saw his sister's vessel, where
She waited for him in great fear,
And saw the strand all covered by
These Greeks, so base and dastardly,
To seek worse paynim he forbore

[19] The *Itinerarium* (p. 186) calls him Willelmus de Bosco Normannus which would translate as William Dubois the Norman. Paris (p. xii) says he was from the Eure. The name is common in England as well as in Normandy.

[20] The *Estoire* here suffers from a lacuna. The *Itinerarium* (pp. 186–88) gives a much better account. After the men had come out of the fort (see note 17), the sailors from the English fleet saw them and started to their rescue. The Greeks opposed them, but were caught between the forces of the sailors from the ships and those come out from the fort. The men from the fort joined their companions on the beach, and the Greeks were defeated. Meanwhile the emperor attempted to persuade the queens to land, but they feared his intentions and procrastinated. While they were still negotiating and making excuses, Richard's ship arrived. The accounts of the *Estoire* and the *Itinerarium* differ considerably on this event, that of the Latin being much superior.

[21] The *Itinerarium* (pp. 184–88) gives a more detailed account of the shipwreck and the landing of the ships. Limassol was the chief port on the south coast of Cyprus. George Jeffrey, in his *Cyprus under an English King*, insists that the spot where this landing took place was not the modern town of Limassol, but the ancient port of Amathus—the modern town not yet having been built. However, as the text of Ambroise, as well as all the other texts of that period, calls the place Limassol, it is needlessly pedantic to argue that the location was Amathus.

And straight betook him to the shore,
Which the tyrant thought to defend,
But dared not the proud king attend.
A Monday morning was the date   May 6, 1191
That God was pleased to designate   1,440
For the king to carry out this deed—
To save the shipwrecked in their need,
To guard his sister from mischance,
To bring his bride deliverance.
'Twas hateful to each noble dame,
The day when to this port she came,
For surely the emperor would
Have seized them both if he but could.[22]
The port the king planned to attack
And fain would capture did not lack   1,450
Defenders; for the emperor
Himself had come down to the shore
With all his own retainers and
All he could hire or could command.

AND IS INSULTED BY THE EMPEROR

The king a legate did select
And had him rowed ashore direct.
The emperor he sought, and he
Requested him most courteously
That he restore what did belong
To the prisoners and redress the wrong   1,460
That on the pilgrims he had wrought,
Which tears to many orphans brought.
The emperor replied with scorn
So great that it surpassed all bourn,
And answered to the messenger
With fury unrestrained: "Tproupt, sir!"

[22] Ernoul (p. 271) and the *Eracles* (p. 160) confirm Isaac's attempt to force the queens to land, but they differ considerably from each other in their accounts of the shipwreck and the fighting. The *Eracles* (pp. 160–63) gives a long story of the slaughter of the shipwrecked pilgrims and a touching incident of the compassion and warnings given them by a Norman soldier in the service of the Greek emperor.

He would not make more fair reply,
But raged and sneered in mockery.
Swiftly the messenger then sped
To the king and told him what was said.   1,470
The king heard the foul word, and then,
"Arm yourselves!" quoth he to his men.
The which they all did straightaway,
Not pausing to make long delay.
To their ships' small boats now they must,
All fully armed, themselves entrust.
With goodly knights the boats were filled,
And with crossbowmen bold and skilled;
Our foemen likewise crossbows bore,
And their men were drawn up on the shore.   1,480
They had five galleys, too, and they
Were armed and ready for the fray.
But seeing our arms, insecure
They felt, and feared discomfiture.

THE ENGLISH FORCE A LANDING

In Limassol, the town wherein
The fighting had its origin,
There was no window left or gate
Or weapon fit to vulnerate
Or tun or cask, or shield or targe,
Nor galley old or ancient barge,   1,490
Board, beam, step, plank of any sort
That they could readily transport,
But that they fetched it to the shore
To do the pilgrims damage sore.
Armed on the strand, more proud by far
Than any living men they are,
With streaming banners and array
Of precious stuffs and colors gay,
Mounted on horse of strength and speed
Or with strong handsome mule as steed.   1,500
Like dogs they hooted us and jeered,

But their pride swiftly disappeared.
Handicapped from the start were we,
Because we came straight from the sea,
And we were sent in skiff and yawl
Of meager size, exceeding small.
By the sea's torment we were torn,
Battered and tossed about and worn.
Each of us was on foot and bent
By weight of his accouterment;   1,510
And they were in their own country,
But more of war by far knew we.
Our crossbowmen their quarrels shot,
And many did not miss, I wot.
Upon the galley men, untrained
In war, their missiles first they rained.
So sore they wounded them and smote
That many leapt from off their boat
Into the water, four by four,
Each tumbling on the one before.   1,520
Then were their galleys overthrown
And captured and placed with our own.
Our archers, likewise our crossbowmen,
Sent clouds of shafts upon their foemen.
The Greeks recoiled before the shock;
Then had ye heard our soldiers mock
Them, as they mocked us short time back
Before we started our attack.
On both sides soldiers shot and threw
Their shafts, and still our oarsmen drew   1,530
On steadily, while thick and fast
Arrows and bolts at them were cast.
All the seashore along the strand
With wild and savage folk was manned.
An undertaking bold ye might
Have seen, and warriors skilled to fight;
When the king saw how sorely put
His company was to set foot

On land, he leapt from out his boat
Into the sea and strongly smote   1,540
The Greeks. The others in his wake
Followed. The Greeks defense did make.
Our men along the beach poured out,
Striking and putting them to rout.

SCATTER THE GREEKS

Then had ye seen the quarrels rain
And the Greeks scatterèd and slain.
They were hard pushed and beaten down
And driven back into the town.
Our troops like lions swift pursued;
At men and horses cut and hewed.   1,550
Before the valiant Latin folk
Greeks and Armenians fled and broke:
Even to the fields they fled in rout,
Our men pressed closely and drove out
The emperor himself, who fled,
And the king straightway followèd
Until, pursuing in his course,
He came upon some mare or horse.
Back of the saddle was a bag,
And hempen stirrups had the nag.   1,560
With a leap, the saddle to bestride,
To the false emperor he cried:
"Come, emperor, and joust! Make haste!"
But he for jousting had no taste.

AND PURSUE THEM INTO THE HILLS

The king gave word to disembark
All of the horses, after dark,
That in his galleys he had brought.[23]
Of this the emperor knew naught,
And had in no way been apprised.

[23] The *Itinerarium* (p. 191) says that Richard landed the horses after the two queens had come ashore.

The horses then were exercised, 1,570
For they were all benumbed and sore
And stiff for the whole month before,
Which they had spent upon the seas
Unable to lie down at ease.
With this small rest, for all their plight
Was such to merit more by right,
At morn straightway mounted the king,
Who had taken in his hand this thing.
Within an olive grove along
The roadside close at hand a throng 1,580
Of Greeks awaited with their banners
And flags of varied hues and manners.
Thence the king drove them forth; then set
Upon his head his steel helmet
And started swiftly to pursue.
Then had ye seen brave men and true!
Closely pursued by our foreguard
They fled; we pressed them fast and hard,
Until our men encounterèd
Their main host. We pursued; they fled. 1,590
Thereat we halted our pursuit,
And they began to shout and hoot,
And made cry so vociferous
(So those who heard the noise tell us)
That in his tent the emperor,
So it is said, heard the uproar
From more than half a league away,
Whither he had withdrawn to stay.
He dined and slept while strife went on;
But they were rudely set upon. 1,600
He and his train then mounted horse
And to the mountains took their course
To see just what their men would do,
Who knew to shoot and naught else knew.
Still shouting, they wheeled round apace,
And our men did not stir from place.

HEEDLESS OF DANGER RICHARD PURSUES

Unto the king an armed clerk came —
Hugh de la Mare was the clerk's name —[24]
And giving to him counsel, "Sire,"
He said to him, "Get hence, retire: 1,610
They have great force past measuring."
The king said: "To your scrivening
Return, sir clerk; go away and write,
And get yourself clear of the fight;
To us leave things of chivalry,
For God's sake and for Saint Marie!"
This man and others spoke him thus,
Seeing the foe so numerous,
While at this hour against that host
There were but forty, or at most   1,620
Fifty, good knights at the king's back.
The brave king stayed not his attack,
But fell upon them with a dash
Swifter than any lightning flash.
As on a lark swoops bird of prey
(All praised who saw the charge that day),
So did the king swoop down headlong
And smite the wicked Grecian throng.
He drove them into disarray,
Struck them with terror and dismay,   1,630
Dealt them confusion and despair,
Meanwhile his own men gathered there.
And as his strength in numbers grew,
So many Greeks they seized or slew,
Not counting those who basely fled,
That none could ever count the dead.
For those of them who were on horse

[24] This Hugh de la Mare is not otherwise known; there were several de la Mares in Richard's host; the name is a common one in Normandy, Yorkshire, or Lincolnshire. Siedschlag (*English Crusaders*, p. 117), lists him as number 58. A "Hugh Clericus," a crusader from Essex or Herts in 1189, appears as Siedschlag's number 55. There must have been many clerks by the common name of Hugh on the crusade.

Up hill, down dale took headlong course;
While footmen, humble folk and plain,
Were all made prisoners or slain.[25]   1,640

HE CAPTURES THE IMPERIAL STANDARD

Great was the battle; all around
Horses were strewn upon the ground.
Hauberk and banner, lance and sword
Lay scattered pell-mell on the sward,
While burdened steeds tottered and fell.
Seeing his men could not repel
Our onslaught and that more and more
Our strength increased, the emperor
Unto the mountain top withdrew [26]
With his Greek and Armenian crew,   1,650
Abandoning to us the ground.
When Richard, king of England, found
That he had thus taken to flight,
Leaving his troops in sorry plight,
The king came on the man who bore
The standard of the emperor
And struck him down, and took in hand
The standard, and gave his command
That it be guarded carefully.[27]
He saw their beaten forces fly   1,660
As flies a whirlwind; many a head
And many a wounded body bled.
He gave no order to pursue:
He could not catch them, well he knew,
Already our Franks, brave and strong,
Had given chase two full leagues long.

[25] The *Itinerarium* (p. 193) tells how Richard personally unhorsed Isaac, but the Greek got a new horse and escaped.

[26] The mountain top here referred to is the plateau region of northern Cyprus; Isaac retreated toward Nicosia, which is in the high country north of the southern plain.

[27] Richard sent this standard as an offering to St. Edmund's Bury monastery. (Dugdale, *Monasticon Anglicanum*, III, 105.)

AND RICH PLUNDER

So, slowly backward he did wend
His way; his soldiers made no end
Of seizing upon costly plate
Of gold and silver, rich, ornate,   1,670
Abandoned by the emperor
There where his tent was pitched before:
His harness and his very bed
And cloth of silk and cloth of red;
Horses and mules so laden down
As if it were a market town;
Hauberks and helms and swords as well
By the Greeks cast aside pell-mell;
Oxen and cows and goats and swine,
Most vigorous and fair and fine;   1,680
And rams and sheep and lambs were there,
And many a goodly colt and mare
And cock and hen and fat capon
And full-fleshed mules who bore upon
Their strong backs quilts embroidered fair;
And robes of rich and costly air
And good steeds that were worth far more
Than ours, exhausted now and sore;
Likewise they seized his dragoman,
Who, I have heard, was named Johan;   1,690
Greeks and Armenians in such number
That they the highways did encumber;
Good wine and food in such amount
None ever knew the tale or count.
The king caused a ban to be cried
Giving safe conduct far and wide
To all the people of the land
Who had no wish for warfare, and
To those who had no wish for peace
He promised no truce or surcease.   1,700

On Saturday of that same week   May 11, 1191
That brought such woe upon the Greek
To Limassol came galleys three
From Cyprus back by way of sea [28]
With the king of Jerusalem;
And much our people gazed at him.
Guy de Lusignan [29] was the king
Who had such grief and suffering
The land of our Lord to defend
That he must leave it in the end;   1,710
Because the king of France was fain—
Which gave unto his heart great pain—
To do him wrong and cast him down
And to the marquis [30] give the crown.
For this he left the land and fled

[28] The *Itinerarium* omits the words "from Cyprus," which make no sense. As it is not used to complete a rhyme, the phrase is meaningless and pointless. Perhaps it should read "from Syria," which would have some point.

[29] Guy de Lusignan, son of Hugh VIII of Lusignan, had become king of Jerusalem through his marriage with Sybelle, eldest daughter of Amaury, king of Jerusalem. Guy came to Syria as an adventurer from the west, driven from home because of his murder of Patrick, earl of Salisbury. His marriage to Sybelle was due to the desire of the lady and was contrary to political dictates. He served as regent for a time under Baldwin IV, but proved incompetent and was dismissed. His elevation to the throne was opposed by most of the barons of Jerusalem, and his reign was unsuccessful, due to civil discord, pressure from Saladin, and a certain natural incapacity of his own. Captured at Hattin, he was released in exchange for Ascalon and began the siege of Acre. As he was opposed by many of his barons and by Philip Augustus, Guy was most anxious to gain the support of Richard and came to Cyprus to present his case to the English monarch and gain his backing.

[30] Conrad de Montferrat, son of Marquis William III, succeeded to the title at the death of his father. His elder brother, William Longsword, count of Jaffa and first husband of Sybelle of Jerusalem, died in 1177 before his father, leaving the succession open to Conrad, the second son. Conrad had gone to Constantinople and thence had come to Tyre while it was being besieged by Saladin. His defense of Tyre was one of the really heroic actions of the war against Saladin. With the baronial party leaderless after the death of Raymond of Tripoli, Conrad became the chief of the party opposed to Guy de Lusignan. He refused Guy admittance into Tyre and held the city, giving but little help to Guy in his siege of Acre. (Ilgen, *Conrad*.)

And to the king of England sped
For succor, lest he should succumb.
The king was glad that he had come;
Straight forth to meet him he did go,
And ye may well believe and know   1,720
That he received him heartily,
For hè was of great family.
His kin bore many a noble name,
And they were with him when he came; [31]
And it was clearly evident
That they were not of base descent.[32]
The king made joy most copious
And did him honors various
And gave him of his property
('Twas wisdom and good courtesy)   1,730
A full two thousand marks, I deem
(A present of no small esteem),
And gave him twenty cups, all told,
Two of them made of finest gold.[33]

[31] Guy had several brothers, of whom Hugh IX was with Richard, Aymeri and
Geoffrey were in Syria. Geoffrey is mentioned as accompanying him to Cyprus to meet
Richard. This Geoffrey was no friend of Richard's, having murdered one of Richard's
familiars in Poitou and having warred against Richard in support of Henry II (Ralph
of Diceto, II, 54). According to the *Gesta* (II, 165) and Roger of Hoveden (III, 108)
Guy was accompanied by Geoffrey, Humphrey de Toron, Bohemond III of Antioch and
his son Raymond, and Leo of Armenia. Beha ed Din (p. 242) says that a hundred and
sixty knights accompanied Guy.

[32] The house of Lusignan was supposedly descended from the serpent woman Mélusine. The first known lord of Lusignan was Hugh le Veneur in the ninth century, whose
son Hugh II built the castle of Lusignan in Poitou. They were among the more important vassals of Poitou before the crusades, but it was in the east that the family rose to
royal heights. The legend of Mélusine was current in France in the Middle Ages and
was given a definite form by Jean d'Arras in the fifteenth century. There is an extensive bibliography on the lords of Lusignan and the Mélusine legend; see especially
E. de Lusignan, *Les Généalogies de soixante et sept très nobles et très illustres maisons*
(Paris, 1586), chaps. xxix–xxxii; L. de Mas Latrie, "Généalogie des rois de Chypre,"
Archivo Veneto, Vol. XXI (1881); Louis Stouff, *Essai sur Mélusine* (Dijon, 1930);
the latest edition of the Mélusine poem is by Jean Marchand (Paris, 1927). The
Itinerarium omits this reference to the Lusignan family.

[33] The *Itinerarium* (p. 195) says that the value of the twenty cups was 105 marks.

RICHARD MARRIES BERENGARIA

Upon the morrow of that day [34]   May 12
Was wedded the fair fiancée;
And there at Limassol was crowned
The fairest bride that could be found
At any time and any place,
A virtuous queen with lovely face.[35]   1,740
Now was the king most glorious,
Because he was victorious
And because he had wed the wife
To whom he pledged his word and life.

RICHARD ORGANIZES HIS FORCES

And now his galleys came, which he
Had waited so impatiently,
And so well armed did they appear
That we had never seen their peer;
And with the other ships the five
That we had won here did arrive.   1,750
And with the others in the port,
To which he had complete resort,
He had of armed ships full two score,
Worth fifty others, mayhap more.
He later took the marvelous
Ship with its great crew valorous—
Eight hundred men, it was surmised,
All Turks and Persians, not baptized.[36]
The king would further fury wreak
On cursed Armenian and Greek.   1,760

---

[34] The *Itinerarium* (p. 195) gives the date as the feast of St. Pancreas; Roger of Hoveden (III, 110) says the 4 Ides of May, both of which are in agreement with the *Estoire*.

[35] The *Itinerarium* (p. 196), Roger of Hoveden (III, 110), and the *Gesta* (II, 167) add details of the marriage and coronation. Present were the archbishops of Bordeaux, Auch, and Apamia, the bishops of Evreux and Bayonne. The marriage was performed by Nicholas, Richard's chaplain, after which the coronation was done by Bishop John of Evreux.

[36] The story of the capture of the ship is told in detail in lines 2140–2298.

He had his host prepared to fight
And caused his guards to watch at night,
Hoping the emperor to seize
In midst of his own properties.[37]

THE EMPEROR SUES FOR PEACE

Following this discomfiture,
When the Greeks such shame did endure,
The emperor was at Nicossie [38]—
Both he and his great company—
Stricken with sorrow, rage, and spite
For all the men lost in the fight,   1,770
For that his troops had fled and run
He found no consolation.
His own land looked on him with hate,
And his fear of England's king was great.
A deputation he did send [39]
Him, promising to make amend.
He would come to him, he averred,
And loyally would pledge his word,
And into Syria would bring,
Mounted, prepared to aid the king,   1,780
Five hundred men, who firm would stand
For God and serve the king's command.
And he did furthermore agree
To give the king more surety,
To pledge his castles as a gage
And with them his rich heritage.
And for men slain because he blundered
Pay marks three thousand and five hundred.

[37] The *Itinerarium* (p. 196) adds a detailed description of Richard's Spanish horse, his saddle and trappings, and of the king's own costume.

[38] Nicosia, the capital of modern Cyprus, lies in the north central part of the island, just south of Kyrenia, on the central plateau. It did not become of first importance until the period of the Lusignan kings, who filled it with Gothic buildings and made it the first city of the island. It is still the chief city and capital and is a treasury of crusader churches and buildings.

[39] The *Itinerarium* (p. 196) says that the conference was arranged by the Master of the Hospital.

And if he served the king's command
Fairly, he should have back his land.[40]   1,790

SWEARS FEALTY TO RICHARD

The king to parley was not loath,
Nor was the emperor, and both
Decided promptly on a date
Whereon they might negotiate.
'Twas in a fig orchard that lay
Between the shore and the highway
To Limassol, it seems to me,
Where they met in full company;
And there were matters told and said
Better than were accomplishèd.   1,800
The king his council did convoke
With his most wise and prudent folk,
And said to those who therein sate,
Whose wish for such a peace was great:
"My lords, ye are my right hand. See
If such a peace as this can be
And see that ye no damage make
To your honor, which here lies at stake,
For if it pleases ye, it will
Be done, but not if it seems ill."   1,810
"We think it goodly, Sire," they said,
"By such peace we are honorèd."
Thereon they went back, and indeed
To all the terms of peace agreed.
And to the king the emperor
The oath of fealty now swore,
Gave him his gage, and solemnly
Kissed him in pledge of loyalty.

AND RECEIVES GIFTS

The king did to the host repair,
Which was hard by; he was soon there.   1,820

[40] According to the *Itinerarium* (p. 198) these terms were offered by Isaac at the conference, not, as here stated, offered as the basis for negotiations before the conference began.

He gave prompt word to load three rich
And very sumptuous tents, the which
He had captured during the disgrace
Inflicted on the Greeks so base
(They were of fustian, and had been
The emperor's own tents, I ween)
And of rich plate great quantities,
And sent them in most friendly wise
To the emperor, who in no way spurned
The plate, and had the tents returned   1,830
To the spot where they before did hold
The parley of which we have told.

THE EMPEROR TREACHEROUSLY FLEES

Upon the very vespertide
When on this peace they did decide,
It happed the emperor had among
His men a knight of evil tongue;
He was called Paien of Caïphas.[41]
Fouler than any dog he was;
He made the emperor think the king
Would make him captive, but the thing   1,840
Was nothing but a shameless lie.
The emperor, setting out to fly,
Mounted a charger swift and came
Forth—Fauvel was the horse's name—
And, making as if on pleasure bent,
He rode away incontinent,

[41] Paien or Paganus of Caïphas, lord of Caïphas (Haïfa) on the coast of Palestine, was one of the most important of the Jerusalemite nobility. He appears on acts as lord of Caïphas throughout the years 1165 to 1191 and is given in Jean d'Ibelin's list of services due as owing seven knights for possessions held in Acre. (Röhricht, *Regesta; Assises*, I, 425.) The chapter on the lords of Caïphas in the *Familles d'Outremer* (pp. 263–71) is badly confused, and is wrong about Paganus. He was of the party of Conrad against Guy and played an important part in securing the hand of Isabelle for Conrad (see below). The aspersions as to his character are merely indications of partisan zeal and should not be taken seriously. Paganus had a fine record in the wars against Saladin, and beyond his adherence to the party of the barons against the Lusignans and Richard there is no reason for him to be condemned. Compare this vilification with the remarks about Balian d'Ibelin and Renaud of Sidon, below.

And left harness and tents behind,
Like one who had quite lost his mind.
He left two horses swift and strong
And desperately fled headlong.   1,850

AND IS PURSUED BY RICHARD AND GUY

When of his flight King Richard knew,
He could not follow or pursue;
For he wished not to make a breach
Of the truce, and had no horse could reach
Him. Yet, on hearing of his flight
He did not wish him to go quite
Scot-free; and so he set about
On land and sea to seek him out.
His galleys, sailing forth that same
Night, soon to Famagusta [42] came.   1,860
The king himself went with them there,
Anxious to settle the affair.
He told the king of Jerusalem
Along the shore to follow them,
To see if he could find the traitor—
This emperor, this violator
Of his sworn oath. Without delay
King Guy set out upon his way,
And after three days' marching he
Reached Famagusta verily,   1,870
From which the citizens had fled.
And there King Richard anchorèd
His ships, and made them carefully
To watch the portals and descry,

---

[42] Famagusta, on the eastern coast of Cyprus, was the chief port of the island in Lusignan times. It became a city of first importance and one of the chief emporia of the world after the fall of Acre, when the trade of Acre was transferred along with much of the population to Famagusta. It suffered from capture by the Genoese, Venetians, and Turks and decayed until it is today merely a small town with many fine ruins but few inhabitants and less trade. The British government has in recent years devoted some thought to reëstablishing Famagusta as a naval center and toward improving its harbor, the best on the island. (Enlart, *Les Villes mortes du moyen âge* and LaMonte, "The Vanished Splendor of Famagusta," in *Butrava* [1940].)

So that their man might not scot-free
Make his escape by way of sea.
Leaving the galleys where they rode,
Three days they in the town abode.

RICHARD REJECTS PHILIP'S PLEA TO HASTEN TO ACRE

During this stay's continuance
There came two messengers from France.   1,880
One was Dreux de Mello,[43] they say,
With him the bishop of Beauvais,[44]
Who came insistently to urge
The king—and pressed him to the verge
Of insult—that to Acre he speed.
For the French king would not proceed
To make attack of any sort
Until he had Richard's support.
They pressed him close, and sorely tried
Him, and they would not be denied,   1,890
Till the king's wrath they did arouse,
Whereon he lifted up his brows,
And words were said that are not fit
Herein to be set down or writ.
'Twas vain to urge him on to haste;
The words they spake were but a waste.
Himself had made swift action,
And, having with the Greeks begun,
The half of Russia's wealth he'd spurn
Before to Syria he would turn   1,900

---

[43] Dreux de Mello, constable of France 1193–1218, was one of Philip's important followers. He was one of those who received large gifts from the king at Messina and it was he who took charge of Philip's share of the spoils of Acre (Roger of Hoveden, III, 121). He is mentioned frequently in *Guillaume le Maréchal* and by Guillaume le Breton. This entire incident of the embassy is omitted from the *Itinerarium*.

[44] Philip de Dreux, bishop of Beauvais, 1175–1217, and cousin of Philip II, is another of our author's villains, due to his championing the cause of Conrad. It was he who pronounced the divorce between Isabelle and Humphrey, and he was prominent in the marriage of Conrad to the princess. He does seem to have forced his ecclesiastical conscience to submit to his political judgment, but he was not the only worldly ecclesiastic of his time.

Till he had crushed the Cypriot
From whose isle rich supplies are got.
Nor would he quit this enterprise
Till he had made of it his prize.
Yet these ambassadors did both
Urge him to put aside his sloth.

AND ADVANCES ON NICOSIA

So, with his host assembled, he
Moved on direct to Nicosie.
Each bore his own arms, and each one
Of food bore full provision.   1,910
The emperor, who close by did hide,
Upon the marching army spied.
The king led the rear guard, for fear
Lest harm come on them from the rear.
Then from the ambush where he lay,
The emperor made swift foray
With force of seven hundred, which
Their cowardice did sore bewitch.
They sent their shafts at the foreguard,
Who let them come straight on toward   1,920
Them; skirmishing about the side,
Like a swift Turcople,[45] did ride
The emperor, and swiftly sped
Toward the rear guard, which Richard led,
And at the king launched arrows two
That had been dipped in poison brew.
Dashing from his battalion,
The king nearly took vengeance on
This wicked emperor foresworn.
But he was by swift Fauvel borne,   1,930

[45] Turcoples were light armed cavalry employed in eastern armies. They were said to have been originally of mixed blood, being descended from Turkish fathers and Greek mothers (Albert of Aix, *Rec. his. crois. Occ.*, IV, 434). They were usually archers and seem to have been developed by the Byzantines, from whom they passed over to the armies of the crusaders. They were used as auxiliaries to the heavy-armed knights and were valuable against the Saracen mounted archers.

And he fled headlong on his horse,
Like a stag running in full course,
And refuge sought, with bitter woe,
In Kantara,[46] his strong château.
The king, since he could not prevent
Him, on toward Nicosia went.

DESPITE THE EMPEROR, NICOSIA ACCLAIMS RICHARD

Our men had captured many strong
Horses, and they had seized a throng
Of Greeks—and some were wounded too—
Who too nigh to the army drew.   1,940
They marched now following the king,
Having no fear of anything.
And so they came at break of day
To Nicosia. There straightway
The citizens with one accord
Hastened to call the king their lord,
And as a father they revered
Him. He had shaven each man's beard.[47]
On hearing this the emperor
Had such great fury and dolor   1,950
He nigh went mad, and did mistreat
Our men and his in ways unmeet:
From his own men who peace did make
With us and ours whom he could take,
Whenever he could catch them, he
Cut hands or feet off cruelly,

---

[46] Kantara was one of the fortresses in the northern mountains of Cyprus. It was the easternmost of the three great castles and dominated the road from Famagusta to Nicosia, as well as guarding the entrance to the Karpas peninsula. Stubbs (*Itinerarium*, p. 201 (erroneously identifies this reference as "perhaps Cape St. Andrea."

[47] The oriental respect for beards was a well-known characteristic. To shave a man's beard was the acme of insult, and the veneration in which beards were held among the orientals caused scorn and amusement from the time of St. Jerome on. William of Tyre (pp. 469–72) tells the celebrated story of how Baldwin of Edessa secured money to pay his soldiers from his father-in-law, Gabriel of Melitène, by pledging his beard as security for the debt, a procedure which greatly shocked and mortified the Armenian.

Cut off their noses, put out eyes,
Finding no vengeance otherwise.
Meanwhile the king received homage
From the most worthy and most sage,   1,960
Who willingly repudiated
The emperor, whom they all hated.[48]

GUY CAPTURES CERINES AND THE EMPEROR'S DAUGHTER

Now of the host the king made three
Divisions, to act separately,
And therewith he laid siege unto
Three castles,[49] quickly taking two.
One army toward Cerines went [50]
And captured it incontinent.
It was the king of Outremer [51]
Who skillfully commanded there.   1,970
Near the stronghold he armed his band,
Besieged it both by sea and land,
Assailed it with a fierce attack;
And since the men within did lack
Support and succor, their defender
Could not do other than surrender.
So they gave up most readily
Their castle to the brave King Guy
With the daughter of the emperor,
Who thereat was distraught so sore   1,980
That he quite lost his sense and mind

[48] The *Itinerarium* (p. 201) says that Richard was taken sick and stayed at Nicosia while he recuperated.

[49] The *Itinerarium* (p. 201) names them: Kyrenia, Dieudamor, Buffavento.

[50] Cerines or Kyrenia was a fortified harbor town on the north coast of Cyprus. Important as a port in the Middle Ages, it is now a peaceful village with the remains of some fine medieval buildings, of which the old fortress (now a government prison) is the most conspicuous. The fort at Kyrenia was one of the strongest of medieval Cyprus and ranked with the great castles of St. Hilarion and Buffavento in the northern defenses of the island. The text has *Ebetines*.

[51] Outremer is the old term for the crusaders' states in Palestine, Syria, and Cyprus. Writers in Europe referred to these eastern colonies as Outremer, while the eastern writers reversed it and referred to Europe by the same appellation. The king of Outremer refers of course to Guy de Lusignan.

And consolation none could find.
So now upon the tower King Guy
The banners of the king raised high.
Guards in the castle he did post,
And to Dieudamor [52] led the host.

THE SIEGE OF DIEUDAMOR

Dieudamor is of too great might
To be taken by storm or fight.
But those defending were so dazed
And so besotted and amazed 1,990
By all the tidings that were told
Them, that 'twas hard for them to hold
The keep; yet they hurled now and then
Great stones downward toward our men.
Safe though they would have been inside
The walls, these folk were terrified.
Withal King Guy besieged it for
Some days, until the emperor
Gave word no longer to defend
It, and bade those within descend. 2,000
When they surrendered to the king,
As I have heard men tell the thing,
'Twas given over to King Guy,
Who ordered that most carefully
Within the tower the maid [53] be watched
That she might not be stolen nor snatched
Away. Then he led back his host,
But found the land most dear in cost.

THE EMPEROR SURRENDERS

King Richard within Nicosie
Had lain, ill of a malady. 2,010

[52] Dieudamor (Dieu d'Amour) was the name given by the crusaders to the fortress castle of St. Hilarion in the mountains just south of Kyrenia. Cyprus was the isle of Venus (the Venusberg was located at Mount Troödos), and this castle was built on Cupid's mountain. The text has Didemus.

[53] That is, Isaac's daughter.

CASTLE AND HARBOR OF CERINES

FAMAGUSTA IN 1933

When that he felt restored, he went to
Besiege the castle Buffavento,[54]
A most exceeding great stronghold.
Hear now the strange adventure told
Of the false emperor to whom
His wickedness brought sorry doom.
Within Kantara's walls he came,
There to give way to grief and shame,
When he learned, trapped as in a gin,
That Buffavento was hemmed in,   2,020
And that we had made prisoner
Within a tower his daughter, her
Whom he loved more than aught alive,
It made him eager to contrive
To make his peace, cost what it might
To extricate him from his plight.
Most grievous was the cost and sad,
To lose the castles that he had
And all his goodly property
Because of his iniquity.   2,030
But what had most undone him was
That his own men had left his cause.
Needs must: no more he did attend,
But from Kantara down did wend
His way and to King Richard gave
Himself, hopeless to shield or save.

BUT BEGS MERCY OF RICHARD

But ere he came he sent to plead
For Richard's pity, and agreed
To grant him all, to be bereft
Of everything and have naught left—   2,040

[54] Buffavento, or the Queen's Castle, lies, like St. Hilarion, in the mountains south
of Kyrenia. It was the center of the three great castles between Kantara to the east and
St. Hilarion to the west, which guarded northern Cyprus. Buffavento is within sight
of St. Hilarion and, like it, stands on a high peak. It is now completely ruined, and
the ascent of the mountain to the ruins of the castle is one of the favorite excursions out
of Kyrenia.

Land, house, or castle any place.
He only craved of him as grace
Not to be gyved by iron chain,
To spare his honor this much pain.
Yielding, the king then had him held
In bonds of silver, and thus quelled
All outcry.[55] So on bended knees
He begged such mercy as might please
The king, who saw he was sincere
And saw his wrongs and losses clear,   2,050
Saw he could do no more to us
And that God willed it to be thus.
And so, to finish this emprise,
He made the emperor to rise
And sit beside him at his right
And of his daughter to have sight.
Seeing her, his joy was more complete
Than if he held God by the feet.
Weeping, he kissed her o'er and o'er
An hundred times. But why tell more? [56]   2,060
With only fifteen days' delay
The king held Cyprus clear—I say
Naught but the truth. To God all thanks
Be given, 'twas mastered by the Franks.

THE SPOILS OF CYPRUS

When the king got the masterhood
Of Cyprus, for God's greater good,
The castles and strong forts he held
From which the Greeks had been expelled.
He found them filled in goodly measure
With every kind of wealth and treasure: 2,070
With silver pots, cauldrons, and kettles,

---

[55] The *Itinerarium* (p. 203) preserves a better sequence of events, as it does not have Isaac placed in his silver chains until after the interview. He was sent to the Hospitaller's castle of Margat, where he remained in prison until his death.

[56] The *Itinerarium* (p. 203) gives the date; Friday after the feast of St. Augustine before Pentecost, i. e., May 31.

Basins and vessels of rich metals,
With bowls and cups and gold ewers,
With bridles, saddles, and with spurs,
Rich stones of precious value—these
Have healing power against disease;
Silk stuffs and scarlet of rich sheen
(Their like I nowhere else have seen),
And other things of quality
Befitting the nobility.   2,080
'Twas for God's work and His domain
That England's king all this did gain.
He sent the host to Limassol,
And urged his men, asking them all
To be prepared to sail in haste
And no more hours of time to waste.
He had the emperor guarded by
The very valorous King Guy.
And his young daughter, a most fair
And lovely maid of beauty rare,   2,090
He had sent to the queen, that she
Might well be taught and fittingly.[57]

THEY LEAVE CYPRUS

So now the army did proceed
Back to the fleet, and made all speed
To load the ships, so that they might

---

[57] The subsequent career of this princess was dramatic and romantic in the extreme. She accompanied the English queen and princess back to Europe after the crusade and lived for some years at Chinon. Her release was one of the terms stipulated by Henry VI for the ransom of Richard, but it was not carried out. Shortly before 1202 she married Raymond VI of Toulouse, but was repudiated soon thereafter when that prince wanted to marry Joanna Plantagenet. In 1202 she was in Marseilles, when the crusading host assembled there for the fourth crusade. A Flemish crusader, a relative of Baldwin of Flanders, met and married her with the intention of forwarding her claims to the throne of Cyprus. They went to Cyprus and demanded the throne from King Aymeri de Lusignan, urging that as he was also king of Jerusalem he did not need the throne of Cyprus. Aymeri was not to be persuaded thus easily, however, and refused to accede to their request. The disappointed couple fled to Armeno-Cilicia, where they disappeared from history. (Ernoul, pp. 352–53; Mas Latrie, *Histoire de Chypre*, I, 56–60.)

Set forth when all was fit and right.
After they had embarked, the fleet
Sailed seaward, when the hour was meet,
And with them too the queens did fare
And all the dromons that were there.   2,100
Upon the isle the king left men [58]
Most skilled in warfare; these men then
Sent on to him provisions—sheaves
Of corn and barley, sheep and beeves,
Of which they had supply profuse
And which in Syria served good use.
And now men overseas did bring
Tidings, and told them to the king,
Of how the siege was well begun
At Acre and how it would be done   2,110
Before he could arrive. Quoth he:
"It is not fit that without me
Another man this town should take!"
Henceforth no more stay he would make,
Save till his comrades who would bear
Him company had gathered there.

            .   .   .

I do not know how numerous.

AND SET SAIL FOR SYRIA

At Famagusta he took ship
And gave the order to equip   2,120
His galleys. And himself took place
In one of great strength, size, and pace.

[58] As regents in Cyprus Richard left Robert de Turnham and Richard de Camville. Robert de Turnham was later given extensive lands in Yorkshire and became seneschal for Poitou (S. Painter). Camville subsequently joined the king at Acre, where he died. Turnham, probably the brother of Stephen de Turnham, the commander of the fleet, was faced by a general rebellion of the Cypriots. King Richard then sold the island to the Templars, who were unable to control it and so turned it back to him. Thus he was able to turn it over to Guy de Lusignan and to pave the way for the settlement of the succession in Jerusalem. (*Gesta*, II, 167, 172; Roger of Hoveden, III, 109, 111, 116.)

No harbor under heaven would not
Be terrified and sore distraught
At ships of war so marvelous
And men at arms so valorous.[59]
Behold, the galleys leave the port,
All fit and of the finest sort,
The king, as usual, light and gay,
Fit as a feather, led the way;   2,130
And swift as any stag that sped,
Across the sea he journeyèd.
Then he saw Margat, on the bord
Of the true country of the Lord,
And then Tortosa he saw next,
Built by a sea storm-tossed and vexed,
And he passed swiftly on his way
Tripoli, Botron, and Infré,
And after that saw Gibelet
With its tower on the castle set.   2,140

A GREAT SHIP OF THE SARACENS

Near Beirut, close by Sidon's shore,
Toward the king a ship there bore
Filled with the men of Saladin.[60]
It was equipped by Saphadin,[61]

[59] Beha ed Din (p. 243) and Ibn al Athir (p. 42) tell how a fleet sent out from Beirut captured five of Richard's ships which he had sent on from Cyprus.

[60] El Malik en Nasr Salah ed Din Yusuf ibn Ayyub, commonly called Saladin, the great sultan of Egypt and lord of Syria, whose conquests precipitated the third crusade. There are contemporary lives by Beha ed Din and Ibn Kallikan (IV, 497–563); the best modern biography is by S. Lane Poole. In the history of the crusades he stands out—the one true *preudhomme*.

[61] El Malik el Adil Saf ed Din Abu Bekr Mohammed, called by the Latins Saphadin and by the Arabs El Adil, was the brother and chief lieutenant of Saladin. He accompanied Shirkuh and Saladin to Egypt and became viceroy of Egypt under his brother. He was also lord of Aleppo and Kerak after their capture. In the struggle with Richard, Saphadin acted as intermediary between the sultan and the English king and seems to have established very friendly relations with Richard, who called him "my brother." After the death of Saladin, Saphadin deposed his nephews and made himself lord of Saladin's empire. He died in 1218, leaving to his three sons the thrones of Egypt, Syria (Damascus), and Mesopotamia. The *Itinerarium* (p. 205) does not mention him in connection with this ship, although Ralph of Diceto (II, 93) says that he sent it.

Manned by the best Turks, chosen from
The finest in all pagandom.
They could not get to Acre, and so
Outside they sailed them to and fro
Till they might safely make the port.
But the king set him out to thwart   2,150
Their plan [62] and swiftly on did drive
His galley, till he did arrive
At where they were; he saw their craft
Was broad and high and of great draft,
Masted with three tall masts: 'twas not
A vessel that in haste was wrought.
And by the pagans it had been
Covered, one side, with felt of green;
With yellow felt, as he descried,
Was covered o'er the other side.   2,160
And all the ship was in such way
Bedecked, as if 'twere work of fay.[63]
And it was filled with armament
Beyond all count or measurement:
And one man spread abroad the bruit
(Who had been present at Beirut [64]
When this ship took aboard this same
Cargo, to be unshipped in shame),
Of seeing arms laden in store,
An hundred camel-loads and more,   2,170
Bow, spear, cross-bow, and arbalist
(Hand, wheel, or twisted, as ye list),

[62] The *Itinerarium* (p. 205) inserts here an episode omitted by the *Estoire*. Richard sent Peter des Barres, the commander of one of his galleys, to hail the ship. Those on board said that they were a French ship belonging to the king of France, but Richard saw that they had neither French nor any other Christian insignia and was suspicious. Ralph of Diceto (II, 94) gives the date for this encounter: 8 Ides June, i. e., June 6.

[63] Richard of Devizes (p. 425) calls it "navem mirabilem, navem qua praeter navem Noae, non legitur major ulla fuisse." The capture of this ship is referred to by Haymarus, ll. 757-80.

[64] Beha ed Din (pp. 249-50) and Ibn al Athir (p. 42) confirm that the ship had been fitted out at Beirut, which was then, of course, in Moslem hands.

And eight hundred well chosen Turks [65]
Sent by the devil for his works,
And more of victuals and supplies
Than one could number or surmise;
Likewise in phials there was Greek
Fire kept, of which men much did speak;
And in the ship were stowed away
Two hundred serpents foul and gray [66]   2,180
('Tis written thus, and by him told
Who helped to stow them in the hold)
Which they planned to set free upon
Our host, and spread confusion.

AROUSES THE SUSPICION OF THE ENGLISH

Our galley close to them did steer
So that to touch them it was near;
Our galley-men then gave them greeting,
Being unaware whom they were meeting,
And asked them whence it was they came
And what might be their seigneur's name.   2,190
They had a French interpreter,
And they made answer that they were
Englishmen on their way to Tyre.[67]
A wind from Arsur then did spire
Which drove them from the galley's side:
A galley-man who closely spied
The ship and crew, and noted how
With eagerness they fain would row
Away, said to the king: " 'Tis plain,
Fair Sire, may I be hanged or slain   2,200

[65] The figures for the number of men on the ship vary widely: Beha ed Din (p. 250) says 650 men; Ibn al Athir (p. 43) says 700; Ralph of Diceto (II, 93) and Roger of Hoveden (III, 112) say 1,500.

[66] The *Eracles* (p. 169) mentions the serpents carried in the ship.

[67] The *Itinerarium* (p. 206) says that they claimed to be Genoese. However, on p. 205 the *Itinerarium* had said they pretended to be French. Roger of Hoveden (III, 112) says they declared they were Frenchmen on their way to Acre from Antioch.

If yon craft is not Turk." Whereat
The king said: "Art thou sure of that?"
"Indeed, Sire, most assuredly.
Do but dispatch now hastily
Another galley in pursuit
And order it not to salute
Their men. Then see what they will do
And if their faith be false or true."
The king gave order: and the galiot
Sped toward them, but it hailed them not.   2,210

WHO ATTACK THE SHIP

Having for our men little use
Their arrows they began to loose
From arbalist and Damask bow.
The king and his men fell on the foe
With swift attack and vigorous,
When that he saw them shoot at us;
And they defended themselves well:
Bowstrings were twanged, and arrows fell
Thicker than hail, and the mêlée
On either side was under way.   2,220
Their ship fared slowly, with small breeze.
Our men came alongside with ease
And often, but they dared not board
It, nor could crush the pagan horde.
A solemn oath the king swore, then
And there, to hang the galley men
If they should weaken or if they
Allowed the Turks to get away.
Then like a tempest on they drove;
And headfirst in the water dove   2,230
Beneath the ship; on the other side
They swam back, and they deftly tied
The ropes that to the helm were bound
Of the pagan ship, so to confound
The infidels, to make them steer

Awry, and cause their craft to veer.
And thereupon they climbed on board
And straight into the ship they poured.
The foe were not left-handed; they
Fell on our men, to cut and slay.   2,240
Those of our folk who were adept
In these things vigorously leapt
Into the ship, while theirs slashed arm
And leg, and did us grievous harm.

AND SINK IT

Our men did battle of such sort
That they drove them into the port;
The pagans, who exceedingly
Feared death, fought back desperately:
In squads upon the deck they mounted,
Squads carefully arranged and counted: 2,250
Fresh soldiers to the battle swarmed,
In bold array, perfectly armed.
And so they fought, and both sides smote
Great blows within the pagan boat.
The Saracens made an attack
So strong they drove our seamen back,
But these in their own galleys drew
Together, and assailed anew.
The king told them to ram into
The ship until they stove it through;   2,260
And so they rammed, and so hard drove
That it at several points was stove.
It foundered through the holes thus wrought,
Ending this battle fiercely fought.[68]
So giving way, the Saracens
Leapt in the sea by tens and tens.
Each of our men slew all he could:

[68] The Arab accounts all agree that the captain of the ship, when he saw that it was
liable to fall into the hands of the crusaders, deliberately foundered his ship by breaking
holes in the bottom of the vessel (Beha ed Din, p. 250; Ibn al Athir, p. 43). Ralph of
Diceto (II, 94) says that the ship was pierced and sunk by a diver from Richard's fleet,

There had ye seen great blows and good
Dealt by King Richard with a will
Fierce to destroy them and to kill.   2,270
However, there were thirty-five
Of them that he retained alive.[69]
Of whom some were good engineers,
Skilled in machines, and some emirs:
The rest were drowned: such end was made
Of Persian, Turk, and renegade.
Had the ship come to Acre, 'tis plain
The town would never have been ta'en,
So much defense it would have brought,
But God, who aids His own, so wrought,   2,280
And England's king, good, valorous
In warfare, and adventurous.

TO THE GREAT DISTRESS OF SALADIN

The Saracens atop the hill
Had seen this thing which served them ill,
And, filled with fury and chagrin,
Sent word of it to Saladin.
And when that Saladin had heard
It, thrice in wrath he tore his beard,
Then like a man distraught, said he:
"God! now is Acre lost to me,   2,290
My men, too, whom I thought secure.
Ye bring me woe hard to endure!"
The pagan army made such wail—
Those who beheld it tell the tale—
That the Turks did cut off their hair
In sorrow, and their clothes did tear,
Because within this ship were lost
Their lords and those they cherished most.

THE FLEET SAILS ON TO ACRE

The king, when he this ship of might
And its crew had captured in the fight,   2,300

[69] Ralph of Diceto (p. 93) says that 200 escaped.

To move him on to Acre yearned;
Thither with joy his course he turned,
His galleys all in fair array,
Who o'er the ship had won the day.
And when he with the fleet set forth
God sent them good wind from the north;
So before Tyre that night they spent,[70]
Both king and soldiers most content;
The noble king, Coeur de Lion,
At morning saw Scandalion, 2,310
Then passed Casal Imbert, then clear
Before him he saw Acre appear,
And the flower of all the world he found
Camped there, and drawn up all around; [71]
He saw the mountains and the vales,
The open plains and hills and dales
Clothed with pavilions and with tents,
And men filled with malevolence
Toward Christendom, to do it wrong,
And they were in a mighty throng; 2,320
He saw the tents of Saladin
And of his brother, Saphadin;
The pagans were so near, almost
They pressed upon our Christian host.
Quahadin, on the other hand,
The seneschal of paganland,[72]

[70] The *Gesta* (II, 169) and Roger of Hoveden (III, 112) reverse the order given by the *Estoire* and the *Itinerarium*. According to the *Gesta* and Roger of Hoveden, Richard sailed from Cyprus to Tyre, where he was refused admission by Conrad's retainers. Richard landed and camped outside the walls of Tyre that night (June 6), resuming his journey by sea the next day and encountering the ship on June 7. The day after the battle with the ship (Saturday, June 8) he arrived at Acre. Ralph of Diceto (II, 94) says that the battle with the ship took place on June 6 and that he reached Acre on June 8.

[71] The order of the forces around Acre is given by Ralph of Diceto (II, 79–80). Diceto distinguishes forty different companies stretched from Mount Musart to below the Tower of the Patriarch. See map of Acre.

[72] The text reads "Quahadin li seneschals de paianie." The *Itinerarium* (p. 211) reads "procurator Paganismi Techehedini." Stubbs identifies him as Taki ed Din Omar, the nephew of Saladin, lord of Hama. G. Paris (p. 558) rejects this identification

Guarded the seacoast and the shore
And on our host waged constant war
Always alert to make attack,
To harry us and force us back.   2,330

RICHARD LANDS AT ACRE

The king viewed all things, and surveyed,
And plans he made and plans he made.
And when he came to land, ye would
Have seen the whole great baronhood
Who came with the French king to meet him
And with most eager welcome greet him.[73]
And many folk were on the strand
To see him. He set foot on land: [74]
Then had ye heard the trumpets ring
To greet Richard, the peerless king.   2,340
And all the host of Christendom
Were happy, for that he had come.
But when he came, the Turks inside
The town of Acre were terrified.
He had so many ships,[75] they knew
That he would put an ending to
Their goings-out and comings-in
Which brought us damage and chagrin.

---

on the ground that when Taki ed Din is mentioned later on he is not referred to as
seneschal. As there was no such office among the Moslems, it is ridiculous to refuse the
identification on these grounds. Taki ed Din is known to have been at the siege of
Acre and to have occupied the position along the shore on the right wing of Saladin's
forces. He was there from September, 1189, to June, 1190, and again from November,
1190, until after April 6, 1191, although he had intended to leave the camp on March
2, 1191. As he had not left by April 6, there is reason to suppose that he may still have
been there as late as June 8. (LaMonte, "Taki ed Din, prince of Hama," in *Moslem
World*, XXXI [1941], 149–60.)

[73] The *Eracles* (p. 170) says: "La fu li rois de France de si grant humilité que
il descendi de son cheval a terre, et prist la meme dou roi Richart entre ses braz et
mist a terre hors dou batel."

[74] The *Itinerarium* (p. 211) gives the date: Saturday before the feast of St. Barnabas
in Pentecost week, i. e., June 8. This date is confirmed by Roger of Hoveden (III,
112), Ralph of Diceto (II, 94), Ibn al Athir (p. 42), and Beha ed Din (p. 248).

[75] Beha ed Din (p. 248) and Ibn al Athir (p. 43) both say he had twenty-five great
galleys.

Now the two kings did side by side
Along their way together ride.   2,350
King Richard came into his tents
And thought him with great diligence
Of what might be the surest way
To capture Acre, with least delay.

THE CRUSADERS REJOICE

The joy was great and clear the night:
No son of mother ever might
See or recount such welcoming
As the host gave unto the king.
For bells they rang and trumpets blew,
Horns, pipes, and other music too;   2,360
Ye had seen folk of every sort
In fulsome joyousness disport
Themselves, with music and with song,
And cup-bearers bear wine along
In fair cups through the streets to all
The people, whether great or small.
The king, by taking Cyprus, had
Made all the army to be glad,
For therefrom would they food derive
To keep the mighty host alive.   2,370
All filled with hope they were and gay,
It was the eve of Saturday;
Wherever you might go or be,
I think that you would never see
Such lights or torches as there beamed,
So that unto the Turks it seemed
As if the valley, all entire,
Were kindled in a blazing fire.
And, learning that our merrying
Was for the coming of the king,   2,380
They filled the vale with great display
Of fighting force when came the day:
These pagan folk, foul and malign,

Skirmished about our trenches' line,
Loosed arrows, harried without rest
The host, and on it closely pressed.[76]

---

[76] The *Itinerarium* (pp. 212–13) here includes an incident omitted by the *Estoire*. The Pisans came to Richard offering their services to him and were accepted. Roger of Hoveden (III, 113) says that Richard allied with the Pisans but refused to accept the alliance of the Genoese because the latter were already allied with Philip of France. Richard's charter to the Pisans, dated October 13, 1191, is published in G. Müller, *Documenti sulle relazione delle città toscane coll'oriente cristiano*, pp. 58–59.

CHAPTER III

Now we shall leave the tale a space
(When come the proper time and place,
If you will follow with me, you
Shall hear me take it up anew)   2,390
Of the coming of the two kings
Of whom I have writ many things
And whom I now to Acre have brought.
Hear now, and hold within your thought
That here I wish and must contrive
To break my thread of narrative,
But it shall be tied close once more
And knotted firmly as before:
For the kings were not the first, but rather
The last who at the siege did gather.   2,400
And therefore to all those who fain
Would know, Ambroise will now explain
Who undertook the enterprise
Of taking Acre, and in what wise;
For he himself saw naught of it,
Having but read that which is writ.
Who first besieged it, and what bold

Attempt they made, shall now be told.[1]
You heard me say—and it is well
That I once more relate and tell—   2,410
When I began this history,
If it come to your memory,
How unto us in Syria came
Most grievous damage, harm, and shame.
'Twas in the time of that king Guy
Who sufferèd so much thereby,
But all men do not know the way
That envy did the king betray.

THE DYNASTY OF JERUSALEM

A king had been reared oversea,
A king whose name was Amaury: [2]   2,420
From him a son, the next king, came,
Baldwin the Leprous [3] was his name.
King Baldwin lived his life's extent
Till he unto the worms was sent.
He had two sisters,[4] ladies fair,
Of virtue, worth, and goodness rare:
These ladies both were wedded, one
To Baron Humphrey de Toron,[5]

---

[1] Here the *Estoire* begins an excursus on the history of the kingdom of Jerusalem and on the siege of Acre before the arrival of Richard. The poet admits frankly that he was not an eyewitness of any of the events chronicled and that he has them on hearsay. This material is Book I of the *Itinerarium.* See Introduction.

[2] King Amaury of Jerusalem, 1162–74, second son of Foulques of Anjou and Melissende of Jerusalem. He succeeded to the throne at the death of his elder brother Baldwin III. He was twice married: to Agnes de Courtenay, from whom he was divorced, and to Marie Comnena.

[3] Baldwin IV, king of Jerusalem 1174–85, was the son of Amaury and Agnes. He was a leper from early childhood, and during much of his reign the kingdom was administered by regents, among whom were Raymond of Tripoli, Guy de Lusignan, and Renaud de Châtillon. Baldwin IV is one of the most tragic and most appealing figures in the history of the crusades. A very sympathetic treatment of his reign is given by Grousset, *Histoire des croisades,* II, 609–759.

[4] Sybelle, daughter of Amaury by Agnes, was own sister of Baldwin IV. Isabelle, daughter of Amaury and Marie Comnena, was merely his half-sister.

[5] Isabelle, the younger daughter, was married as a child to Humphrey IV de Toron, lord of Toron, Banias, Kerak, and Montreal. The marriage was arranged in 1180 and solemnized in 1183 while Saladin was besieging Kerak. Humphrey was the

The other to a noble lord,
A Count William, yclept Longsword,[6]   2,430
And lord of Jaffa by the sea,
Brother of Montferrat's marquis.
By him was born unto the dame
A male heir: Baldwin was his name.[7]
The young man lived, but the count died,
For thus it pleased fate to decide.
Guy de Lusignan coveted
The countess, and to her was wed.
The child was king, but scarce was king,
For God thus governs everything.   2,440
When ill fate overtook the youth,
'Twas to the lady that in truth
The kingdom fell, and right this was,
And with good reasonable cause.
The crown was taken by King Guy,
And much of strife was caused thereby.[8]

---

grandson of the great Humphrey the constable, whom legend credited with having knighted Saladin. Humphrey IV's mother, Stéphanie de Milly, lady of Kerak and Montreal, married Renaud de Châtillon after the death of Humphrey's father, and young Humphrey IV was brought up by his step-father. Humphrey IV is referred to in rather slighting terms by his contemporaries, who scorned him for his lack of military valor. He was lacking in vigor and ambition, though not lacking in personal courage, and his refusal to strike for the crown (as described below, note 8) caused him to be looked down upon. Humphrey was a devoted adherent of Guy and served with him throughout the war against Saladin.

[6] William Longsword, eldest son of Marquis William III of Montferrat, died before his father and so was never himself marquis, the title passing to his younger brother Conrad. William came to the east, where he married Sybelle in 1176, and he received the counties of Jaffa and Ascalon with his bride. He died within a year, leaving his wife pregnant with the child who became Baldwin V.

[7] Baldwin V, son of William Longsword and Sybelle, was crowned king of Jerusalem during the lifetime of his uncle Baldwin IV, in 1183. The barons feared that the succession might go to Sybelle and her husband Guy and so put through the coronation of the child Baldwin, who was only about six years old. In 1185, at the death of Baldwin IV, Baldwin V became sole king under a regency. Raymond of Tripoli was made governor of the realm, while the personal custody of the child king was entrusted to his maternal great-uncle Joscelyn de Courtenay. Baldwin V died in 1186, aged nine, and the throne was seized by his mother and step-father.

[8] When Baldwin IV died and the regency had been established for Baldwin V, the barons agreed that in any case of accident occurring to the young king the regency should continue in the person of Raymond of Tripoli until the question of the succes-

THE TREASON OF RAYMOND OF TRIPOLI

Betwixt Count Raymond,[9] false and fell,
And Saladin, of whom I tell,
There long had been alliance made
Of which in Syria much was said.   2,450
This Raymond craved the kingdom, which
He thought to have, for he was rich,
And he was count of Tripoli,
But he secured it not, thanks be
To God. When Guy was crownèd king,
Chosen by God for honoring,
Unto his coronation
He called his barons, every one.

---

sion could be settled. It was agreed to leave the succession to the decision of the pope, the emperor, and the kings of France and England, and to await their decision before proceeding with any coronation. When, however, Baldwin V died, Joscelyn de Courtenay and the court party seized Jerusalem and other domain cities while Raymond was away and carried through a *coup d'état* whereby Sybelle was crowned and then conferred the crown upon her husband. This stroke was the work of Joscelyn, Renaud de Châtillon, the patriarch, and the Master of the Temple. Raymond summoned the barons to meet with him at Naplouse, and they refused to accept the *fait accompli*, urging the claims of Isabelle and her husband, Humphrey. Humphrey, however, fled to Jerusalem, where he took the oath to Guy and threw himself on Guy's mercy. The baronial opposition collapsed, and most of the barons made their peace with the new king and queen. Raymond, however, sulked and refused to perform homage to Guy. Baldwin d'Ibelin also refused to accept the new monarch, and after a perfunctory homage, which was necessary to retain his fiefs, he turned his lands over to his son and went to Antioch. It was through fear of an attack by Guy that Raymond drew closer to Saladin and strengthened the treaty between them, an action which gave rise to the charge that he had treasonably sold out Christianity to the Moslems. (Baldwin, *Raymond III*, pp. 69–82; LaMonte, *Feudal Monarchy*, pp. 33–37; Röhricht, *Königreichs*, pp. 415–20; Grousset, II, 759–76.)

[9] Raymond III, count of Tripoli and regent of Jerusalem during the reign of Baldwin V, was a second cousin of Sybelle and Isabelle, being the son of Hodierne, the younger sister of Melissende, the grandmother of the queens. He stood nearest the throne in line of succession and would have inherited had Sybelle and Isabelle both died without heirs. There is nothing to indicate that Raymond actually ever aspired to the crown, however. He was lord of Tiberias and prince of Galilee through his wife, Eschive of Tiberias, and as such was chief vassal of the king in the principality of Jerusalem. We have already noted Ambroise's hostility to Raymond and the reasons for his partisan denunciation of this able leader.

Among them he sent summons to
The count of Tripoli, but you   2,460
May ask in vain what heed was paid
And what insolent answer made.
The messenger returned indeed,
And the count promptly did proceed
To make his plaint to Saladin,
Saying that he could not stay in
His land, because King Guy who sate
Upon the throne did greatly hate
Him. So much did he say and lie
That Christendom took harm thereby . . .   2,470
And asked him, for his dear love's sake,
To help him full revenge to take.[10]
My lords, 'twas at that meeting-place
That there was planned the treason base
That brought all Christendom such loss
And made us lose the Holy Cross.
The count once more was summonèd
To court, and much with him they plead
To come. He said that he would not,
Nor from King Guy would he hold aught.   2,480
The king sent a third time, with plight
To render him his every right.
And so he came. Ill come he was
For he was certain to compass
The ruin of the land. Therein
He did the evil work begin.

[10] We have already discussed this matter in a previous footnote. The *Estoire* and the *Itinerarium* are the chief sources for this charge of treason against Raymond, which is entirely unfounded. William of Newburgh (I, 255–58) repeats these accusations and even reports a rumor that Raymond poisoned Baldwin V. Bar Hebraeus (pp. 322–24) also accuses Raymond of treason and of going over to Saladin at the coronation of Guy. It was apparent to anyone familiar with the situation that some sort of treaty with Saladin would be imperative as long as such an incompetent as Guy remained in control in Jerusalem. Raymond tried to salvage what he could out of the wreckage he knew Guy would make of the kingdom. Marshal Baldwin, in his *Raymond III* (pp. 156–60), has given a full discussion of the charges against Raymond and shown the ridiculousness of them.

But when he died, great shame befell
Him, as the history doth tell.[11]

SALADIN INVADES THE KINGDOM

Ye have heard many times before
The tale, and heard it o'er and o'er,   2,490
How, when he had been crowned, King Guy
Did not let two full months pass by
Before he ordered to convoke
Throughout all Syria his folk
To gather and to bear him aid;
For Saladin's men did invade
The country, and at his command
Swept in full force into the land,
Dealt to Guy's men a sore defeat.
An hundred knights of the élite,   2,500
And Jacques de Mailly there were slain,[12]
Which caused the Temple grievous pain.
And it was this discomfiture
That started the misadventure
That has so long brought misery

[11] The method of Raymond's death is not known. Beha ed Din (p. 114) says that he died of pleurisy, but Conder's note claims he was killed by the Assassins (p. 113). Ibn al Athir (p. 687) reports that he died of anger and grief. Röhricht (*Königreichs*, p. 446) and Baldwin (*Raymond III*, p. 138, n. 17) collect the various sources dealing with Raymond's demise. One western annalist says that he was murdered by his wife. That he died very soon after the fall of Jerusalem is evidenced by the mention of his death as a recent event in a letter announcing the fall of the city (Ibn Kallikan, IV, 524).

[12] Jacques de Mailly, marshal of the Temple, is said by the *Itinerarium* (p. 7) to be a native of Touraine. The story of the battle of Nazareth of May 1, 1187, is best told by Ernoul (pp. 144–48) and the *Eracles* (pp. 37–44). El Afdal, Saladin's son, requested of Count Raymond permission to hunt in the territory of Tiberias for one day. Raymond acceded to the request on condition that the Saracens were not to enter any town or house or to plunder the countryside in any way. While the Saracens were peacefully hunting they encountered a party of Templars and Hospitallers who were coming as an embassy from Guy to Raymond. The knights fell upon the hunters and a battle ensued in which the Christians were almost wiped out. Roger des Moulins, the Master of the Hospital, and Jacques de Mailly, the marshal of the Temple, were slain, and Girard de Ridefort, the Master of the Temple, barely escaped with his life. That evening the Saracens rode back across the border in accordance with their promise to remain in the country only one day. (Baldwin, *Raymond III*, pp. 86–91.)

On holy Christianity.
The count of Tripoli gave out—
His lip hung always in a pout—[13]
That to King Guy he would proceed,
And lend him succor in his need.   2,510
He came to him, and made accord;
But people recalled afterward
That 'twas a false accord he made
And that he suddenly betrayed
Him in the height of battle-tide
When so many good people died.
It well may be he did, although
It may be that he did not so.[14]
But most men testify and say
He played him false in the mêlée;   2,520
If so, grim fate he merited.
Now Saladin had summonèd
His men to come from his nine realms [15]
With bows, with hauberks, and with helms,
And they arrived, in mighty throng,
And none held back, nor weak nor strong.
Many emirs of great rank came
And noblemen of mighty name,

[13] This peculiarity of Raymond's is not noted by any other writer, and we incline to the opinion that it was inserted in the *Estoire* merely for the rhyme. William of Tyre (p. 1012) describes him: "The above mentioned count was a man of slender body, lean, of modest stature, with an aquiline face, straight hair, medium dark, sharp eyes, erect shoulders, of composed mind, extremely far-seeing, and strenuous in his actions, sober beyond most in eating and drinking, liberal in giving . . ."

[14] Bar Hebraeus (pp. 323–24) says that Raymond deliberately deserted at Hattin because he had advised against the battle and would have been put out had the Christians won a victory against his counsel. Baldwin discusses the question of Raymond's treason, pp. 156–60.

[15] The identity of the nine realms is obscure: William of Newburgh (I, 241) says eight; the *Itinerarium* (p. 11) gives: Egypt, Damascus, Edessa, Al Jezira, and Hither India as the countries ruled by Saladin. The letter from Saladin to Frederick Barbarossa, published in the *Libellus* (pp. 259–62), includes among Saladin's domains: the lands of the Bedouins and of the Turkomans, Egypt, Damascus, maritime Jerusalem, Al Jezira, Edessa, India, and overlordship over the caliph of Bagdad. Saladin signs this amazing letter with the title "Soldani Sarracenorum et paganorum."

Prepared to part from their country
To damage Christianity.   2,530

AND OVERWHELMS ITS ARMY AT HATTIN

Now King Guy, with his Christians,
And with them some Venetians,
Had made into two parts his force,
Both his foot-soldiers and his horse:
One to the port of Tabarie
He sent, and one to Saforie.
That force to their good fortune went
Who on Tabarie made descent,
For though they lost their bodies there
Straight unto God their souls did fare.   2,540
The count of Tripoli, who planned
To play them false, had their command.
Our men did not suspect him; they
Did only harken and obey.
And so he wrought, and so he strove
That the enemy's army drove
Ours to the sea of Galilee,
Where water had they none. Then he
Caused them to drink, in his falsehood,
Of the sea, which is sweet and good.[16]   2,550
When it was time for him to lower
Lance and do all in his power,
He fled away; they who were left
Were of the body's life bereft.
Who smote on whom I do not know,
Nor who escaped, who was laid low,
Because I was not at the fray;
But truly, this to you I say,
That God arranged what happened here,
Because unto Him it was clear   2,560

[16] This passage makes little sense. Perhaps it should be read allegorically to mean
the sweet water of martyrdom. The Christian army suffered intense thirst in the long
dry march to Hattin. Men threw away their armor and many surrendered in return for
a drink.

That in the world was so much sin
And people reveling therein,
That had not this occurred, unto
Him would have come but very few.
It was at la Marescallie,[17]
Which lies alongside Tabarie,
That King Guy battled with his men
And slew full many a Saracen,
But our men, suffering many a wound,
Lay dead and headless on the ground.   2,570
There was no hope of rescuing,
For the foe rushed upon the king,
And wounded him, and overbore
Him to the earth, and beat him sore.
Within his arms the Holy Cross
He held clutched tight, for insult gross
They might have done It, had he not: [18]
But God, it seems, had given it thought.

HE OVERRUNS THE LAND

When came the finish of the fray
Which God decreed should end this way;   2,580
And both the king and cross were ta'en,
And almost all the army slain
(Wherefore so many took the road,
Leaving their goods and livelihood).
Then Saladin, just as it pleased
Him, had the whole land seized,
Save Tyre and Ascalon (God thus
Gives His land, then takes it from us)
And save Jerusalem, but he

---

[17] The *Itinerarium* (p. 14) and the *Libellus* (p. 223) agree that the battle was fought at Marescallia (modern Lubya). However, most accounts refer to the fight as occurring at the Horns of Hattin just north of Lubya. See map and discussion in Baldwin, pp. 106 ff.

[18] Not King Guy, but the bishop of Acre bore the Cross into battle. When he was killed, the Cross was carried by the bishop of St. George of Lydda. (Schlumberger, *Renaud de Châtillon*, pp. 285–86, 292.)

Conquered that also speedily.[19]   2,590
He laid his siege to Ascalon
Thinking it would be lightly won;
But they held out courageously
Against him, and most stubbornly.
And many Saracens there died
Before that he might come inside,
Until he caused his men to bring
And show before their walls their king.
He offered, for the citadel,
To yield the king, who sent to tell   2,600
The town's defenders not to make
Any surrender for his sake:
But they, who could no more endure,
Must take what terms they might secure.
For him they gave up Ascalon
And with their chattels left the town.[20]

GUY'S RELEASE AND RAYMOND'S DEATH

And upon these terms was King Guy,
The book says, set at liberty:
To quit the realm he must agree
And straightway to go oversea.   2,610
He took to sea, in all due form
So that he might his oath perform,
And to Tortosa's isle he came,
Which did its people much inflame.
There Saladin a message sent—
A Saracen intelligent
He was, and knew the king had been
Ill-fated, but not harsh nor mean,
And wished not on himself to bring
The danger of another king—   2,620
That he would quit him of his vow.[21]

[19] Jerusalem capitulated to Saladin on October 2, 1187.

[20] Ascalon surrendered on September 4, 1187.

[21] It is worth noting that the *Estoire*, partial as it is to Guy, includes this extremely uncomplimentary explanation of Saladin's motive for releasing the king.

The king retraced his footsteps now
To Tripoli, on the marine.
And there he found his wife, the queen,
And the count, who hated him, and who,
Men say, had done him treason too.
But now he gave the king, whate'er
His inward thought, a greeting fair.
It little serves to give account
Of this corrupt and traitrous count,   2,630
Who made an orphan many a child,
And Christianity defiled:
Dearly he paid the treachery
That he did, and the villainy,
For it brought on him, by God's grace,
Swift death, and death with sore disgrace.

SIEGE OF TYRE

Nor shall I tell the siege of Tyre
Which gave Saladin pain and ire,
And where William de la Chapelle [22]
Battled most valiantly and well,   2,640
And where the brothers Tabarie,[23]

[22] G. Paris (p. 544) ventures the suggestion that this William de la Chapelle may have been the famous "Green Knight" whose heroism is recorded by the *Eracles* (p. 106). But after making this suggestion Paris admits that the probability is that the Green Knight was Sanchez Martin.

[23] The brothers Tabarie were Hugh, William, Oste, and Ralph of Tiberias, sons of Walter de St. Omer and Eschive of Tiberias, and step-sons of Raymond of Tripoli. They were with Raymond in his escape from Hattin in 1187 and went to Tyre, where they helped defend that city. Hugh became the second in command to Conrad after Conrad assumed the control in Tyre, but went with Guy to Acre in 1190–91 and accompanied Richard in his Jaffa campaign in 1192. After the end of the third crusade the brothers are found among the vassals and councillors of Henry of Champagne, Ralph being seneschal of Jerusalem 1194–98; but the death of Henry brought disaster to the family. Queen Isabelle, left a widow, sought a husband, and Ralph of Tiberias became a candidate for her hand. In 1197 Hugh gave up the lordship of Tiberias to Ralph, to strengthen his position as a candidate for the throne, but Ralph was passed over in favor of the more powerful Aymeri de Lusignan, already king of Cyprus. A feud developed between Aymeri and Ralph in which Ralph was guilty of conspiracy against the new king and was forced to leave the country. William of Tiberias seems to have died about this time, as his name last appears on an act of 1192 and he was not mentioned in a

Who guarded the town gallantly,
Were so devoted and so loyal
To God and to His kingdom royal.
Nor of the marquis shall I tell
Who there began stoutly and well.
Already was the land invaded
When he came, but somewhat he aided
God's work. He started valorous
And ended false and treacherous.   2,650
I would not stray too far, nor turn
From King Guy, who is my concern;
Who now from his imprisonment
Is freed. On him my mind is bent.

GUY PREPARES TO RENEW THE WAR

That he was back in Tripoli
Pleased men of high and low degree.
Now poverty and woe did hem
In Guy, king of Jerusalem,
As one who comes from prison forth.
He took no more than his just worth,   2,660
For he had nothing he could take,
And some expense he needs must make;
And he knew that the enemy
Had taken Acre, which was the key
To his land, and driven out his force,
And he knew not where to take recourse.

letter from Pope Innocent III to Hugh and his brothers Oste and Ralph in 1199 (Potthast, *Regesta pontificum*, Vol. I, no. 909). Ralph, Hugh, and Oste all fled to Armenia,
where Oste joined Raymond Rupin and Leo, appearing with them in acts from 1210 to
1216. He last appears on an act of 1218 in Cyprus. (Röhricht, *Regesta*, doc. 912.) Hugh
and Ralph went to Constantinople in the wake of the fourth crusade and settled in the
new Latin Empire. There Hugh died about 1205, but Ralph returned to Jerusalem after
the death of King Aymeri and resumed his office of seneschal, 1207–10. He participated
in the crusade against Damietta and is last heard of in Acre in 1220. Ralph was the
leading jurist of his time, and it was from him that Philip de Novare learned the science
of the laws. It may well have been Ralph who transmitted to Constantinople the laws
of Jerusalem which formed traditionally the bases for the Assizes of Romanie. The
lordship of Tiberias passed to Eudes de Montbéliard, the husband of Ralph's daughter
Eschive.

To God his sorrows he confided,
And the Lord God full well provided.
When the bell rang, one morning, there
The prince of Antioch forth [24] did fare,   2,670
And to seek out King Guy he went
To ask of him that he consent
To go with him, and to return
To Antioch, and there sojourn
Till he could gather and unite
His men, and arm them for the fight,
And know where best to fall upon
The Turks, that something might be won
From them. The king went with the prince
To Antioch in his province.[25]   2,680
A little time he sojourned there
And meanwhile he shed many a tear
When he bethought him of the clime
Once his, now lost in his own time.
Then back to Tripoli he went,
Made ready men and armament;
He gathered and united all
The men he could contrive to call
With what loan he could gather, for
He did not wish to linger more.   2,690

AND IS JOINED BY HIS BROTHER GEOFFREY

And while he stayed there, all intent
On gathering men and armament,
Geoffrey de Lusignan, his own
Brother, came there. He was well known
As the land's strongest vassal, for
He had been nourished well on war.

[24] Bohemond III of Antioch, 1163–1201, son of Raymond of Poitiers and Constance of Antioch. Bohemond played a rather sorry role in the war against Saladin, plundering the refugees who came to his country. He is chiefly conspicuous for the length of his rule and for his marital difficulties.

[25] The *Eracles* (pp. 124–25) says that he went to Tripoli, where were the ships of King William of Sicily.

It was at Tyre he first put in
But there he did not find his kin,
For the marquis and his escort
Forbade him entry to the port.   2,700
So, having been rebuffed and spurned,
To Tripoli he now returned.
There did his brother find King Guy,
Who welcomed him most heartily.
And when the king had well prepared
For war his soldiers, forth they fared.
He came to Tyre along the strand:
Few knights and men were in his band.
He found the portals all were barred
To him and his men by the guard: 2,710
The marquis, base and insolent,
To let him in would not consent;
He did an ill-inspired thing,
Barring his own realm to the king.[26]
The king, his entry thus denied,
Declared that he could not abide
Such insult. There he took firm stand
And had his tent pitched on the sand.

DESPITE CONRAD, MANY JOIN GUY

Outside of Tyre gathered the host,
And know ye that it sorely cost   2,720
Him that the town to him was banned;
But this affront had all been planned
By Montferrat, the false marquis—
The valiant Conrad's son was he,[27]
Who was captured in the mighty fight.
Never could he have done such spite:
Loyal was he, and chivalrous,

[26] Conrad's refusal to surrender Tyre to Guy is told in more detail in the *Eracles* (pp. 123–34).
[27] This is a mistake. Conrad was the son of Marquis William III of Montferrat. William had been taken prisoner by the Saracens, who offered to surrender him in return for Tyre. Conrad refused any suggestion of capitulation. (Ernoul, pp. 236–37.)

Whereas his son was treacherous.
The men of Tyre who well did love
Their God and placed God's work above   2,730
All else, left the town straightaway
And sought the king without delay.
There were the noble Germans who
That year served loyally and true,
And the good brothers Tabarie,
Syria's loyalest company,
And the Pisans, who to serve the Lord
Most valiantly gave hand and sword;
Their homes they had abandonèd
And much of wealth as well. They led   2,740
Their wives and children too, to fare
To Acre, where the Saracens were.

THEY MOVE TO THE SIEGE OF ACRE

Having his brother's aid did bring
Great happiness unto the king,
The true tale tells that he sojourned
Four months before he was returned
To Tyre upon the sand, the town
Which in all justice was his own.
When he had brought from the whole land
The soldiers under his command,   2,750
Together with his brother's forces—
Who formed large share of his resources—
He had four hundred knights, and counted
But seven thousand men unmounted,
To besiege Acre.[28] I surmise
None else would dare such enterprise;
'Twas marvel that such feat he tried
—Save that he knew God on his side—
To attack a force that numbered more
Than his, by an hundred men to four.   2,760

[28] The *Eracles* (p. 125) says that Guy had but a few men and that the Saracens in Acre outnumbered the besiegers four to one. Beha ed Din (p. 156) estimated that Guy had 2,000 horse and 30,000 foot when he began the siege.

But God willed all that did befall
The host that came to Acre's wall,
Which Saladin most mightily
Endeavorèd to fortify,
For he was sure of an attack
From those who fain would win it back.
The king set forth his God to serve,
From Whom his trust did never swerve.
What men he had, though they were few,
He led along a road he knew: 2,770
The host passed swiftly through the dire
Pass that doth lie 'twixt Acre and Tyre,
The pass called Scandalion; thereby
The host was guided by King Guy.
But Saladin was unaware
Of this; had he known the affair,
The host had quickly been destroyed.[29]
Nor could all Russia's gold avoid
Such fate. God willed it otherwise.
Thus was begun the enterprise   2,780
Of saving Christianity,
Which grew with great rapidity.
Now in the Blessed Body's name
That we Christians adore, there came
The king's army to Acre. Thereon
The king mounted atop Toron.[30]
And now the Christian host that went
From Tyre to Acre made the ascent
Of Toron. Ye may know aright
That they climbed there in dark of night: 2,790

[29] Saladin fought several skirmishes with the Frankish army in July 1189 and was hurrying to Acre when he heard that the army was at Scandalion, where "a body of Franks had disembarked" to join the Franks of Tyre and the King's army (Beha ed Din, p. 153).

[30] This is not the fief of Toron. The word *toron* simply meant a hill (modern Tell). The *Eracles* (p. 125) says that this was a *toron* in the lands of St. Nicholas outside Acre.

They dared not in the wood remain,
Hence higher ground they must attain.

SALADIN DEFENDS ACRE

And when at dawn the Turks did fare
Forth from the town, and saw them there,
Behold, all Acre was disturbed,
Its knights excited and perturbed.
They sent to tell Saladin then
That a handful of Christian men
Had moved upon them foolishly
And that he should come hastily   2,800
To cut their heads off and to spare
Not one, because they would not dare
Defend themselves. Exceedingly
Was Saladin rejoiced thereby;
He was at Beaufort, which he pressed
With vigor and sought to invest.[31]
He called reserves, and gave command
Through all the reaches of his land
That they to Syria should make
Their way at once, for plunder's sake.   2,810
Too many came, may God confound
Them, Who made earth and heaven around.
Had we been chopped up inch by inch,
Each one would not have had his pinch.
The third day that our men were on
The lofty summit of Toron
(Where all night long they kept their arms
To ward off Saracens' alarms),
Behold, the men of Saladin,

[31] Saladin had been delayed for some time by the siege of Beaufort (Belfort, Kalaat es Schekif) which had been prolonged through the guile and trickery of Renaud of Sidon. Renaud was sent to prison, and the negotiations were broken off in August, but the castle did not surrender until the following April (Beha ed Din, pp. 141–43, 150–53, 174). The *Eracles* (p. 125) says that Saladin was at Roche Guillaume when he had this news from Acre.

Persian and Turk and Bedouin,   2,820
Who came, intent to occupy
The land in its entirety.
Upon the third day of the week [32]
Came Saladin himself to wreak
The vengeance swift he coveted
And cut off every Christian head.

THE SIEGE BEGINS

'Tis not a matter for surprise
If they must watch with open eyes
And if travail and pain they gave
In their attempt their heads to save.   2,830
For where they were on Toron's height,
The Turks assailed them day and night—
So oft attacked them, with such heat,
That scarce could they make shift to eat.
Geoffrey de Lusignan did most
Great labor to defend the host.
Erstwhile he was both brave and bold,
Now even more his fame is told.
From Monday until Friday thus [33]
They dwelt in plight most perilous.   2,840
Now shall ye hear with what regard
God cares for those He wills to guard:
Nothing can do him harm or ill
Who gives himself to serve His will.

JACQUES D'AVESNES ARRIVES WITH REINFORCEMENTS

While thus they dwelt in fear and doubt,
The king and those with him looked out
Upon the high sea far away,
And fervently to God did pray

[32] Tuesday, August 29 (15 Rejeb). The date is given by Beha ed Din (p. 155).
Saladin moved up to el Kharruba.

[33] Monday, September 18, to Friday, September 22. Saladin held his men back until
Saturday, September 16, then cut through the besiegers and opened the way to Acre. The
heavy fighting took place the following week, as our author states. (Beha ed Din, pp.
157-59.)

For such succor as might avail
Them, when, behold, coming full sail,   2,850
A splendid fleet of vessels manned
With people coming to the land!
Jacques d'Avesnes there was, of Flander.[34]
I do not think that Alexander
Or Hector or Achilles were
Men of more noble character.
'Twas Jacques who sold, or gave as gage,
Or pledged, his goodly heritage
And, selling all his property,
Most wisely and most loyally,   2,860
Heart, soul, and body did bequeath
To the King Who rose to life from death.
And fourteen thousand with him came,
Men fully armed and known to fame.
These vessels were the Danish fleet: [35]
There many a castellan ye might meet
From Cornwall, and la Marche as well,[36]
So those who know the story tell.
Excellent steeds of war had they,
Sturdy and swift, both brown and bay.   2,870
When they were close to land, ye had
Seen the Turks growing well-nigh mad
With rage; along the shore they dashed,
Some even in the water splashed.
And mad were those within the town,

[34] Jacques d'Avesnes, a Flemish baron, was one of the spectacular heroes of the crusade. He came with a large following to Acre early in the siege in 1189 and at once assumed a position among the most important leaders. His death is loudly lamented by Ambroise further on. He had previously gained celebrity through a revolt against his lord, the count of Flanders. (Meyer's note, *Guillaume le Maréchal*, III, 40.)

[35] Ten or twelve thousand Danes set out from Denmark in May, 1188, sailing to Palestine via Lisbon and Messina. At Messina they met Jacques d'Avesnes and his Flemings with whom they joined company. Under the command of Avesnes they arrived at Acre just in time to take part in the battle in September. The *Eracles* (p. 127) says that there were fifty or more ships in all. The *Itinerarium* (p. 74) says that the Danes were led by the nephew of the Danish king. (Riant, *Expéditions des Scandinaves*, pp. 277–83.)

[36] The *Eracles* (p. 128) refers to Frisians, Germans, and Bretons.

Who shot thick rain of arrows down.[37]
But those on Toron made descent
And to assail each flank they went,
Where, charging, they made fierce attack.
The Turks, however, drove them back   2,880
With heavy firing. Nonetheless
Our soldiers landed with success.
Seeing the host come, Saladin, pleased,
Said: "Now our booty is increased."

PRELIMINARY SKIRMISHES

When the high King, Whom we bow down
To worship, saw His army grown
Till it was somewhat firm and strong
Which might not have endurèd long . . .
They all took heart in unison
And made their way down from Toron;   2,890
Making their shelters, pitching tents,
The siege of Acre they did commence.
While on both sides their foes molest
Them, and they too are sorely pressed.
Holding themselves upon the strand
The Pisans made a valiant stand,
Gallantly guarding the sea-board
Against the cruel paynim horde,
So that they might not damage or
Capture the ships that came to shore.   2,900
One morning—Friday was the day—
Took place a spirited affray
Off yonder toward Mount Musart [38]
And soldiers slain on either part.
Those in the town made a sortie
And into Acre brought forcibly

[37] According to the *Eracles* (pp. 127–28) it was on the arrival of Avesnes that Saladin reinforced the garrison in Acre, sending Karakush in as commander.

[38] Mount Musart was a hill to the north of Acre. It lay outside the inner circuit of walls, but was included in the outer circuit.

A caravan of goodly size
Of camels laden with supplies,
And unto Saladin they brought
The plunder for which they had fought.   2,910
They came and left the city quite
At ease, as those who have the might.
Those who held Acre to repel
Us, were not peasants, mark ye well,
Taken away from cart or plough;
For later we learned well enow
That of all those who disobey
God, none were more stalwart than they
To storm a castle, none more bold
To guard a city and to hold.   2,920

WESTERN CRUSADERS AUGMENT THE FORCE

'Twas no more than a fortnight when
Arrived there the count of Brienne; [39]
His brother Andrew [40] with him came,
Son of good sire and of good dame.
And the seneschal of Flanders,[41] who
Brought a full score of barons too.
And the landgrave of Germany [42]—
Goodly horses from Spain had he—
Likewise the bishop of Beauvais [43]—
No aged man, infirm and gray—   2,930

[39] Erard II, count of Brienne 1161–92. He was the father of Walter III, count of Brienne and Lecce, and of John, king of Jerusalem and emperor-regent of Constantinople. (Mas Latrie, *Trésor de chronologie*, p. 1576.)

[40] Andrew de Brienne, lord of Ramerupt, was killed October 4, 1189.

[41] Helin de Wavrin was the seneschal of Flanders, with which title he appears on acts from 1176 to 1189. He appears several times in the *Guillaume le Maréchal*.

[42] Louis II, landgrave of Thuringia 1172–90. According to the *Itinerarium* (p. 68) it was he who persuaded Conrad to come to the assistance of the army at Acre. He died on his way home from the crusade. Ralph of Diceto (II, 82–83) accuses him of treason, asserting that he and a number of the other leaders accepted money from Saladin to allow the destruction of the siege towers and the prolongation of the siege.

[43] Philip de Dreux, bishop of Beauvais, see above, chap. II, note 44. He is another of the barons charged with treason by Diceto.

And his brother, Count Robert,[44] a bright
And vigorous and sturdy knight.
The count of Bar [45] arrived, and there
Was none more courteous anywhere;
And many another grave and wise
Man came to join the enterprise.[46]
Strangely, the more they came, the less
They gave the foe fear or distress,
Who drove and harried their defense
And pressed in even to their tents.   2,940
The townsmen sallied forth on us,
And the others grew more numerous
Each day and filled the land. Almost
They had surrounded our brave host;
However, without wavering
They held firm for their Heavenly King.
While before Acre raged the fight,
No deacon, priest, nor clerk could write
Or tell the anguish and the pain
The Christian troops had to sustain,   2,950
Their hardships and their martyrdom,
Until the kings were thither come
The kings of England and of France
And their men of good valiance,
Who loved God in all faith and trust
And brought the walls of Acre to dust.

[44] Robert II, count of Dreux 1184–1218, brother of Philip, and cousin of King Philip II. He was a persistent crusader, and took the cross a second time in 1211. He is another of Ralph of Diceto's traitorous barons. He was the father of the famous Peter de Dreux, duke of Brittany.

[45] Henry I, count of Bar-le-Duc 1170–91, died at the siege of Acre. He was cousin of Henry of Champagne.

[46] The *Itinerarium* (pp. 73–74) gives a different list of arrivals: the count of Ferrers (i. e., earl of Derby), Narjot de Toucy, Ancelin de Montreal, Geoffrey de Grenville, Otho de Fosse, William Goez, the viscount of Château Erald, the viscount of Turenne, the castellan of Bruges, the archbishop of Pisa, Count Bertulf, Count Nicholas of Hungary, Count Bernard, Count Joscelyn, Count Richard of Apulia, Count Aldebrandus, Ingelremmus de Vienne, Hervé de Gien, Thibaut de Bar, Count John of Leogria, Count John of Seis, Guy de Dampierre, the bishop of Verona, the nephew of the king of Denmark, and others.

THE TURKS ATTACK BUT ARE REPULSED

It was one Friday in September [47]
There happened, as I well remember,
A mishap that befell on us
Most harmful and calamitous.   2,960
The Saracens each day assailed
Our men; no single day they failed.
The Christians armed themselves to stand
Each in his rank, at the command
Of the commander of the troops,
Which were divided into groups.
The Hospital and the Temple, too,
Were on the seashore, where the crew
Of Saracens was numerous.
The fighting always started thus: 2,970
In the center the count of Brienne [48]
Took his position with his men,
There the landgrave of Germany
Took post with his great company
Near the Mahomerie,[49] on guard,
For which they merited reward . . .
The troops from Pisa and King Guy
And others of great gallantry,
Upon the right, to keep watch on
The Turkish forces, held Toron.   2,980
The Saracens came fiercely; you
Might many a fine contingent view.
The Templars and the Hospital
Charge and upon the vanguard fall,
Break through their ranks, undo them quite,

[47] According to Beha ed Din (pp. 162–66) and Ibn al Athir (pp. 10–12) this battle
took place early in October.

[48] The *Eracles* (p. 129) says that the count of Brienne commanded the rear guard,
with the Templars in the van. Guy and Geoffrey guarded the camp as stated by the
Estoire.

[49] The Mahomerie (al Birah), a casale which belonged to the Church of the Holy
Sepulcher just outside Acre. Stubbs (p. 455) defines a "Mahomerie" as a mosque; it was
rather a Moslem village.

And follow when they take to flight.
So do our other troops. All round
The Saracens break and give ground.
But in such numbers were the foe
That not a Christian man might know   2,990
In what way they might turn about,
Nor could the Turks impede the rout.

UNTIL AN ACCIDENT TURNS THE TIDE IN THEIR FAVOR

Close to the mountain-side were they,
When the devil, entering the fray,
Did a most evil deed, which cost
The lives of many of our host.
It happened through a German's horse
That ran away from him. Full course
He and his fellows followèd,
But could not catch it where it fled.   3,000
The horse fled toward the city. Hence
An hundred thousand Saracens
Thought we were fleeing. By the token
They thought the Christian ranks were broken.[50]
They charged upon us. To the fray
They turned, and drove us so that day
That those whose wont it was to guide
The host, themselves were sorely tried.
The foe fought hard and overbore
Us: we were one to twenty-four.   3,010
And those who club or mace could wield
Left many dead upon the field.

CHRISTIAN CASUALTIES

There was Andrew de Brienne slain:
May his soul suffer not in pain!
Never died knight so unafraid
Or so quick to lend others aid.

[50] The *Eracles* (p. 129) relates this same incident. Guy left the camp in order to save the battle, and the Turks from Acre attacked the camp, which was defended by Geoffrey with only a small company of men.

The pagans hemmed in the marquis
De Montferrat so close that he
Might well have perished, were it not
That King Guy succor to him brought.   3,020
The Master of the Temple died [51]
Amid the raging battle-tide.
'Twas he who said the noble word
Learned in the good school of the Lord
When at this onslaught, timid folk,
And fearless folk as well, bespoke
Him thus: "Come, sire, come, leave the fight,"
And had he willed to, well he might
Have come. "May God forbid," said he,
"That elsewhere I may ever be,   3,030
Or any man ever upbraid
The Temple, that I fled afraid."
He fled not, rather perished thus,
Born down by Turks too numerous.
Five thousand humbler folk were slain,[52]
Whose naked bodies strewed the plain.

AND HEROISM

Then when the foe within the town
Learned that our men were beaten down,
They mounted on their Arab horses,

[51] Girard de Ridefort, Master of the Temple 1186–90. He had been a marshal of the
kingdom of Jerusalem in 1179 and had arranged with Raymond of Tripoli to have
the hand of the next heiress whose marriage was within the power of the prince. When,
however, the fief of Botron and the hand of its heiress became available, Raymond sold
the lady and the land to Plebanus, a Pisan, who paid a high price for them, and Girard
was passed by. He entered the Temple, became seneschal (1183) and Master of the
Order (1186), and was one of Raymond's most vigorous opponents. He was one of
the men responsible for the coronation of Guy and for the disastrous march to Hattin,
against the advice of Raymond. The *Itinerarium* (p. 70) calls him "Bideford," a spelling which Stubbs accepts. Ibn al Athir (p. 12) records this battle under the date of
October 3 and says that the Master of the Temple was taken and executed. The *Eracles*
(p. 130), however, agrees with the *Estoire* that he was killed in battle.

[52] Ibn al Athir (p. 12) estimates ten thousand; Beha ed Din (p. 167) says that
seven thousand were reported to have been slain but that he doubts there were quite so
many.

Came forth, and fell upon our forces   3,040
With a rush so impetuous
That ill would have befallen us,
Had we not stoutly fought them back;
Our men withstood the fierce attack,
Did noble deeds, and mighty blows
They dealt upon their hated foes.
The king fought sturdily and well,
King Guy, of whom ye have heard tell.
Geoffrey de Lusignan likewise,
Who suffered sore in this emprise,   3,050
And Jacques d'Avesnes, the bold, whose hand
Did such great prowess in the land,
And others too. So well they strove
That back to Acre the foe they drove.

THE CRUSADERS ENTRENCH THEMSELVES

Thus it befell upon that day
When Fortune turned her face away.
The Saracens were cheered anew
(God curse them, and I curse them too!)
Thereby to harass and molest
Our Christian soldiers, and they pressed   3,060
And harried our men more than e'er.
When that our leaders were aware
Of this, the barons thuswise spake:
"Lords, little profit do we take.
Let us contrive some tactic, good
To fend away this devil's brood
Who all day vent on us their spite
And steal our horses in the night."
This was the resolution which
They took: they caused a mighty ditch   3,070
To be dug—deep and broad and wide—
And many targes set inside
The ditch, and timber-ends and shields,
And thus they did divide the fields.

But still the Saracens molest
Our men, and do not let them rest.

CORPSES POLLUTE THE WATER

Hear now the great confusion
Resulting from the slaughter done
Upon the Franks, of which I treated
But now, when they were sore defeated.   3,080
Upon the morrow of the day
Of this calamitous affray,
When all the host's élite was battered
Down, and their strength rent and shattered,
When many poor folk, who had hied
Them hither in God's service, died;
Saladin caused each slaughtered corse
To be thrown in the water course
Of Acre, and thus sent back to us.[53]
It was a sight most hideous: 3,090
The bodies, floating down, were tossed
Ashore by the stream among the host;
The pile of dead grew great. Therefrom
Such foul and noisome stench was come
That all the army thither fled
Until the slain were burièd—
And even long after had to shun
The fetor and corruption.

TRENCH WARFARE

The Christian army now had made
The trench that served as barricade;   3,100
And sheltered them within it when
Attacked by forces Saracen,
Who every day assailed them, whether
Torrid or chilly were the weather.
About the trench was fought the battle
'Twixt God's men and the pagan cattle:

[53] Beha ed Din (pp. 167–68) confirms this evidence that the bodies of the dead were thrown into the stream.

To make it firm was our employ,
While they endeavored to destroy.
On this spot ye might see, therefore,
Five hundred thousand shafts and more   3,110
Which the trench-diggers handed thence
To those who fought in their defense;
There ye might see on either part
Men of good courage and stout heart;
There ye might see men fall, roll under
Others, torn and ripped asunder;
Fierce blows were dealt throughout the fight,
Which did not cease until the night.

THE LANDING OF THE PILGRIMS

Between the time when first the host
Laid siege to Acre upon the coast   3,120
And the holy feast of All Saints' day,
I know, and oft I have heard say,
That men came thither without end,
Each one prepared his aid to lend.
The count of Ferrers [54] came, through whom
More than five score Turks met their doom;
He was an archer of such craft
That none could better speed a shaft;
And Guy de Dampierre [55] came, the one
Who had such fair castles of stone;   3,130
The bishop of Verona [56] came
Who had such good and honored fame.
And all these folk who had come thereto
Were martyrs and confessors, too.
For I dare say those of greatest ease
Suffered a martyr's miseries

[54] William Ferrers, earl of Derby, arrived at Acre in 1186 and died 1190 (Siedschlag, *English Crusaders*, p. 126, no. 170).
[55] Guy de Dampierre, an important baron of France, was one of the barons accused of treason by Ralph of Diceto (p. 82). He held fiefs as vassal of the count of Champagne.
[56] Adelardo Cattaneo, bishop of Verona 1188–1214, cardinal 1214–28.

With ceaseless vigil and with fright
And toil unending, day and night;
For rest they dared not, nor could they
A moment in their labor stay,   3,140
Until the trench was all complete
That witnessed many a bloody feat.

A SARACEN FLEET ARRIVES FROM EGYPT

The day preceding All Saints' eve
There happed a thing that made to grieve
The host, a mishap marvelous—
Most hurtful and disastrous.
The while the Christian troops were bending
Beneath the weight of cares unending,
Those who took stand on Toron's height
Toward Caïphas turned their sight.   3,150
Coming therefrom a mighty fleet
Of galleys armed their eyes did greet.
This fleet was come from Babylon,[57]
Who strove with Acre in unison.
The fleet moved on in fair array,
And news thereof was straightaway
Throughout the Christian army told,
How it was coming swift and bold.
And some of them there were who thought,
Though no man in the host knew aught,   3,160
That 'twas a Pisan fleet, and some
That it had from Genoa come,
Venice, Marseilles, or Sicily,
To help them win their victory
And storm the town. While thus they guessed,
The galleys ever closer pressed,
And closer still, so that in short
They made their way into the port

[57] Babylon of course is the medieval Babylon in Egypt, i. e., Cairo. Beha ed Din (pp. 181–82) reports the arrival of the great fleet from Egypt and the battle with the Christians as occurring on June 12. If this is the same fleet and battle as that described by the *Estoire*, there is a great discrepancy in the dates.

Of Acre. Before they reached the town,
One of our ships they made their own,   3,170
Which bore both soldiers and supplies,
And rapidly they drove their prize
Inside the city's barriers. Then
They seized the food and slew the men.

TURKISH ATROCITIES

Now hark ye to the evil works
Done to our God by these fell Turks.
The day of that feast honorèd,
When many pious tears are shed,
The day we celebrate the feast
Of all the saints whom He has blest   3,180
In Heaven, these wretches spitefully
Hanged to the walls of Acre on high
The bodies of those Christians ta'en
Within the ship and basely slain.
Preachers may surely tell and state
That such as these participate
In the eternal bliss that doth transcend
All others and is without end,
The bliss of those to whom we pay
Devotion on that holy day.   3,190

CONSTRUCTION OF SIEGE MACHINERY

This fleet of which ye heard me tell
Guarded the port and road so well
Against God's men that by its guard
The road and harbor both were barred,
So that no succor could arrive
To those who for their God did strive.
And as the winter time came on,
They had made no provision.
They had dug their trench, but then by main
Force it was later filled again.   3,200
That winter they made wooden towers

And mangonels and great stone throwers,
Cat castles, sows, shields great and strong,
On which they gave hard toil and long.
While workmen on the other side,
Full thirty thousand, fortified
The town with gates and towers too,
And barbicans sturdy and new.
So strong they made it and so stout
That they could keep the whole world out.   3,210
And Saladin, who had no care
To lose the city, set up there
So many mangonels, such store
Of stone throwers and machines of war,
So many craftsmen with deft hand,
Both foreign and from his own land,
Greek fire in jars so numerous,
So many weapons murderous,
That, as we later came to know,
Never had city or château   3,220
Weapons so copious and good
Or such a vast supply of food.
Thus was it that this winter passed,
Till the sweet spring was come at last.
And then, as Ambroise doth present
The story, it was during Lent
The German soldiers used their skill
To build the very first windmill
That Syria had ever known,[58]
While God's accursed gazed from the town   3,230
Thereon and were bewilderèd
And filled with terror and with dread.

DOLÒR AT THE DEATH OF FREDERICK BARBAROSSA

And now unto God's army there
Came tidings that at first were fair,

[58] The *Itinerarium* (pp. 78–79) says mills operated by horse power. The common
type of mill in use in Syria was the water mill, of which some fine examples still stand
along the banks of the Orontes.

But later were most dolorous,
Unwelcome, drear, and piteous:
The emperor of Germany,
A good man, with strong company
Moved toward the Sepulcher by land
To beg for grace from God's own hand.   3,240
He died, and 'twas a bitter loss,
At a river that he strove to cross
By a ford unknown and untried.
Thus did the will of God decide.
When those inside of Acre had
Received this news, they were so glad
They could think of naught else.[59] They beat
Their drums, cut capers in the street,
Rushed to the watch-towers and mounted
Thereon, and to our men recounted   3,250
The news that Saladin had heard
And given to them, word for word.
There perched upon the walls aloft
They shouted to us loud and oft,
And renegades they sent us, bound
To say: "Your emperor is drowned."
Then did the Christian army mourn,
So grief-stricken and so forlorn,
They felt small cheer for the crusade,
Save for the hope of coming aid   3,260
And save for promises held out
And through the army spread about
Of the great kings now coming towards
The land, and of our potent lords,
The kings of England and of France
Who later brought deliverance:
Thereby the host was comforted.

[59] Beha ed Din (p. 184) reports the receipt of this news in June; Ibn al Athir (p.
28), however, says that it was received only on July 26, the day after the great battle.
He was drowned on June 10, according to Tageno, and as Saladin had scouts watching
every move of his army it is reasonable to believe that the news of his death would
have reached the sultan quickly and that Beha ed Din's date is the correct one.

A CHRISTIAN FLEET ARRIVES FROM TYRE

Behold, the tidings now are spread,
A little after Easter day,
That the great fleet was on its way   3,270
From Tyre, and soon it came to port.
Then might ye think of a cohort
Of ants, who from their anthill pour
From every portal, aft and fore.
Forth from the town, at the alarm,
The Turks poured out, in just such swarm.
Ten thousand armed men came to view,
Covered, they and their galleys too,
With carpets and with cloth of pure
Silk, and with buckram and velours.   3,280
Against the fleet they sallied forth,
The fleet, which sped before the north
Wind and drove swiftly toward the strand,
Where the others waited to withstand
The onslaught. With impetuous dash
Each force moved forward to the clash
And one upon another fell,
Fighting most valiantly and well.
'Neath the marquis of Tyre's command
Were fifty vessels armed and manned,   3,290
With their equipment all complete,
That moved against the Turkish fleet.

AND DEFEATS THE SARACEN FLEET

There many banners had ye seen
And men of bold and steadfast mien,
Swift and disposed for knightly gests!
The foe first shot their arbalests.
And thus the battle was engaged
Which soon between the navies raged.
No coward folk were such as these:
The Pisans and the Genoese   3,300
Were stormed upon their ships and barges

By men with arbalests and targes.
Close up beside our men they got,
And then were bolts and missiles shot
Until we drove the Turks' fleet back
And captured, with a strong attack,
A galley which we brought to port.
Ye would have heard then great disport!
Ye would have witnessed dames and wives
Who bore within their hands great knives,   3,310
And, seizing Turks by hair and tress,
Inflicted on them sore distress
And then cut off their heads and bore
Them back in triumph to the shore.
Upon the fleets still the mêlée
Continued; each one oft gave way,
And then toward the other drew
Again; they both Greek fire threw.
Both burned, and both made shift to smother
The flames, and when they bumped each other   3,320
Most desperately they fought and strove
Until within the port they drove.
No man before had ever seen
A battle such as this had been.

BUT THE TURKS ATTACK BY LAND

But it was our besieging host
Of God who paid the dearest cost,
Because the Turks, more numerous
Each day, were made so furious
And were so filled with rage and spite
At losing their ship in the fight   3,330
That while the fight was being fought
At sea they made such fierce onslaught
Upon our trench, that none among
The Christians, high or low, or young
Or old, though known to fame and stout

In war, could save himself, without
Great effort, from the Turks that stormed
The trench; for like to flies they swarmed,
Using all means they could employ
To fill the trench up and destroy.   3,340
Ye might have seen there all the plain
Like to a field of fresh-reaped grain,
From here to where the hills began
Covered and darkened with the clan
Of Turks, who ever forward pressed
Without a moment's pause or rest:
Into the trench's depth they rushed
So thickly that they fell and crushed
Each other. Black men hideous
There were, to God obnoxious   3,350
And Nature, wearing red head-dress:
Beasts of more dreadful ugliness
God never made, and they were plentiful
And cruel and unmerciful.
They seemed, as they moved fearsomely
With their red headdresses on high,
Like ripely laden cherry trees.
And many more Turks were with these—
Five hundred thousand men there rallied,
'Tis said. Forth from the city sallied   3,360
The other Turks. Their banners sailed
On high. On both flanks they assailed
Our men. So deadly was the fray
That many times during the day
The Christian soldiers were in doubt
If they could make shift to hold out.

BUT THE CHRISTIANS ARE TRIUMPHANT

The foes, whose heads in red were dressed,
Had one flag around which all pressed.
It was the banner of Mahomet

And bore the image on its summit [60]   3,370
In whose name they had thither come
To crush and break down Christendom.
These wicked miscreant people fought,
Using great stones that they had brought.
Such was the attack that sorely tried
Our host upon the landward side.
While on the seaward side the fight
Lasted until the fall of night;
But, by God's mercy, finally
Our navy won the victory,   3,380
For groups of barons, day by day,
Had been established to relay
Each other in the ships—groups formed
Of very valiant men, well armed,
Who fought with courage and resource
And drove the foemen by main force
Within the harbor chain; and thus
Our fleet wrought harm so serious
Within the city walls among
The Turks—then forty thousand strong—   3,390
That they could not come forth or gain
Succor either from land or main;
And as their food supply grew less
They knew great famine and distress.

THE CRUSADERS ATTACK THE TOWERS

The Thursday of Ascension [61]
When our holy procession
Recalls how God arose to Heaven,
As Scripture's truth to us is given,
In His name Whom we worship, all

[60] This is a common mistake among medieval writers who looked on Moslems as
pagan idolators. Moslem law strictly forbids not only any representation of God or
Mohammed, but of any human being, as man is made in the image of God. The Moslem
troops carried heraldic devices on their banners.

[61] The *Itinerarium* (p. 85) says that it was Saturday after Ascension, i. e., May 5.

Our men would fain storm Acre's wall.   3,400
Against the foe's Greek fire we had
Towers with armor strongly clad.[62]
There were three such, of mighty size,
Built by three nobles' enterprise:
The marquis with the Genoese,
The landgrave, and King Guy were these.
When that the time came to begin
The assault, these three nobles were in
Their towers. And to the walls above
The defenders climb, while forward move   3,410
God's troops. The attack met strong defense
From those who had small sustenance,
And who, defending steadfastly,
Made us pay dear their misery.
Defenders ne'er fought with such might
As did these limbs of Satan fight:
Some beat the tabor, some made speed
To rush where there was greatest need.
Down from the hills the Turks did swoop
Upon our trenches, troop on troop,   3,420
And fell on them and leaped inside
When they saw we were occupied
With the assault. So we must thence
Both storm the walls and make defense.
Fiercely and long we stormed the wall,
From break of dawn till evenfall.
At evening we must needs desist,
So strong the paynim did resist.
Upon the three towers the Turks cast
Greek fire and burned them, so at last   3,430

[62] Beha ed Din (p. 178) describes these towers: "The enemy had erected three towers, built of wood and iron, and had covered them with hides soaked in vinegar, to prevent their being set fire by the combustibles hurled at them by the besieged. These towers were as huge as mountains; we could see them from the place where we were; they commanded the city walls. They were set on wheels, and could each, according to report, accommodate more than five hundred men; their roofs were broad, and were constructed to carry one mangonel on each."

Perforce we gave them up. They burned
And all their might to ashes turned.[63]

FAMINE IN THE CITY IS RELIEVED

In Acre the unbelieving brood
Of dogs long suffered lack of food,
And, as the time passed, even more
They lacked and greater famine bore.
And they were in such parlous state
Of dearth and hunger desperate
They had to kill their beasts and eat
Them, heads and necks, entrails and feet.   3,440
Out of the city gates they flung
Captives, infirm and old. The young
And vigorous and the adults
They kept to work their catapults.
They suffered such acute distress
And pain and want and hungriness,
That there is no way to portray
It, until after Saint John's day;
And then the devil, to protect
Them, sent three vessels, which were wrecked;   3,450
And many of the Turks were killed,
But they salvaged the stores that filled
The ships.[64] This gave them fresh supply,
And they were greatly cheered thereby
And made fresh sortie and attack,
Hemming us in, both front and back.

THE CHRISTIAN FOLLY LEADS TO DEFEAT

There came a day which dearly cost
The men of God's devoted host:
The day was that of Saint John's feast [65]

[63] The burning of the towers is described at length by Beha ed Din (pp. 178–79).
[64] It is at this point that Beha ed Din describes the naval battle between the Christian
ships and the fleet from Egypt which our author relates above, p. 151.
[65] This date is wrong. It should be St. James day, July 25. Beha ed Din (pp. 193–96)
describes the battle under that date, and the *Eracles* (p. 151) dates it "la feste de Saint
Jaque qui est a xv jors de juignet."

But the devil, who had never ceased 3,460
His work, was able to encumber
The army and reduce its number.
I lie! The devil it was not.
The Lord God willed it so, I wot,
Because it was His will to gain
More martyrs for His high domain.
The very finest sergeantry
That men have seen or e'er may see—
Poor folk they were, whose lot was hard—
Set out without sufficient guard. 3,470
They sought their sufferings to appease;
The army gives men little ease.
Ten thousand well-armed men were they
Who set forth, all in fair array,
In closely drawn battalions,
In squads and in divisions.
Toward the Turkish tents they went,
For it was there that they were bent.
When the Turks saw them coming straight
Toward them, they did not dare wait. 3,480
Our men arrived; of all the best
That they could find there they possessed
Themselves. Thus heavy laden they
Were for the Turks an easy prey,
Who swiftly down upon them bore,
So that seven thousand men and more
They left who were not succorèd
Save by some knights who thither sped;
But being few they strove in vain,
And so the footmen all were slain. 3,490
'Twas there died Thoril de Mesnil,[66]
Who fought with courage and with zeal.
We mourned him. This woe did betide
The host and many more beside.

[66] Thoril de Mesnil has not been identified beyond this reference. A Peter de Mesnil appears as witness on an act of John's at Rouen, Sept. 8, 1197 (Landon, *Itinerary*, p. 122).

CHAPTER IV

HENRY OF CHAMPAGNE BRINGS REINFORCEMENTS

Upon God's host the infidel
Made many an onslaught dire and fell,
And God, through His own company,
There suffered misadventures many.
God put His people to the test
Just as He tried the saints, those blessed   3,500
Who many trials did abide,
As in a furnace gold is tried.
Those men who to the Savior offered
Themselves full many a hardship suffered.
'Mid this their bitter sufferance
Behold the baronage of France.
Starting in August, when the time
Was ripe, before the winter's rime
There came Count Henry of Champagne [1]
With a great company of men;   3,510
And Count Thibaut of Blois [2] came too,

[1] Henry of Champagne, son of Henry the Liberal and Marie of France, was nephew of both Philip Augustus and Richard. He inherited the county of Champagne in 1181 and came to Acre late in July, 1190. Selected king of Jerusalem and husband of Queen Isabelle at the death of Conrad in 1192, he ruled Jerusalem until his death in 1197. Ibn al Athir (p. 28) reports his arrival on July 28; Beha ed Din (p. 197) says it was just before the first of August.

[2] Thibaut, count of Blois 1152–91, younger brother of Henry the Liberal, uncle of Henry of Champagne, king of Jerusalem. His death is reported by Haymarus (1. 654).

But he did not live three months through.
Nor did Count Stephen [3] long time bide:
He came, and presently he died.
The count of Clermont,[4] whose knighthood
To God and to the world seemed good;
The count of Chalon [5] came, a strong
And sturdy noble, tall and long.
So many came of good renown
The number never has been known.[6]   3,520

A MIRACLE

Before Acre, during the space
That these staunch men of noble race
For their salvation's sake there dwelt
And for God's love, which they all felt,
There took place gallant deeds and stout
Adventures, and God brought about
By His might many a miracle
That has been writ in chronicle.
The host had catapults for throwing
Stones, and men were always going   3,530
To and fro thereabout. Events

[3] Stephen, count of Sancerre, younger brother of Henry the Liberal and Thibaut of Blois, was a celebrated jurist. His death at Acre is noted by Haymarus (l. 654).

[4] Ralph, count of Clermont c. 1162–91, first cousin of Henry of Bar, was constable of France (Cartellieri, *Philipp II August*, II, 106).

[5] William II, count of Chalon-sur-Saône, 1168–1203. Richard entrusted to him the defense of Jaffa in November, 1191.

[6] The *Itinerarium* (pp. 92–93) gives in addition: Manserius de Garlande, Bernard de Saint Valery, John count of Ponthieu, Erard de Castigny, Robert de Bove, Alan de Fontanis, Louis d'Assela (Ascla), Walter d'Arzillières, Guy de Châtillon with his brother Lovellus, Guy de Meisières, John de Montmiral, John d'Arches, the lord of Camte in Burgundy, Gaubert d'Aspremont, Clarembald de Noyers, the bishop of Blois, the bishop of Toulon, the bishop of Ostia, the bishop of *Mordrensis* (?), the bishop of Brescia, the bishop of Asti, the patriarch of Jerusalem, the bishop of Cæsarea, the bishop of Nazareth, the bishop-elect of Acre, the archbishop of Besançon, Baldwin archbishop of Canterbury, Hubert bishop of Salisbury, the archdeacon of Colchester, Ralph de Hauterive, the abbot of Scalons, the abbot of *Esterpen* (Esterp); from Normandy came Walchelin de Ferrières, Robert Trussebot, Richard de Vernon and his son, Gilbert de Tillières, Ivo de Vipont, Ranulf de Glanville, Gilbert Malleman, Hugh de Gurney.

There took place and strange incidents,
Which, at the hour they happened, seemed
Like miracles, and so were deemed.
Within the city walls there were,
As doth the chronicle aver,
Full many a stone-throwing machine
The like of which was never seen,
And one there was that aimed so well
That it did damage dire and fell: 3,540
It smashed to pieces from afar
Our engines and machines of war,
For rocks of such huge size it threw—
As if borne on by wings they flew—
That all of two men's strength it took
To draw its sling, so saith the book;
And when the stone thus swiftly sent
Struck on the earth in its descent,
The missile sank into the ground
A full foot deep, and there was found.   3,550
This same machine it was that smote
A man upon the back. Take note
That never could a tree of wood
Or marble column have withstood
Such blow, but would have split in two,
So straight and hard the missile flew.
But the man did not even know
That he was struck. God willed it so.
One needs must in a God believe,
Who can such miracle achieve.   3,560

THE SAVING POWER OF HOLY WRIT

As time went on its way apace
Many an incident took place.
While April into May did change
There happened an adventure strange
Unto a sergeant in the host
Who held within the trench his post,

In coif of mail and hauberk clad,
And doublet broidered rich he had.
One of the foes who spurn God's name
Behind a loophole took his aim,   3,570
And a swift bolt from his arbalest
Struck our man full upon the breast.
It cut the coif, the doublet, too,
And then it pierced the hauberk through.
Upon his neck the sergeant wore,
Thank God, a brief that saved him sore
Mishap, for written on it were
God's names, and those who saw aver
That they saw plainly how the dart
Rebounded when it struck this chart.   3,580
God worketh in this wise: those whom
He guards need fear no evil doom.

A GROTESQUE INCIDENT

As time went on its way apace
Many an incident took place.
One day it happened that outside
The trench a knight was occupied
In yielding to a need of nature
Felt by every living creature.
And while he bent down to appease
His craving and to take his ease,   3,590
One of the Turks in the vanguard,
To whom he had paid small regard,
Drove on toward him at full pace;
It was most cowardly and base
To take a knight thus unaware
While occupied in such affair.
He had left the vanguard far behind,
And rode, lance leveled and aligned
Upon the knight, intent to slay
Him, when our men began to say,   3,600
"Flee, my lord, flee!" with hasty cries.

He scarcely had the time to rise
But managed to get to his feet
And left his duty incomplete.
Fast as his horse could run the foe
Bore down and thought to lay him low,
But failed, thank God, because, adept
And agile, the knight sidewise leapt.
He took in either hand a stone
(Hear how God doth avenge His own)   3,610
And when the Turk had turned his horse
And toward the knight retraced his course,
The latter took most careful aim,
And as the Turk toward him came
He smote him, just as he had planned,
With one stone that he had in hand,
Beneath his helmet, on his head:
Upon the spot the Turk fell dead.
The knight then took in hand the rein
Of the horse of him whom he had slain.   3,620
And then the person who recounted
The tale to me saw how he mounted
Thereon and rode back to his tent,
And kept his prize in great content.

A HEROIC WOMAN

As time went on its way apace
Many an incident took place.
Again there happened an affair
That merits to be told with care.
Many were those men who assailed
The walls, and many times they failed.   3,630
And some, to fill the moat, brought store
Of stones which eagerly they bore,
While with war horse and sumpter mule
The barons helped them, as a rule;
And many women bore their share,
Taking delight the load to bear.

One woman took especial joy
In laboring at this employ.
An archer Saracen inside
The wall saw this dame occupied 3,640
To set her fardel down, and when
She sought to rise erect again,
He shot at her a shaft, which found
Its mark, and she fell to the ground.
The dame was wounded mortally
And all the people hastily
Gathered about her where she lay
To mortal agony a prey.
Her husband came at once, and then
She to the dames and worthy men 3,650
A final solemn prayer did make
That for God and for their souls' sake
Her body should be used to fill
The moat where she with such good will
Had labored. For she would not lend
Her corse to any other end.
'Twas carried there with grief and dole
When God had rapt away her soul,
And, as the story telleth, no man
Ever should forget such woman. 3,660

RETRIBUTION OVERTAKES AN EMIR

As time went on its way apace
Many an incident took place.
There happed adventures in great plenty
During the siege—not one, but twenty
And more; but I cannot recall
Them or enumerate them all.
One day came forth from Acre a Turk
Battalion, seeing our men at work
Gathering forage, which they needs
Must have in wartime for their steeds. 3,670
An emir led them from the town,

A great man and of high renown,
For strength and valor known to fame.
Bellegiminus was this emir's name.[7]
The barons who watched o'er the men
Went out against the Saracen.
That day our army was pressed hard
For they had not sufficient guard,
So many having gone to seek
The forage, that the host, made weak,   3,680
Was periled by the fierce attack
That smote them both in front and back.

. . .

Natheless our men repelled them all
Save the emir, who stayed behind
With this one purpose in his mind:
It was the height of his desire
To set our war machines on fire,
Could he but reach them as he willed.
He has in hand a vial filled   3,690
With Greek fire; and he thus essays
To set the engines in a blaze.
A knight then smote him down, intent
To deal him fitting punishment:
He stretched the Turk upon the earth
And on his vitals fire poured forth
From out the vial overturned,
So that his genitals were burned;
And though the men with him were fain
To extinguish it, they strove in vain.   3,700

THE REWARD OF SACRILEGE

As time went on its way apace
Many an incident took place.

---

[7] Bellegiminus, emir of Megisimus, is given by the *Itinerarium* (p. 13) as one of the emirs who came to assist Saladin. I am unable to identify him.

It ofttimes happened and befell
That soldiers of the infidel,
Who against God did occupy
The town, mounted the walls on high,
And from the churches these men oft
Brought crosses, which they raised aloft,
And these they basely would mistreat
And spit upon, befoul, and beat   3,710
To show the bitter hate they bore
The Christian faith: they loathed naught more.
A Turk one day began to pound
A wooden cross that he had found
And on the walls set up erect.
He beat it with base disrespect
And, not quite satisfied with this,
He sought to foul it and bepiss.
A good crossbowman, to arrest
Him, put string to his arbalest   3,720
And notched the quarrel firm and tight,
Wishful to venge this deed of spite
Upon the Turk who fouled the rood.
He shot, and, as his aim was good,
Toward the Turk's belly swiftly flew
The bolt and pierced his entrails through.
He fell dead with his legs upraised,
Whereat his friends were wellnigh crazed
With rage. Thus God avenged the vile
Offense that did His cross defile.   3,730

A DUEL

As time went on its way apace
Many an incident took place.
One day there happened an adventure
That Ambroise telleth in his scripture.
A Turk came forth, intent to fire
His shafts at us, nor would retire;

A Welshman of some skill and craft
Set out to match him shaft for shaft.[8]
The Welshman was named Mariduc:
He was not son of king or duke.   3,740
The Saracen was called Graïr,
A strong man, firm, and without fear.
Now with their bows each set to work.
Turk shot at Welsh, Welsh shot at Turk.
The Turk made query and demand
Whence came the Welshman, from what land.
"I come from Wales," our man replied,
"And you were mad to come outside."
The Turk said: "You shoot skilfully.
Will you now make a match with me?   3,750
Let me shoot first, and you abide,
Nor make a move to either side.
And if I miss you, I shall stand
And wait, nor move to either hand."
With such persistence did he plead
That the Welshman at last agreed.
Thereon the Turk took aim and shot
But slipped, and so he struck him not.
The Welshman said, "Now hold thee so
While I shoot." Said the other, "No,   3,760
Let me but once more shoot at thee,
And then thou twice mayest shoot at me."
"Gladly," the man from Wales replied,
And while his foe was occupied
Taking a shaft from out his quiver,
Standing close to the unbeliever
The Welshman, who would have no part
In such terms, shot him through the heart.
"You kept the pact not," so he spoke,
"So, by Saint Denis, mine I broke."   3,770

[8] These individual matches seem to have been rather common. Beha ed Din (pp. 161–
62) describes how the soldiers would set boys on to engage in mock battles and trials of
strength.

VAIN ATTACK ON THE TOWER OF FLIES

The Pisans and the others who
The craft of seafaring well knew
A tower on galleys did devise
And ladders twain of goodly size;
They clad the tower and the outside
Of all their ships of war with hide.
The Tower of Flies [9] they now assailed
And many missiles thereon hailed,
Its garrison fought without fear
And sold their lives extremely dear.   3,780
And from the galleys of the town
More than two thousand there came down,
Of Saracens full armed for battle
To lend aid to their fellow cattle;
These men flung shafts and numerous
Lances and sharpened darts at us
And crushed our shields and spears with great
Huge rocks of most terrific weight.
Those in the tower never failed
To make defense when ours assailed.   3,790
We shoot well: many a missile falls
Among the foe who man the walls.
There had ye seen the Turks constrained
To take to shelter, while thick rained
The spears, and valiant men relayed
Each other and fierce onslaught made.
Then the two ladders were directed
Against the tower and there erected
With mighty effort and great cost,
For those within the tower tossed   3,800
Huge beams on Christian man and knight

[9] The Tower of Flies was located out in the harbor at the very end of the break-
water. The *Itinerarium* (p. 75) explains the name by the story that the rock on which
it stood had been used in very ancient times as a place of sacrifice and that flies had been
attracted thereto by the blood and flesh on the rock. Beha ed Din (pp. 210–12) records
the attack on this tower as on September 24.

Who placed the ladders thus upright.
They did not take the coward's way
But ever came back to the fray.
Upon our tower they cast Greek fire
Which kindled it into a pyre
And made its occupants descend,
And so destroyed it in the end.
But ere this there was heavy slaughter
Of Turks who perished in the water.   3,810
They burned our tower down amain
And likewise burned our ladders twain
And the ships that carried them. These works
Gave cheer and comfort to the Turks,
Who shouted loudly when they saw
That they had made our men withdraw
And jeered at those who had sworn oath
To God, the host whom they did loathe.

THE CRUSADERS' ENGINES ARE DESTROYED

The host of God was sore distraught
By this, but good comfort was brought   3,820
By barons who came bringing aid
To Syria for the crusade.
The archbishop of Besançon [10]—
Let us speak first of him—thereon
Ordered his men 'fore Acre to make
A great ram that would breach and break
The walls. It was costly, clad around
With iron and most tightly bound
Both fore and aft, above, below,
And feared not what machines could throw;   3,830
For the archbishop had in mind
To use the best of every kind.
Count Henry built another one
Of great cost and proportion,

[10] Thierry de Montfaucon, archbishop of Besançon 1180–91. His death is recorded
by Haymarus (l. 666).

And baron, nobleman, and count
Built more machines than my account
Can say. But I would tell the fate
Of that built by the archprelate—
The one of which I told ye first—
When it essayed the wall to burst.   3,840
With care the barons of the host
Arranged the attack, and so disposed
The engines and gave word to haul
Each one his own before the wall.
The archbishop had drawn ahead
His ram, of which but now ye read,
Which was so made and cost so dear
That it would have the right to fear
Naught in the world. 'Twas underneath,
As 'twere, a kind of house or sheath.   3,850
Therein a great ship's mast it had,
Knot-free, with each end ironclad,
And underneath the ram were those
Who were to deal the wall stout blows
And well might feel themselves secure.
The Turks, whose hatred doth endure,
Of dry wood brought provision,
And then they cast Greek fire thereon,
And with their catapults they flung
Whole mighty columns down among   3,860
Us, shafts of marble and hard stone;
And trees and heavy beams were thrown.
Then from great vessels they had filled,
Jugs, jars, huge tuns, and casks, they spilled
Sulphur and tallow, tar and pitch,
Followed by wooden logs, the which
Mahomet's minions, fell and dire,
Kindled to blazing with Greek fire,
Till those within the ram, their plight
Being hopeless, took at last to flight.   3,870
The Turks, the while they thus opposed

Our ram, upon the walls exposed
Themselves. Then archers and crossbowmen
Sent well-aimed shafts among the foemen;
Then combat fierce ye had descried
And wounded men on either side;
Ye had seen many a vassal brave
Hasten to rescue and to save
The ram and the debris to haul
Therefrom. And ye had seen Turks fall   3,880
With their gay, fair accouterments
Headlong from off the battlements.
At last the missiles from above
Rained down so thickly that they stove
The ram and crashed its armor through
And shattered all its framework too;
Once more they cast upon it fire
Until the ram was burned entire.[11]
Natheless their victory cost them dear,
For in it they lost an emir   3,890
And of their finest men fourscore.
But we, too, suffered damage sore.
Thus ended the attack that day,
Since none could haul the ram away
And none could put the fire out:
The Turks jeered us with mocking shout.

DEATH OF QUEEN SYBELLE

At end of August to our teen
There died, within the host, the queen
Of Jerusalem; it was most ruthful
That one should die who was so youthful.   3,900
God to her soul be gracious!
For she was known as valorous.
And also died two maidens fair;

---

[11] Beha ed Din (pp. 215–18) tells of the burning of this ram and the cat on October 4. He gives a detailed description of the ram, whose head was "in form like the great axle of a mill-stone."

Both daughters of King Guy they were.[12]
By death of these two princesses,
The kingdom's rightful heiresses,
The king lost afterward that realm
Which cost him such blows on the helm.

A NAVAL BATTLE

October followeth on September,
And toward the Kalends of November [13]   3,910
From Alexandria a grand
And prideful fleet drew nigh the land.
Our men, by whom the ships were seen
And counted, said they were fifteen.
These ships were on their way to bring
Succor to the Turks suffering
In Acre, where, so long immured,
Great misery they had endured.
Three dromonds of the largest kind
Came following straightway behind   3,920
The fleet, and, as they shoreward drew,
Our seamen kept them close in view.
When those who sailed their ships caught sight
Of ours, they were distraught with fright.
Brave though he were, none could forbear
To wish that he were otherwhere;
For the evening sky was overcast
With dusk, and the wind blew fierce blast,
So that the Christians dared not meet
Or draw nigh to the pagan fleet,   3,930
For each had all that he could do
To ride the raging tempest through.
Now while the Saracens, full sail,

[12] Ernoul (p. 267) says that Sybelle and her *four* children all died. The *Eracles* (p. 151) names only her daughters Alice and Marie, and it adds "dont le roiaumes eschie par dreit heritage a Ysabeau la feme de Hanfroi." Sybelle's death occurred sometime before October 1, 1190. (LaMonte, *Feudal Monarchy*, p. 39, n. 1.)

[13] The *Itinerarium* (p. 114) says not long after the feast of St. Michael (Sept. 29). Beha ed Din (pp. 209–10) reports the arrival of the fleet from Egypt on September 17, but says it consisted of only three ships.

Came, driven swiftly by the gale,
And crossed the chain, not without grief,
To bring their paynim friends relief,
Upon their vessels mishap came
Which they could not avoid, and shame
As well: they crashed, with dire effect,
Upon the rock, where they were wrecked.   3,940
And there two of their ships were lost,
And they were stoned by all the host.
The ships split when they ran aground,
And of their crews the most were drowned.
Jeering, the Christians rushed to slaughter
Such pagan dogs as 'scaped the water.
One galley, driven on the strand,
They captured where it came to land:
Great store of food therefrom they drew,
And all the pagan dogs they slew.   3,950
But the other craft made shift to cross
The chain and anchor without loss
Where the Turks waited loyally
With swords and lances held on high
And lanterns lighted, by whose guide
The Saracens came safe inside.
These Saracens who came ashore
Helped the defenders to restore
Their strength. They thrust forth the inept
And weak; the strong and stout they kept.   3,960

THE CRUSADERS ADVANCE TO THE DOC

The great day of Saint Martin's feast,
When food supplies were much decreased,
The host was summoned for next morn—
In name of Him by Mary born—
To move on toward the mountain's height
And meet the Turks in open fight.[14]
First was there benediction

---

[14] Beha ed Din (pp. 223–31) recounts this battle, but elaborates. The actual battle was on Wednesday, November 13; the campaign lasted through Saturday.

And general absolution
By the archbishop of Canterbury [15]
And other bishops of great glory.   3,970
Then to each lord and baron post
Was given to lead and guide the host.
When morning came our soldiers mounted,
And there was many a squadron counted
Of Christian fighters of such fitness
That none their like did ever witness,
Drawn up in ranks as close and strong
As if bound tight by chain or thong.
The army's van was broad and large
To withstand many a battle charge;   3,980
The rear guard had such company
Of good knights that one scarce could see
How far their line stretched out until
One climbed upon some lofty hill;
You could not throw a plum that might
Not strike some brightly armored knight.
The line moved on straight toward the Doc,[16]
And you could not have cooked a cock
Before Saladin was aware
That he for battle must prepare   3,990
If he continued to await
The Christians. He chose to vacate
His mountain stronghold that same night,
Broke camp, and yielded up the site.[17]

AND FORAGE TOWARD CAÏPHAS

Into our host came now a spy,
Who said our hated enemy
Had come down from the mountaintop,

[15] Baldwin, archbishop of Canterbury 1184–90. He was a Cistercian who became successively bishop of Worcester (1180) and archbishop of Canterbury (1184). He was most active in preaching the crusade in England and came to Acre with the first English contingent. He died at the siege November 19, 1190. (*Dictionary of National Biography*, III, 32.)

[16] The "Doc" is a bridge over the Belus river. Beha ed Din (p. 227) calls it "Dauk," and it is today the Nahr Namein bridge over the Wadi Halzun.

[17] Beha ed Din (p. 227) says that he withdrew to his position at El Kharruba.

Were in full flight, and would not stop
Till they were far away from us.
Almost we followed. Dangerous   4,000
Pursuit would have been, and mistaken,
For they could not be overtaken.
Finding no battle, our array
Went on toward Caïphas straightway,
Where, it was said, there was great store
Of victual, that was needed sore.
To Recordane now came our troops;
Whereon, more swift than falcon swoops
On duck, the Turks came to annoy
And plague them. First they would deploy,   4,010
Return, loose shafts, skirmish about,
Beat on their tabors, roar and shout.
At vespertime, the pilgrims made
Their camp, pitched tents, and there they stayed
Until the morn at break of day;
Then they proceeded on their way
Onward to Caïphas to fare.
But the provisions were not there
Of which they heard there was such trove.
The Turks had seen fit to remove   4,020
These stores at dawn, when they marched out.
Now, when the Christians looked about,
All the Turks in the world they found,
It seemed to them, gathered around
To hem them in. Above, below,
Right, left, the land was covered so
Therewith that ours could not forbear
To wish that they were otherwhere.
Never were such great droves and swarms.
Our soldiers took them to their arms,   4,030
And made them ready for the battle,
But the Saracens, the baseborn cattle,
Did not dare to begin the fray
Against so goodly an array.
The pilgrims turned about, their aim

Being to go back whence they came,
But suffered woe and turbulence
Before they came back to their tents.

RETURNING, THEY ARE HARASSED BY THE SARACENS

Where that stream has its source whose water
Flows toward Acre, there was great slaughter 4,040
Ere the fight ended, and there died
Many a knight on either side.
By Templars the rear guard was manned
That day, and men from the command
Of England's king: and that rear guard
Had much to do and labored hard.
For God ne'er made snow, hail, or sleet,
Or rain in May, that heavier beat
Or came to earth more dense and quick
Than the shafts which poured down fast and thick 4,050
Upon the Christian host that day
Before the end of the mêlée.
At last, in good order, they started
Back, and toward Acre departed.
Our army took the stream's left bank;
Theirs took the right. So flank to flank
They marched, and, marching, sought to bother,
Annoy, and harass one another.
On our side there were some who made
Their way to us and brought us aid. 4,060
Our foot sergeants, who had to ward
Off the attacks on our rear guard
And who followed the army's traces,
Marched on but always kept their faces
Turned toward the Turks. Their lot was pain
Before the host was safe again.

THE BATTLE OF THE DOC

'Twas very early in the morning
When our men set about returning
To Acre and to its blockade.

But the Turks set an ambuscade   4,070
Beside the Doc bridge to waylay
Us, since we had to pass that way.
They strive to wreck the bridge, but ere
They break it down, our men appear;
But it was manned and guarded, so
That the pilgrims were hard put to know
How they could force their way or pass
Through such a strong embattled mass.
Geoffrey de Lusignan took lead
And, having mounted a fresh steed,   4,080
With five good knights as company
Charged down upon the enemy
So fiercely that he overbore
Full thirty of the foe or more
Into the stream, where they were drowned,
Though close their friends were massed around.
With such force did they cleave and hew
That they were able to cut through
And come without more accident
Back to the siege in great content.   4,090

FAMINE IN THE CAMP

Now came the end of the fair season,
When few, of great or little reason,
Came overseas to join the host;
And yet a few of them still crossed.
And as their number grew supply
Of food diminished constantly.
And as the time passed less and less
There was of food, and the distress
Increased. Then at last they had none,
Save when ships brought provision.   4,100
The rich still had sufficient store,
But direst want assailed the poor,
Who made complaint and cried out much
At being gripped in famine's clutch.

And many, for the violence
Of their distress, wished to go thence.
When shipments came they were detained
At Tyre, and there the food remained,
Because the marquis was disposed
To stop its coming to the host.   4,110

SEEKING THE CROWN, CONRAD MARRIES ISABELLE

Now shall ye hear of the treacherous plot
Of the false marquis, who had sought,
By wealth and dealings underhand
With men of power, to rule the land.
And, with his skill in wile and cheat,
He so maneuvered his deceit
That a sister of the queen who died
Within the army at that tide,
The wife of Humphrey de Toron,
A lord of high position,   4,120
Was separated from the said
Humphrey, so that she then might wed
The marquis.[18] Whereon he agreed

[18] The *Estoire* here reduces to its simplest form a political move which was carried through by Conrad in conjunction with the Syrian baronial leaders. The *Itinerarium* (pp. 119–23) gives a more detailed account of the affair, but the best source is the *Eracles* (pp. 151–54). The real reason for Isabelle's divorce from Humphrey and her marriage was, of course, entirely political. Humphrey had shown himself unfit as a leader, and the Syrian barons had no intention of accepting him as their king. Isabelle had inherited the throne, and there was every prospect of a queen once more attempting to foist off an unacceptable husband as the king. Conrad, who aspired to the royal title, built up a party among the barons, using bribery where persuasion failed, and secured the adherence of the bishop of Beauvais, the legate, and other ecclesiastics, as well as Balian d'Ibelin, Renaud of Sidon, Paganus de Caïphas, and others of the baronial faction. The *Itinerarium* says that Raymond of Tripoli would have been a party to the scheme had he still lived. Isabelle was at first reluctant to acquiesce, but was finally won over. The *Itinerarium* (p. 121) says that she consented willingly, but the *Eracles* states definitely that "elle ne le vost consentir por ce que ele amoit Hanfroi son mari," but that she was brought around by the argument that she would lose the throne unless she consented to give up her husband. At any rate, the action was begun when Marie Comnena, Isabelle's mother who was remarried to Balian d'Ibelin, brought suit for annulment of the marriage on the grounds that Isabelle had been married to Humphrey when she was only eight years of age and so below the legal age of consent. Humphrey

His men should to the host proceed
Without fail. He took her for spouse
'Gainst God and law in his own house.
The archbishop of Canterbury
Was wroth and so refused to marry
Such pair.[19] The bishop of Beauvais
Made legal a great sin that day,   4,130
Because the marquis had already
Two wives, each one a fair young lady.[20]
One was in Constantinople,
A lovely woman, fine and noble;
The other, in his country; now
Unto a third he pledged his vow.
For this the good archbishop [21] and

---

contested the suit, urging that Isabelle had consented to the marriage and that she was
well contented therewith. Guy de Senlis then challenged Humphrey to a judicial duel,
alleging that Isabelle had never truly consented to the marriage, which had been arranged for her by Baldwin IV. Humphrey, "qui estoit failli du cuer et norreture de
feme," refused to accept the challenge; Ernoul (p. 268) claims that he was bought
over by the bishop of Beauvais "per deniers donans." Alberic, archbishop of Pisa, the
Apostolic legate, then pronounced the marriage void, and Isabelle received the homages
of the barons as queen of Jerusalem. Her first official act showed her real feelings in the
matter; she confirmed to Humphrey the fief which his grandfather had held, making
him one of the wealthiest lords of the land. Then on November 24 Isabelle and Conrad
were married by the bishop of Beauvais. The date for the marriage can be determined
from two sources: the *Itinerarium* and the *Estoire* both say that Guy de Senlis was
captured on the very day of the marriage. Haymarus (l. 521) in a rubric says that Guy
was captured on the morrow of St. Clement's, which places it on November 24.

[19] Archbishop Baldwin opposed the marriage of Isabelle and Conrad and was able to
prevent its accomplishment as long as he lived. As Stubbs points out (Roger of Hoveden, III, cxxiv, n. 1), the marriage was celebrated immediately after his death, which
occurred on November 19, 1190 (Röhricht, *Königreichs*, p. 540, n. 2).

[20] This is not exactly the truth. Conrad had had two wives, but certainly the first
and probably the second was deceased before his marriage with Isabelle. The evidence
about his former marriages is found in Nicetas, who says (p. 317) that he was a widower when he married Theodora, the sister of Isaac Angelos, in Constantinople. Ilgen
(*Conrad*, p. 39) suggests that his first wife may have been that sister of the king of
Scotland whose proposed marriage to one of the sons of the marquis of Montferrat is
mentioned in a letter by John of Salisbury in 1167. It would seem from the statements
of Nicetas that he was again a widower when he left for Tyre.

[21] This is obviously a mistake. As Archbishop Baldwin died five days before the marriage took place, he could not excommunicate Conrad after the ceremony. Baldwin
may have threatened Conrad with excommunication in case he should marry Isabelle,

The other clerks and bishops banned
The match, which they abominated.
At once they excommunicated   4,140
Him and informed him, clear and bold,
He did adultery threefold,
And God would not vouchsafe consent
To such unholy sacrament.

THE SARACENS RAID THE WEDDING FEAST

After the marquis had espoused
Her who so long his lust had roused,
He made feast and festivity.
Of living wives he now has three,
One in the host, one in his land,
And a third ready to his hand.   4,150
Such match would bring great disarray
And harm: they came that very day.
For when those who were at the feast
Had drunk as deeply as they pleased,
Into the meadows forth they went
For jousting and for tournament.
Thereon the Saracens, who lay
In ambush, made a swift foray.
The host was roused, but nonetheless
The Saracens had marked success: 4,160
For Guy, the butler of Senlis,[22]
Was captured, and none knew if he
Was killed, or whither he was ta'en;
But a score of ours were seized or slain.
Thus for the wedding feast they paid.

---

and the ban have fallen on him when he was married, but certainly the archbishop did not personally excommunicate him after his marriage.

[22] Guy de Senlis, butler of France, was the nephew of the count of Clermont (Cartellieri, *Philipp II*, p. 178). Haymarus (l. 521) gives the date of his capture as the morrow of St. Clement's, i. e., November 24. The fact that it was he who championed the divorce of Isabelle against Humphrey (see note 18, above) made his capture on the day of the wedding a significant fact to the opponents of the marquis.

CONRAD RETURNS TO TYRE

Those of the host were much dismayed;
The prudent leaders felt misgiving,
Though some of them kept on believing
That the marquis's word was good
And that he would send store of food   4,170
Unto the host, to keep his oath.
But he departed, taking both
His armed contingent and his bride,
And though he was amply supplied
With food, whereof the host felt sore
And grievous need, he sent naught more
Save to those who had so degraded
Themselves that they his marriage aided.

"LIKE THE HEROES OF OLD"

My lords, of Alexander's [23] death,
Which had such parlous aftermath,   4,180
Or of the mission of Balan,
Or the adventures of Tristan,
Or of Paris and Helen, those
Two who for love suffered such woes,
Or of Arthur of Brittany,
His deeds and his bold company,
Of Charlemagne, or of Pépin,
Of Agoland, or Guiteclin,
Or of the songs of battles old
That jongleurs with delight have told,   4,190
I cannot tell ye lie or truth
Or say if they be false or sooth;
Nor can I find a man so wise
To tell if they be truth or lies.
But what so many saw, the things

[23] The persons referred to in the following lines are all heroes of the romances and epics and are put in by our author to show his familiarity with the contemporary popular literature. The Arthur of Brittany is, of course, King Arthur of the Round Table, not Richard's nephew, Arthur Plantagenet.

They witnessed, and the sufferings
That men at Acre underwent,
The countless mishaps to torment
Both head and heart, the heat, the chill,
The sickness, every kind of ill,   4,200
These things I can recount as true
And ye may well hearken thereto.

FAMINE AND HIGH PRICES

When winter bringeth in its train
At Advent bitter wind and rain,
Within the host at Acre complaint
And famine grew without restraint
'Mid folk of modest means or small,
Whose miseries continual
Seemed, as the days passed, to increase,
And they lamented without cease.   4,210
They made shift, of a verity,
Somehow, till the Nativity;
But then began the listlessness,
The famine, and the sore distress:
After the feast of Jesus' birth
More piteous became the dearth.
Heavy the peck of grain that cost
An hundred besants in the host
And that a man could bear with ease
Beneath his arm. Drear days were these!   4,220
The price of flour and grain was high.
It cost twelve sous one hen to buy.
So hard were times that one must pay
For but one egg six deniers.[24]

[24] Beha ed Din (p. 223) says the scarcity was so great that even at Antioch a sack of grain cost 96 dinars of Tyre; Ibn al Athir (p. 32) gives the price of 100 besants a sack in the crusader camp; the *Eracles* (p. 150) says that grain cost 20 besants Saracen, beef or mutton could not be had at any price, a chicken cost 60 sous, and an egg 12 pence. The men ate mostly the meat of horses, mules, or donkeys. Roger of Hoveden (III, 69) reports that a loaf of bread which normally cost but a penny sold at the height of the famine for sixty shillings. Further evidences as to the famine are to be found in Haymarus (ll. 141-92, 469-80).

But most the starving people sought
For bread, and for it strove and fought,
And much they did vituperate
The marquis who had caused this state.

THEY EAT HORSES

My lords, do not believe I joke:
So that there might be flesh for folk   4,230
To eat, they skinned full many a steed
Of war and ate thereof with greed;
Crowds gathered round when one was flayed,
And for the meat high price was paid.
All winter long high was the price:
They sold it for ten sous a slice.
A dead horse sold for more by far
Than any living steed of war.
They found all pleasing to the taste,
Even ate entrails, naught did waste,   4,240
And greatly did vituperate
The marquis who had caused this state.

AND HOARD THEIR PITTANCE

Hard were the times, the need was sore
For everyone, both rich and poor;
Yet he who had wealth and who could
Thereby provide himself with food,
Though he were generous, did not dare
Divide with other men his share:
So many people came for aid
That each clung tight to what he had,   4,250
And much did they vituperate
The marquis who had caused this state.

THEY SUBSIST ON GRASS AND HERBS

Had it not been for herbs and plants,
Which they sowed to get sustenance
And reaped for broth which they contrived
To cook, they could not have survived.

You had seen sergeants, men of worth
And valor, men of noble birth
Reared among wealth and gentleness,
Who, in starvation and distress,   4,260
Would feed upon the grass where'er
They saw its growth of green appear.
And then did they vituperate
The marquis who had caused this state.

SCURVY ATTACKS THE HOST

Then came a malady that fell
Upon the host, as I shall tell:
The rains came, with such dense downpour
As never had been seen before,
Flooding the host with waters; folk
Began to cough and hoarsely spoke,   4,270
And swellings grew on legs and head.
Each day there were a thousand dead.
As sickness made their faces swell,
From out their mouths teeth dropped and fell.
And some, unable to discover
Any food, never could recover.
And then they did vituperate
The marquis who had caused this state.

THEY STEAL BREAD

My lords, for need men often do
Things that bring blame and censure, too.   4,280
Men of all lands could not but dread
The shame of begging for their bread,
And so they robbed the bakers' store
Rather than charity implore.
One day it happed a man was made
A prisoner in such a raid,
And he who caught him stealing food
Tied him as tightly as he could:
Since nothing safer could be found,

Both arms behind his neck he bound.   4,290
The bakers bustled here and there,
Each one intent on his affair,
Giving the captive little heed.
Then God, Who aids His people's need,
The fetters from his hands removes.
He lies upon a pile of loaves:
The servants drowse and watch the street,
While he eats all that he can eat
And puts a loaf beneath his arm
While a chair hides him safe from harm.   4,300
Contented with the circumstance
He lay and waited for his chance,
Then, fleeing, to the host repaired
And told his friends how he had fared,
And with them, who were well-nigh dead
With hunger, freely shared the bread
That he had brought with him. For brief
Time this afforded them relief.
Though they were helped by the repast,
Their satisfaction could not last.   4,310
Now is their lack of sustenance,
Their want and hunger, so intense
That much they did vituperate
The marquis who had caused this state.

SOME DENY THEIR FAITH

Most direful sufferings were felt
By those who in our army dwelt,
And no one ever could recount
How high the misery could mount
That our companions had been made
To suffer during this crusade.   4,320
Hear now the ruin and the damage
Of men whom God made in His image:
How great was wretchedness to make

These starving men their God forsake!
Within the host so much the lack
Of everything did try and rack
Our men that many now forsook
Their God, went forth, and refuge took
Among the Turks. They said that plain
It was no God would ever deign   4,330
Be born of woman; they denied
Baptism and God crucified.

A PENNYWORTH OF BEANS

There were two comrades in the host,
Poor sergeants, who no wealth could boast
Save but one penny angevin,
Which brought them little but chagrin.
In truth, they had no bite of food
Nor any other sort of good,
Except the clothing that they wore—
That, and the armor that they bore.   4,340
So they devised how they might best
Their single angevin invest
In victual so that the outlay
Might bring them somehow through the day.
They sought for omens that might guide
Their conduct in their cloaks of hide
And gave thereto such careful thought
That thirteen beans at last they bought.
One of the beans they found was bad
And to exchange it one man had   4,350
To cross a seven-acre field.
When to the merchant he appealed
To change it for a good one, he
Exchanged it most reluctantly.
He came back and they ate with greed,
Driven well-nigh insane with need.
Then when the beans were gone, behold,

Their misery increased twofold;
And then they did vituperate
The marquis who had caused this state.   4,360

THEY DRINK TO EXCESS AND REPENT

Within the host of God was sold
A thing called carobs,[25] I am told.
Easy to get they were: the meat
Thereof was sweet and good to eat.
And many bought them who could pay
For a full measure one denier.
Many, with these and nuts, contrive
Somehow to keep themselves alive;
But those who lay ill and supine
And who drank often of strong wine,   4,370
Of which supply was plentiful,
Grew bloat with wine and overfull,
Besides which they ate nothing save
The food their stomachs did not crave:
And so they died in squads, while those
Who exercised and shunned repose
Lived and regained their force a little,
But, since they had no sort of victual,
These men did much vituperate
The marquis who had caused this state.   4,380

AND EVEN THEY EAT FLESH IN LENT

Hardship and famine were their lot
Before renewed supplies were brought:
There is no scourge like hunger's whip;
And when the lack of bread doth grip
A man, then each day his distress
Increaseth as he eatheth less;
So during Lent they avidly
Ate flesh, committing sin thereby.

[25] Carobs are a kind of bean which were, and still are, one of the chief products of Cyprus and which form an important part of the diet of the natives.

'Twas at the time when every man
Must fast, the time when Lent began;   4,390
But when God sent more sustenance
Later, they all did penitence;
When they recalled how they had sinned
And eaten flesh, they were chagrined,
And then they did vituperate
The marquis who had caused this state.

AND ALWAYS THEY CURSE THE MARQUIS

So, to the winter's end, remained
The famine, great and long sustained,
Which people in the host that sought
To aid their God endured and fought.   4,400
Truly they had no way to mend
Their lot from Christmas to the end
Of Lent. I know myself their plight
Was such they shunned each other's sight,
While charity had turned so cold
That avarice grew many fold;
And even the most generous
Now became avaricious,
And avarice, without largesse,
Made many die of their distress,   4,410
Who, dying, did vituperate
The marquis who had caused this state.

CHARITY OF THE CLERGY AND NOBLES

So long endured this suffering
That great complaint and murmuring
Were heard. 'Twas God's will to make clear
That men should both love Him and fear.
The bishop of Salisbury [26] then
Called sons and brothers. To these men

---

[26] Hubert Walter, bishop of Salisbury 1189–93, archbishop of Canterbury 1193–1205, justiciar of England 1193–98, Apostolic legate 1195–1200, regent of England 1199, chancellor 1199–1205, one of the leading statesmen of the century and one of Richard's trusted advisors. (*Dictionary of National Biography*, XXVIII, 137–40.)

In God's name nobly he did preach
And by goodly example teach.   4,420
The bishop of Verona, who
Was worthy of his tonsure, true
And steadfast, ever did his part
Of preachments that went to the heart;
He of Fano in Lombardy,[27]
A bishop of great sanctity,
Preached eloquently to the throng.
And after this it was not long
Ere they collected gold to feed
The poor who suffered greatest need.   4,430
The fund grew great: each did his best
To swell it and give the distressed
And hungry all he could afford.
The poor folk gave thanks to the Lord,
While they ate the provisions which
Were given to them by the rich.
Walchelin de Ferrières [28] was one
Who gave in great profusion.
The hands of Robert Trussebot [29]
With human kindness overflow.   4,440
Likewise Count Henry of Champagne
Gave largely and gave not in vain.
Sir Joscelyn de Montoire [30] must be
Recorded in this history.
The count of Clermont courteous

[27] Monaldus, bishop of Fano, 1178–1214.

[28] Walchelin de Ferrières, a Norman knight from the Eure (Paris, p. xii), distinguished himself at the battle of Arsur. Richard granted him a charter at Mortain in April, 1190 (Cartellieri, p. 296, no. 106). He was with Richard at Speyer in 1194 and died in 1201 (Powicke, *Loss of Normandy*, pp. 494–95).

[29] Robert Trussebot, identified by Round as of the family of "Trusebot of Warter," Yorkshire. Roger of Hoveden (III, 129) tells how at the battle of Arsur he demanded as his hereditary right the honor of carrying Richard's banner into the fight, but Richard had given the banner to Peter de Préaux, and Trussebot's claims were ignored (Siedschlag, p. 124, no. 130).

[30] Joscelyn de Montoire was probably of the cadet line of the counts of Vendôme (S. Painter).

Was warmhearted and generous.
The good bishop of Salisbury
Gave without trace of penury.
And many more who served God lent
Their hand to aid the indigent.   4,450
The funds thus gathered and provided
Among the needy were divided
Among the great and small, poor wights,
And sergeants, foot soldiers, and knights;
And to the famished folk they gave
According as the want was grave,
And succor to each one they offered,
Based on his rank and what he suffered.
God saw that with sincerity
His folk were moved to charity,   4,460
And, since they acted in such fashion,
He gazed upon them with compassion.

A SHIP BRINGS FOOD

It may be that ye are informed
Of the great miracle performed
By Heaven's King; those who have heard
It should rejoice with one accord.
Into the port of Acre a barge
Arrived: 'twas neither long nor large.
Within this barge was grain.[31] And now
Ye all may hear the tale of how   4,470
The Lord God succored Christendom
And out of dearth made plenty come.
The dearth came not from scarcity,
For there was food in quantity,
But from the merchants' avarice,
Who held it to get higher price.
But when God, Who is charity
And fountain of humility,

[31] Haymarus (ll. 393–404) describes the arrival of this ship and (ll. 709–20) the fall in prices when the new supplies had been obtained.

Saw His own people's wickedness,
He gave command that the distress   4,480
And famine should come to a stop
And that the price of grain should drop.

AND PRICES DROP FORTHWITH

'Twas Saturday before the nones
That this barge brought provisions.
And there was not much heard or said
Of how it lay in the roadstead,
Except by those who sold the grain
And thought of nothing but their gain.
The ship came on a Saturday,
I think, some time after midday;   4,490
'Twas God Himself who brought it there.
By Sunday He took in His care
What corn the granaries contain—
A hundred besants cost the grain—
And from a hundred cut the rate
To four. Well doth negotiate
A merchant who thus lowers price.

A PUNISHMENT OF A PROFITEER

Hear how the Lord God did chastise
A vassal for his insolence
And did so with expedience: 4,500
There was a Pisan in the host
Who held his grain at so high cost
That none without great wealth or treasure
Could buy from him a single measure.
The Lord, Who every man doth know,
Dealt now a well-deserved blow
To his rapacity that dwindled
Not, for into flames were kindled
His house and all that it contained,
So all that he by greed had gained   4,510

Was burned. He lost his wealth entire,
For no man could put out the fire.

RESTORATION OF PLENTY

When people saw God working thus,
Charity grew more generous.
Each gentleman more liberal
Grew, and with others shared his all.
The poor and starving offerèd
Thanks unto God that they were fed.
Those who had eaten flesh in Lent
Confessed their sin and, penitent,   4,520
Had absolution, since their need
Had driven them to such misdeed.
Three strokes dealt with a rod upon
Their backs, and lightly, had each one;
The bishop of Salisbury gave
Them, like a father, kind and grave.

THE KING OF FRANCE ARRIVES WITH HIS HOST

God had wrought thus, and it was past
The day of Easter, when at last
Philip, the French king, came and made
His entry into the crusade;   4,530
The count of Flanders came beside
Him, who caused great stir when he died;
And the count of Saint-Pol [32] came, whose neck
A shield most bravely did bedeck;
And there came William of Garlande,[33]
Whose followers were a mighty band;
And likewise came William des Barres,[34]

[32] Hugh IV, count of St. Pol, 1174–1205. His wife Yolande, was the sister of Baldwin V of Hainault, not, as G. Paris asserts, of Flanders.

[33] William de Garlande, one of Philip's chief advisors, was conspicuous at Bouvines in 1214. In 1190 Philip had named him among those who were to assist in the government during his absence (Cartellieri, p. 100).

[34] William des Barres, count of Rochfort (d. 1233), had quarreled with Richard at Messina and incurred the anger of the English king. Richard subsequently forgave him

A valiant knight, well skilled in war;
My lord, Sir Dreux d'Amiens,[35] came,
For wealth and prowess known to fame;   4,540
A knight named William de Mello,[36]
Whom I admire, arrived also;
The count of Perche,[37] too, who deprived
Himself of everything, arrived;
And with the Frenchman there returned
The marquis, as I truly learned.
But why should I enumerate
Them all? No man of high estate
There was in France who did not fare
To Acre, intent to do his share.   4,550
The king of France, therefore, with all
The Christian forces at his call,
Brought his retainers to the host
From Easter until Pentecost; [38]
Then England's king, who with firm hand
Had taken Cyprus, reached the land.[39]

---

because of his great bravery. (Roger of Hoveden, III, 93–94.) William appears frequently throughout the *Guillaume le Maréchal*.

[35] Dreux d'Amiens was one of the nobles sent as envoy by Philip to Richard in 1191 (Roger of Hoveden, III, 123).

[36] William de Mello accompanied Dreux d'Amiens as envoy to Richard; he had been one of Philip's envoys to Genoa to arrange for the passage. He is mentioned frequently in both Rigord and the *Guillaume le Maréchal*. (Cartellieri, p. 119.)

[37] Rotrou II, count of Perche 1144–91, who had been given the castle of Bellême by Henry II. He died at the siege of Acre. He was the husband of Mahaut, sister of Henry the Liberal of Champagne, and was thus uncle to Count Henry.

[38] Philip arrived at Acre on April 20, 1191 (Beha ed Din, p. 240; Ibn al Athir, p. 181; Roger of Hoveden, III, 100). Rigord (p. 108) says March 13 and Ralph of Diceto (p. 92) says Easter the 12 Kalends of April! He stayed until August 1 (*Itinerarium*, p. 239; Roger of Hoveden, III, 126). Easter was April 14, Pentecost on June 2.

[39] Richard arrived June 8, 1191 (Roger of Hoveden, III, 113; Ralph of Diceto, II, 94; Ibn al Athir, p. 42; *Itinerarium*, p. 211).

CHAPTER V

THE NARRATIVE RETURNS TO RICHARD'S ARRIVAL

Now I must needs take up again
The tale and make the story plain
Of Acre's siege. Ambroise would give
Continuance to his narrative,   4,560
Resume the story that he left,
And tie once more the knot he reft,
Recount in what way the two kings
Arrived at Acre, relate the things
They did, tell the whole history
As he hath it in memory,
How Acre was taken, in such wise
As he beheld it with his eyes
When he came to the Holy Land.

RICHARD'S LARGESSE

As I recounted aforehand,   4,570
Richard, the king of England, wrought
Such deeds of courtesy as ought
Be told, for he showed nobleness
As well as valor and largesse.
The king of France had pledged that he
Would give from out his treasury,
To every man who owed obeisance

Unto him, three golden besants.
This action brought him much acclaim.
So, when King Richard thither came   4,580
And heard of this, he had it cried
Throughout the army far and wide
That he would give to any knight
From whatsoever land who might
Accept his pay the sum of four
Gold besants taken from his store.
This was the rightful pay and fair
Given to men for service there.[1]
Behold, when this promise was noised
Abroad, how the whole host rejoiced.   4,590
And they of low and humble state,
With those whose rank was moderate,
Who had been there a long time, said:
"Lord God, when will attack be made?
Now there has come the gallantest
Of kings in Christendom, who best
Can storm a town with strength and skill.
Now may the Lord God do His will!"
King Richard had their confidence.

RICHARD'S MALADY CAUSES DELAY

Then sent him word the king of France,   4,600
Who had comported himself fair
Since Eastertide, when he came there,
That they should cry the attack and start
To assail the enemy's rampart.

[1] This would mean more if the *Estoire* stated the period of time for which the knight
served for his four besants gold. The gold besant was worth four "besants saracen," and
the annual pay of a knight in the kingdom of Jerusalem, as inferred from the amount
of revenue produced by money fiefs, was about 500 besants a year. (LaMonte, *Feudal
Monarchy*, pp. 149–50.) If we can presume that Richard was offering four gold besants
(i. e., 16 besants blanc) a week, it would figure to about 800 besants a year which was
very good pay indeed. Philip was at all times more conservative financially than Richard. Richard of Devizes (p. 426) records that Henry of Champagne left the service of
Philip and transferred to that of Richard because the French monarch would lend him
money only against the security of his county of Champagne, while Richard freely gave
it to him.

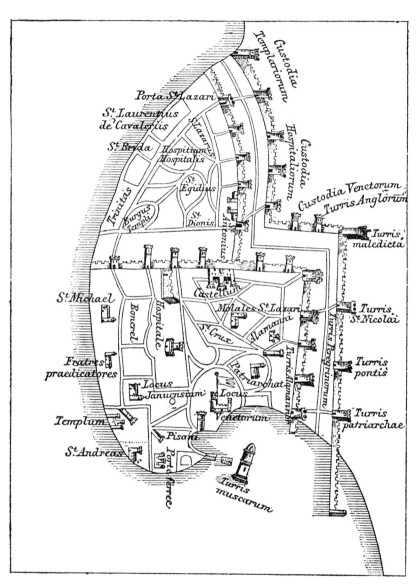

Custodia Templariorum
Porta St Lazari
St Laurentius de Cavaleriis
St Brida
Lazarus
Hospitium Hospitalis
Custodia Hospitaliorum
Trinitas
Burgus Templi
St Egidius
St Dionis
Antonius
Custodia Venetorum
Turris Anglorum
Turris maledicta
St Michael
Bonorel
Hospitale
Castellum
Molales St Lazari
St Crux
Alamani
Turris St Nicolai
Fratres praedicatores
Locus Januensium
Turris Alamanorum
Patriarchat
Turris Peregrinorum
Turris pontis
Locus Venetorum
Turris patriarchae
Templum
Pisani
St Andreas
Porta ferrea
Turris muscarum

MEDIEVAL ACRE, AFTER THE PLAN OF
MARINO SANUDO

But King Richard was ill: he bore
Much pain from mouth and lips made sore
By an accursèd malady,
Which people call "léonardie." [2]
He sent word thereof to the king,
And that the fleet, which was to bring   4,610
His barons to him, still remained
At Tyre, because it was detained
By what is called the Arsur wind,
Which had caused it to fall behind;
That his machines, now on the way,
Will come with little more delay;
That when his forces all arrive
He very willingly will strive
To capture Acre with all his might.

THE FRENCH MOVE TO THE ATTACK

Natheless, the king of France in spite   4,620
Of this—God help me—would not bide
Further, but had the onslaught cried.
They armed themselves at break of day,[3]

[2] G. Paris identifies this *léonardie* as alopecia, a disease wherein the hair falls out both from the head and the face. This does not at all fit the symptoms described by Ambroise. The *Itinerarium* (p. 214) explains these same symptoms "ex ignotae regionis constitutione cum eius complexione minus concordante." The *Gesta* (II, 170) and Roger of Hoveden (III, 113) both tell that Richard and Philip were taken sick with the "aegritudinam quam Arnoldiam vocant" of which the symptoms were that the hair fell out "in qua ipsi fere usque ad mortem laborantes capillos suos deposuerunt." This is alopecia, but it is not what Ambroise and the *Itinerarium* describe. From the symptoms given by our author it would seem that Richard was afflicted with the disease which is common today under the name of Vincent's infection or trench mouth. Vincent's infection is often due to malnutrition and the absence of vitamin C. "Dietary deficiencies, and particularly scurvy, have been frequently emphasized," says Dr. H. M. Williams in a recent article in the *Texas State Journal of Medicine* (March, 1939). Knowing the conditions under which Richard's army was fed and the inadequacies of the commissariat of any medieval army, it is not at all improbable that the crusader kings suffered from this disease, common in camps today, in its more virulent form. Thanks are due to Dr. Laurence Chenoweth, of the University of Cincinnati, for a "long range diagnosis" of Richard's ailment.

[3] The *Itinerarium* (p. 215) gives the date: Monday after the Nativity of St. John the Baptist, i. e., July 1, 1191.

For they were eager for the fray.
There were so many armed that ye
Could scarcely count their company;
What press of hauberks of fair seeming
Ye had seen! What helmets brightly gleaming,
And steeds of battle all bedight,
And what display of cloth of white   4,630
And chosen knights! None could behold
Or had beheld so many bold
And gallant gentlemen, endowed
With courage, mettlesome and proud,
So many streaming flags and banners,
Embroiderèd in diverse manners!
Then they disposed the forces which
Were to mount guard upon the ditch
Against Saladin's men, for fear
He might attack them from the rear.   4,640
Then God's men toward the citadel
Moved forward, and assailed it well.
Whenas the Turks in Acre saw
The army of the Christians draw
Nigh to the walls, they rent asunder
The air with din like God's own thunder,
With basins and with bells and tabors;
For some performed no other labors,
Save, from the palacetop on high,
To watch upon the host and spy   4,650
And give the alarm, by smoke and din,
To those who followed Saladin
And summon them for needed aid.

HEROISM OF GEOFFREY DE LUSIGNAN

Then had ye seen them make a raid
Upon the trench! They sought to fill
It, but they could not work their will,
For Geoffrey de Lusignan, who
In bravery was ever new,

Came to the barrier which they
Had captured in their first foray,   4,660
And in fierce onslaught he repelled
Them; with the battle-ax he held
He sent ten foes into their grave,
Dealing them blows so stout and brave
That no knight e'er deserved such praise
Since Oliver's and Roland's days;
So was the barrier won back
Which the foes took in their attack,
But ere 'twas won, there was great shout
And strife and fighting all about.   4,670

THE ATTACK FAILS

And those assailing Acre meanwhile
Had filled the moats with many a pile;
They nonetheless found it was meet
To change their tactics and retreat,
So they abandoned the attack
And to their own quarters [4] went back.
Thus fruitless the attack remained:
The people cried out and complained,
And bitterly vituperated
The kings they had so long awaited.   4,680
"Lord God," said each before his tent,
"How little has our waiting meant!"
Now while our men their armor doffed,
The Saracens hooted and scoffed;
And seeing ours had changed attire,
The Saracens once more set fire
To the machines of war the king
Of France built for the capturing
Of Acre; this filled his heart with fury
('Twas well known, and I heard the story),   4,690
And he fell sick, too sick to ride
Upon his battle steed astride.

[4] The text has "quarels," which is meaningless. G. Paris renders it "camp."

THE BESIEGERS ARE HEARTENED BY REINFORCEMENTS

So was the host in mournful state,
Dismal, forlorn, and desperate,
With the kings, who were to take the town,
By malady both stricken down;
And with the count of Flanders dead,[5]
Greatly they were discomforted.
Why should I write more long account?
With the kings ill, and dead the count,   4,700
The host was in such sore distress
That they could find no happiness.
And their despair had been complete,
Save for the coming of the fleet;
The bishop of Evreux came then,
Bringing his stalwart fighting men;
There came Roger de Teoni [6]
With knights in goodly company;
The several brothers Cornebu,[7]
Sons of a single sire, came too;   4,710
And Robert de Newbroke [8]—I ne'er
Have known a gentleman more fair;
And there came Jordan de Homez [9]

[5] The count of Flanders died June 1, 1191 (Roger of Hoveden, III, 111).

[6] Roger de Teoni was from Norfolk, according to Siedschlag (p. 125, no. 139). Powicke (*Loss of Normandy*, p. 517) says Roger de Tosny held lands near Les Andelys. An English branch of the family held an honor in Worcestershire. S. Painter writes me that a Roger was lord of Painecastle under Richard, but thinks that Roger the crusader was Norman.

[7] The brothers Cornebu were, according to G. Paris, John, Richard, and Thomas de Tornebu, Normans who came from the Eure, on whom see also Powicke, *Loss of Normandy*, p. 157. Siedschlag (p. 128, no. 167) suggests William de Cornebure (or of Cornbrough), Walter de Cornebure, and Simon de Cornebure, who appear on a charter of St. Mary of Monkton Church in Yorkshire.

[8] Robert of Newbroke, or Neubourg (Eure), was according to Round (*E.H.R.*, XVIII, pp. 478–79), a member of the great house of Beaumont and held lands in fief from Henry de Neubourg, earl of Warwick. S. Painter says he held lands in Dorset and Somerset, half of the old fee of Gerbert de Percy.

[9] Jordan des Homez, constable of Séez, had been one of the guarantors of the treaty between Richard and Philip at Messina in 1190 (Roger of Hoveden, III, 62). G. Paris (p. xi) locates him as from La Manche, but Powicke (*Loss of Normandy*, p. 492) says he was lord of Cleville in the Calvados.

Who was the constable of Séez;
At the same time the chamberlain
Of Tancarville [10] joined the campaign;
Robert of Leicester [11] had before
These other nobles come ashore;
And Gilbert Talbot,[12] too, was come,
A knight of fairest vassaldom;   4,720
And Ralph de Taissons [13] came, a lord
Whom we must not fail to record;
And the viscount of Châteaudun [14]
Arrived, and Bertrand de Verdun; [15]
And also came the Tozelais,[16]
Bold knights and courteous in their ways;
There came Rodin de Herdecourt,
The king's friend and one of his court;
And those of Préaux [17] came, the ones
Who were the king's companions;   4,730
Garin Fitz-Gerold came,[18] and he

[10] William II de Tancarville (Seine-Inférieure), chamberlain of Normandy and governor of Poitou for Henry II, is well known as the cousin of William Marshal, in whose home the young Marshal was educated. The *Guillaume le Maréchal* contains many references to him. (Meyer's note, III, 13; Powicke, *Loss of Normandy*, p. 514.)

[11] Robert IV, earl of Leicester, steward of England and Normandy, received his earldom at Messina (Siedschlag, p. 123, no. 124).

[12] Gilbert Talbot of Linton, Herefordshire. The *Itinerarium* calls him "Girard." (Siedschlag, p. 116, no. 41.)

[13] Ralph de Taissons, lord of St. Saveur-le-vicomte in Normandy, for a time seneschal of Normandy under John, held 45 fees in Normandy, also lands in Kent, Gloucestershire, and Nottinghamshire. He joined Philip against John and lost his English lands (Powicke, *Loss of Normandy*, p. 513). He took the cross in 1188 (Cartellieri, *Philipp II*, p. 54) and later was one of the constables who led the pilgrims to Jerusalem after the truce.

[14] This viscount of Châteaudun is identified by Paris as Ralph.

[15] Bertrand de Verdun, of Staffordshire, seneschal of Ireland, sheriff of Warwick and Leicester, was left in charge of Acre when Richard left that city. He was also commissioned to look after the queen (Siedschlag, pp. 113-14, no. 20).

[16] The brothers Tozelais, or Tosolensis, are unidentified.

[17] William, John, and Peter de Préaux, three Norman knights, all rendered distinguished service under Richard on the crusade. John, the head of the house, was lord of Préaux in Normandy. All three played important roles under King John. (Powicke, *Loss of Normandy*, pp. 499, 510.)

[18] Garin Fitz-Gerold was one of the barons of the Exchequer in England. One of the

Brought with him a fair company;
And likewise came he of la Mare,[19]
Richly and well equipped for war;
And many more I do not name
To aid the Lord God thither came.[20]

SIEGE MACHINERY BATTERS THE WALLS OF ACRE

Thus the two kings were stricken down
By illness while they sieged the town.
God willed them not to die, but live
And succor to the city give.   4,740
The king of France was well and cured
While still the other's ill endured.
The engines toward the wall released
Their missiles, and they never ceased.
The king had one called Male Voisine,
But in Acre was one named Male Cousine
Which ever damaged it and wrecked.
The king would then set it erect
Once more, and it would beat and maul
Until it breached the master wall   4,750
And did great damage as it beat
Upon the tower called Maudite.[21]

---

greatest of the English lords, he held several great honors including the Courci lands. He served throughout the third crusade and may have returned to the east on the fourth. (Siedschlag, p. 127, no. 157; p. 136, no. 56.)

[19] Paris notes that two brothers, Robert and William de la Mare, are mentioned in the *Guillaume le Maréchal* and that they are probably the persons here referred to. Siedschlag (p. 123, no. 125) suggests Robert de la Mare of Norfolk and Suffolk. Robert de la Mare was constable of Tickhill in 1194. (Landon, *Itinerary*, p. 85.)

[20] The *Itinerarium* (pp. 217–18) names in addition to those mentioned by the *Estoire*: Hugh Fitz-Nicholas; Ernauld de Magna Villa; N. de Stuteville; William Martel; William Malet; William Bloez; Chotard de Loreora; Roger de Satya; Andrew de Chauvigny; Hugh le Brun; Geoffrey de Rançon; Ralph de Mauléon; William de Roches; Geoffrey de Lancellis; Hugh la Fiette "who was in Cyprus at its capture." Most of these men are mentioned by the *Estoire* later on in the poem.

[21] The *Tour Maudite* was a strong tower at the corner of the defense wall of Acre. The *Itinerarium* (pp. 75–76) says it received its name from the fact that in it were minted the thirty pieces of silver for which Judas betrayed Christ, wherefore it has ever since been termed accursed.

And also wrought most valiantly
That of the duke of Burgundy.
The Templars' engine missiles sped
That smote on many a Turkish head;
While that owned by the Hospital
Dealt blows that satisfied them all.
A stone thrower was on the site—
The Stone Thrower of God, 'twas hight—   4,760
For which a good priest, with fair voice,
Preached well and made the host rejoice.
And he collected, by the power
Of words, such wealth, that near the tower
Called Maudite full two perches length
Of wall were shattered by its strength.
The count of Flanders had one, too,
While he was still alive, and you
Could find no better mangonel:
This to the king of England fell.   4,770
He had a smaller one, along
With this, reputed to be strong.
These two began to concentrate
Upon a tower above a gate
Where the Turks gathered, and so well
They aimed that half of the Turks fell.
The king had had constructed two
More engines, both so stout and new
That those who worked them were protected
The while their missiles they projected;   4,780
He built a belfry of great height
Which filled the Turkish foe with fright;
It was so clad and sheathed outside
With wood, with cordage, and with hide
That it feared not the Greek fire's blast
Or any stone or missile cast.
He also builds two mangonels,
Of which one with such force propels
Its stones that they pass o'er the wall,

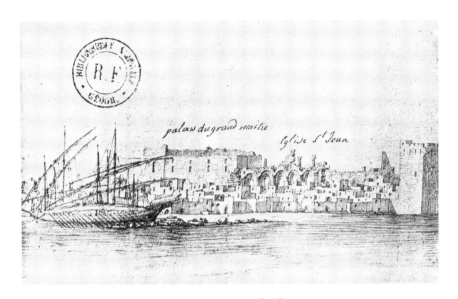

ACRE IN 1686

ACRE IN 1933

And on the Butchery [22] they fall.   4,790
So day and night the engines send
Their bolts, and never make an end.
'Tis just as true as we are here
A bolt aimed by one engineer
Killed twelve men with a single stone,
The which to Saladin was shown.
'Twas by the English king's command
Such stones were brought into the land;
Sea rocks they were, brought all the way
From Messina, Saracens to slay.   4,800
But still the king lay ill in bed,
Most wretched and discomforted.
He did come forth to witness battle
Against the Saracens' base cattle,
Who on our army's trenches pressed
So closely; he was more distressed
Because his part he could not take
Than by the ill which made him quake.

THE SARACENS DESTROY THE ENGINES

To capture Acre was difficult,
And they made many a catapult   4,810
Which cost them very heavy price
And only barely did suffice,
For when they turned aside their gaze
The Saracens set them ablaze.
The king of France made for the host
A cat castle, at heavy cost,
And a testudo, richly clad,
Whose end was direful and sad.
'Neath the testudo oft would go
The king himself with his crossbow   4,820
In hand, and made his quarrels fall

[22] The Rue de la Boucherie was one of the important streets of Acre running down
to the harbor. In 1229 Frederick II had to pass through it to reach his ships and was
pelted by the inhabitants with pieces of meat and tripe. (Philip de Novare, p. 91.) The
word in our text is "macacre."

Among the Turks who manned the wall.
One day while his men watched his cat
And those who laborèd thereat,
The Saracens cast on it dry
Brushwood, the which they heaped on high
On cat and on testudo, too
(Ambroise himself this sight did view),
Then, with an engine, hurled Greek fire
Thereon and turned it to a pyre,   4,830
So that the cat castle was burned
And all destroyed and overturned,
While the testudo of rich price
Was burned and shattered in a trice.
The king, made angry and morose
Thereby, heaped curses on all those
Who ate his bread but would not then
Avenge him on the Saracen.
He had the assault cried out that night.
The morrow morn dawned hot and bright.[23]   4,840

THE FIGHT AT THE TRENCH

So bravely on the morrow started
Forth our soldiery stouthearted.
Those who that day guarded the trench
No danger would make cringe or blench,
For the world's finest men were found
There, met and gathered all around.
There was great need thereof that day,
For Saladin was heard to say
He would be first to enter there
And of his presence make us ware.   4,850
He came not, but his people came
And stormed the trench with deadly aim:
Dismounted and on foot they fought.
Then was the battle fierce and hot,

---

[23] Roger of Hoveden (III, 117) says that the battle occurred on the third day of
the month; Beha ed Din (p. 258) dates it 7 Jomada II, which would be July 2.

And mighty blows with sword and mace
Were dealt. The strife went on apace,
For the Turks outside with fury raved
When those in Acre called and waved
At them the flag of Saladin.
It was the emir Saphadin   4,860
Who stormed the trench with such a will [24]
That he managed at first to fill
It up. But our men drove them back,
While those assigned to the attack
Of Acre bravely assailed the wall.
May God's reward upon them fall!

THE WALL IS BREACHED

The sappers of the king of France,
Who pledged aid in this circumstance,
Had dug so deeply underground
That the wall's fundaments they found,   4,870
Which they shored up with beams and frames.
These they now kindled into flames
Till a great section of the wall
Fell but nigh caught them in its fall;
For in its tottering it veered,
And all our men were sore afeared.[25]
The foe, in numerous array,
Rushed where they saw the wall give way.
There had ye seen all sorts and manners
Of pagan pennants, flags, and banners   4,880
Borne by the hosts of wickedness
That thither crowd, and thickly press,
And move upon us in a dire
Attack, and on us cast Greek fire;
Ye had seen onslaughts violent
Where ladders 'gainst the wall were leant.

[24] The *Itinerarium* (pp. 221–22) says that the army was commanded by Kahadin, which Stubbs takes to mean Taki ed Din. (See p. 115, above.)

[25] The *Itinerarium* (pp. 222–23) says "magna pars muri subsedit, paululum inclinans, nec prorsus ad terram decidens."

There was performed by Aubery
Clément [26] a deed of bravery,
Who had said that he would die that day
Or into Acre make his way,   4,890
Nor did he lie; he was to come
That day into his martyrdom.
Atop the city wall he went
To fight the Turkish rabblement
Who hemmed him in; unterrified
He fought with them; fighting he died.
For those who in his footsteps stormed
The walls, and on the ladder swarmed
Caused it to bend and fluctuate
And then collapse beneath their weight.   4,900
So down into the moat they fell,
Making the Turks to hoot and yell.
Some of our men escaped from 'neath
The wreckage, some there met their death.
Great sorrow came upon the host
When Aubery Clément was lost.
To mourn and honor him, the assault
On Acre now came to a halt.

After the day that saw him die
Not many more days had gone by   4,910
Before we undermined the feet
Of the aforesaid Tower Maudite,
And sapped and shored it till its state

---

[26] Aubery Clément of Metz in Gâtinais was the first marshal of France. His father
was the Robert Clément who had been a councillor of Louis VII and had been one of
Philip's early councillors (G. LeBarrois d'Orgeval, *Le Maréchalat de France*, I, xix,
16–20). The *Itinerarium* (p. 224) says of Aubery: "maxime quippe fuit vir auctori-
tatis et nominis et eximiae virtutis." His death is reported by Rigord (p. 115), the
Itinerarium (pp. 223–24), Ernoul (p. 273), Roger of Hoveden (III, 117), and
Haymarus (ll. 797–804). The *Eracles* (p. 157) tells of his death before the arrival
of Richard.

Was dangerous and desperate;
The Turks for their part likewise tried
To dig a tunnel from inside,
Until each met the other one;
They ceased their digging thereupon.
There Christian captives were constrained
To dig the tunnel, gyved and chained,   4,920
And when they met our men, they spoke
With them, and from their bondage broke
Away. When their escape was learned
The Turks with angry fury burned;
And hastily closed up the gape
Through which they had made their escape.

RICHARD, THOUGH ILL, DIRECTS THE ATTACK

As I related to ye, still
King Richard in his bed lay ill,
Yet 'twas his will that, though he ailed,
The town of Acre should be assailed   4,930
'Neath his command. He had a fine
Testudo drawn up to the line
Of trenches, whence his good crossbowmen
Sent well-aimed missiles at their foemen.
Wrapped in a silken counterpane,
So help me God, despite his pain,
He caused himself then to be carried
'Neath the testudo, whence he harried
The Turks with many a bolt, which he
Aimed at the tower skilfully.   4,940
His engines that same tower attack,
And all the while the Turks fight back.
His sappers never left off boring
Deep underneath the tower, and shoring
Up the walls, until by this means
And by the pounding of machines
'Twas battered over to one side.
The king of England then had cried

By his own crier throughout the host—
The crier upon a wall took post—   4,950
That two gold besants would the king
Give to whoe'er a stone would bring
From out the tower; then three, then four
He promised. Sergeants by the score
Rushed thither. Many there were hurt

．　．　．

So many fell on the terrain
That the rest did not dare remain
Or 'neath their shields in safety hide.
The wall was very high and wide.   4,960
Natheless they made effectual
Attempt to pull stones from the wall.

THE TURKS RESIST STOUTLY

The Turks shot bolts where they could see
The stones pulled forth. So eagerly
They sent their shafts and bolts at those
Who dug that they must needs expose
Themselves. One Turk had recklessly
Donned the armor of Aubery
Clément and in full view stood there.
Whereon King Richard struck him fair   4,970
Upon the chest with well-aimed shot,
And he fell dead upon the spot.
The Turks, to make up for this loss,
Stood forth in fashion hazardous
And flung themselves into the fight
And smote and shot with all their might.
Defenders ne'er so stoutly fought
As these: one marvels at the thought.
Armor, however strong and sound,
Could not protect a man from wound: 4,980
Hauberks and breastplates double both
Availed no more than colored cloth

Against the heavy quarrels cast
By their machines so thick and fast.
Against our sappers the foe delves
So well that they can save themselves
Only by hying to the rear;
The Saracens make mock and jeer.

AN ATTACK BY THE SQUIRES

When after furious onslaught
This tower to the ground was brought   4,990
And when the smoke had cleared and left
Apparent many a gap and cleft,
The squires, courageous and light,
Armed themselves ready for the fight.
Behold the banner of the count
Of Leicester, which on high did mount;
My lord, Andrew de Chauvigny [27]
Was also of the company;
Richly appareled, my lord Hugh
LeBrun joined them; the bishop, too,   5,000
Of Salisbury, and many a lord
From many a land with one accord
Came there. 'Twas at the dinner hour
That they drew up before the tower.
The noble squires now assailed

.   .   .

Their sentinels, seeing us storm
The walls, cried loudly the alarm:
Now all the citadel was stirred
And startled when they heard the word,   5,010
And the Turks poured into the breach.

[27] Andrew de Chauvigny is mentioned frequently in the *Guillaume le Maréchal*, where he is called "uns chevaliers des gens le comte de Peitiers" (l. 8633). He was one of the custodians of property left by deceased crusaders according to the arrangements made at Messina, and was one of the outstanding heroes of the crusade. After his return to the west he became lord of Châteauroux. He became the hero of a fourteenth-century poem on the crusade (G. Paris).

The squires, who greatly craved to reach
Their goal, moved on with rapid feet.
Then had ye seen the forces meet
And clash in violent mêlée
And strike and smite and wound and slay.
Our squires attacking were but few,
While the foe's numbers ever grew.
They carried blazing fire to burn
Us, seeing which we had to turn   5,020
Back, for we dared not to attend
The flames, which forced us to descend.
I do not know how many met
Their death in this hard-fought onset.

AND BY THE PISANS IS BADLY TIMED

Then armed themselves the Pisans, who
Were warriors of derring-do,
And swarmed upon the wall and scaled
It, but the Saracens assailed
Them very fiercely. So the battle
Betwixt the Pisans and these cattle   5,030
Waxed so ferocious and intense
That such a valorous defense
And brave attack were never known;
The Pisans had to clamber down.
Had we but known how matters lay,
Acre would have been ta'en that day;
But the main portion of the host
Were seated dining, and engrossed
Therein. Unplanned was the onslaught,
Which faltered, and then came to naught.   5,040

TREATY BETWEEN CONRAD AND GUY

Within the host of the crusade [28]
Council was held and concord made

---

[28] In the *Itinerarium* this incident occurs in Bk. iii, chap. 20 (pp. 235–36), after the surrender of Acre, which would correspond to the *Estoire*, l. 5244. The former is a far more logical place for it to be, and it seems to be out of place here.

Betwixt the marquis and King Guy—
A concord wished for ardently.
The marquis, in this circumstance,
Was upheld by the king of France,
The while King Richard took his stand
Beside the monarch of the land,
The true king of Jerusalem.
Since there was no love between them   5,050
And since they both were covetous
Of the realm, it was decided thus:
That King Guy should remain the king,
But that they should share everything
Therein, as rents and revenues; [29]
Meanwhile the marquis for his use
Should have Beirut, Sidon, and Tyre
To make the peace sound and entire.
And if it happened that King Guy
Should chance to be the first to die,   5,060
The marquis then should have the crown
And Geoffrey should have Ascalon
And Jaffa [30] . . . and that he then should
Do with the land as seemed him good.
But the marquis, his whole life through,
Was envious of these brothers two.

THE VALIANT DEFENDERS OF ACRE ARE DISHEARTENED

Proud were the men and glorious
Within the town, and marvelous:
And had they not been miscreants,
None had surpassed their valiance.   5,070
Nevertheless they were afeared
At what they saw, for it appeared
As if the whole world did unite,
Intent to crush them with its might;

[29] The *Itinerarium* does not mention this sharing of the revenues.
[30] Roger of Hoveden (III, 174) and the *Gesta* (II, 227) say that Geoffrey was given Jaffa and Cæsarea *after* Richard fortified them.

And they beheld their strong walls crashed
And broken through and breached and smashed.
They saw their strength reduced amain,
So many wounded were and slain.
Nevertheless, within the wall
Were still six thousand men in all,   5,080
Mashtub [31] and Karakush [32] likewise;
But these beleaguered enemies
No longer had hope of relief,
And well they knew the wrath and grief
Which all our host felt, consequent
On the death of Aubery Clément;
They knew the death of sons and brothers,

[31] Saif ed-Din abu l'Hasan Ali ibn Ahmad ibn Ali al Haija ibn Abd Allah ibn Abi
'l-Halil ibn Marzuban al-Hakkari al Mashtub was one of Saladin's most trusted emirs.
Ibn Kallikan says of him (I, 164): "None of Salah-ad-din's emirs were on an equality
with him, nor even approached him, in rank and influence. They used to call him the
grand emir, this being the title by which he was known, and which was borne by no
other." He accompanied Saladin to the siege of Acre and was sent into the city to command its defense in 1191. He negotiated the terms of the surrender of Acre and became
the prisoner of Richard, who kept him closely confined at Acre. He was finally released
upon payment of a ransom of 30,000 dinars and rejoined Saladin on June 14, 1192.
The sultan appointed him governor of Naplouse but he did not long enjoy the position,
for he died less than a hundred days after his release, in Jerusalem on November 1,
1192. (Ibn Kallikan, I, 164, and Beha ed Din, passim.)

[32] Beha ed Din Karakush ibn Abd Allah al-Asadi was a former servant of Shirkuh's
who rendered signal services to Saladin in the occupation of Egypt. He was created
governor of the palace and later lieutenant of the sultan in Egypt, and it was he who
built the citadel of Cairo. In 1189 he was appointed governor of the citadel of Acre,
and he commanded that fortress throughout the siege. With the surrender of Acre he
became the prisoner of Philip, who turned him over to Conrad at Tyre. Conrad sold
him to the duke of Burgundy, who in turn gave him to Richard in payment of a debt
of 1,500 lbs. of silver which he owed. (Roger of Hoveden, III, 126–28, 181.) He was
ransomed in October 1192 for a considerable sum: Beha ed Din (p. 395) says 200,000
gold pieces; Ibn Kallikan (II, 521) says in one place 10,000 dinars and in another
30,000 pieces of gold. Bar Hebraeus (p. 340) tells an anecdote to the effect that
Karakush's ransom had been fixed at 8,000 gold pieces, but that when he heard that
al Mashtub had been charged 30,000, he felt it beneath his dignity to allow himself to
be ransomed for an inferior figure. He died at Cairo in April, 1201. Both Ibn Kallikan
(IV, 498) and Bar Hebraeus say that he was a eunuch, the latter asserting that he was
a Greek. He had a reputation for pomposity and stupidity which caused him to be
caricatured after his death, but as Ibn Kallikan remarks, he could not have been so
stupid or Saladin would not have trusted him as he did.

Of uncles, nephews, and of fathers,
And cousins-german, too, who fell
At the hands of the infidel   5,090
Had made us hate them bitterly;
And they knew most assuredly
That the armed men of Christendom
Would either die or overcome
Them. They could not break the blockade.
Across the city they had made
A wall dividing it in two.
Most truthfully I say to you
That they hoped to resist our force;
But God inspired them to a course   5,100
Which brought great honor unto us,
To them disaster ruinous,
And thus Acre fell to us, though not
A blow was struck, nor fired a shot.

THEY PLEAD WITH SALADIN FOR AID

Now, at a meeting held inside
The walls, the Saracens decide
To ask us for safe conduct, so
That word to Saladin may go;
For he had pledged his word and sworn
That, should their lot grow too forlorn,   5,110
He would make such a peace with us
As they demand: he had sworn it thus.
So, having asked us for safe passage,
They sent to Saladin a message,[33]

[33] There are considerable differences in the various accounts of these negotiations.
The *Itinerarium* (pp. 228–30) says that Mashtub and Karakush asked for a truce,
while they might ask help from Saladin, and promised that if help were not forth-
coming they would surrender the city. Philip granted this request, but Richard refused.
Saladin promised them help when he heard that they had opened negotiations, but
was unable to supply it. The *Eracles* (pp. 171–74) is more favorable to Saladin and
less so to Richard. According to its account the envoys from Acre came to Philip with
the offer to surrender if their lives and property would be spared. While the envoys
were still with Philip, during the truce granted by the French king to facilitate the
negotiations, Richard attacked the city. Philip was so enraged at this act of bad faith

Praying that in their sore distress
He cling fast to his nobleness;
And that the law, of old set forth,
Given by Mahomet to the earth,
Should not be ruined or laid waste
By any Christians, nor abased;   5,120
That he should take swift counseling
And pay heed to no other thing
Save to relieve those warriors who
At his command had gone into
The town of Acre and there kept guard
Till nigh they touched the foeman's sword;
That he think on the miseries
Of their deserted families,
Whom, since the armies set forth three
Years gone, they had no chance to see;   5,130
That he should rescue them and theirs,
Nor let them die for lack of cares;
That he should keep his plighted word,
Else they would make, as they averred,
Peace with the Christians on as good
Terms and conditions as they could.

---

on the part of Richard that hardly was he prevented from himself attacking Richard. Karakush appealed to Saladin for aid, but the sultan replied that he could render none, so Karakush offered the surrender of the city, the Cross, and the prisoners, at the mercy of the Franks. Ibn al Athir (p. 44) reports that the Moslems in Acre tried negotiations, but were refused by the Franks who dealt direct with Saladin. The sultan offered the return of the Cross and the exchange of prisoner for prisoner to redeem the inhabitants of Acre, but the Franks refused. This account is supported by Bar Hebraeus (pp. 335–36), who says that the Franks demanded the return of *all* the places and prisoners captured by Saladin; and when Saladin offered only 3,000 prisoners in exchange for the people in Acre, the Franks stormed the city and took it. The most detailed account is that of Beha ed Din (pp. 259–67). Mashtub and Karakush wrote to Saladin on July 2 that the city could not hold out. The sultan attempted to relieve it by attacking the crusaders' camp, but the attack failed. Mashtub then sought out Philip and offered terms which were rejected, the Franks demanding the return of all cities and prisoners. The Moslems then offered to surrender the city if the lives of the inhabitants were spared, and added the surrender of the Cross. The Franks still rejected the offer, and on Friday, July 12, Saladin received word that the city had surrendered.

SALADIN PROMISES SUCCOR

Saladin hearkened to the plaint
Of his men, suffering and faint;
He heard their woe and their distress—
Their sorrow and their feebleness.   5,140
He made reply to those aggrieved
As best he could: he had received,
He said, tidings from Babylon
That many a battalion
Of fighting men, whom he therefrom
Had summoned, in swift ships would come
To save the gallant company
Of Acre; he would not let them die.
He said the caliph [34] had replied
That succor they should have inside   5,150
The week. If this aid did not save
Them, then the promise that he gave
Them would be kept; he would make peace
With Christendom for their release.
The messengers went back into
The city. There misfortunes grew.
The engines day and night still dropped
Stones on the walls, nor ever stopped,
And the Turks were so filled with fright
That they would climb the walls at night   5,160
And from that height would headlong fling
Themselves, to end their suffering. [35]

[34] The text has "Amulaine." The *Itinerarium* (p. 230) gives "Muleinae," variants
on the word "Miramolin," which was the ordinary Christian word for the Arabic
"amir al-mu 'minin," commander of the faithful, a title employed by the caliphs.
G. Paris says that this refers to the caliph of Cairo, but unfortunately for this identification the caliphate of Cairo had been suppressed by Saladin and existed no longer.
Stubbs identifies this as the caliph of Bagdad. Beha ed Din (p. 171) tells how he had
been sent on an embassy to the caliph En Nasr li Din Allah Abu el Abbas Ahmed ibn
el Mostadi bi-Amr Illah at Bagdad to ask his help when Saladin learned of the approach
of the army of Frederick Barbarossa.

[35] The *Itinerarium* (p. 230) says that many sought Christian baptism, but that their
conversion was due rather to fear than to true religious conviction.

WHICH HE IS UNABLE TO SEND

Messengers went and came once more
And unto Saladin they bore
The word that death would end their grief
Unless they had peace or relief.
Saladin, seeing clear and plain
The sorrow, suffering, and pain
And sore misfortune of his men,
Took counsel with his barons then,   5,170
Asking what course he should pursue
In that which he was asked to do.
The emirs and the wealthy lords
Replied in firm and measured words—
They were the close friends and the kin
Of the defending troops within
The town, and wished for their release—
That he could do naught but make peace
On the best terms that he could make,
Lest matters sorrier turn should take.   5,180
When the sultan heard this request
By all his noble lords expressed,
When he learned Acre's suffering,
To which he no relief could bring,
Whether he willed or not, he told
The messengers—good men and bold—
That, since defense was impotent
To save the town, he would consent
To its surrender. They agreed,
Before the messengers proceed,   5,190
Upon the terms of peace which they
Intend to bring to the parley
With Christendom. With gladsome air
The messengers to Acre repair.
The city's chiefs and ours now gather
To hold a counseling together:
Ours hearkened to what theirs proposed,
'Mid silence on the host imposed.

With an interpreter to aid,
The Turks set forth the offer made;   5,200
To wit, that they proposed to give
The Cross in which Christians believe,
The city, too, and of the throng
Of captives they had held so long
Two thousand noble prisoners,
Likewise five hundred commoners;
That Saladin would give command
To have sought out through all his land [36]
Their arms and gear and everything
They owned; and that no Turk should bring   5,210
With him aught but his shirt for cover
When came the moment to give over
The town of Acre and come outside.
Also, they promised to provide
A full two hundred thousand besants
To give to the two kings as presents.
And they proffer as guaranty
Hostages, Turks of dignity
And rank and wisdom, those best known
And best reputed in the town.   5,220
Our men held counsel to discuss
The terms which the Turks offered us,

---

[36] The exact terms of this offer differ in the various accounts. The *Itinerarium*
(p. 232) says that they first offered 250 noble captives and then increased the offer to
2,500. Ralph of Diceto (p. 94) gives 1,500 captives, Haymarus (ll. 834–35) states
1,500 ordinary captives and 100 chosen nobles. The *Eracles* (p. 177) and Ernoul
(p. 274) say that the nobles were to be ransomed and the common prisoners were to
be exchanged head for head. Rigord (p. 115) states that the offer was all the Christian captives and the Cross. The terms given by the Moslem historians emphasize
money payments. Beha ed Din (pp. 266–67) and Ibn al Athir (p. 44) give substantially the same terms: 100 noble prisoners to be selected by the Franks (Athir says
500); 500 common prisoners; the Cross; 200,000 dinars to the crusader chiefs;
4,000 (Athir gives 14,000) dinars to Conrad de Montferrat, who had been instru-
mental in securing the surrender. When these sums had been paid and the prisoners
surrendered, the inhabitants of Acre were to be allowed to leave the city with their
families and personal possessions. From this comparison of the various accounts it can
be seen that Ambroise had a very clear and accurate knowledge of the terms.

And, finding they were excellent,
To such a peace they gave consent.[37]

THE PITIFUL STATE OF THE CITY

The day when Acre was surrendered,
As I have heard the story rendered,
Four years had passed since that day when
'Twas captured by the Saracen.
My memory doth not betray
Me; it took place upon the day   5,230
After that of Saint Benedict,[38]   July 12, 1191
Despite the race God's interdict
Hath cursed. May He the curse maintain!
I cannot from these words refrain.
Then had ye seen the piteous state
Of Acre's churches desolate!
The ruptures and the damages
Done to the holy images!
The crucifixes overthrown,
Crosses and altars battered down,   5,240
To mock at our fidelity,
To do their base idolatry,
And celebrate Mohammed's rite.
But they paid dearly for their spite.[39]

PHILIP PLANS TO QUIT THE CRUSADE

Just at this time,[40] when unto us
The Turks were to give up the Cross
And Acre was surrenderèd,

[37] The *Itinerarium* (pp. 232–34) here inserts a chapter dealing with the proud aspect of the Moslems as they came out of the city and with the entrance of the Christian army into Acre. It tells also of the division of the chief captives—Mashtub to Richard, Karakush to Philip—and of Philip's occupation of the house of the Templars and Richard's taking over the royal palace.

[38] The date, Friday, July 12, is given by the *Itinerarium* (pp. 232, 234), *Gesta* (p. 178), Roger of Hoveden (III, 120), Beha ed Din (p. 267), Ibn al Athir (p. 44), Ralph of Diceto (II, 94), Haymarus (l. 848), *et al.*

[39] Ibn al Athir (p. 44) says that the Franks pillaged and destroyed the city, but the *Eracles* (pp. 175–76) tells how Philip and Richard restored their properties to the former Christian inhabitants of Acre.

[40] The *Itinerarium* (p. 236) says it was at the end of July.

Behold, throughout the host were spread
The tidings that the king of France,
In whom the folk had confidence,   5,250
Wished to go home and now was making
Things ready for such undertaking.
God's mercy, what a time to leave!
And what an ill thought to conceive,
To leave his men when to maintain
And lead them was his duty plain!
The king declared, say what one may,
That illness made him go away; [41]
But none can any proof adduce
That malady is an excuse   5,260
From serving that King Who doth guide
All earthly kings both far and wide.
I do not say he was not there,
Nor gave of wood and steel full share,
Silver and gold, pewter and lead,
Nor many people succorèd,
Like to the Christian king in worth
And rank supreme upon the earth.
This should have caused him to remain
And do his best without chicane   5,270
In this unhappy land which hath
Been tried so sore by pain and wrath.

INCURRING THE REPROACHES OF THE CRUSADERS

The news was now freely discussed
And openly, throughout the host,

[41] Ernoul (p. 278) and the *Eracles* (pp. 179–81) give diametrically opposed explanations of Philip's motives in desiring to return home. Ernoul maintains that his anxiety
to leave was that he might reach France in time to gain control over the lands of the
deceased count of Flanders before they could be occupied by the count of Hainault.
The *Eracles*, on the other hand, says that Philip was sick unto death with "double
tercine fever." Richard, realizing that he had consistently played Philip false and not
wishing that he remain alive to reproach him, plotted his death. He went to the French
monarch with the tidings of the death of Philip's son Louis, hoping that the shock would
kill him in his badly weakened condition. Philip, however, suspected guile and verified
the news from Europe, learning to his joy that no such word had been brought. His
haste to return home was the result of his sickness and a desire to protect his life.

How the king planned to go away
And made things ready every day.
Behold the whole French baronage
Disconsolate and filled with rage
Because they saw such will in him
(The head, of which each was the limb)   5,280
That longer he would not remain,
However much they weep and plain.
And when they saw they could not make
Him change his purpose for their sake,
Truly I say that most severely
They blamed him, and they very nearly
Denied their king and lord—so great
Had grown their discontent and hate.

HE ENTRUSTS HIS MEN TO THE DUKE OF BURGUNDY

The king of France prepared his way,
Unheeding what his men might say   5,290
Who urged upon him tarriance
Before he took him back to France;
Barons and soldiers went along
With him: they formed a mighty throng.
He yielded the lieutenancy
Unto the duke of Burgundy
With all the people of his land,
And of King Richard made demand,
Requesting that two ships be lent
To him. Down to the seaport went   5,300
His men. King Richard as a gift,
Gave him two fine ships, stout and swift;
It was a gift he freely made
And for which he was badly paid.

AND SWEARS TO KEEP PEACE IN THE WEST

King Richard, who to serve God's will
Remained in Syria, was still
Mistrustful of the French king, just

As their two fathers with distrust
Had viewed each other, and each one
Unto the other harm had done.   5,310
Richard required him to swear
On holy relics and give fair
Assurance not to lift his hand
Against him or attack his land
While he was on his pilgrimage
To save the Lord God's heritage;
And after he was back in France
To give him warning in advance
By message forty days before
He moved against him or made war   5,320
Or harmed him by a hostile act.
The king took oath to keep this pact;
And pledges of his faith he gave,
As we recall, great men and brave
Such as the duke of Burgundy,
Count Henry, and a company
Of five or more of goodly fame,
Although the rest I cannot name.

DISPOSITION OF PHILIP'S HOSTAGES

The king of France now took his leave;
I tell ye, and ye may believe,   5,330
That more of malediction
He took with him than benison.
He and the marquis seaward made
Their way to Tyre,[42] where they conveyed
Their share of captives Saracen—
Karakush was among these men.
A hundred thousand besants he
Demanded for their liberty,
On which he counted to provide
His army until Eastertide;   5,340

---

[42] The *Itinerarium* (p. 239) says on the day of St. Peter in Chains, August 1. Roger of Hoveden (III, 126) says that he left Acre July 31 and sailed from Tyre August 2.

But all these hostages did sicken,
And many died who thus were stricken,
So that from them he had not any
Profit, not a sou or penny,
Or anything to make him rich
Except one-half the booty which
They had found in Acre. In discontent
His soldiers often made lament
That they had got no more reward,
And therefrom came extreme discord.   5,350
But later, at the duke's request—
Who got therefrom a manifest
Advantage—there was made a loan
Of silver marks five thousand on
The hostages.[43] King Richard made
The loan: the French troops thus were paid—
But 'twas much later this befell.

RICHARD CARRIES ON

King Richard now perceived full well
That, since the French king had gone hence
And would not stay, toil and expense   5,360
He must assume now in full measure.
So he had taken from his treasure
Silver and gold in great amount. He
Gave with great freedom of his bounty
Unto the French, and thereby gladdened
Them all, for they were greatly saddened.
To others he was generous,
That they might quit their pledges thus.
The king of France has to his land
Returned. King Richard took in hand   5,370
The task. He will not waver from the side
Of God. He had a summons cried

[43] Roger of Hoveden (III, 181) says that 1,500 lbs. of silver were loaned by
Richard to the duke, for which he later accepted Karakush as payment (March, 1192).

In the host, who had a fortnight's wait,
And then a week, beyond the date
Agreed. For Saladin fulfilled
Not—or it may be that God willed
It thus—the pledge that he had made;
It was for this the host delayed.
The king made ready for the trip,
And loaded and prepared to ship   5,380
His mangonels and engines, for
The summertime was almost o'er,
And he wished all to be prepared.
He had the walls of Acre repaired
Beyond their former strength and measure.
While he himself ofttimes took pleasure
Watching the workmen laboring;
For 'twas the great hope of the king
To win God's land and make it safe
For us. This waiting made him chafe.   5,390
And, save for envy which impeded
Him, well would he have succeeded.

THE SARACENS PROCRASTINATE

Now had arrived the time to act
And to fulfill the oath and pact
Sworn by the Saracens unto
The Franks; but still the Christians knew
Not that with wiles and vain pretense
They were put off. The Saracens
To find the Rood said they required
Time; and ever our men inquired   5,400
About It and demanded news.
But it was God's will to refuse
To guard or save those in whose stead
It was to be surrenderèd.
One man reported: "It is here!"
Another: "This man saw It clear

Who went among the Saracens!"
But this was all lies and pretense.[44]
Saladin did not aid or cherish
The hostages, but let them perish;   5,410
For, with the Rood, it was his thought
That peace more fitting might be bought.[45]

CONRAD'S TRUCULENCE

While still they linger and pretend
The Christian chiefs a message send
To the marquis who is at Tyre,
Of whom they now ask and require
That he should thither come and bear
The hostages and take the share
Belonging to the king of France—
One-half, as read the covenants.   5,420
The bishop of Salisbury, who
For company had barons two—
Count Robert, and loyal Pierre
De Préaux, brave and debonair—
These three lords bore the embassage.
The marquis, who was filled with rage,
Gave answer he would do not so,
For to the host he dared not go,
Having more fear of Richard than
Of any other living man;   5,430
And, furthermore, if he should yield
The Turkish prisoners he held,
He asked that the True Cross be split,
That he might have his share of It.
If this were done, he would obey
And give them up without delay.
They heard the answer truculent
Made by this marquis insolent,

[44] Beha ed Din (p. 270) says that the Cross was in the camp.
[45] Haymarus (ll. 856–60) and Ernoul (p. 276) agree that Saladin refused to return the Cross.

And thought the less of him in truth;
Natheless they did their best to soothe   5,440
Him. One of them, they said, would here
Remain as hostage. Without fear
The marquis could thus come before
The king. But once again he swore
He would not take a single stride
That way. They took no leave, but hied
Them back to Acre and to the king
Told all, nor altered anything.

HE REFUSES TO JOIN THE HOST

The king, raged by this perfidy,
Sent for the duke of Burgundy,   5,450
And for Lord Dreux d'Amiens he sent,
A noble lord and excellent,
And Robert de Quincy.[46] Now when
Into his presence came these men,
He set before them the abuse
Of reason, the crime, and the excuse
Sent, whereby the marquis explained
Why he came not but still detained
The captives; he would share the realm
Without e'er bearing shield or helm;   5,460
He had cut off their victualing,
So that to Tyre there came no thing
That was not stopped and capturèd.
"This is insensate folly," said
The king. "Sir duke, to him must you
Now go; if folly we pursue,
We shall accomplish naught of worth."
The duke of Burgundy set forth;
Robert de Quincy, staunch and true,
And my lord Dreux d'Amiens went, too.   5,470

[46] Robert de Quincy (Quency) of Long Buckby, Northhants, was the nephew of Earl
Robert of Leicester, being the son of Saer de Quincy, first earl of Winchester, who held
half of the honor of Leicester by marriage with the sister of Earl Robert. (S. Painter;
Round, *E.H.R.*, XVIII, 480; Siedschlag, p. 124, no. 127.)

To the marquis at Tyre they came
And gave him summons in God's name
And in the name of England's king
That he aid in reconquering
And winning back Syria's land,
Since part of it he did demand.
These men addressed him civilly;
And he made answer scornfully
He would not set foot in the host,
But would guard his city. He made boast　　　　5,480
That there he feared no man alive.
So for some little time they strive.
But these three noble personages
Led him to yield his hostages,
And back with them incontinent
To join the host at Acre they went.

SALADIN FAILS TO REDEEM HIS HOSTAGES

Thus were the hostages regained,
The ones who were at Tyre detained;
And by a fortnight's time, and more,
Had passed the date established for　　　　5,490
The enemy to keep the sum
Of pledges which to Christendom
Were made.[47] The sultan Saladin

---

[47] The *Itinerarium* (p. 241) says that the truce expired with the terms unfulfilled on August 12. The *Gesta* (p. 189) and the *Eracles* (p. 177) both blame Saladin for failure to come to the appointed meeting with Richard. There seems to have been considerable misunderstanding about the exact terms of the treaty. Beha ed Din (pp. 271–72), Ibn al Athir (pp. 44–45), and Bar Hebraeus (p. 336) all give approximately the same story of the affair. Saladin had been allowed three installments in which to pay the money and prisoners agreed upon. The first payment was 100,000 dinars, the Cross, and 1,600 prisoners. The dates at which these payments were due are given differently by the three authors, Beha ed Din stating that he had three months for the entire payment, Ibn al Athir giving two months, and Bar Hebraeus giving only thirty days. As this was just a month after the surrender of the city it was probably, as Beha ed Din says, the end of the first term of a month. Saladin had collected the Cross and the 100,000 dinars, but had not yet been able to gather together those prisoners who were especially demanded by the Franks. He offered to turn over the money and the prisoners which he had and to give hostages for the rest, if Richard

Was false and recreant therein,
Failing to ransom or recover
The men whom he to death gave over,
And losing all that good renown
Which up till then had been his own;
For in the world there was no court
Where he enjoyed not fair report.   5,500
For God sometimes suffers His foe
A space, and then He lays him low;
The while He doth exalt His friend
And guide his labor to good end.
But Saladin was nevermore
To be exalted as before,
For all the victories that he
Had gained o'er Christianity
Were won because through him God chose
To work, and through his work bring those   5,510
His people who had gone astray
Back once more to the righteous way.

WHO ARE SLAUGHTERED BY THE CHRISTIANS

When King Richard was ware at last
That it was true and certain, past
All doubt, that he was being fooled
By Saladin and ridiculed
By dallyings deliberate,
He was regretful and irate
That the host had not made more quick
Departure; when he learned the trick   5,520

would surrender the prisoners whom he was due to have released at this time. Richard refused either to give up his prisoners or to give hostages as a guarantee that he would later surrender them. Saladin asked the Templars to guarantee the return of the Moslem prisoners if he would immediately release his Christian captives, but the Templars refused as they mistrusted their allies. Rebuffed in every suggestion, Saladin refused to give up any of his prisoners or treasure. The *Gesta* (p. 189) says that he executed his prisoners after the failure of this negotiation, and that only after the execution of the Christians did Richard massacre his captives. The consensus of evidence shows, however, that Richard was the first to execute his prisoners.

And how Saladin would do naught
Nor give to those men further thought
Who had guarded Acre in his stead,
Richard a council summonèd
Of nobles, and to them confided
The case. They took thought and decided
That they would slay the greater share
Of the Saracens, and only spare
Those of most noble family
Wherewith our hostages to buy.[48]   5,530
Now King Richard of England, who
Ere this so many pagans slew,
No further would his mind concern
With them,[49] and so, to overturn
The Turks' pride and iniquity
And to venge Christianity,
Two thousand seven hundred, all
In chains, were led outside the wall,[50]
Where they were slaughtered every one;
And thus on them was vengeance done   5,540
For blows and bolts of arbalest.
For this be the Creator blessed!

RICHARD PLANS TO MOVE SOUTHWARD

The summons through the host doth ring
For sunset hour of evening . . .

[48] The names of the important prisoners who were spared are given by the *Gesta* (pp. 189–90) and Roger of Hoveden (III, 128); Mashtub; Karakush; Hessedin, the son of Caulior; Hessedin Jordic of Aleppo; Passelari, constable of Concon; Camardoli, the treasurer of Acre; and Kahedin, a writer of Acre.

[49] Beha ed Din (pp. 273–74) says that some reported that the massacre was to avenge Christians slain, while others thought that Richard planned to advance toward Ascalon and wished to rid himself of the burden of guarding the prisoners.

[50] The *Estoire's* 2,700 prisoners is fairly close to the 3,000 reported by Beha ed Din (p. 273) and Haymarus (l. 861). Bar Hebraeus (p. 336) gives only 1,800, while the *Eracles* (p. 178) gives the preposterous figure 16,000. Cartellieri ("Richard," p. 11), accepts the figure 2,600. The massacre occurred on August 20 (Roger of Hoveden, III, 127; *Gesta*, p. 189; Beha ed Din, p. 273; Ibn al Athir, p. 46). Abu Chamah (pp. 32–33) says that Saladin returned the captives whom he had collected to their previous owners and kept the money in his war chest. He also kept the Cross.

And in the name of God, the Giver
Of all good, they should cross the river
Of Acre and then should ride straight on
Until they came to Ascalon,
To get the seacoast in their power.
They loaded on biscuit and flour,   5,550
Wine, meat, and other kinds of store.
Command was given, furthermore,
That each man bear ten days' supply
Of food. The mariners hard by
Along the coast would bring their barges
With them, all laden with their charges.
And then the galleys should proceed
To follow after them with speed.
Both food and soldiers would be shipped
In them, well armored and equipped.   5,560
Thus in contingents twain they planned
To make their conquest, one by land
And one by sea, because there was
No other way to win their cause
And conquer Syria, which hath lain
Beneath the Turks' rule and domain.

THE MARTYRS OF THE SIEGE OF ACRE

The army had at Acre lain
One whole summer and winters twain
And nearly till mid-August,[51] torn
By strife and cost, sick and forlorn,   5,570
When the king ordered to be killed
Those who deserved it by their guilt
Toward God and toward His pilgrims, thus
Making orphans so numerous.
For many a damsel without aid
Was left, and many a widow made,

---

[51] The *Itinerarium* (p. 244) says "usque ad medium autumnum." Beha ed Din
(p. 276) says that they left Acre Thursday August 22 (29 Rejib); Ibn al Athir (p. 48)
gives the day previous.

And ruined many a heritage,
And broken many a lineage,
And bishoprics and churches left
Alone and of their pastors reft.   5,580
There has been written an account
By a good clerk of prince and count
Who died there, and he has set down
The names of those of some renown,
But not the minor folk or small;
For had he wished to name them all,
So far the list would have extended,
His work and writing ne'er had ended.
And in this manuscript he wrote
Are six archbishops, ye may note,   5,590
As well as bishops twelve who died
And the patriarch,[52] to leave aside
The priests and clerks, of whom none may
With surety the number say.
Likewise the clerk's script doth contain
The names of forty counts there slain.
And five hundred great landed lords
Who sought their God the script records.[53]
May God absolve and grant them grace
To find within His realm their place!   5,600
For all the folk who perished there,
And all who thitherward did fare,
For simple hind and castellan
Who helped God's army to maintain—

[52] The *Gesta* (p. 147) names some of these ecclesiastics: Heraclius, patriarch of Jerusalem; Baldwin, archbishop of Canterbury; (Letard?) archbishop of Nazareth; (Thierry de Montfaucon) archbishop of Besançon; (Pierre d'Isnard) archbishop of Arles; (Carus? or William?) archbishop of Monreale; (Eudes) bishop of Sidon; (Eudes?) bishop of Beirut; the bishops of Acre, St. George of Lydda, Hebron, and Tiberias.

[53] Abu Chamah (p. 28) quotes a letter from Saladin in which he estimated 50,000 Christians to have been killed. The Latin Continuator of William of Tyre enumerates: one patriarch, a queen and her two daughters, five archbishops, twelve bishops, five hundred and fifty dukes, counts, and barons (Salloch, p. 141).

For every man who did his part
We all should pray with all our heart
That God will welcome them among
His own, in His celestial throng,
Where to sojourn is marvelous,
As He hath promised them and us   5,610
For their welfare and ours: so may
Each man a paternoster say.

RICHARD'S PRECAUTIONS

When those base dogs were slain who held
Acre so long and who repelled
Us oft, the king took from the ditch
His tents and gave command to pitch
Them on the land near the rampart
While waiting for the host to start.
He found it was expedient
To mass foot sergeants round his tent: 5,620
The treacherous Saracens would come
And launch attacks most troublesome,
Shouting and fighting fierce and hard,
When least our men were on their guard.
The king was used to these alarms
And was the first to leap to arms
To assail the hated enemy
And to do deeds of chivalry.

THE CAPTURE OF TWO CHRISTIAN LORDS

One day it chanced that they pursued
Them, and the mêlée was renewed.   5,630
The king and all of his array
Took arms and plunged into the fray.
With them a count of Hungary [54]
And great troop of his yeomanry;

[54] This count of Hungary is Nicholas, who came to Acre in 1189, according to the *Itinerarium* (p. 74). See above, p. 140*n*.

They sallied forth against the Turks,
And some of them did gallant works,
But following their foemen's flight
Too far, fell in an evil plight.
They seized the count of Hungary—
A man of eminent degree—   5,640
And also took a lord named Hugh,[55]
A gentleman born in Poitou
Who was the marshal of the king.
So thitherward did Richard fling,
Thinking to rescue Hugh, but they
Had taken him too far away.

ARMS AND TACTICS OF THE SARACENS

For the Turks have a serious
Advantage, which cost dear to us:
The Christians were with armor clad,
And heavily. The Saracens had   5,650
Mace, bow, and sword, and bore a spear
Well sharpened, and no other gear
Except a knife that little weighs.
When to pursue them one essays,
Their steeds unrivaled like a swallow
Seem to take flight, and none can follow;
The Turks are so skilled to elude
Their foemen when they are pursued
That they are like a venomous
And irksome gadfly unto us.   5,660
Pursue him, he will take to flight;
Return, and he renews his spite.
Thus did the pagan folk molest
And plague King Richard without rest:
He rushed upon them, and they fled;
He turned about, they followèd—
Sometimes they followed to their cost;
Sometimes they gained more than they lost.

[55] Can this be Hugh de Lusignan?

THE WORLD, THE FLESH, AND THE DEVIL

King Richard was within his tent
Waiting the host, while forth it went;   5,670
To cross the moat they were most slow,
And slowly did their number grow,
While Acre's walls scarcely contained
The crowd of men who there remained.
Three hundred thousand men, past doubt,
There were inside the town and out.
Sluggish they were beyond all measure,
Because the town was filled with pleasure.
There were good wines and bountiful
And many damsels beautiful;   5,680
And with the wines and women they
Caroused in vile and shameful way.
There was such wickedness within
The town, and so much lust and sin,
That decent, worthy folk were fraught
With shame at what their fellows wrought.

ONWARD CHRISTIAN SOLDIERS

The host was summoned; forth it came.
Just as a sheltered candle flame
Goes out when blown by gusty wind,
So must be quenched and left behind   5,690
The folly that had come upon
The host, for its corruption;
Because the women all refrained
From going; in Acre they remained,[56]
Save for the good old dames who toiled,
And dames who washed the linen soiled
And laved the heads of pilgrims—these
Were good as apes for picking fleas.
Behold the host at break of day
Armed and drawn up in fair array.   5,700

[56] The *Itinerarium* (p. 248) says that the council ordered that the women must
remain in Acre and not accompany the army.

The king took post in the rear guard
To ward off mishaps untoward.
That day small distance was traversed:
When by the pagan folk accursed
The army's going forth was known,
Ye had seen them like the rain pour down
The hills, here thirty, here a score;
For they were grieved and angered sore,
Because they had seen slaughterèd
Their kinsfolk, who were lying dead; 5,710
Therefore they followed without rest
The host, and harried it and pressed.
But, thank God, their malevolence
Availed naught. Ours departed thence,
Across the stream of Acre made
Their way, pitched tents, and there they stayed
And waited; for there still were some
Left inside Acre, who had not come
From the city. It was hard to make
All at one time the town forsake. 5,720

CHAPTER VI

THE CRUSADER HOST

'Twas Friday when the Christian host,[1]
Whose story I am telling, crossed
The stream; the morrow was a feast,
When every man his labor ceased;
'Twas of our Lord's disciple, who
Is known as Saint Bartholomew.
The Monday following this day
Was just two years since the array
Of Christians came here and assailed
Acre, where at last their force prevailed.[2]
On Sunday, then, the host set out
In God's name, Who doth guide throughout
All things. The chiefs arose at dawn
And drew up each battalion.
There had ye seen fair chivalry,
The bravest young nobility,
The noblest and best chosen men
E'er seen before or seen since then;

Aug. 23, 1191

5,730
Aug. 25

---

[1] Friday, August 23, which agrees with the date given by Beha ed Din. The chronology of Richard's march is given in Appendix C.

[2] Monday, August 26, which disagrees with the date given by Ibn al Athir (p. 6), who says that the siege began on August 29, 1189.

So many tried men in fair fettle,
And armor of such sturdy metal;   5,740
So many sergeants firm and bold,
For valor worthily extolled;
Ye had seen so many pennants streaming,
So many lance blades brightly gleaming;
Ye had seen so many floating banners
Broidered and worked in divers manners;
So many hauberks and fair helms,
Their like was not in full five realms;
Ye had seen an army drawn up here
Well fitted to inspire fear.   5,750
Now in the fore guard went the king,
With men who feared not anything.
It was the Norman knights who bore
The standard,[3] as ofttimes before.
The duke, leading the proud French nation,
Within the rear guard took his station;
But in their march was such delay
As nearly made them go astray.

THE SARACENS HARRY THE HOST

Along the seashore moved the host;
Leftward, among the dunes disposed,   5,760
The cruel army Saracen
Observed the progress of our men;
In the meanwhile a fog arose,
Which harmed the host and helped their foes.
The line of march thinned and grew weak
And at one point was like to break—
Just where the carrier wagons went
Bearing supplies and nourishment.
The Saracens swooped down headlong
And on the wagon drivers flung   5,770
Themselves. Horses and men they slew

---

[3] The *Itinerarium* (p. 249) gives a detailed description of this standard.

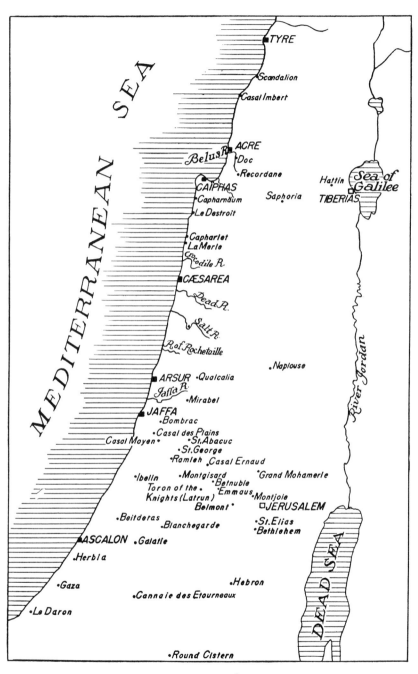

REGION OF RICHARD'S CAMPAIGNS
IN PALESTINE

And carried off provisions, too.[4]
They broke straight through our ranks and scattered
Them and drove them sorely battered
Down to the margin of the sea.
Here, where they battled sturdily,
One of our sergeants, named Evrard,
Had his hand struck off fighting hard—
He was my lord of Salisbury's man—
But neither gave his ground nor ran.   5,780
Being of his right hand bereft,
He took his sword into his left,
Firmly took stand against his foes,
And safely warded off their blows.
Now was the army sore distraught,
While King Richard thereof knew naught.

BUT ARE REPELLED

The rear guard had come to a halt,
Amazed and stunned by this assault;
Then John, the son of Lucas,[5] spurred
His horse, and bore the king quick word.   5,790
The king rode thither speedily
With his most trusted company;
From the vanguard he rode until
He reached the Turks hard by the hill;
'Mongst them like thunderbolt he flew.
I know not how many he slew
Ere he was known. They would have had
A harmful neighbor and a bad
Had he known sooner how things stood.
One Frenchman fought with lustihood—   5,800
William des Barres, whose valiant work

[4] Beha ed Din (pp. 274–75) says that Saphadin attacked the Christian army on its first day out, but was unable to check it seriously though he very nearly cut off one division.

[5] John, the son of Lucas, was according to Round (*E.H.R.*, XVIII, 477) and to Siedschlag (p. 118, no. 65) John Fitz-Luke, a baron of Devonshire. Round suggests that he may have been another John who was butler in 1187.

Stretched on the ground full many a Turk.
So well he labored in the fight
That the king pardoned him outright
And quite gave up a grudge he bore
Him, and was ill-disposed no more.
They drove the Turks back up the mount;
Of those slain I know not the count.
Saladin was right close at hand,
Leading a mighty pagan band,   5,810
But seeing how his soldiers made
Retreat, he lingered and delayed,
While our ranks that were broken through
Resumed their ordered march anew
Until they reached a river's side
And wells of water, which they tried.
There they pitched tents upon the ground [6]
In a great open place they found
Where Saladin had lain. For here
It very clearly would appear   5,820
Had camped a huge and marvelous
Array of pagans impious.

THE CRUSADERS MARCH TO CAÏPHAS

And thus it happed on the first day
That the host marched upon its way,
The Turks took toll from them; but so
It is when men to conquer go.
God did this for their welfare's sake
That they might make no more mistake,
But march in ranks more firm and serried
Than when they were thus fiercely harried.   5,830
After this time more sober care
Was given to the host's welfare.
But 'gainst more obstacles they worked;

[6] But they did not stay all night apparently, as they moved on to Caïphas that same day. Both the *Estoire* and the *Itinerarium* would seem to indicate a stop at this place, but the chronology shows that it was not over night and that they reached Caïphas the first night. See note 7 below.

For just beyond the mountain lurked
Saladin, leading his abhorred
And unbelieving pagan horde,
Manning the small gaps where they knew
Our soldiers must maneuver through.
They had so well planned their campaign
That all our army would be slain   5,840
Or taken captive beyond doubt,
Or would at least be put to rout.
The Christian army moved away
From the stream; but went not far that day.
'Neath Caïphas they camped, and so
Awaited those whose pace was slow.[7]

WHERE THEY REST

'Neath Caïphas along the coast
Was camped the proud and valiant host.
Divided in two parts were we
Between the tower and the sea.[8]   5,850
Two days we sojourned,[9] to repair
Our armor and supplies with care,
Abandoning all that useless seemed
And keeping that which we esteemed;
For the foot soldiers, those of less
Importance, suffered great distress,
Being burdened in such painful wise

---

[7] Stubbs and Norgate (*Richard*, pp. 178–79) both maintain that the army camped the first night at Saladin's former camp and then went on the next day to Caïphas. The rubric of the *Itinerarium* (p. 252) says, however: "Castra nostra a flumine Achon ad Cayphas perveniunt." The chronology of the march demands that the army have reached Caïphas by the first night. They stayed there two days—i. e., the night they arrived and the next day, Sunday night and Monday. See Appendix C for the itinerary of this march.

[8] The *Itinerarium* (p. 252) says *oppidum Cayphas*, more definite than the *Estoire*.

[9] Ambroise in common with most medieval writers follows a system of counting unfamiliar and confusing today. This method counted the day of arrival at a place as a day spent there. Thus when he says they stayed two days he means they arrived there one day and stayed over the next. For the stay at Caïphas this would be: arrival Sunday evening, stay over Monday, leave Tuesday—a stay of two days. This is proved by his later statement that they left Tuesday.

With weight of weapons and supplies
That many, who could not abide
The heat and thirst, perished and died, 5,860

CONDITIONS OF THE MARCH

When that the host of God at length
At Caïphas had gathered strength,
On Tuesday they took up their way Aug. 27
Marching in orderly array.
The Temple were the *avant-garde;*
At the rear the Hospital kept ward.
All those who saw the ranks move forth
Could judge that these were men of worth;
The host was led with skill—far more
Than it had had the time before— 5,870
And they must needs complete a long
Day's march, being rested and made strong.
But they found all along the bank
Thick briers, herbage dense and rank,
Which struck the footmen's faces, making
Most difficult their undertaking.
The land was all one desert place;
There had ye witnessed many a chase,
For all along the shore they found
Wild game in plenty. From the ground 5,880
It rose up at their very feet,
And they took much of it for meat.

THE CASAL OF THE NARROW PASS

At Cafarnäum, the château
Which those we hate most had laid low,
The king arrived; there he descended
And dined, and there the host attended;
And all those who were so inclined
Dined likewise; after they had dined,
The casal of the Narrow Pass
They sought. Narrow indeed it was. 5,890

Thither without more incidents
They came, and camped, and pitched their tents.   Aug. 27
Each eve, when they had shelter got,
Before the army slumber sought,
There was a man who would cry out,
Cheering the whole host with his shout,
For his voice sounded far and wide;
"Help, Holy Sepulcher!" he cried.
And all would echo his loud cry,
Lifting their hands toward the sky,   5,900
Tears flowing from their eyes. And then
The man would cry out once again,
Till three times he had raised his voice
And all the army would rejoice.

SERPENTS AND SCORPIONS

By day there was security
But in the night's obscurity
They were distraught by many swarms
Of tarantulas and stinging worms,
Which in great numbers came among
The pilgrim folk, and bit and stung   5,910
Them, and at once those bitten swelled.
But those who led the host dispelled
With theriac their malady
And drove out its malignancy.
Still the tarantulas assailed
Them, but wise judgment now prevailed,
And when the vermin came and when
They were within the sight of men
Such din within the host arose—
Witness thereof I call Ambrose—   5,920
Such noise, such tumult, and such clamor,
Such fearsome riot; men would hammer
On helms and on chaplets of steel;
On saddle, tub, and board would deal
Great blows, on basin, pot, and kettle,

On shield and targe of sounding metal.
Whereat the vermin fled, afeared
By this great uproar that they heard.
And when habitually they
Made noise, the vermin went away.   5,930

THE FLEET BRINGS PROVISIONS

At the casal where it had stayed
The host its preparations made
To fight its hated foes and quell
The onslaughts of the infidel.
The place where they had stopped was wide,
And the king made the host to bide
Two full days in inaction   Aug. 28–29
While waiting for provision.
Then came the fleet, and with them were
Galleys and ships with provender;   5,940
They had followed close along the coast
Carrying victual for the host.
To the casal our troops returned.
At the Merle,[10] where the king sojourned,   Aug. 30
He had arranged all things, decided
The marching order, and provided
That he would take the fore guard, thus
Making the van secure for us,
And that the Templars should take care
Of the rear guard [11] and keep watch there;   5,950
Because the Saracens close by
Harassed the army constantly.

[10] Rey identifies this Merle as the village of Tantourah (p. 422). It was the seat of a bourgeois court belonging to the lord of Arsur (*Assises*, I, 420). The *Estoire* would imply that the army returned to the Casal des Plains while Richard was at the Merle. This is contradictory to the statement of the *Itinerarium* (p. 255) which says "procedebat exercitus ad oppidum Merlam dictum, ubi rex pernoctaverat una praedicatorum noctium." The *Estoire* seems to be in error on this point.

[11] Beha ed Din observed the army after it left Cæsarea and reported that Guy commanded the vanguard, Richard the center, and the Temple and Hospital the rear (p. 282).

CÆSAREA AND THE RIVER OF CROCODILES

The king of England battled hard
That day, and great fame should reward
Him. He would have done noble work
Had others not preferred to shirk.
The king and his men charged the foe;
But others, slothful, did not so,
And thus incurred reproach that night,
Which they had merited aright.   5,960
For whosoe'er followed the king
Had done a very splendid thing.
Natheless he made the Turks fall back,
While the host painfully made track
Along the sand with heavy feet;
For most excessive was the heat,
And their day's march was far from brief
And full of heaviness and grief.
Many there were who met their death
Struck down by the sun's torrid breath.   5,970
And these they buried. Those sore stricken
Whom toil and pain had made to sicken,
The weary and the footsore, who
No longer could the march pursue—
And often they were numerous—
To these the king was generous.
He sent them to the camping place
In ships and galleys, by his grace.
That day they marched with painful tread.
The harbingers had gone ahead   5,980
To Cæsarea, where the foe
Had been, who had laid the city low,
And fiercely battered it and sundered
The while they pillaged, spoiled, and plundered.
But when our soldiers made descent
Thereon, they fled incontinent.
So we pitched tents upon the ground

Beyond a river that we found.
Even to this day men call this stream
The River of Crocodiles. I deem   5,990
Therein two pilgrims bathed, and they
Were eat by crocodiles that day.

THE FLEET JOINS THE HOST

To Cæsarea, walled and wide,
Where God good labors multiplied—
For often on this seacoast He
Dwelt with His well-loved company—
The king ordered his ships to fare
After him, and rejoin him there.
At Acre he ordered to convoke
By public cry the slothful folk,   6,000
Commanding them that with the fleet,
In God's name, they should come to meet
The host; and there came a large part
Of them before the host could start.
The great fleet came, one eve, to moor
At Cæsarea, near the shore;
It took its place beside the barges
Which had sailed close along the marges
Of the land, and which had fed us well
Despite the hostile infidel.   6,010

THE DEATH OF AYAS AL TAWIL

The host, at high tierce—this Ambrose   Sept. 1
Beyond all peradventure knows—
Fully equipped and well prepared
For marching and for battle, fared
Them forth in ranks. They would proceed
A short day's march, it was agreed,
Because the Saracens' recurrent
Onslaught smote them like a torrent
Whene'er they moved.[12] This day severe

---

[12] Beha ed Din (p. 282) describes the host on the march: "I saw some of the Frank

Was the attack, but one emir   6,020
Was killed, a man of gallantry
And of such strength and mastery
That there was no man who could beat
Him, and none even dared compete
With him. He had so huge a lance
There were no larger two in France;
He was Ayas al Tawil.[13] So
I heard him named by those who know.
The Turks mourned him with cries and wails
And from their horses cut the tails,   6,030
And had the Christians not by force
Stayed them, they had carried off his corse.
Then the host moved again, and wended
Its way, till it at last descended
To the Dead River, which had been
Covered by the base Saracen.
But we uncovered it and drank,
And spent two nights upon its bank.

RICHARD SUFFERS A SLIGHT WOUND

After they had two days reposed   Sept. 1–2
Beside the stream, the gallant host   6,040
Set out. Slowly and without haste
They crossed a land barren and waste.   Sept. 3
This day into the hills they bore
Their course, because they found the shore
So cumbered and inimical

---

foot soldiers with from one to ten arrows sticking in them, and still advancing at their ordinary pace without leaving the ranks . . . These men exercised wonderful self-control, they went on their way without any hurry, whilst their ships followed their line of march along the coast . . . One cannot help admiring the patience displayed by these people, who bore the most wearing fatigue without having any participation in the management of affairs or deriving any personal advantage."

[13] Ayas al Tawil, one of Saladin's mamelukes, was called "Ayas Stoi admiralus Carracoensis" by the *Itinerarium* (p. 13). Beha ed Din (pp. 284–85) tells of his death in this skirmish and says he was buried by his friends near Birka. Ibn al Athir (p. 50) maintains that he was killed near Arsur.

That they could not pass through at all.
Likewise they kept more close array
Than they had any other day.
The rear guard were the Templars, who
Their temples scratched that eve in rue,   6,050
Because so many horses there
They lost that they were in despair;
The count of Saint-Pol bore the cost
Likewise of many horses lost;
For much he suffered from the fell
Maraudings of the infidel,
And so well thwarted their forays
That all the army gave him praise.
The king of England, to descry
The Turks, that day approached them nigh;   6,060
And one Turk, when the king drew near,
Struck him in the side with a spear,
But his wound was not serious
And he assailed them furious,
While javelins on either side
Flew thick, and horses reared and died.

HORSE MEAT

The javelins fell thick as rain,
So that ye might have sought in vain
Where the host went and never found
Four full feet of uncovered ground;   6,070
And thus the host was set upon
All day until the set of sun,
And bitter suffering they knew,
Until at eve the Turks withdrew.
Our men made camp upon a site
Near the Salt River's [14] bank that night.   Sept. 3
Then crowds surrounded the best fed
And fattest horses that lay dead,

[14] The *Itinerarium* (p. 258) dates this on Tuesday after the feast of St. Gilles (September 3).

Slain in the day's fight, and still fresh.[15]
The sergeants bargained for the flesh,⠀⠀⠀⠀⠀⠀⠀6,080
Paying high price for what they bought,
And to obtain it fiercely fought;
The king heard this, and caused a ban
To be cried, that, if any man
Whose horse had died would give the meat
To his good soldiery to eat,
He would give that man a live horse.
The soldiers thus had free recourse
To them; they flayed them with a will
And of the good parts ate their fill.⠀⠀⠀⠀⠀⠀⠀6,090

THEY PASS THE FOREST OF ARSUR

Here for two days the host abode.[16]⠀⠀⠀⠀⠀⠀Sept. 3–4
The third, at tierce, upon the road⠀⠀⠀⠀⠀⠀Sept. 5
It moved, in order ranged for battle;
For it was said the pagan cattle,
The unbelieving black-faced brood,
Had hid themselves in Arsur wood,
Which that day they would set on fire,
Kindling it to a blaze so dire
And fearsome that 'twould burn and roast
Our army. Nonetheless the host⠀⠀⠀⠀⠀⠀⠀6,100
Through Arsur forest made its way.
I think that no man can gainsay
That 'twas a march as fine and fair
As has been witnessed anywhere.
They went straight on and had no cause
Ever to make a halt or pause.
So through the wood they came at last
And by the Mount of Arsur passed,

[15] Beha ed Din (p. 279) reports this famine in the Christian camp as he learned of it from Christian captives.

[16] Neither the *Estoire* nor the *Itinerarium* mentions an incident which Beha ed Din says happened while Richard was encamped on the Salt River. Richard requested a conference with Saphadin and asked for peace, but as he demanded the return of all the Christian territory conquered by Saladin, the negotiations were impossible.

Emerging into the champaign,
Where they camped in an open plain   6,110
Beside the River Rochetaillée,
Despite the circumcised array
Who had gathered in such mighty force
That one who saw the vast concourse
And gazed upon it with his eyes,
Striving to estimate its size,
Judged them three hundred thousand strong
And thought his judgment not far wrong.
While our host Christian numbered then
Only a hundred thousand men.   6,120
Beside the River Rochetaillée
The Lord's own faithful army lay.
'Twas Thursday [17] when their camp they made   Sept. 5
And all day Friday there they stayed.   Sept. 6

RICHARD DISPOSES HIS TROOPS FOR BATTLE

On Saturday,[18] when it was dawn,   Sept. 7
Ye had seen each and every one
Make ready to defend his head;
For to them plainly had been said
That till in battle they had met
These dogs, no farther they could get.   6,130
The foe, in many an ordered band,
Drew nigh the host on every hand,
And, seeing this, the Christian host
Against them in such wise disposed
Itself that naught had to be changed
Nor any squadrons rearranged.
Richard, the king of England, who
So well the art of warfare knew,
Ordered in his way who should man
The rear guard, who should take the van.   6,140

[17] The *Itinerarium* gives the date: Thursday before the Nativity of the Virgin, i. e., September 5.

[18] The *Itinerarium* gives the date: Saturday the eve of the Nativity, i. e., September 7.

He made twelve great divisions [19]
And ordered the battalions,
Composed of valiant men whose worth
Had no superior on earth,
And whose hearts were intent to serve
Their God, nor ever flinch nor swerve.
The vanguard was by Templars manned;
In the rear the Hospital took stand.
Methinks Bretons and Angevins
Followed the van; then came the prince,   6,150
King Guy, with soldiers from Poitou
(I am assured that this is true);
The Normans and the Englishmen,
Who bore the dragon, followed; then,
Following these, the Hospital
In the rear guard rode last of all.
The rear guard that day was composed
Of noble barons, and they closed
Their ranks in serried companies,
Riding together in such wise   6,16.
That were an apple 'mongst them cast
It could not but strike man or beast.
And it extended from the host
Of Saracens down to the coast.
There had ye seen fair banners wave
And men with countenances brave.

THE LEADERS OF THE HOST

Ye had seen the count of Leicester there,
Who would not have been otherwhere;
And there was Hugh de Gurnay [20] found
Whose men were well famed and renowned;   6,170
William de Borris,[21] who was reared

[19] The *Itinerarium* (p. 260) says in five divisions.
[20] Hugh de Gurnay held a large border fief in Normandy and also lands at Wendover, Bucks. He was given the custody of Richard's prisoners at Acre. (Siedschlag, p. 117, no. 56; and S. Painter.)
[21] William de Borris is identified by G. Paris as a Norman knight who is referred

There in the country, too, appeared;
Also Walchelin de Ferrières,
With divers soldiers, did his share;
Likewise Roger de Teoni
With knights in goodly company;
And Jacques d'Avesnes, of knightly fame,
Who that day into heaven came;
And Count Robert de Dreux. No few
Good men were in his retinue.   6,180
Likewise the bishop of Beauvais,
Who had joined his brother for that day;
Lord des Barres and lord de Garlande
With strong contingents were at hand;
While Dreux and William de Mello
Had numerous followers also;
This noble gathering of Franks
Rode side by side in close-knit ranks—
So close that it were hard to make
In their firm line a breach or break.   6,190
Count Henry de Champagne kept guard
Upon the army mountainward:
He kept in surety the flank
Marching beside the army's rank,
While the foot sergeants were aligned
Back of the host and close behind.

---

to in the *Guillaume le Maréchal* and of whom it is said that he was "en chevalerie
norri" (*G. Maréchal*, ll. 4521–22). Paris suggests that the line of the *Estoire* which
says that he was reared in Syria is a mistake and that in place of the phrase "qui de la
terre estoit norris" it should read "qui de la guerre estoit norris." The *Itinerarium* does
not include this phrase to characterize him at all. The fact that William is mentioned
in our text among a group of European crusaders, added to the facts that a person
of that name was known to be in France at this time (*G. Maréchal*, III, 53) and that
there was no one of that name prominent at that time in Syria, makes us incline to
accept Paris's identification. There was a William de Barra who appeared on documents of Jerusalem 1142 to 1156 (*Regesta*, docs. 210–321), but there is no mention
of him later than 1156, so that it is extremely improbable that he would be the man
here referred to. But though we may agree that William was a Frenchman, not a
Syrian, as the text clearly says "de la terre" the literal meaning has been preserved
in the translation.

The harness and provisions,
Carts, sumpter beasts, munitions,
So that no mishap should betide
Them, were moved to the water's side.   6,200

THE SARACENS, MANY AND FIERCE

Thus did the army with its freight
Slowly and at an easy gait
Move forward, marching steadily;
The king, the duke of Burgundy,
With gentlemen honored and tried
In front and rear and on each side,
To right and left, marched with the host
To view the Turks, see how disposed
They were, and guide the host aright.
They fell into a grievous plight,   6,210
Because, an hour before tierce,
They were assaulted by a fierce
Onslaught and hemmed in by their foemen,
Who had more than two thousand bowmen.[22]
Following these a black race came—
Noirets is their most common name,
Or Saracens of the *berrue*—
Loathesome, and black as soot in hue,
Foot soldiers swift and agile, armed
With bows and with light shields. They swarmed   6,220
Upon the host, and closely pressed
The assault, with neither cease nor rest.
Ye had seen great bands of Turks, who ride
In squadrons through the countryside,
With numerous rich pennons streaming
And flags and banners of fair seeming;
And thirty thousand Turkish troops [23]
And more, ranged in well-ordered groups,
Garbed and accoutered splendidly

---

[22] The *Itinerarium* (p. 262) gives ten thousand.
[23] *Ibid.* (p. 262) says here twenty thousand.

Dashed on the host impetuously.   6,230
Like lightning sped their horses fleet,
And dust rose thick before their feet!
Moving ahead of the emirs
There came a band of trumpeteers,
And other men with drums and tabors
There were, who had no other labors
Except upon their drums to hammer,
And hoot, and shriek, and make great clamor.
So loud their tabors did discord
They had drowned the thunder of the Lord.   6,240
And thus the infidel dogs closed
Tumultuously upon the host;
For two leagues round there was no scrap
Of earth as big as my own lap
That was not filled with them, no place
Unoccupied by their foul race.

ASSAIL THE HOST AND WELLNIGH BREAK ITS RANKS

On either flank, the sea, the land,
They fought to gain the upper hand,
Assailing so ferociously
That they made us lose heavily;   6,250
And horses in great number fell
Beneath the onslaught infidel.
That day our excellent crossbowmen
Fought nobly and did service yeoman,
And the good archers, who from aft
The host sent many a well-aimed shaft.
These were so hard beset that they
Were nigh to break in disarray
And had no hope they would survive
This combat or emerge alive;   6,260
And I will tell ye truthfully
That craven folk and cowardly
Threw down their arrows and their bows
And sought a refuge from their foes

Among the host. Those who remained,
And in the rear the host sustained,
Were pressed so fiercely by the foe
That backwards they perforce must go;
And thus, more oft than not, they went.
There was no man so excellent   6,270
Who would not gladly have had done
The pilgrimage he had begun!
But at this I am not astounded,
Because the host was so surrounded
Upon the left hand and the right
That army in such grievous plight
And by such fearful onslaught torn
No man has seen who e'er was born.
That day ye might have witnessed plain
How knights, whose horses had been slain,   6,280
Fought, when compelled thus to dismount,
'Mid the archers. Well can I recount
That neither rain nor snow nor sleet
In winter's depth did ever beat
More thickly or more densely fly
(Many can tell ye if I lie)
Than did the foemen's shafts, which flew
Upon us and our horses slew.
In armfuls ye might there have found
And gathered them upon the ground   6,290
Like thatch upon a stubble field,
So fiercely did the paynim wield
Their weapons. Scarce could we sustain
The attack upon our baggage train.
Word from the Hospital was brought
To the king that they were sore distraught
And that they could not undergo
More stress unless they charged the foe.
They must hold fast, replied the king,
And thus endure their suffering;   6,300
So they endured the attack perforce
And painfully pursued their course.

THE CRUSADERS DEFEND THEMSELVES VALIANTLY

That day, as God's omnipotence
Decreed, the heat was most intense,
The heat was fierce, and furious
Were the foes who now closed in on us.
Now must the verity be told
That no man, howsoever bold
He be, seeing the quantity
Of foes and the ferocity   6,310
And daring with which they were filled
And which the devil had instilled
In them, could fail to think our state
Was parlous, dire, and desperate,
Unless he knew their ways. As falls
On the anvil at intervals
Of heat the blacksmith's hammer, so
Their men with oft recurrent blow
Upon our rear guard beat and smote.
That day 'twas led by men of note.   6,320

.   .   .

And they did not take heed aright,
Although it was their duty clear,
And so these did them harm severe,
Driving upon them hard with maces.
There had ye witnessed empty places
Round divers men who might have been
Elsewhere, but thought they would demean
Them ill, if they were to fall back
Or shrink before the Turks' attack.   6,330
And so they did the contrary,
Fighting with dauntless bravery,
While still the foe went on to press
The attack, 'mid fear and sore distress.
But nobody should be confounded
By this, bewildered or astounded;
For all the force of pagandom—

From Damascus unto Persia, from
The sea unto the orient—
Contained no warrior eminent,   6,340
Sturdy, or valiant, or bold,
For prowess or for worth extolled,
Whose service Saladin had not
Begged or required or sought or bought,
And so persuaded to remain
With him and help thwart the campaign
Of God's folk and their enterprise.
But all of these could not suffice,
Because the flower of chivalry
And gentle-born nobility—   6,350
Men bred and nurtured for the fight—
Had now arisen in their might
From all over the Christian world
And on the pagan army hurled
Themselves. Brave men of the élite
They were; and he who could defeat
This host would have the right to say
That none could dare to bar his way.

RICHARD PLANS A DELAYED ATTACK

The heat was great and thick the dust;
God's men in valor were robust,   6,360
Warding off blows with hardihood,
While savage were the devil's brood.
The Turks were massed in denser order
Than thickly close-grown hedge's border.
The Christians marched along their track,
With the foes charging at their back
And doing them but little harm.
Ye had seen the Turks, the devil's swarm,
Enraged, who shouted at us then
And cried that we were iron men,   6,370
Because our armor made secure
Our men, and helped them to endure

With little fear the foes' attacks.
They slung their bows upon their backs
And with their maces dealt great blows.
More than a score of thousand foes
Smote the Hospital like a forge,
Whereat one knight cried out: "Saint George,
Will you allow us thus to come
To grief? Now well may Christendom   6,380
Collapse, since no man will do battle
Courageously against these cattle!"
The Master of the Hospital,
Garnier de Naplouse,[24] thus did call,
And spurring toward the king, he said:
"Sire, we are sore discomfited
And suffer shame and bitter pain;
Our horses all are being slain."
The king replied: "Master, despair
Not: one cannot be everywhere."   6,390
The Master went back and rejoined
His troops; the Turks pressed close behind,
While count and prince felt, every one,
Shame and humiliation,
And cried out: "Let us charge, good sirs!
Lest we incur reproach and slurs
As cowards. Ne'er was seen such shame.
Ne'er has our host incurred such blame,
Yielding before the infidel;

[24] Garnier de Naplouse, Master of the Hospital, accompanied Richard on the crusade from England. Born in Syria, he had served the Hospital in many capacities: castellan of Gibelin, 1173–75; Grand Preceptor of the Order, 1176–77, 1180–84; Prior of the Langue of England, 1185–90; also Prior of the Langue of France, 1189–90; Master of the Order, 1190–92 (Delaville LeRoulx, *Hospitaliers,* pp. 105–6). Col. King (*Hospitallers,* p. 136) says that he was the son of Henry de Milly, while Round ("Garnier de Nablous," *Archaeologia,* LVIII [1903], 384) says that he was descended from the family of the viscounts of Naplouse. We can find no evidence for either of these statements. (LaMonte, "Viscounts of Naplouse," *Syria* (1938), pp. 272–78.) A confusing statement in the *Itinerarium* (p. 372) caused Stubbs to become badly confused on Garnier, but Round (*loc. cit.*) and G. Paris corrected Stubbs's mistakes. Garnier died August 31, 1192.

And if we haste not to repel   6,400
With valiance the miscreant throng
We might perchance delay too long."
God! What loss, what adversity,
What grief and what calamity
Befell the host upon that tide!
How many Saracens had died
Had sin not gained the upper hand
To thwart the countercharge we planned!
Our men took careful counsel, weighed
Their chances of success, and laid   6,410
A plan to charge, most likely to succeed
If everyone had given heed.
Before our squadrons dashed headlong
On theirs, three spots were fixed among
The host; six trumpets thence would blow
The signal to attack the foe.
Two in the vanguard were to stay,
Two in the rear, and two midway.
And if each man had done his work
Aright, we should have crushed the Turk.   6,420

A PREMATURE CHARGE

But two men, who could not refrain
From charging, made our efforts vain.
Before the rest they dashed ahead
And left two Turkish soldiers dead.
One of these two knights martial
Was marshal of the Hospital,[25]
The other, Baldwin le Caron,[26]
Bold as a lion, companion
Of the English king, 'neath whose command

[25] This marshal of the Hospital is identified by Paris as William Borrel, who is known to have held the office in 1193. He might however have been Lambet, who was marshal in 1188. (Delaville LeRoulx, *Hospitaliers*, p. 410.)

[26] Baldwin le Caron is identified by Paris as a Flemish knight who is listed among the Flemish knights at a tournament in the *Guillaume le Maréchal* (ll. 165, 4571). Norgate (*Richard*, p. 187) calls him a Norman.

He had come hither from his land. 6,430
In the King Almighty's Holy Name
These two first into battle came,
Calling "Saint George!" with mighty shout;
The Lord God's men then turned about
At once, with one accord, their horses
And charged the fearsome pagan forces.
The Hospital, who had borne the brunt
Of the attack, with solid front
Swept on. And my lord of Champagne
With the fine barons in his train 6,440
Joined in; and likewise Jacques d'Avesnes
With all his kinsfolk, doughty men;
And also Count Robert de Dreux
Joined the charge. This I know is true.
With him the bishop of Beauvais
Threw himself into the affray.
While leftward, toward the seacoast's marge
The count of Leicester made his charge.
Into the fight the rear guard flung
Itself: no cravens were among 6,450
These men.[27] Then charged the Angevins,
The Bretons, Manceaux, Poitevins,
And every other company
With them. Truly it seems to me
That these bold men who rode to smite
The Turks charged on them with such might
That each man drove his lance into
An enemy and pierced him through
And through, and from his saddle cast
Him down. Their soldiers stood aghast; 6,460
For we descended on the foes
Like thunder, and great dust arose;
And all those who, dismounted, fought
On foot and with their bows had shot

---

[27] Roger of Hoveden (III, 124) claims that the duke of Burgundy fled from this battle, but the *Eracles* (pp. 185–86) says that he left for Acre *after* the battle.

Shafts that to our great damage sped—
All those had their heads severèd:
As soon as the knights overthrew them,
The sergeants followed them and slew them.[28]

ROUTS THE ENEMY

The king, seeing his men break away
From line and charge into the fray,   6,470
At once drove spurs into his steed
And forced him to his swiftest speed:
Charging without delay, he made
All haste to lend these first troops aid.
Swifter than crossbow bolt doth fly
He rode, with his bold company
Toward the right, where with fierce hand
He fell upon a pagan band
With such impetuous attack
That they were mazed and taken back   6,480
And from their saddles hurled and thrown,
So that like sheaves of grain thick strewn
Ye had seen them lying on the earth;
And England's king, of valiant worth,
Took after them and close pursued
Them, with such skill and fortitude
That round him all the road was filled
With Saracens who had been killed.
Both fore and aft, both sides, they lay
In heaps. Others fled or gave way.   6,490
For nigh a half a league of space
The trail of corpses marked his trace.
Down crashed full many a Turk accursed;
Ye had seen Saracens unhorsed,
And ye had seen thick dust clouds fly.
Our men were greatly harmed thereby,
Because, so thick the dust did smother,

---

[28] The *Eracles* (p. 184) mentions the heroism of Gautier de Bethsan and the death of the count of Auvergne.

They could not recognize each other
When they came forth from out the press,
The which redoubled their distress.   6,500
They smote to left and smote to right:
Then were the Turks in sorry plight.
Ye had seen men of valor wield
Their arms, men bloody leave the field;
Ye had seen many a rich-hued flag
Droop down into the dust, and drag;
Many a good sword had ye seen
And many a javelin sharp and keen;
Ye might have picked up on the place
Arrow and quiver, bow and mace,   6,510
Quarrels and bolts and shafts and darts
Enough to fill a score of carts.
Ye had seen bearded Turks lie slain,
As thick and close as sheaves of grain.
While those of them who still held out
Against us, fiercely laid about;
And others still who had been tossed
From out their saddles and had lost
Their mounts fled midst the bushes. These
Sought refuge, climbing into trees: 6,520
They were pulled down therefrom, and filled
The air with shrieks when they were killed.
And some gave up their mounts to flee
As best they could toward the sea,
And flung them from the cliff tops steep
Full ten ells down into the deep.
They suffered a most fearsome rout,
So that for two leagues all about
Fugitives filled the countryside,
Who once were boastful in their pride.   6,530
For all our men had turned upon
Them. Those who bore the gonfalon
(The Normans, men of surety)
Moved with great perspicacity,

Withholding their attack until
The fray would have to turn most ill
Before great harm could come to them,
If I judge right their stratagem.[29]

THE SARACENS RALLY

The gallant men of God's crusade,
After they made their onslaught, stayed;   6,540
And when they stayed, the Saracens
Rallied, and reformed their defense.
So, armed with maces, came a score
Of thousand infidels and more
To rescue those whom we had felled.
Then was our soldiery repelled
And battered hard and driven back;
Their archers took up the attack
With arrows which they shot in swarms.
Their maces smashed our heads and arms   6,550
So that they bent our knights down over
Saddlebows. When we could recover
Our strength and catch our breath anew,
Into the fray once more we flew
And smote their companies afresh,
Rending them like a flimsy mesh.
Ye had seen saddles whirled about,
Turks driven back and put to rout.
Then they assailed us in such strength
We could not go a bowshot's length,   6,560
And had our companies not stayed
Their drive, dearly we would have paid.
There was the emir Déquedin,[30]

---

[29] This passage is somewhat clearer in the *Itinerarium* (p. 272), which explains that the Normans and English guarded the standard and so remained in the rear of the fighting lines to establish a rallying point for the Christian soldiers.

[30] This certainly means Taki ed Din Omar, lord of Hama, Saladin's nephew, but there are reasons to believe that he could not have been at this battle and that this reference is an error. Perhaps his banner was carried into battle by some of his vassals from Hama who were serving in Saladin's army, but even this seems improbable under

Who was kinsman to Saladin
And who bore high aloft his banner
Emblazoned in fantastic manner.
It bore a blazon in the guise
Of breeches: this was his device.[31]
He was the Turk who felt most hate
For the entire Christian state,   6,570
And he had in his company
Seven hundred of known bravery,
For they were Saladin's élite
And very hard men to defeat.
Each squadron of these men of valor
Carried a flag of yellow color
With streamer of a different hue.
So fiercely charged this pagan crew,
With such dash and such recklessness,
Upon the men of righteousness—   6,580
Who back toward their standard went,
Bearing their weight of armament—
That even the most mettlesome
Had much to do not to succumb
Before this onslaught desperate.
Bravely our men the charge await.
Bold was the charge, stout the attack,
And after it each side drew back.
Our men fought their way toward the host,
The while the Saracens opposed   6,590
Us, and we staggered 'neath the blows
Dealt on our helmets by our foes,
Who checked our progress with their might.

---

the circumstances, as he was engaged in a campaign in the north. (LaMonte, "Taki ed Din, prince of Hama," *Moslem World*, XXXI [1941], 149–60.)

[31] Lane-Poole (*Saladin*, p. 320) explains this as a misunderstanding of a heraldic device representing an Egyptian cartouche. Mayer (*Saracenic Heraldry*, pp. 21, 243), considers trousers as a possible device and accepts this description, but suggests that probably the banner was a shield with bends badly disfigured.

BUT ARE REPULSED ANEW WITH GREAT LOSS

William des Barres, the doughty knight,
With his men launched a charge that won
The praise of each and every one;
With courage undismayed they fell
Upon the hated infidel
So fiercely that I do not know
How many Turks their charge laid low   6,600
Who never fought in battle more.
Richard, the king of England, bore
The charge, with his courageous band,
Mountainwards, where rose the land;
He rode Fauvel, his Cypriot steed
(There was no horse of such good breed
From here to Ypres); so mightily
He smote the loathsome enemy
That with bewilderment they viewed
His chivalry and fortitude.   6,610
Our men fought well till they came through
Safely to where the standard flew,
And rallied each battalion.
Once more in order, they rode on
To Arsur, where they stopped and dressed
Their tents, and made ready to rest,
For 'twas the hour to repose.[32]
Some wished to plunder that night. Those
Betook them to the battlefield
To gather all that it would yield.   6,620
When they returned therefrom they said
That of the Saracens there dead
Were thirty-two emirs and lords,[33]
Whose corpses the foe afterwards
Sought out; and on the field had died

[32] The *Itinerarium* (p. 274) adds here the account of an attack by the Turks from
Arsur, which was repulsed by Richard with fifteen companions.

[33] Beha ed Din (p. 292) mentions Museh, the grand emir of the Kurds, Kaimaz el
Adeli, and Lighush.

Full seven hundred Turks,[34] beside
Those who, sore wounded in the fray,
Died, and in nearby meadows lay;
They lost ten times as many men
As we, and even ten times ten.[35]   6,630

THE DEATH OF JACQUES D'AVESNES

Ah God! What great calamity—
What mishap and adversity—
Befell us when the Saracen
Troops charged anew upon our men,
For they were able to surround
And overwhelm a lord renowned!
'Twas Jacques d'Avesnes they caught thuswise—
God make him saint in paradise!—
And 'twas his horse's fall that brought
Upon the host this evil lot.   6,640
But he resisted stout and bold;
For we have been informed and told
That at the finish of the battle
When he lay 'mid the pagan cattle,
The gentlemen who, with intent
To seek his corse, were thither sent,
Within a little space of ground
About his fallen body, found
Fifteen Turks cut to pieces, whom
He slew in vengeance for his doom.   6,650
Three of his kinsmen shared his fall,
And they received no aid at all
From some, in this dire circumstance—
Which caused much talk. A lord of France

[34] The *Itinerarium* (p. 275) says seven thousand.

[35] There is no possible doubt of the significance of this battle or of the completeness of Saladin's defeat. Abu Chamah (p. 38) tries to gloss it over, saying, "if they had not taken refuge behind the walls of Arsur, the Franks would have been entirely destroyed." But Beha ed Din (p. 293) admits that the Moslems took only one prisoner and tells of the sultan's grief over the defeat, while Ibn al Athir (pp. 49–50) states frankly that the Franks did not realize how completely the Saracens had been routed in the fight.

It was—the count of Dreux, men said,
With the retainers whom he led.
So many censured this neglect
That I cannot their views reject.

BRINGS GRIEF TO THE HOST

At Arsur camped the host. The foe
Had suffered a most crushing blow   6,660
And would have been defeated quite
Had orders been obeyed aright.
Now the news spread among the host
Of those of our men who were lost;
They were not lost, but found, for they
Had fallen following God's way.
'Tis Jacques d'Avesnes and all his train
I mean, who were cut up and slain.
The host of God was lost in thought,
So disconcerted and distraught   6,670
None ever saw the like of it
Since Adam in the apple bit:
No one man's death e'er caused such plaint
Or such regret or such lament.
So valiantly had he served
His God, that he this plaint deserved.
And he had fixed, ere his demise,
A chosen place in paradise
Beside his patron saint, Saint James
The Apostle. They bore the same names.   6,680
Before the Turks he did not deign
To flee, this martyr Jacques d'Avesnes.

JACQUES D'AVESNES IS BURIED AT ARSUR

At Arsur the host occupied
Its camp by the great river's side,
And there they rested until morn,
For they were tired out and worn
With giving and receiving blows;

There they were fain to take repose
Until the third day dawned, and then
They felt themselves restored again.   6,690
The battle was on Saturday;   Sept. 7
And Sunday, as none can gainsay,   Sept. 8
Was feast day of the Glorious,
The Mother of God, the Precious.
'Tis celebrated in September,
As history tells and ye remember.
The Hospitallers and likewise
The Templars donned their panoplies;
With turcopoles most valorous
And other soldiers numerous,   6,700
They took them to the field where they
Who perished in the battle lay.
Throughout the battlefield they sought,
And they ate naught and they drank naught
Until at last the corse they found
Of that good vassal, fair-renowned
Jacques d'Avesnes. He was uncovered
At last, but they had not discovered
Him until they had laved his face,
Where mortal wounds had left their trace;   6,710
Wounds that he got in the defense
He made against the Saracens.
They covered up the corse and cared
For it, and back to Arsur fared
With it. There was great company
Of men-at-arms and chivalry
Who forth to meet the body went,
Making such wailing and lament
That no man ever could have heard
It and not been to pity stirred.   6,720
One mourned for his courageousness,
Another wept for his largesse.
The king of England and King Guy
At his interment stood close by,

Within Our Lady's church. And may
Our Lady to Her Sweet Son pray
For him whose body there was laid
To rest. After the mass was said,
The priests did all the subsequent
Rites in a manner reverent;   6,730

.   .   .

The noble lords then took the corse
In arms and gave it to the keeping
Of earth. Ask not if there was weeping! [36]

THE LOSSES OF THE SARACENS

Now let us for a time forbear
To write more words of this affair
Or to tell more, though it shall not
Be dropped from our mind or forgot,
For in our tale it has its place.
We must turn back now for a space,   6,740
And now 'tis of the infidel
Who smote us that we needs must tell.
These folk, to evil dedicated,
Had been, as I before related,
Discomfited and put to rout:
[They had not done what they set out
To do.] Loudly they had proposed
To the sultan and made great boast
To crush and wholly overcome
And slaughter hostile Christendom,   6,750
Thinking, beyond all fail or fault,
They would accomplish this result.
Matters went otherwise. Ah, might

[36] The *Eracles* (pp. 185–86) says that on the evening of the funeral of Jacques d'Avesnes, the duke of Burgundy called the French together and suggested their returning to Acre on the grounds that they, the French, had no interest in helping Richard win glory through the conquest of Jerusalem, when their own lord, Philip, had not remained to partake of the glory. Ernoul (pp. 278–79) gives the same motivation for the withdrawal of the French.

Your eyes have seen the mountain height
Where the Turks fled! We have been told
By those who did the sight behold
That when their soldiers fell on our
Troops, we repelled them with such power
That with their baggage train they fled,
Leaving so many camels dead,   6,760
So many horses, brown and pied,
With mules in thousands who there died,
And suffering such a heavy loss
In men when they were charged by us
That had we but pursued their rout
And followed on them close, no doubt
The whole country would have been won
And made Christian dominion.

SALADIN JEERS AT HIS MEN

After the army of the Turk
Was vanquished, after this day's work   6,770
Was known to Saladin, who still
Kept to his quarters on the hill,
After he learned that his élite,
His finest troops, had met defeat,
In wrath and fury manifest
His chosen emirs he addressed:
"Where is my household, that was wont
So pridefully to boast and vaunt?
Now at their will the Christians ride
Throughout the Syrian countryside   6,780
With none to hinder them or stay,
And I meanwhile know not what way
To turn. Where are those threatening words,
Those blows of maces and of swords,
Which, blustering, ye said would be
Dealt when ye met the enemy?
Where is the fulsome talk and prattle
Of rich conquest and mighty battle?

Where are the great disasters told
In scriptures written down of old—   6,790
So runneth the narration—
Which our forefathers wrought upon
The might of Christian insolence?
Badly doth this affair commence,
For the world holds our valor light
In warfare, battle, or in fight.
Our ancestors, who gave us birth,
Were valiant; we are nothing worth."

WHO PAY TRIBUTE TO RICHARD'S VALOR

Now did the Saracen emirs
Hearken to these, Saladin's jeers,   6,800
Reproaching them for their disgrace,
And not one lifted up his face
Save one, Sanguin d'Aleppo,[37] who
Upon his steed sat straight and true.
And said: "Sultan of justice, hear
Me now. With bitter and severe
Reproach you hold us up to shame.
But wherefore cast on us the blame
Without knowing the reason why?
You do not look with reason's eye.   6,810
We did not fail for any lack
Of bravery in our attack.
We launched, with fearless hearts and leal,
Upon the Franks iron and steel;
Before their blows we did not quail,
But naught against them can prevail,
For they are safely girt about
With armor strong, secure, and stout,

[37] Abu el Fath Ghazi abu Mansur el Malek ez Zaher Ghiath ed Din, son of Saladin (b. 1173, d. 1216), governor of Aleppo. Beha ed Din (p. 359) says of him: "The sultan was very fond of him and showed a marked preference for this son, for he saw in him all the signs of a man favored by fortune and gifted with great talents together with a capacity for administering affairs." His biography is given by Ibn Kallikan (II, 443–46). The incident reported here is probably entirely fictitious.

Which guards them from our weapons' shock,
As firm and solid as a rock,   6,820
Impervious to all our blows.
Who has to deal with men like those,
How shall he gird him to fulfill
His task? And more astounding still
Is one Frank of their company
Who slays our people terribly.
Such man we never saw indeed:
At all times he is in the lead.
At every point he wields his might
Like a well-tried and stalwart knight.   6,830
It is before him that we fall
In sheaves: Melek Richard they call
Him. Such a melek should hold land,
Win wealth, and spend it with free hand." [38]

SALADIN ORDERS THE DESTRUCTION OF FORTRESSES

Then Saladin, enraged, irate,
As ye have heard me here relate,
Called Saphadin, his brother, to
Him, saying: "Now I wish to show
What faith I have and confidence
In my men. Mount in haste. Get hence,   6,840
Tear down the walls of Ascalon:
'Twere futile to make stand thereon.
As if 'twere wood, break down and fell
The town of Gaza's citadel.
But Le Daron I bid you spare,
For thither may my men repair.
Destroy me Galatía's fort,
Lest the Franks find there a support.
Raze me the Fig Tree, so that they

[38] Compare this speech with one attributed to Saphadin by Richard of Devizes (pp. 445–48). There is no question but that Richard was greatly admired among the Moslems; Ibn al Athir (p. 43) says of him: "For he [Richard] was the most remarkable man of his times for his bravery, his ruse, his activity, his patience; because of him the Moslems were visited by a calamity without parallel."

May find it no fit place to stay   6,850
And let La Blanchegarde be destroyed,
All peril therefrom to avoid;
Raze Jaffa. See you raze it all;
Raze Casal des Plains and Casal
Moyen; raze Saint George to the ground
And Ramleh, the great town we found,
Beaumont upon the mountain's crown,
Casal Ernaud and the Toron;
Likewise Beauvoir and Mirabel,
And every mountain citadel—   6,860
Destroy them all. 'Tis my desire
That not a one remain entire.
Castle and fort and fortress must
Be razed and cast down to the dust,
Save Le Crac [39] and Jerusalem.
'Tis my will; be this done to them."
Thus Saladin the order gave.
His brother now his leave did crave,
For well he understood the word.

THEY RECONNOITER THE POSITION OF THE HOST

Then loud spoke up a Turkish lord,   6,870
An emir, Caïsac by name,[40]
A Saracen of goodly fame,
And unto Saladin said: "Sire,
No man should so believe his ire
Or heed his wrath as you have done.
Summon your spies and send them on
To Ramleh's plains and hills. These scouts
Should spy upon the whereabouts
Of the Franks, and strive their plans to learn

[39] Le Crac may mean either Crac of Montreal in Transjordan or Crac des Chevaliers in northern Syria near Homs. Neither is at all appropriate here, as all the other places are near Jerusalem.

[40] Alem ed Din Kaisar, governor of Ascalon, later commander of Daron. Beha ed Din (pp. 296–97, 337) confirms that he was ordered to destroy the walls of his city and calls him "one of the chief mamelukes and a man of good judgement."

And, having done so, should return 6,880
With tidings and inform us where
The enemy intends to fare;
For they perchance may take some path
Where we may wreak on them our wrath.
By our adored Mohammed, one
Should choose time and occasion
Before one puts his men to shame.
You should not cast on us the blame;
By chance of warfare men may meet
With misadventure and defeat. 6,890
I shall not hesitate to say
That if I have a good array
Of men I'll hold them short and make
Them think their coming a mistake."
Then they chose out thirty emirs,
Great noblemen and lofty peers:
Each one had in his company
Five hundred Turks of gallantry
Who went, at Saladin's command,
Down to the Arsur river's strand, 6,900
And there they placed themselves, and spied
Till God's men were disposed to ride.

THE HOST PROCEEDS TO JAFFA

The host of God, who had well fought
And who had beaten down somewhat
The haughtiness and insolence
Of the Saracens, departed thence
On the third day.[41] They had to go
Through a land stricken sore with woe.
In good order they rode. Their aim
Was to avenge the Lord God's shame. 6,910
The Templars that day, while they fared,
Mounted the rear guard, well prepared;
For the peasant says who guards with care

[41] The *Itinerarium* (p. 281) says that it was on Monday; i. e., September 9.

Will not be taken unaware.
But this time they did rear guard work
For naught. All day they saw no Turk,
And, till we reached the stream at night,
Not one of them appeared in sight.
And there they made attempt to press
Upon us, but without success.   6,920
A little while they shot and fired
At us, and then they all retired.
Beside the Arsur stream our host
Made camp that night, and there reposed.
Next morn set forth the harbingers,   Sept. 10
Together with the commoners
Who with great effort were restrained;
These at an early hour attained
To Jaffa, which lies on the sea.
But the Saracens so cruelly   6,930
Had beaten, shattered it, and wrecked,
Left it so ruined and abject
That the host could not there abide.
So they camped on the left-hand side
In a fair olive grove, among
The trees. But why the tale prolong?
I say only that there had passed
Three weeks [42] before they came at last
From Acre to the point where they
Were now. Matters befell that way.   6,940

WHERE THEY LEARN OF THE DEMOLITION OF ASCALON

Before Jaffa, 'mid gardens fair,
The host of God flung to the air
Its banners in the olive grove;

.   .   .

There was great wealth of pasture ground,
And there did grapes and figs abound,

[42] Actually twenty days. See Appendix C.

Almonds, and pomegranates too,
Which in such great profusion grew
And which so copiously did fill
The trees that all might eat at will.   6,950
This gave our men strength to support
Their woes. The fleet came into port:
Vessels plied back and forth with shipment
Of fresh provisions and equipment
From Acre to Jaffa. The displeasure
Of the base pagans knew no measure.
And Saladin, who did not dare
To fight, gave the command to tear
Down walls and towers of Ascalon.[43]
One day, about the hour of noon,   6,960
The host learned of this situation
Through humble folk of lowly station,
Who said, having fled thence at night,
That Ascalon was in dire plight,
All undermined and sapped and made
To stand upright by stanchions' aid.
Some folk, when these tidings spread through
The host, believed them to be true;
Whereas to other men they seemed
A lie, a jest, a fancy dreamed   6,970
That Saladin such feebleness
Should show, for whatsoe'er distress
Or whatsoever it might cost.
Therefore King Richard and the host
Dispatched a mission to find out
The truth. Borne by a galley stout
Sir Geoffrey de Lusignan went
—Who for God suffered great torment—
With him Sir William de l'Estanc,[44]

[43] Ibn al Athir (p. 51) says it was because the men refused to defend it; Beha ed
Din (p. 296) claims that the Moslems were unable to protect it, so had to destroy it.
[44] William de l'Estanc (de Stagno) is mentioned in the *Guillaume le Maréchal*
(1. 10138) as a companion of the marshal in 1194. He held lands at Verneuil and
Mortain. (Meyer's note, III, 133–34.) He was subsequently seneschal of Poitou

A worthy knight of noble rank,   6980
And with these two went several more.
These gentlemen halted before
The citadel and at it gazed
Till they were sure 'twas being razed.
Thereupon they returned and stated
The truth. The lords deliberated
As to what way they should proceed,
Whether to aid the city's need.

THE CRUSADER COUNCIL ELECTS TO FORTIFY JAFFA

The council gathered to decide
Their course, near Jaffa, just outside   6,990
The wall; there words diverse were said
And many a plan was offerèd.
For in their ages far apart
Are they, and each has his own heart:
Some barons wished to undertake
What others thought were a mistake.
They ought not to have disagreed
But joined to make their cause succeed.
It was advised by some of them
To move on toward Jerusalem;   7,000
While others, if it could be done,
Would drive the Turks from Ascalon,
For 'twas a good place to repair.
Ye had heard the parties twain declare
Their views in harsh, reproachful words,
Speaking like great and potent lords.
Then spoke his mind the English king,
Who had been reared on warfaring,
Unto the French in company
And to the duke: "It seems to me,   7,010

(Powicke, *Loss of Normandy*, p. 228). He was one of Richard's intimate companions; his name appears in the king's charters throughout the reign, and he was one of Richard's five companions when he returned from captivity. (Landon, *Itinerary*, p. 70 and *passim*.)

My lords, that we have different wills,
And this may bring us grievous ills.
The Turks, who dare not clash head-on
With us, now cast down Ascalon.
Let us not let them overthrow
It. Thither every man should go.
'Twere wise to save this citadel,
Meseems." What further can I tell?
Save that the Frenchmen,[45] who with reason
Repented thereof in good season,   7,020
Replied 'twere well that they remain
And have Jaffa rebuilt again,
Because the shortest road doth wend
Thence to their pilgrimage's end.
'Twas ill-thought opposition
That held them back from Ascalon.
Had they been willing to proceed
Thereto, the land would have been freed
Entire. But all they could decide
Was to have Jaffa fortified.[46]   7,030

THEY FORTIFY JAFFA

When this decision had been made,
The Christian host at Jaffa stayed.
So that the fort might be erected
Once more, a great tax was collected.
They cleared and dug anew the moat,
And built the walls up round about.
Therein the host took up abode.
And there each day made more inroad
Amongst them vice and wickedness
And evil and lasciviousness.   7,040
Back to the host the women came

[45] According to the *Eracles* (pp. 185–86) the duke of Burgundy and most of the French had gone back to Acre after the battle of Arsur and had not accompanied Richard to Jaffa at all.

[46] Ibn al Athir (pp. 51–52) quotes a letter from Conrad to Richard taunting him on his failure to capture Ascalon.

And plied the trade of lust and shame:
They went into the ships and barges.
God's pity! These were evil targes
And evil shields wherewith to wage
A war to win God's heritage!
How wrongfully did those behave
Who unto evil-doing gave
Themselves, and lost the precious price
Of pilgrimage through their own vice.   7,050

BUT VICE AND SLOTH DELAY THE HOST

During the last days of September,
It seems to me, as I remember,
That Jaffa was, to some extent,
Rebuilt.[47] Forth from the gardens went
The host while many a prince and duke
Pitched tents around Saint Abacuc;
But divers causes had been thinning
The army's ranks since the beginning,
For many took the backward road
To Acre and in the taverns bode.   7,060
When the king learned the slothfulness
Of the pilgrims, and their wickedness,
He sent to Acre, commanding them,
Through the king of Jerusalem,
That to the host they should return
And keep the pact which they had sworn
To God. But for King Guy they made
Sluggish return. Indeed they stayed
Till King Richard himself, who then
And later suffered for his men,   7,070
To Acre went, where in such wise
He spoke, that to the enterprise
Many returned. He brought the queens
To stay in Jaffa with their trains.

[47] Roger of Hoveden (III, 174) says that Richard gave Geoffrey de Lusignan the
cities of Jaffa and Cæsarea.

The time it took these folk to fare
Obliged the host to tarry there
Six weeks, two months; later we bore
Most grievous penalty therefor.

CHAPTER VII

RICHARD FALLS INTO AN AMBUSH

When the king forth from Acre had cast
His men and they rejoined at last   7,080
The host, the strength thereof was grown
To more than it before had known.
But ye shall hear how at this tide
The host was very sorely tried,
As he who writes this tale observed.
Sad fate might well have been reserved
For it; when he who doth command
A host in a strange foreign land,
Like that of Syria, is lost,
Confusion seizes on that host.   7,090
And this I say because the king
Of England, reconnoitering,
Went toward the Saracens to catch
Them unawares; [1] but careless watch
Was kept, and too small complement
Of men this time with the king went.
He went to sleep during this venture:
Meanwhile those enemies of nature,
The Saracens, kept guard close by,
And to the king they drew so nigh   7,100

[1] The *Itinerarium* (p. 286) says, "Cum falconibus suis spatiatum."

He scarce was waked in time to rise.
Lords, 'tis no matter for surprise
If the king rose in haste. When thus
Hemmed in by foes so numerous
One man alone is far from safe.
To him did God such grace vouchsafe
That he could mount, and his men, too,
What few he had—they were too few.
Seeing them mounted, the Turks fled
Incontinent, and the king sped   7,110
After them to their ambuscade.
And there a swift attempt they made
To hem the king in. On his brand
Of steel the king then put his hand,
And, seated firm on Fauvel's back,
He waited for the Turks' attack.
Each of them wished to seize him, though
None of them dared to risk his blow.
Perchance they might have overthrown him
And captured him, had they but known him.   7,120

THE SACRIFICE OF WILLIAM DE PRÉAUX

Then William de Préaux, a knight
Most faithful, loyal, and upright,
Cried: "Saracens, melek am I!"
The word "melek" doth signify
The king. The Turks upon the spot
Seized him and to their army brought
Him back.[2] There died Renier de Maron,[3]

[2] This episode is noted by Beha ed Din (p. 302), Ibn al Athir (p. 52), and Abu Chamah (p. 44). Beha ed Din says that the man who saved Richard was killed in the fight.

[3] Renier de Maron and his nephew Walter are identified by G. Paris merely as knights who accompanied Richard. We are inclined to think that they were really native Syrian-Frank nobles who had attached themselves to the crusader host. Maron was a fief of the kingdom of Jerusalem, held as an arrière fief of Naplouse by Philip de Milly. Philip ceded it to the crown in 1161, and it remained in domain until 1182, when it was granted to Joscelyn de Courtenay. In 1183 King Baldwin took it back in exchange for a revenue of 1,000 besants and some smaller properties, but in 1186

Stouthearted and a noble baron,
And Walter too, his nephew, who
Was also a brave man and true;   7,130
And also Lucas and Alain
De l'Estable [4] in this fray were slain.
As soon as these tidings were known [5]

.   .   .

Happy and gay, so says the book.
And in pursuit none undertook
To go, for with great speed they made
Escape, and with them they conveyed
William; for these base people thought
They had seized the king. But this was not   7,140
The will of God, Who was his guard.
The Turks had made off mountainward,
Thinking the king was in their power.
Meanwhile back to the army our
Men came. The king and all the host
Grieved much for William, who was lost.

King Guy again granted it to Joscelyn. (LaMonte, "Rise and Decline of a Frankish Seigneury," *Rev. hist. sud-est européen.*) In 1229 Frederick II granted the investiture of Maron to the Teutonic Knights who had purchased it from the heirs of Joscelyn (*Regesta*, doc. 1003). Renier de Maron appears on documents of Conrad de Montferrat's at Tyre in October, 1187 (*Regesta*, docs. 665, 667, 668). As the fief was in the seigneury of Joscelyn at that date, Renier could not have been lord thereof, but he may well have come from there. A Pontius Marranus appears on acts of the years 1168-75 (*Regesta*, docs. 453, 525) and Peter de Marone is found on an act of Agnes de Scandalion in 1274 (*Regesta*, doc. 1399). Walter is unknown save for the reference to him in the *Estoire*. There is not enough evidence to prove the existence of a family of Maron, but there is enough to show that Renier may very possibly have been a Syrian rather than a western crusader. S. Painter says that the name is not one with which he is familiar, and he doubts that it is either Norman or English.

[4] Lucas and Alain de l'Estable are identified tentatively as English by Siedschlag (p. 118, no. 73, p. 112, no. 6), since the name is an English one, but Painter writes me they were probably French.

[5] The *Estoire* here has a lacuna of several lines, which in the *Itinerarium* recount the anxiety of the host and its joy at Richard's return.

RICHARD SPURNS THE COUNSELS OF CAUTION

When God had been so generous
As to conserve the king's life thus
Who led the host upon its way,
Various men made bold to say,   7,150
Who for completely fearless knew him
And dreaded lest some harm come to him:
"Sire, for God's mercy, from such raids
Refrain! Avoid such ambuscades:
Protect yourself and Christendom.
You have good men and mettlesome.
Go not alone upon such works.
When 'tis your will to vex the Turks,
Let your troop be most amply manned.
Our life and death lie in your hand—   7,160
Our death, if harm should come upon
You; for when once the head is gone,
The limbs alone cannot suffice,
But fail and perish in a trice;
Swift come mishap and accident."
So worthy men great effort spent
Counseling him to mend his way;
But when 'twas said and done, each day
When he saw combats—and but few
Of them could be kept from his view—   7,170
He flung himself into the fight,
And with such valiance did smite
The Turks that ever he did gain
The victory, with many slain
And captured. And God brought him back
In safety from each fierce attack.

THE HOST MARCHES OUT FROM JAFFA

When, with great effort and great cost,
All was made ready in the host,
Order and summons to them came

In God the Son of Mary's name   7,180
That they should go to the Casal
Des Plains and strengthen tower and wall,
So that the host's head might withstand
Attack. The king then gave command
That men in Jaffa should remain,
So that they strongly might maintain
The town, and garrison the port,
And let no men of any sort
Go forth, save merchants for supplies.
The bishop of Evreux, likewise   7,190
The count of Châlon, and Sir Hugh
De Ribole,[6] with their retinue,
Remained in charge of this affair:
They put the town in good repair.
Now the host mounted and moved on; [7]
No man e'er saw a finer one
Nor one more sumptuously arrayed.
Only a short day's march they made.
They stopped between the casals twain
And there they pitched their tents again;   7,200
I have good reason to believe
And know that it was All Saints' Eve   Oct. 31
When we encamped ourselves that day;
The Turkish host at Ramleh lay,
And thence made forays vigorous
And raids and onslaughts upon us.

RICHARD RECONNOITERS

Leaving Casal des Plains, our men
Were 'twixt there and Casal Moyen
A full fortnight or more. They found
The foe had razed it to the ground.   7,210
The king had it rebuilt once more

---

[6] Hugh de Ribole is said by G. Paris to be otherwise unknown.
[7] The *Itinerarium* (p. 289) says that Richard defeated the Saracens in a small skirmish on the Wednesday before All Saints' Day. On the next day, the eve of All Saints, the army camped between Casal des Plains and Casal Moyen (October 31).

Stronger than it had been before,
While the Templars built once more
The other. The Turks pressed us sore.
One day there drew nigh us a force
Of a full thousand men on horse.
And our host stirred at the alarm
Like to an anthill all aswarm.
The king and many another knight
Mounted and made what haste they might;   7,220
And the Turks—may the devil lead
Them!—turned about and fled full speed;
And so swiftly their horses sped
That, whatsoever way they fled,
The king could never overtake
Them, with the best speed he could make.[8]
Nevertheless he still pursued
Them, but in vain, until he viewed
The town of Ramleh in full sight
And the fell pagans massed in might;   7,230
Then back to his main army he
Returned with his brave company.

THE SARACENS ATTACK A FORAGING PARTY

On the sixth day of the great fete   Nov. 6
Of All Saints,[9] which all celebrate,
The squires left the host, with courage,
And sallied forth to seek for forage.
On this occasion those brave lords,
The Templars, acted as their guards.
The foragers went far and wide
And scattered through the countryside.   7,240
A search most diligent they made
For fresh grass, and ofttimes they paid
A heavy price to get this food
(Having to buy it with their blood).

[8] The *Itinerarium* (p. 290) gives twenty-six killed and sixteen captured.
[9] The date, November 6, is confirmed by Beha ed Din (p. 318).

The Templars watched them as they fared,
But just when they were least prepared,
Four companies of Saracens
Swooped down on them with violence.
They were four hundred, rightly counted,[10]
And every man well armed and mounted;   7,250
They issued forth from towards Bombrac
And on the Templars made attack,
Hemmed them in, cutting off retreat,
For in the world are none so fleet;
Closely they press, and swift they ride,
Coming at us from every side.
The Templars, seeing this concourse
So nigh, each baron from his horse
Dismounted. They did valiant work,
Each with his face toward the Turk,   7,260
Back toward his brother; every one
Might have been the same father's son.
The Saracens with might and main
Attacked us, so that three were slain.
Ye might have seen great blows; ye might
Have heard helms ringing, caught the light
Of sparks as steel smote steel. No lack
Was there of parry and attack.
The Turks were minded to surprise
Us, hemmed and closed as in a vise;   7,270
They strove to seize us with their hands,
When from our host there rode forth bands
Of men. They drew nigh at full speed.
'Tis said—and 'tis pure truth indeed—
That first Andrew de Chauvigny,
With fourteen in his company,
Charging the Turks full tilt essayed
To bring the hard-pressed Templars aid.
With fearless valor forth he came,
And his companions did the same.   7,280

[10] The *Itinerarium* (p. 291) says four thousand.

There was a fierce encountering,
But 'twas not hidden from the king.

RICHARD SENDS REINFORCEMENTS

The king was occupied just then
In rebuilding Casal Moyen,
And he had summoned there two counts
Who should be in all good accounts,
The counts of Leicester and Saint-Pol.
With them the king was pleased to call
William de Caieu,[11] who that day
Did valiant work throughout the fray;   7,290
Likewise Otto de Trasignies [12]—
All men of noble families.
Now to them came the noise and shout,
The which the foragers sent out.
Thereon straightway the king addressed
Unto the said counts the behest
That they go to the Templars' aid,
While in his armor he arrayed
Himself. As swiftly as he might
He donned his armor for the fight,   7,300
And they rode forth at rapid pace.
When they drew nigh unto the place,
Forth from a river bed emerged
Four thousand enemies, who surged
In two diverse directions. Some
Toward the Templars fiercely come;
The others on the barons fell.

[11] William de Caieu was a vassal of Flanders, but closely attached to Richard. He served the king on several occasions, acting as one of the guarantors of the treaty of Messina and as envoy to Conrad at Tyre. He was one of the persons addressed by Richard in his *chanson* from prison. He was captured by the French at Bouvines (G. Paris in *Romania*, XXI (1892), 263-64; Powicke, *Loss of Normandy*, pp. 163-64).

[12] Otto de Trasignies (Traseigni) is identified by Siedschlag (p. 119, no. 82) as having revenues from Kent. He was sent together with William de Caieu by Richard as his envoy to Conrad when the king consented to Conrad's elevation to the throne of Jerusalem in April, 1192 (*Itinerarium*, pp. 334-35).

The barons ordered themselves well,
And to the advancing Turks opposed
Ranks firmly knit and tightly closed.   7,310
The count of Saint-Pol then enrolled
The count of Leicester, who was bold,
In a mad venture, wild and rash;
To wit: he with the Turks would clash,
With the other guarding, from the right;
Or else his friend would start the fight,
While he on guard would be intent
Whate'er he did, where'er he went.
The count accepted this bold plan,
And, with his followers, began   7,320
A charge that brought him at full pace
Among the ranks of the dark race,
And with such fortitude he came
That for his prowess he won fame
And rescued two knights, but 'twas not
Without a struggle fiercely fought.

AND COMES IN PERSON TO THE RESCUE

The battle tide was at its height
When Richard, the king skilled in fight,
Arrived and saw the ring of foes
Which pressed on all sides to enclose   7,330
Our men. His company was small,
But men stouthearted one and all.
"Faith, sire," thus unto him now spoke
Certain of those among his folk,
"You risk a sore mishap indeed,
And surely you will not succeed
In rescuing our comrades yon.
'Twere better they should die alone
Than you risk death in this attack.
Therefore 'tis well that you turn back;   7,340
If misadventure should befall
You, 'twould result in the downfall

Of Christendom." He listened to
These words, and his face changed its hue.
Then said he: "Since 'twas I who sent
Them there, and at my prayer they went,
If without me they perish there,
May I a king's name never bear!"
He drove the spurs into his horse,
Loosened the rein, gave him free course,   7,350
Like to a falcon, swift to stoop.
And then he charged into the troop
Of hostile Saracens to pierce
Them with an impetus so fierce
That if a thunderbolt had driven
Clear through them it could not have riven
Them more. He cut and smote and smashed
Through them, then turned about, and slashed
And sheared off arm and hand and head.
Like animals they turned and fled.   7,360
But many could not flee. There were
Many slain or made prisoner.[13]
Our men pursued them with a will,
And drove and followed them until
The time came to return at last
To camp. And thus this day was passed.

RICHARD OPENS NEGOTIATIONS WITH SALADIN

These two casals were fortified;
While his men were thus occupied,
The king perceived they were athirst
To fight the Saracens accursed.   7,370
He summoned envoys thereupon,
Wise men of high condition,
And he sent them to Saladin

---

[13] The *Itinerarium* (p. 294) says that Richard slew an emir named Aralchais. This
is probably the emir Aiaz el Mekrani whose death in this battle is reported by Beha ed
Din (p. 319). The *Itinerarium* adds that the battle was won with no help from the
French; also that three Turks surrendered and through fear accepted Christian baptism.

And to his brother Saphadin,
Making demands imperious,
Rich, noble, and most marvelous:
The realm of Syria, from end
To end, where'er it doth extend,
And all belonging thereto when
It was the leprous king's domain,   7,380
And, as to that king had been done,
He asked tribute from Babylon.
He claimed this as his heritage
By conquest of his lineage.
These messengers, when they had sought
The sultan, all this message brought.
He told them he would not do such
A thing, that the king asked too much.
He sent reply by Saphadin,
His brother, a wise Saracen,   7,390
That all the land of Syria he
Would give him, peacefully and free
From strife, from the river to the shore
Of the sea, and never claim it more;
But this was on condition
That none should rebuild Ascalon,
Neither Christian nor Saracen.
This word he sent by Saphadin.[14]

[14] The *Itinerarium* (p. 296) adds details: when Saphadin reached the camp, Richard was being bled and was unable to receive him. Saphadin was entertained by Stephen of Turnham until the next day, when Richard granted him an interview. On this occasion Saphadin presented Richard with seven camels and a tent. Both the *Estoire* and the *Itinerarium* omit any mention of a romantic interlude which is stressed by the eastern authorities. Beha ed Din (pp. 308–12, 324–28), Ibn al Athir (pp. 52–53), Abu Chamah (pp. 45–46), and Bar Hebraeus (pp. 337–38) all relate the episode of the proposed marriage of Richard's sister Joanna to Saphadin. According to this account, Richard demanded all the lands as far as the Jordan. When this was refused, he suggested that Joanna, his sister, marry Saphadin and that they should be given the former kingdom of Jerusalem. The Moslems negotiated on these lines to secure time. Joanna refused to accept the agreement unless Saphadin should accept Christianity. This was met by Richard with the suggestion that as Joanna was reluctant, his niece should be substituted. Other proposals for a treaty which were made at this time included the suggestion that Richard be given the Cross and that each should keep the lands then in his possession; also that Richard be given Jerusalem except the Holy Sakhra area.

BUT, MISTRUSTFUL, REJECTS HIS TERMS

The king, however, paid no heed
To the words of this deceitful breed   7,400
Who by false lies strove to decoy
And block him, that they might destroy
And wreck their places fortified.
Ill fate their stratagem betide!
For Saphadin so far deceived
The king that he his gifts received.
Messengers came and went to bring
These gifts and presents to the king.
For this reason the king incurred
Reproach; and comments harsh were heard.   7,410
But Saphadin had brought him to
Believe that he had peace in view,
And peace the king would readily
Have had, were honor gained thereby,
The glory of our faith to enhance;
Also because the king of France
Had left, which made him much misdoubt,
Knowing that that king loved him not.
Messengers came and went: the king
Was kept a long time parleying,   7,420
Until he learned the fraudulence
Of the deceitful Saracens
So false and hypocritical.
He wished the Crac of Montreal
To be destroyed. Not otherwise
Would he conclude hostilities.
Since they refused, he caused to cease
This present effort to make peace.

HOSTILITIES ARE RENEWED

When this attempt at peace had failed,
On right and left the Turks assailed   7,430

All this time Saladin was negotiating for a separate peace with Conrad. The negotiations ran on throughout the month of November before they finally were abandoned.

The host with onslaught violent,
On damage and destruction bent.
The king fought them, dealt blows for blows,
And by example showed to those
Who had reproached him and were grieved
Because the Turks' gifts had deceived
Him that he lacked not loyalty
To God and Christianity.
The Turks he oft encounterèd
And hewed off many a Turkish head   7,440
Which he displayed within the host,
And surely the host nothing lost
Because these gifts came to his hand;
He would have saved the Holy Land
But for the obstacles perverse
Of those who often robbed his purse.

THE HOST ENCAMPS AT RAMLEH

When they had made shift to restore,
Rebuild, and fortify once more
The strongholds, and the king had well
Manned them with guard and sentinel,   7,450
The summons through the host was cried
Convoking them at eventide,
And the next morn they took to horse
And soberly pursued their course,
Moving directly toward Ramleh.
As soon as we were on our way
And Saladin learned that he must
Abandon Ramleh to our host
Because he dared not fight, the town
Was at his hest wrecked and torn down,   7,460
While up to Toron of the Knights [15]

[15] The *Itinerarium* (p. 298) here reads "Darum," which Stubbs points out must
be an error for "Toron," as Daron is not in the mountains and as it lies in the wrong
direction. Beha ed Din (p. 303) and Ibn al Athir (p. 52) tell of Saladin's retreat
from Ramleh to Latrun (Toron of the Knights) which they date on the 13 Ramadan
(October 4).

He fled in haste. In mountain heights
He placed his trust. Down on the plain
Our host continued the campaign.
On horses that had had their gorge
Of barley, we came 'twixt Saint-George
And Ramleh in two days.[16] And then
Camped there awaiting food and men.
And there we had to undergo
Once more fierce onslaughts from the foe,   7,470
While very heavy rains that fell
Checked us and helped the infidel.
So steadily these rains came down
That we took shelter in the town
Of Saint-George, likewise in Ramleh; [17]
We camped there, and we made a stay
Of six entire weeks,[18] no less,
In great discomfort and distress.

THE EARL OF LEICESTER LEADS A RAID

During the sojourn that we made
In this place where we were delayed,   7,480
There was a combat bravely fought
Which should not rightly be forgot;
The count of Leicester, doughty knight,
Leftwards, near Saint-George, fought the fight
Against the Turks, who often closed
In, carrying our Christian host

---

[16] The *Itinerarium* (p. 298) says that the army pitched its tents between St. George and Ramleh and stayed for twenty-two days.

[17] The *Itinerarium* (p. 298) gives several details omitted by the *Estoire.* The host with King Guy camped at St. George, while the count of St. Pol went to the Casal of the Baths. On the eve of St. Thomas (December 20) Richard made a foray against Blanchegarde, which had just been reinforced by three hundred Turks. On the night of the Holy Innocents (December 28) the Hospitallers and Templars carried out a raid in the hills near Jerusalem and brought back 200 oxen as booty. King Guy and Stephen of Turnham left the host and went back to Acre.

[18] Ibn al Athir (p. 54) and Abu Chamah (p. 48) agree that the Franks went to Ramleh on November 22. Abu Chamah says that they stayed there seven weeks, until January 10 (p. 49).

From that direction frequently;
The count, with a small company,
Went to pursue them as they fled,
Wearing his steel helm on his head.   7,490
Three knights, all reckless of mischance,
Proceeded rashly in advance
And dashed among the Turks full speed.
All three had perished there indeed,
Had not the count, who was concerned
To save their lives, thitherward turned
His horse, and hurled himself among
A hundred Turks or more, and flung
Them backward till they crossed a stream;
He charged with vigor too extreme,   7,500
For now four hundred Turks advance
Well armed with Turkish bow and lance,
Who, keen to seize him, interposed
Themselves between him and the host.

HEROES OF THE FRAY

They had now beaten to the ground
Garin Fitz-Gerold. Many a wound
They dealt that made his body bleed.
Ye had seen many a gallant deed
Performed there where Sir Garin fell.
And to the count still worse befell;   7,510
He was hemmed in and overthrown
And sorely hurt and beaten down.
And from his horse they cast down Dreux
De Fontenil; [19] in short time, too,
Robert Néel [20] had lost his mount.
Such press swarmed in upon the count—

[19] Dreux de Fontenil (called Drogo de Fontenillo Putrellis by the *Itinerarium*) is not known beyond this incident. (See Edwards.) The *Histoire des ducs de Normandie* (p. 166) mentions Amaury de Fontenil among the important barons who took part in Louis VIII's expedition against England.

[20] Robert Néel is also unidentified beyond this reference. Painter does not find him in the family of Nesle which was headed by the counts of Soissons.

Turks, Persians, renegades, surround
Him so—that he seemed nearly drowned; [21]
Scarce could they beat him to the earth.
There battled men of sterling worth.   7,520
Henry Fitz-Nicholas there got [22]
Lessons in war most harshly taught.
So, too, did Robert of Newbroke:
No gentler man of noble stock
E'er breathed. He was most tall in stature
And of such brave and stalwart nature
That 'midst the paynim foul, undaunted,
Down from his charger he dismounted,
And gave the count his horse, and thus
Saved both from shame opprobrious.   7,530
Also in the count's company
There was Sir Ralph de Sainte-Marie.[23]
Had Ernaut du Bois [24] not been there
Defeat had surely been his share.
William and Henry de Melloc [25]
With him endured the battle shock.
Saol du Breuil [26] was there likewise.

THE BATTLE RAGES

I think that never mortal eyes
Viewed such prowess as was displayed

[21] The *Itinerarium* (p. 300) says that the count was unhorsed and very nearly drowned in the river. See Introduction, p. 16.

[22] Henry Fitz-Nicholas held a fee of a knight and a half in Dorset and Somerset (Siedschlag, p. 116, no. 46).

[23] Ralph de Sainte Marie is claimed by G. Paris as possibly Norman.

[24] Ernaut du Bois was one of the chief vassals of Leicester (Siedschlag, p. 114, no. 23; S. Painter).

[25] William and Henry de Melloc are identified by Paris (p. xii) as Normans from the Eure. The *Itinerarium* (p. 301) gives a different form: Henry de Melloc, William and Saulus de Breuil, which makes William a Breuil instead of a Melloc. This is wrong; that our text has the correct form is shown by the *Scripta de feodis,* which lists both William and Henry as holding lands in Normandy.

[26] Saol du Breuil was sent back to Palestine in February, 1194, to inform King Henry that Richard was still planning to return there (Roger of Hoveden, III, 233; Landon, *Itinerary*, p. 83).

By these bold knights, who unafraid   7,540
Held out against the Turkish horde.
For none knew battle-plan nor word,
Nor how, through the thick press, to hew
His way. The book says—and 'tis true—
That the count fought against his foes
So long, and got so many blows
Dealt by the Turks, that in his dire
Distress he came nigh to expire,
And his companions had like fate.
Upon their chargers' necks prostrate   7,550
On toward the Toron [27] they were led,
When forth to meet them full tilt sped
A stalwart Christian company,
Leaving our host as they drew nigh.
Andrew de Chauvigny in the fray
Took part, also Henry de Gray,[28]
Pierre de Préaux, too, a knight
Most valiant and skilled to fight,
And many more who were not named
To me, of men for valor famed.   7,560
Each one of these fair men of worth
Laid low his Turk upon the earth.
But that Turk smitten by Pierre,
Though he lost soul and body there,
Was so strong that it cost travail
And pain ere Pierre could prevail
O'er him. Though fiercely they did strive,
They could not bring him back alive;
Pierre and his men overthrew him,
And then, after a hard fight, slew him.   7,570

[27] The *Itinerarium* (p. 301) says "Darum" again.
[28] Henry de Gray was, according to Paris (p. xi), a Norman knight from Calvados. Round (*E.H.R.*, XVIII, 476) says that he settled in Essex after the crusade. S. Painter says that he was lord of Codnor in the honor of Peverel (Notts) and of Thurrock (Essex). His name appears frequently on Richard's acts (Landon, *Itinerary*).

THE SARACENS ARE PUT TO ROUT

Hear ye, my lords, of a strange joust:
Valiant is that man who can thrust
And strike as did my lord André!
Meeting an emir on his way,
He pierced his body through, and the blade
Of his lance was at his back displayed;
But as André charged, the emir
Held with so firm a grasp his spear
That it pierced André's arm and broke
It, with the vigor of the stroke.   7,580
So did that combat end, and so
It was the emir was laid low.
Many good men were saved and shielded
There, and many a lance was wielded
Gallantly, and many a spear.
The first group would have paid most dear
If the others had not lent them aid.
Ye should have seen what brave stand made
The count of Leicester in this fight
And how he smote to left and right,   7,590
While 'neath him there were slain two steeds.
Those who were there and saw his deeds
Say no man of his age e'er fought
More gallantly, and no man got
Aid rendered in more noble way
Than the aid given him that day.
Such succor rushed forth from the host
That not one of our men was lost:
They all were rescued safe and whole.

·   ·   ·   7,600

We broke their ranks, drove and pursued
Them, scattering, till in lassitude
We gave up following their track
And to our tents at last went back.

SALADIN REPAIRS TO JERUSALEM

'Twas now that Saladin did learn,
And very clear he might discern
It, how our army did prepare
And make itself ready to fare
To the Holy City. When he knew
Beyond a doubt that this was true,   7,610
That but two leagues away we pressed
His men, giving no truce nor rest,
At once he caused to be torn down
Four or five towers of the Toron,[29]
And to Jerusalem he straight
Betook himself, so men relate.[30]
The Turks into the mountains hied
Themselves. We held the countryside.

PILGRIMS' PROGRESS

When that the Turkish force had gone
And when our army had moved on,   7,620
The cry went forth throughout our host
And all was ordered and disposed
That we should to the mountain's base
Proceed, and make camp at that place,
There to await supplies and food,
And duly was this plan pursued.
Thereon we mounted on our horses
And in battalions ranged our forces.
Before Betnuble ye might behold
Us soon.[31] 'Twas cloudy and most cold,   7,630
And there was heavy rain and storm,
Which did our animals great harm,
Because the rain so thickly poured

[29] The *Itinerarium* (p. 305) again says "Darum."

[30] Saladin went to Jerusalem from Latrun on December 12 (Abu Chamah, pp. 48–49).

[31] The Franks advanced from Ramleh to Latrun on December 22 (Ibn al Athir, p. 54) or December 23 (Roger of Hoveden, III, 174). According to Hoveden, Richard spent Christmas at Latrun.

It passeth all belief or word.
The rain and hail came so intense
That to the ground they beat our tents.
Before and after Christmastide
Such number of our horses died;
So much biscuit was made unfit
To eat, by water soaking it;   7,640
So much of salt pork was made rotten
Through damage by the storms begotten;
And hauberks rusted by the rain
That scarce could be made clean again;
So many clothes were ruinèd,
So many people went unfed,
That in their bodies many woes
They felt. Yet still their hearts uprose.
The hope that they were drawing near
The Sepulcher gave them good cheer.   7,650
So much they craved Jerusalem
That they brought all supplies with them
To hold out through a siege. Then came
Great gathering of folk whose aim
Was prowess, and who joined the host
Rejoicing, for good works disposed;
While those by illness stricken down
At Jaffa or some other town,
Firm and determined in their thought
And mind, took litters and were brought   7,660
In crowds to join the host. But they
Encountered, swarming round the way
Where they were borne with cheering words,
The infidels' harassing hordes,
Who spied their march and charged into them
Most cruelly, and killed and slew them.
These were true martyrs beyond doubt,
Since in the good faith they set out,
And since upon their way they fared,
Guided by the firm hope they shared   7,670

With one and all, foolish and sage,
Of fulfilling their pilgrimage.
Now in the host was great content
And noble joy and merriment.
Ye had seen many people make
Their hauberks roll, and others shake
Their heads, saying: "God, grant us aid!
Aid us, Saint Mary, Virgin Maid!
God, may we now our voices raise
In thanks, in worship and in praise!   7,680
Now we shall see Thy Holy Tomb!"
No man felt any grief or gloom
Or any sadness or distress;
For all was joy and happiness
And men did nothing but rejoice.
They all cried with a single voice:
"Lord God, it is Thy grace that hath
Conducted us. We tread the righteous path."

OPPOSITION TO THE ADVANCE ON JERUSALEM

But there were those who little heeded
These words, and who the march impeded.   7,690
It was the Templars, wise men all,
And the good knights of the Hospital,
And those who in the land were bred,
Who to the king of England said
That in their true opinion
If they on this occasion
Should lay siege to Jerusalem,
Saladin would descend on them
The while our men were busied by
The siege. The Turks would occupy   7,700
The road between the sea and hills,
And we should suffer many ills
In case our host were in this wise
Cut off from all source of supplies.

But if they did not seize the road
And in this manner discommode
Us, if the city fell to us,
Still was the plan most perilous
Unless the city were straightway
Peopled with folk who there would stay.   7,710
Since every pilgrim, dolt or sage,
Having performed his pilgrimage
Would promptly to his land return,
Back to the home where he was born;
And, with the scattering of the host,
The land would once again be lost.[32]

TWO SERGEANTS ARE AVENGED

The new year came, and on the third   Jan. 3, 1192
Morning a destined thing occurred:[33]
The Saracens, base folk and brown,
Near Casal des Plains had come down   7,720
Among the dunes and camped among
Them; there they spied the whole night long.
They came forth with the morning light
Upon our road, and these caught sight
Of sergeants twain who passed that way.
[These they attacked and smote till they]
Were cut to pieces. But God's will
Would not leave unavenged this ill;
For knowing of this ambuscade
And of the camp the Turks had made,   7,730
The king of England had repaired
To Casal des Plains, well prepared.
Geoffrey de Lusignan was there
As well. The third of the New Year
It was. Each one his war horse drives,

[32] The *Itinerarium* (p. 306) says that this advice was not heeded.

[33] The *Itinerarium* (p. 306) gives an elaborate date: 1192, a leap year, with the Dominical Letter D, the third day after Circumcision.

Hoping to save the sergeants' lives;
But they were slain and butchered; so
The Turks, who well had come to know
King Richard's swiftness and his manner
Of doing battle and his banner,   7,740
By side roads that we knew not well
Sought safety. On toward Mirabel
Fourscore departed in one band,
While others scattered through the land.
Seven were taken prisoners
Or slain. And the king drove his spurs
In his good charger's flanks, and chased
Those fourscore Turks who fled in haste
Seeking refuge in Mirabel.
He rode that day upon Fauvel,   7,750
Who bore him with such speed that he
Could catch up with the enemy
Before the men in his command
Could join their forces to his hand.
Before they came he overthrew
Two Saracens, whom he then slew.
If the pursuit had been more skilled,
Still more would have been seized or killed.
Natheless they took or slew, before
They went back to the camp, a score.   7,760

THE LEADERS DECIDE TO TURN BACK TO ASCALON

When it was past Epiphany,   After Jan. 6
The leaders and nobility
In council met. They asked advice
Of gentlemen discreet and wise
Born in the land, making request
For counsel whether it were best
To turn back or pursue their way.
The answer came without delay—
Temple and Hospital agreed
With them—'twere unwise to proceed   7,770

At that time to Jerusalem,[34]
And, if the choice were left to them,
To strengthen Ascalon were far
More wise, to guard the road and bar
The Saracens from travel on
It with supplies from Babylon
To give Jerusalem good aid.
Therefore was the decision made
To travel back to Ascalon
And rebuild wall and bastion.   7,780

NOT KNOWING THE SORE STRAITS OF THE SARACENS

When there was noised abroad this plan,
And swiftly through the host it ran
How to the leaders it seemed meet
To withdraw (I say not retreat),
The host, that so much craved to press
Ahead, was so filled with distress
That never since the Lord God made
The world was such deep grief displayed—
Such sorrow and unhappiness,
Such heartache and such wretchedness,   7,790
Such bitterness and misery—
And as for all the revelry
That erstwhile made their hearts to stir
Thinking to reach the Sepulcher,
'Twas naught beside their present grief;
And some in harsh words found relief.
They cursed this stay with violence,
And cursed the day they pitched their tents,
But had they but known the distress
In Jerusalem, the feebleness   7,800
From which the Turks suffered, the woe
They were obliged to undergo
From snow that filled the mountain passes

---

[34] Ibn al Athir (pp. 55–56) says that the Syrian Franks dissuaded Richard from his proposed march on Jerusalem.

And brought about the death in masses
Of steeds and animals, 'tis clear
And true as that ye all are here
That, had their mishaps dolorous
And sufferings been known to us, . . .
The Turks would have been put to death
At once and the town seized forthwith.   7,810

THE SLOUGH OF DESPOND

On Saint Hilary's day it was   Jan. 13
That the host grieved and mourned because
They had to turn back on their way.
Every pilgrim cursed the day
When he into the world was born,
Being heartsick at this return.
The army was in grievous state,
Sore burdened, and disconsolate.
They were most desperate for lack
Of means to bear provisions back,   7,820
For their pack beasts, by manifold
Dense rains and by the bitter cold,
Had been made weak and caused to sicken
With fever, whereby they were stricken;
When they were burdened with a load
Of goods and through the thick mud strode,
They stumbled to their knees and fell.
Then to the devil down in hell
Men cursing gave themselves. My lords,
Think not that these are idle words: 7,830
Never was goodly company
So deeply sunk in misery;
And many of the lesser folk,
Who were bent down beneath the yoke
Of illness and were sore distraught,
Would have been left upon the spot
If England's king had not with care
Caused search to be made everywhere

Till he had rescued everyone.
So all the expedition   7,840
Turned back. Upon the selfsame day
Of the return, they reached Ramleh.

THE HOST BEGINS TO DISINTEGRATE

At Ramleh, as I have just said,
Lay the host, much discomforted.
And there, a prey to grief and care
And disappointment and despair—
Despair which could not have been worse—
The army started to disperse;
For many French, dissatisfied
And angry, scattered far and wide.   7,850
Some of these men for Jaffa made,
Where for a little while they stayed;
Others went back to Acre, where
The cost of victual was not dear;
Others to Tyre, led by the lures
Of the marquis's overtures.
Some with the duke of Burgundy,
In shame and animosity,
Sought the Casal des Plains, where they
For one entire week did stay.   7,860
The king, with the indignant host
Which had in numbers greatly lost,
And Count Henry of Champagne, too,
His nephew, and their retinue
Betook them straight to Ibelin,
And found such poor shelter therein
At eve, and on such bad roads passed
That they were sullen and downcast.

WRETCHEDLY, THEY COME TO ASCALON

At Ibelin now lay the host,
Dissatisfied and ill-disposed;   7,870
And in the morn before 'twas dawn

Those men went forth who traveled on
Ahead to view the land and scout.
Having struck tents, the host set out
And, fully armed, rode on their way
Once more: by living man no day
Shall be described or told more fraught
With woes. The day before was naught
Compared with this one. They traversed
Full many an evil pass accursed,   7,880
And when their pack beasts fell it cost
Them much in victuals that were lost.
It was the will of God to try
Them thus, and thus to testify
That He grants not His joy to those
Who for Him do not suffer woes.
Betwixt midday and nones, anon
We find them come to Ascalon.[35]
They found it so severely wrecked,
So battered, beaten, and abject,   7,890
That climbing the debris to come
Inside the walls was troublesome
And hard. Such mishaps they had had
There was not one who was not glad
To rest. But later on they got
In plenty the repose they sought.

A STORM DELAYS THE ARRIVAL OF SUPPLIES

Now Ascalon lies on the sea
Of Greece. Thus was it named to me.
I never saw a town located
Fairer, or better situated,   7,900
If only it had port or entry,
For round about is all good country;
But the water is so perilous
At that point, so tempestuous,
That no vessel could ride secure

[35] The *Itinerarium* (p. 312) gives the date, January 20.

Therein. Our men must needs endure
Therefore hardship and suffering,
Because no ship could come and bring
Supplies and food into the place
By way of sea, for eight full days.   7,910
So while the storm raged, they had naught
To eat, except what they had brought
Along with them and had to hand.
No man or beast upon the land
Dared move. None ventured to set out,
For close upon them round about
Hovered their cruel enemies,
Until, with clear weather, supplies
Were brought from Jaffa to the shore.
But then the storm began once more   7,920
To rage at sea, and so severe
That food became extremely dear;
For ships and galleys that had gone
To bring them back provision
Were battered, wrecked, and cast aground,
And most of those who manned them drowned,
And all our good transport ships cast
Ashore and shattered by the blast.
These, torn down by the king's command,
Were used to build longboats. He planned   7,930
To use them, thus rebuilt anew,
But this he could not carry through.

SALADIN DISBANDS HIS ARMY

Saladin, through his spies and scouts,
Learned of our army's whereabouts
Scattered along the seacoast. Then
He told his people Saracen
To go to their own lands and stay
At home until the month of May,
When once more 'twould be time to fight.
It was not needful to incite   7,940

Them. They went with great willingness,
For they had suffered sore distress
In Syria for four entire
Years, had borne the summer's fire,
Endured the winter's bitter chill,
For which nature equipped them ill
And whereby many of them died.
Many there were who wailed and cried
In angry and resentful words,
Emirs and Persians, Turks and Kurds,   7,950
And other tribes from lands afar
Who oftentimes had gone to war
Before, and never had sustained
Such loss. Departing, they complained
And wept in lamentation
For kinsfolk slain and damage done
In Syria. Saladin's fate
Was to incur more bitter hate
Than any man. The Saracens
Reproached him with great violence   7,960
For all the Turks at Acre whom
He left unsuccored to their doom,
When such great number of them died.
So their hosts scattered far and wide,
Save those who must perforce remain,
Being of the sultan's own domain.

RICHARD REUNITES THE HOST

'Twas about Candlemas that those [36]   Feb. 2
Of our host and those of the foes
Divided, taking ways diverse,
Each man pursuing his own course.   7,970
Thereupon, to the French, who went
The first of all, King Richard sent,
Summoning them to Ascalon,
So that our forces might be one,

[36] The *Itinerarium* (p. 315) says at the end of January.

And to hold counsel and to scan
The situation, and to plan
What way to turn, and in what wise
They should pursue their enterprise;
They might far better take one path
Than separate in sinful wrath.   7,980
They sent him messages to say
That they would come and they would stay
With him only till Eastertide,
But this they also specified:
That should they at that time think best
To leave the host, and so request,
He in his turn should grant them leave
To go, and they should then receive
Safe conduct given by his hand
To go to Acre or Tyre by land.   7,990
The king yielded to their desire,
Granting their every wish entire;
Thus he contrived to reunite
The host, and made the joy more bright.

THEY REFORTIFY ASCALON

When all to these terms had acceded
And when once more the host proceeded
To reunite at Ascalon—
The accord was broken later on—
All men together therein bided.
Then they took counsel and decided   8,000
To fortify the town once more.
But all the barons were so poor
Who there within the town sojourned
Since to the host they had returned,
They dwelt in indigence so drear,
So unmistakable and clear,
That no man could observe their state
And fail to feel compassionate.
All set to work without delay,

Natheless, and cleared the base away 8,010
From one gate. Each put forth his best,
And all were marveled and impressed
At all that they accomplishèd.
From hand to hand of good knights sped
The stones; sergeants and squires as well
All labored on the citadel.
Each gave his best. None tried to shirk.
So many toiled, layman and clerk,
That great was their accomplishment;
And then, after a time, they sent 8,020
For masons, who for this were hired
And who a lengthy time required.

THE TOWERS OF ASCALON

There once had been at Ascalon—
Though now they all were broken down—
Full fifty-three fair towers, beside
The turrets, strongly fortified;
And of these, five the names still bore
Of those who founded them of yore.
Hark to the builders' names, as told
To us by those who did unfold 8,030
The tale and knew its verity:
In old days of antiquity
There reigned a man, Ham was his name,
Mighty and proud and known to fame.
He was the son of Noah, by whom
The ark was built and all from doom
Was saved. By this Ham were begotten
(Tell it if it be not forgotten)
Thirty-two sons who carried on
His reign, and who built Ascalon. 8,040
And these sons sent through every land
Under their power and command,
Through burg and city, to collect
Men skilled their towers to erect.

The Tower of the Maids was made
And built by damsels, it is said;
Whereas the knighthood of those days
The Tower of the Shields did raise;
The Tower of Blood was built sometime
By fines for different sorts of crime;   8,050
Likewise the emirs, it appears,
Built up the Tower of the Emirs;
The Bedouins raised their own tower,
Massive and strong and of great power.
These were the towers' names, as told
By those who knew the tale of old;
While other folk, of diverse sort,
Built other portions of the fort.

RICHARD ASSUMES THE COSTS

As soon as came the masons, they
Were hired without the least delay,   8,060
And the king gave himself entire,
Before all else, to pay their hire;
Nor did the greater lords forbear
To do, each one, his proper share.
But when, at times, naught else availed,
Or when the other barons failed,
The king then had the labor done
And finished, as it was begun.
And when the barons' force was spent
Or fell short of their complement,   8,070
The king, to give them cheer, conveyed
Wealth of his own to lend them aid;
He gave them so much of his own,
As it was understood and known,
That three-fourths of the city were
Paid by the king's own exchequer.
The king built up the citadel,
And later 'twas through him it fell. . . .
Of the French, who so failed him when

At Jaffa he with his brave men   8,080
Leaped from his galley to the sea,
There he displayed his gallantry,
As we, at the right time and place,
Shall show and prove so well our case
That, following our memory,
No lie shall blemish history.

· · ·

May God admit me to His glory.

RICHARD RESCUES CHRISTIAN CAPTIVES

Hear ye a strange adventure. It
Is well deserving to be writ,   8,090
And a miracle most evident.
Saladin in a group had sent
A thousand Christian captives [37] on
The road that leads to Babylon,
Guarded by men from his own ranks.
These were both Syrians and Franks;
They came to Le Daron. The Lord,
Who unto Lazarus restored
The breath of life when he was dead,
Brought succor unto them and aid.   8,100
Now hark, and ye shall hear what way.
King Richard had gone forth one day
From Ascalon, 'twixt noon and nones,
With his own brave companions,
Had gone to look at Le Daron,
The which he captured later on
And which gave peaceful sanctuary
To Saracens who used to carry
Provisions to Jerusalem
From Babylon and sheltered them   8,110
Ere Le Daron was capturèd.

[37] The *Itinerarium* (p. 318) gives 1,200 captives.

Thither these prisoners were led
And led to die a death of shame.
But why tell more! When the king came
Upon them with his company
Of knights of intrepidity
And the Turks saw his banner, they
Were filled with terror and dismay;
Into the citadel some hied
Themselves, meanwhile leaving outside   8,120
The captives, whom they did not dare
Retain, seeing the king draw near.
These prisoners unfortunate
Took refuge in a church to wait
Their fate. The king came, set them free,
And put to death each Turk whom he
Was able to lay hands upon.
Many a battle steed he won
That day, and of living Turks a score
He took, and he slew many more.   8,130
Had God not led him with His hand,
The next day all that captive band
Would have been marched away and sent
To Babylon. Imprisonment
And death therein had been their lot,
Had not the king's men succor brought.

CONRAD REFUSES TO JOIN THE HOST

When God had freed His people whom
The foe were leading to their doom,
And to King Richard given the grace
He granted in Saint Leonard's case [38]   8,140
Of setting captives free, and when
God had been thanked by all our men,

---

[38] St. Leonard was the saint who especially delivered prisoners. Bar Hebraeus (p. 339) says that Saladin sent Richard 24,000 dinars for the redemption of Saracen prisoners during the winter of 1191.

To the marquis the king addressed—
And not for the first time—request
That he should come to take his post
At Ascalon among the host
And merit thus that portion fair
Of the kingdom which fell to his share,
As sworn by oaths and covenants
In presence of the king of France.   8,150
The king sent message of this sort.
Whereat the marquis made retort
That in the host he would not set
His foot until they two had met
And spoken. This, meseems, was done
At Casal Imbert later on.

DISAFFECTION OF THE DUKE OF BURGUNDY

During the sojourn our men made
At Ascalon, where they delayed
In order and with ranks unbroken,
Harsh and reproachful words were spoken   8,160
Betwixt the duke of Burgundy
And the king. Trouble arose thereby.
The French came to the duke to ask
Their pay and took him much to task;
He did not have wherewith to pay
Them, so he went to make essay
Whether King Richard would consent
To lend more wealth than he had lent
The French upon the share that fell
To them from Acre's citadel   8,170
Last summer. No more loan the king
Would grant them. So, what with this thing
And others, they said many a word
Which I shall not write or record;
This caused the duke, angry at heart,
And many Frenchmen, to depart.

CIVIL WAR IN ACRE

To Acre straightaway they went,
And there they found in fierce dissent
The Pisans and the Genoese.
The Pisans, by their loyalties,   8,180
Continued faithful to King Guy,
Whereas the Genoese stood by
The marquis, through the circumstance
Of his oath to the king of France.
Therefore in Acre was turbulent
Disorder and embroilment;
And shouting and confusion filled
The town, and men were slain and killed.
So that the duke, 'mid these alarms,
And his French soldiers took to arms.   8,190
Observing this armipotence,
The Pisans made a brave defense,
Inflicting shame and infamy
Upon the duke of Burgundy.
Beneath the duke they slew his horse,
Making him go on foot perforce,
And then they rushed at once to close
The gates, wishing to shut out those
Who would have done great damages
Within. Because the Genoese   8,200
Unto the marquis had made known
That they would render him the town.
Thither the marquis came, with fleet
Of galleys and men armed complete
To take the city by surprise.
Then had ye seen the Pisans rise
Boldly and proudly to repel
Them with machine and mangonel.

RICHARD RESTORES ORDER

Three days in battle thus were spent,
Until in haste the Pisans sent   8,210

To seek the king of England. He
Had already set out to see
The marquis. He went overland
To Cæsarea, I understand.
The envoys found him there. He bode
Not, but swiftly onward rode
And came to Acre in dark of night;
And when the marquis learned aright
That King Richard was here again,
Nothing there was that could restrain   8,220
Him. Straight to Tyre he went apace—
From Arsur this is five leagues space [39]—
The duke of Burgundy with his
French troops had gone there before this.
And when the king, who that night lay
At Acre, was so informed, next day
He rose at dawn [40] and took in hand
The whole affair, and so well planned
That he made all the strife to cease
And gave to both contenders peace,   8,230
And reconciled the Pisans to
The Genoese, for well he knew
That if he made not peace, distress
Would follow and great harmfulness.

CONRAD SOWS DISSENSION

When in this wise the Genoese
And Pisans had been brought to peace,
After long strife, so fiercely pressed,
The king of England made request
Of the marquis, by messenger
At Casal Imbert to confer   8,240
With him, and try if some accord

[39] This verse makes no sense. G. Paris translates it: "For now the Arsur wind prevailed." This makes little better sense, and we have adhered to the literal translation
of the text. The line is omitted in the *Itinerarium*.

[40] The *Itinerarium* (p. 322) dates this as on the day after Ash Wednesday (February 20).

Between the two could be restored.
So they foregathered there: the king
And marquis held long parleying
Together, and at length consulted.
But naught, meseems, therefrom resulted.
For the marquis at once evaded
The pledge he gave the king, persuaded
By the duke of the Burgundians
And various companions   8,250
Who, urging on him to forsake
The ways of peace, caused him to break
His word. When the king learned of this,

. . .

It was most rightfully decreed
That since the marquis gave no heed
To serving God, nor sought to earn
His share of the country, in return
They should seize on his revenues
And keep the income from his use.   8,260
And hence there rose hostility
'Twixt the king and the nobility
Of France and the marquis, who drew
The French as he was wont to do.
Throughout the land this did foment
Such trouble that three-fourths of Lent [41]
(I judge, and well my words I weigh)
The king of England had to stay

. . .

In Acre, nor dared depart therefrom.   8,270

A SUCCESSFUL RAID

Three days before Palm Sunday some   Mar. 27
Of the young men of Christendom
From Jaffa rode toward Mirabel,

---

[41] The *Itinerarium* (p. 324) says from the day after Ash Wednesday (February 20) until the Tuesday before Easter (March 31).

And they were fortunate. They fell
Upon rich booty and fair sack
And with them brought it safely back.
And thirty Saracens they slew
And they took fifty captives, too.
To Jaffa they returned, where they
Kept for themselves one-half their prey,   8,280
Of which they scarce knew the amount;
The other half was for the count.[42]
The sergeants' portion then was sold
For besants Saracen, 'tis told,
Fourteen hundred or more, all sound
And of the proper weight and round.[43]

A RAID INTO EGYPT

The Saturday which followed on   Mar. 28
This day, came forth from Ascalon
All who had horses, to pursue
And capture prey of which they knew   8,290
By information gleaned from spies.
They carried out their enterprise.
Those tell, who saw this episode,
How into Egypt these men rode.
Four leagues past Le Daron they sped;
Horses and mares they capturèd.
Of sheep and cattle large and small
They took seven hundred, and withal
Took thirty camels and a score
Of asses. They took, furthermore,   8,300
More than ninescore of miscreants,[44] men
And women and small children. Then,
In satisfaction and content,
Straight back to Ascalon they went.[45]

[42] The *Itinerarium* (p. 324) calls him the count who governed the city. This would be Geoffrey de Lusignan, count of Jaffa and Ascalon.

[43] *Ibid.* (p. 325) gives 8,000 besants Saracen, "probatae monetae."

[44] *Ibid.* (p. 325) reads "fere ducentos," with their wives and children.

[45] *Ibid.* (p. 325) tells how Richard knighted the son of Saphadin, "ad hoc transmissum," on Palm Sunday.

CONRAD SUMMONS THE FRENCH

Ye have heard what I erstwhile writ
Of the disunion and the split
That caused the barons to discord.
The marquis and the duke sent word
To the host at Ascalon from Tyre,
And they did summon and require 8,310
All Frenchmen there to come straightway
To Tyre, and cleave to and obey
The marquis, by the allegiance
That they owed to the king of France.
And then did men clearly discover
And grow aware of the maneuver,
The cunning, and the trickery,
And cruel mortal enmity
Of the false marquis, and the oath
That he and the French monarch both 8,320
Swore at the time when that king started
Homeward. Thereby the French were parted
Out from the English king's command,
Who sought the welfare of the land,
As, if it please ye to give ear
A little, I shall tell ye clear.

RICHARD GRANTS THEM ESCORT

Upon Tuesday of Holy Week Mar. 31
When men to do their penance seek,
The king, wrathful and discomposed
In mien, once more rejoined the host. 8,330
On Wednesday the French barons came
Before him, to request and claim
That, as he had made covenant
To do, he unto them should grant
An escort and observe his vow.
This he accorded to them now,
And gave them of his Angevins,
His Manceaux, and his Poitevins,

And his barons of Normandy.[46]
Himself went forth in company   8,340
With them, and, shedding tears, he made
Every effort to persuade
Them to stay with him and the host
And to continue at his cost.
Seeing that he could not obtain
His will, that they would not remain,
And that his earnest prayer was spurned,
To Ascalon he now returned
And sent, without the least delay,
To his generals at Acre, to say   8,350
That all the Frenchmen should be banned
From staying there, by his command.

SALADIN RECONVENES HIS ARMY

That Thursday on which men are shrived   April 2
Was the day when sinfulness deprived
Us of the French nobility.
Deep was the host's despondency
And deep the gloom and heaviness
Of heart. Their numbers were made less
By more than seven hundred knights,
Brave, noble, trained in many fights,   8,360
Who dared not stay there with their peers.
Ye had seen many men shed tears
Because of this discord that split
Them. When the paynim learned of it,
Their gladness was immoderate,
And those who witnessed it relate
That Saladin in his content
Had letters writ at once, and sent
To the emirs of every land
That war had brought 'neath his command,   8,370
Summoning them to Syria, for

[46] The *Itinerarium* (p. 326) says the Templars, Hospitallers, and Count Henry of Champagne.

The Franks would conquer there no more;
Because, from knowledge he had gained,
Such enmity among them reigned
That he thought once more to acquire
By wealth and skill Acre and Tyre.[47]
These men obeyed, but they were loath
To come and therefore came with sloth.
They came natheless so numerous
That there were too many for us.   8,380

THE HOLY FIRE

The Saturday ere Easter Day,   April 4
Says he whose story I convey
To you, the sultan Saladin

                    .   .   .

Jerusalem at the Sepulcher;
And many a Christian prisoner,
Latin and Syrian, in chains
Was there, suffering grievous pains.
Tender and tearful moan they made
And with their tears to God they prayed   8,390
Mercy for Christianity
Thus fallen in adversity.
During the time these captives prayed
Amid the sweet tears that they shed,
Behold, the fire of heaven came,
In manner and in guise the same
As it is wont, into the lamp;
And as a man's eyes leap and ramp,
So all the people, young and eld,
Christian and Saracen, beheld   8,400
It kindled, and they all discerned
That in its wonted way it burned.
The people, at this spectacle,

---

[47] The *Itinerarium* (p. 327) reports Saladin as saying that the French had departed and "terram deserentes jam fere vacuam."

Were thrilled to see such miracle.
The Saracens amazed perceived
The sight. They said and they believed
The lamp had been enkindled by
Some magic or some sorcery.
Saladin wished to know the entire
Truth; he then ordered that the fire   8,410
Be quenched. So his men put it out
At once. But this availed them naught,
[For all they did could not restrain]
The lamp from kindling once again.
He had it quenched once more. The Lord
God wished that His own truthful Word
Should beyond any doubt appear
In His own city, bright and clear,
So a third time He lit the light.
When Saladin perceived aright   8,420
That faith to which the Christians hold,
Then, in all truth, he spoke and told
His Turks that he was soon to die,
Or that the city would not lie
Much longer under his command,
And, as I learn and understand,
He did not long survive, but died
Before the next year's Lententide.[48]

EASTER AT ASCALON

At Easter,[49] that high feast and great,   April 5
The king held mighty court of state   8,430
To make his people less forlorn,
And caused his banners to be borne
Outside of Ascalon, and spread. . . .
Each man on what he pleased was fed.
The court was held for but one day:
The morrow, without more delay,

[48] Saladin died on Wednesday, March 4, 1193.
[49] The *Itinerarium* (p. 329) says this was on April 5.

The king had work resumed upon
The walls, and took up that begun
By the French soldiers, but which they
Abandoned when they went away.   8,440
Also he saw to the repair
Of all that fell to his own share.[50]
Ye heard me tell the tale but now,
Those who were pleased to listen, how
The convoy of the barony
From Poitou and from Normandy,
From Maine and from Anjou,[51] had gone
And convoyed the French barons on
To Acre, and then returned once more.

THE FLESHPOTS OF TYRE

Now shall ye hear how the French bore   8,450
Themselves at Tyre, whither they went
During the time that there they spent,
What good derived from their affair,
What they sought to accomplish there,
What tasks and expeditions,
What pains and tribulations,
They for the love of God endured.
Those who were present there assured
Us that they danced through the late hours
Of night, their heads bedecked with flowers   8,460
Entwined in garland and in crown;
Beside wine casks they sat them down
And drank until matins had rung;
Then homeward made their way among
The harlots, swearing great oaths, breaking
Gates and portals down, and making
Loud cry of foolish words and strife—
Such was, forsooth, their way of life.

[50] The *Itinerarium* (p. 330) here inserts a short chapter which tells how Richard reconnoitred St. George on Easter Tuesday and Daron on Wednesday.

[51] These are not mentioned by the *Itinerarium*, which had stated that Templars and Hospitallers formed the escort.

I do not say that all of these
Men did and said such villainies,   8,470
Because the good men, who there dwelt
And stayed against their wishes, felt
Most grief-stricken at this disaccord,
Which was not ended by the Lord.
To great disgust such acts incited
Them. But wicked folk delighted
At the discord and severance
Of the barons and the king of France.

BUT WHERE ARE THE SNOWS OF YESTERYEAR?

When Charlemagne, that king so great
Who conquered many a realm and state,   8,480
Set forth to wage his war in Spain,
Leading with him that gallant train
Whom Ganelon, to the dismay
Of France, to Marsile did betray;
Again, when he in Saxony
Did such great feats of gallantry,
When he beat Guiteclin and broke
The power of the Saxon folk
With his companions mettlesome;
And when he led his host to Rome   8,490
When, with a great force, Agoland
At Reggio came from sea to land
In that rich realm, Calabria;
In the other war, when Syria
Was lost and conquered and invaded,
And Antioch likewise blockaded;
And 'midst the strife and fierce onslaught
Of battles 'gainst the paynim fought,
Where many of them lost their life,
There was no quarreling or strife   8,500
In those old days for men to quench
Of who was Norman and who French,
Manceau, Burgundian, or who

Was Breton, who was from Poitou,
And who from England, who from Flanders.
Then were no bitter words or slanders
Cast, or tauntings harsh with scorn.
But by each man was honor borne,
And all were called Franks, whether they
Were white of skin, or brown, or bay.   8,510
And when sin caused them to discord,
The princes harmony restored,
And since they dwelt in peace among
Themselves, the strife endured not long.[52]
Even thus should these our men have done
And, acting with discretion,
Given a good example, rather
Than vex and harass one another.

[52] This harmony among Charlemagne's paladins does not seem to have had any marked effect on Ganelon; nor does the record of the quarrels among the leaders of the first crusade, especially the Normans and Provençaux, bear out this rather idealistic picture of the "good old days."

CHAPTER VIII

ILL TIDINGS FROM ENGLAND

Past Easter Day, at the great passage,[1]   April 5
Unto King Richard came a message   8,520
Which to our army was the cause
Of woe. The prior of Hereford [2] 'twas—
In England lies this priory—
Who sought the king out speedily
In Syria, and to him there
Brought tidings neither good nor fair.
The letters that he bore,[3] all sealed
And written in great stress, revealed
That the lieutenants he had placed
In England in his stead were chased   8,530
From out their stronghold and domain;
And in the land folk had been slain
The while his men were thus expelled;
And this the prior had beheld.

---

[1] The two great annual expeditions to Syria went from the west in the spring and the autumn, usually in March and September. The contracts and regulations which prevailed for the *passagium* to Syria among the Genoese are discussed in E. H. Byrne, *Genoese Shipping*, pp. 49–58.

[2] This prior of Hereford has been identified by Stubbs as Robert, who later became abbot of Munchelaey (Siedschlag, p. 123, no. 121).

[3] The *Itinerarium* (p. 333) says letters from William, bishop of Ely, the chancellor.

The letter then went on to say
His chancellor was sent away
From England by the king's own brother; [4]
And in no treasury or other
Strong place, save a church, was aught
Left for safekeeping that was not   8,540
Despoiled by his rapacity.
With criminal audacity
He so mistreated and oppressed
The chancellor, a lord and priest,
Master and bishop, too, that he
For refuge fled to Normandy.
Also there was another thing:
He strove hard to betray the king,
During the latter's pilgrimage,
By asking of the baronage   8,550
Of England oaths of fealty
[And sought to get illegally] [5]
What the exchequer could collect.
"Fair sire, I pray you with respect,"
The prior said, "and I bespeak
You to come home and vengeance wreak
On those who have wrought all this ill,
Else they will do more evil still:
When they have seized the whole domain,
Not without strife shall you regain   8,560
Your land." My lords, now marvel not
If the king, who so bravely wrought
For God in far-off lands, where he
Endured such woe and misery,
Was sorely troubled in his heart.
For who doth such ill news impart

---

[4] The *Gesta* (pp. 207–25) and Roger of Hoveden (III, 134–55) give details of the rebellion in England against the rule of William Longchamp, the chancellor-justiciar.

[5] The *Itinerarium* (p. 333) tells how John seized the castles and revenues in England. The lacuna here is probably only one line, not two as G. Paris suggests, for the verse permits only a lacuna of one or three lines.

Disheartens any fair and frank
Good man who fears to lose his rank.
Now were these tidings far diffused;
No men were ever so confused,   8,570
Grief-stricken, and disheartened quite
At thinking of one man who might
Make his departure from the host;
For they believed their cause were lost
If the king left them to their fate,
And they were in precarious strait,
A prey to strife and to discord.
And peace would never be restored
'Twixt those of Tyre and Ascalon.

RICHARD ASKS COUNSEL OF HIS BARONS

The next day, between tierce and none,   8,580
The king summoned the baronage
And told them of the embassage
That came from England to his hand,
How men essayed to steal his land
And how they had deposed and reft
Of power the chancellor he left
To govern for him in his place;
Therefore he must his steps retrace.
He said, if it should happen so
That he were thus obliged to go,   8,590
That he would leave, at his expense,
Three hundred knights of excellence
In Syria, two thousand, too,
Of sergeants, loyal, brave, and true.
He said it was his wish to know
And to be answered who should go
Homeward with him to share his fate.
He set them to deliberate
Whether to go or to remain,
For he wished no man to constrain.   8,600

THE BARONS ASK THAT CONRAD BE MADE KING

The nobles in that gathering
Spoke and took counsel on the thing
Which the king laid before them thus.
Each one of them was at a loss
To know what he should do or say.
They thought of all the disarray
And how there was in all the land
No single master leader's hand,
For that the realm was split in twain,
Nor could King Guy ever attain   8,610
To mastery of his own share,
And the marquis would not repair
To the host, whatever pledge they made,
But always with the Frenchmen stayed,
So all was strife and altercation.
When they recalled this situation,
They went back to the king and told
Their thought, nor did they aught withhold:
To wit, unless he left a lord
Whom all could trust, with one accord,   8,620
And who was skilled in arts of war,
Where'er he came from, near or far,
The knights would all, abandoning
The realm, fare homeward with the king.
The king, thinking to go his way
At once, asked them without delay
Which of the kings they wished for sire
And which one they did not desire,
Whether the marquis or King Guy;
And one and all they made reply,   8,630
Kneeling before him as they spoke,
The small, the great, the middle folk,
And prayed and asked with but one word
That the marquis be made their lord,

For it was he who was most fit
To aid the realm and succor it.

RICHARD, ACQUIESCING, SENDS COUNT HENRY TO TYRE

When the king saw that everyone
So willed, without exception,
He blamed those present who erstwhile
Were wont the marquis to revile;   8,640
Since all the same desire expressed,
He yielded now to their request,
And noble barons straightway sent
To fetch him there in great content,
And fetch, too, the whole company
Of French, and bring back amity.
This choice that ye heard me relate
Was not a thing of little weight,
But one which fools and wise men shared;
Now the ambassadors prepared   8,650
Themselves. Count Henry of Champagne
There was, and with him in his train
My lord Otto of Trasignies,
Both men of noble family,
And William of Caieux, also.
They set helms on their heads, and so
Went forth their messages to bear
To the marquis, and bring him cheer,
And give him welcome news, of such
A sort as would delight him much   8,660
And make the French at Tyre content.
They took to horse and forth they went.
When they arrived [6] what things befell
Ye presently shall hear me tell.

CONRAD'S EARLIER NEGOTIATIONS WITH SALADIN

'Tis true and past all doubt that when
The French barons and noblemen

---

[6] The *Itinerarium* (p. 336) says that they were to go to Tyre by galleys.

Beside the marquis took their stand,
And when King Richard gave command
So many times (as it has been
Related and as ye have seen)   8,670
That he, to win the land, should come
And join the host of Christendom,
The marquis would not come, wherefore
He merited misfortune sore.
Now shall ye hear what he was fain
To do, to trammel God's campaign.
Against the honor of the crown
And 'gainst the host of Ascalon
With Saladin he had assured
A peace, on these sworn terms procured: 8,680
That the marquis was to proceed
To Saladin; the terms agreed
Gave him half of Jerusalem.[7]
He had already settled them
Like one of treacherous repute.
Also he was to have Beirut,
Sidon was to be his likewise,
With all the land that round them lies;
And in addition to all this
One half the realm was to be his.   8,690
This was agreed by Saladin.
But 'twas the emir Saphadin

[7] Details of the negotiations conducted by Conrad are given by Beha ed Din (pp. 303–30). In September 1191 Conrad had offered the sultan his friendship and alliance if Saladin would grant him the lordship of Sidon and Beirut as well as of Tyre. Before Saladin was willing to surrender his cities to Conrad, he insisted that the marquis give evidence of his good faith by releasing all his Moslem prisoners and attacking Acre. While these negotiations were in progress, Richard offered the proposed marriage of Joanna with Saphadin, and Saladin preferred to treat with Richard if possible. When, however, it was found impossible to arrange any terms with Richard, the negotiations with Conrad were resumed. Saladin offered the marquis the lordship of any city he could take from the Franks, but with the stipulation that all Moslem prisoners should be released. It was further stipulated that should Richard grant Conrad the kingdom of Jerusalem, any treaty between Richard and Saladin should have precedence over the agreements between Conrad and the sultan.

Refused consent to such a pact.
Later 'twas told us as a fact
That to the sultan thus he spoke:
"God forbid, sire, that you should make
A peace with Christianity,
Whate'er the importunity,
Save with the king of England. (There
Is nowhere Christian knight more fair.)   8,700
I neither wish it nor consent."
So the affair no further went,
Yet it was spread abroad and known,
And spoken of by everyone,
For Steven of Turnham, a man
Sent as envoy to the sultan,
Was in Jerusalem when came
These men, whom many knew by name:
There was Balian of Ibelin,[8]
Falser than any fiend of sin;   8,710
There was Renaud of Sidon,[9] who
Had come to seek and to pursue
A peace unclean and foul and lewd.
By dogs he should have been pursued.

[8] Balian d'Ibelin, lord of Ibelin and Rama, was one of the leading barons of the native Frank nobility. At the death of King Amaury, Balian had married his widow, Marie Comnena, and had received with her the city and fief of Naplouse. Balian was of the party of Raymond of Tripoli as opposed to Guy de Lusignan, and later supported Conrad as the most suitable candidate for the throne. As the step-father of Princess Isabelle, he played an important part in securing her divorce from Humphrey and her marriage to Conrad. Balian was highly respected by Saladin, who conferred upon him the territory of Caïmont in 1192 (*Eracles*, p. 198). His friendship with Saladin made him valuable as an envoy, and he was employed not only by Conrad on this occasion but also later by Richard when the final peace was drawn up (*Eracles*, p. 199 variant; Beha ed Din, p. 384). Balian died around 1193–94, leaving his fiefs to his sons John d'Ibelin, later lord of Beirut, and Philip, who became regent of Cyprus (LaMonte, "John d'Ibelin," *Byzantion*, XII [1937], 420–24).

[9] Renaud of Sidon, lord of Sidon and Beaufort, 1165–1200, was another leader among the Franco-Syrian nobility who supported Raymond of Tripoli and later Conrad. He was connected with the royal house and with the Ibelins through marriage, having married first Agnes de Courtenay and second Helvis, the daughter of Balian d'Ibelin and Marie Comnena. Beha ed Din tells at length of his attempts to outwit Saladin by futile negotiations when the sultan was besieging Beaufort (pp. 142–43, 150–53) and mentions him as Conrad's ambassador (pp. 317, 321–22).

CONRAD RECEIVES THE NEWS OF HIS ELECTION

The messengers we told about
And whom we witnessed setting out
Rode on their mission day by day
As they had planned, and in this way
They came to Tyre in proper course.
There each dismounted from his horse   8,720
And sought the marquis, to declare
The purpose that had brought them there.
They greeted him with courtesy.
While he and all his company
Into great peals of laughter broke
For greeting. Then Count Henry spoke
And said, in all good will disposed:
"The king, Sir Marquis, and the host
Of Christian knights at Ascalon
Upon you have bestowed the crown   8,730
And realm of Syria. Come, lead
Your marshaled host. You shall succeed
In conquering it gallantly."
Then, says the story truthfully,
Such joy throughout his heart was spread
That, while his lords hearkened, he said,
With hands raised toward the firmament
(Which later many did resent):
"Oh, fair Lord God, Who did create
Me [and with soul illuminate],   8,740
Thou Who art King of truth and good,
Since, Sire, Thou knowest mine aptitude
To rule Thy kingdom righteously,
Let now the crown be given me;
But if Thou feel I am not fit
Do not give Thy consent to it."

PREPARATIONS FOR CONRAD'S CORONATION

Now were the tidings heard and told
And spread broadcast in the stronghold
That the marquis would rule the land

As king: such was the host's demand.   8,750
Now was rejoicing marvelous,
And eager men were anxious
To make them ready to set out.
In search of gold they went about,
And silver; each man sought a loan,
Since each man must provide his own.
You had seen the arms of many a knight
And helms and chaplets furbished bright,
And many a squire had you now seen
Making the sword blades fair and keen.   8,760
You had seen many hauberks rolled,
Sergeants and knights in postures bold,
To smite upon the hated foe,
And men of fortitude, I trow,
If God, Who knew how they were made
Better than we, had given His aid.
Ye had seen many men delight,
Yet it is well to learn aright,
And ye should learn that joy or pleasure
Should not be carried beyond measure,   8,770
Nor should grief cause too much distress.
All felt good will and gladsomeness
And joy at this conclusion;
Count Henry now to Acre had gone
To seek loans, with the baronage
Who with him bore the embassage.
There they made ready and disposed
Themselves to go back to the host,
When the event, of which I tell
The very purest truth, befell.   8,780

CONRAD IS ASSASSINATED

It happed that the marquis one day
Dined with the bishop of Beauvais,
And having taken leave, he went
Forth in great solace and content

And walked before the money-changers.
Hear now how joy, beset with dangers,
Is swiftly turned to desolation.
He walked along in great elation,
When two youths, lightly clad, who wore
No cloaks and each a dagger bore,   8,790
Made straight for him and with one bound
Smote him and bore him to the ground,
And each one stabbed him with his blade.[10]
The wretches, who thuswise betrayed
Him, were of the Assassin's men:
They killed one of them there and then;
Within a church the other sought
For refuge. It availed him naught,
For he was seized and hauled outside
And dragged about until he died.   8,800
But those who gathered there inquired
And asked of him, ere he expired,
How the marquis had done them ill
And what impelled them thus to kill
Him, and what man had sent them there.
Thereon, the traitor did declare
—And later it was verified—
That long since they had come to bide
Close to the marquis, but that they
Had not contrived a means to slay   8,810
Him till that day when their emprise
Brought tears into so many eyes.
The Old Man of the Mount, in hate,
Had sent them to assassinate
The marquis. He commands to kill
All whom he hates or wishes ill,
As it shall presently appear
To all those who are pleased to hear.

[10] The murder of Conrad occurred on April 28 (Beha ed Din, p. 333; Roger of
Hoveden, III, 181; Ernoul, p. 290; Ralph of Diceto, II, 104; Abu Chamah, p. 52).
Ibn al Athir (p. 58) says incorrectly April 29.

THE ASSASSINS

The Old Man of the Mountain's way,
Which each doth to his heir convey,   8,820
Is to have many children brought
Into his house, and reared and taught
In arts and ways of every sort,
Till they learn wisely to comport
Themselves. And there they dwell among
Wise men, till they know every tongue
Spoken in every land throughout
The world. And their faith is so stout,
So dark, so cruel, so ingrained
By the care wherewith they are trained,   8,830
That when they are called before the Old
Man of the Mount, and by him told
That they, to prove their penitence
For sins and win his confidence,
Must slay some man of high renown,
They deem it as their lifework's crown.
Then each receives a dagger, keen
And sharp and bright and polished clean;
Thereupon they go forth, and spy
On this man, and with him ally   8,840
Themselves, and with smooth tongue they win
A place among his men and kin,
Until they end his life. In turn,
'Tis their conviction that they earn
The highest joys of paradise.
This cannot be in any wise.

DESPAIR AT CONRAD'S DEATH

My lords, drawn from this kind of folk
Were these two men of whom we spoke,
Who slew the marquis, as we told.
His followers in their arms took hold   8,850
Of him and raised him from the ground
Gently; from where he got his wound

To the house wherein he dwelt they bore
Him. Then was lamentation sore
And the crowd gathered round outside.
He lived a brief time, and then died.
But not before he had confessed
His sins, and as a last behest
Said to his wife, the marchioness—
Seeing her weeping in distress—   8,860
That she must guard Tyre as her own,
With care, nor render up the town
Save to the king of England or
The country's lawful governor.
He died, and in the earth was laid.
Laymen and clerks great mourning made;
They went to the Hospital to bury
His corse, 'midst grief extraordinary.
Never were folk more dolorous
Than they: but God had willed it thus.   8,870
Now are the tidings spread, destroyed
The gladsomeness that overjoyed
Us, and that had such short duration
In the land that looked for its salvation
In him who was so soon to leave
It. The land took itself to grieve,
So stricken and disconsolate
As no man ever could relate.

THE FOUL BREATH OF CALUMNY

Hear now how laboreth the devil
And how he doth engender evil,   8,880
The which, adroitly multiplied,
Doth spread its fell contagion wide
And far. Hear how his increased power
Did lasting damage at this hour,
And all because of words that folk
Most envious and accursèd spoke.
These folk, hating the noble King

Richard, belittled everything
He did.[11] They should have been cast out.
They said Richard had brought about   8,890
The murder of the marquis by
The ways of stealth and bribery,[12]
And sent to tell the king of France
To guard himself with vigilance
'Gainst the Assassins, at whose hand
The marquis fell; to the sweet land
Of France four had been sent, prepared
To murder him, so they declared,
By order of the English king.
God! What a loathsome slandering!   8,900
How basely did they work who sent
Such message and admonishment,
Which made so many men a prey,
Later, to grief, woe, and dismay!

[11] The *Itinerarium* (p. 341) says that it was the French.

[12] The guilt for the assassination of Conrad has provided matter for considerable speculation. Contemporaries were in no agreement on the question, and Richard, Saladin, and the Old Man of the Mountain, head of the religious sect of the Assassins, were all blamed according to the taste of the writer. Abu Chamah (pp. 53–54) accepts Richard as the guilty party and praises God that the infidels thus destroy each other. Bar Hebraeus (p. 339) reports that the murderers at first said they were employed by Richard, but later admitted that they had been sent by the Old Man of the Mountain. Beha ed Din (p. 333) merely states that the assassins claimed to have been sent by Richard; Ibn al Athir (pp. 58–59), however, maintains that Saladin himself hired the assassins to kill either Richard or Conrad, and that they killed Conrad, not wanting to relieve Saladin of the threat of Richard's presence. The most detailed accounts are given by Ernoul (pp. 288–90) and the *Eracles* (pp. 192–93). According to their version Conrad had seized a merchant ship belonging to the Assassins when it came into Tyre and had refused any compensation or satisfaction when the Old Man objected. The Old Man, insulted and indignant, thereupon dispatched two of his men to avenge himself on the marquis. There were, however, rumors that the murder had been done at the order of Richard, and King Philip experienced considerable uneasiness therefrom. A letter, supposed to have been written by Sinan, the Old Man of the Mountain, in which he definitely stated that it was by his order that Conrad met his death, deserves no credence. It is dismissed by Ilgen as probably a product of the English chancery in an attempt to exonerate the king. However, Ilgen, who devotes an entire appendix to the question of the guilt, comes to a positive conclusion that Sinan, not Richard, was to blame. (Ilgen, *Markgraf Conrad von Montferrat*, pp. 127–35.)

Later this treacherous lie was reason
Wherefore the king was put in prison,
And all his deeds of gallantry
In Syria brought him enmity.

COUNT HENRY IS ELECTED KING

When the marquis was laid to rest
And men their mourning had expressed   8,910
As by their duty they were bound,
The lords of France were to be found
In their tents, outside the city wall,
More than ten thousand, great and small;
The great held parley and addressed
Unto the marchioness request
That she surrender peacefully
The town to them in amity
To govern for the king of France.
She answered without hesitance   8,920
That when the king returned thereto
She would yield it, without ado,
To him, unless some other lord
Were chosen. This their anger spurred.
While they were arguing and striving
And in this fashion were contriving,
As I relate, to seize on Tyre,
Count Henry came, the noble sire,
Approached the town and entered it—
So he whose tale I tell hath writ.   8,930
Soon as the people saw him, they
Without postponement or delay
Chose him as king, and so decided;
Thus had the will of God provided.
They came before him, and they spoke
To him, to pray him and invoke
Him to be lord and sovereign
Of Syria and its domain,
And wed the widowed marchioness,

Who was the realm's inheritress.   8,940
Delaying little his reply,
He made all haste to satisfy
Them: that since God had called him there
And they had chosen him as heir
To have the kingdom's government,
He wished to have the full consent
Of his uncle, who was England's king.
So he sent messengers to bring
The king's will, so that he might voice
His thought upon the barons' choice.   8,950

RICHARD HEARS THE NEWS

In May, when leaf and flower revived
Afresh, the messages arrived
At where King Richard was, to tell
Him tidings of what fate befell
The marquis, as our tale explains.
The king was then on Ramleh plains,[13]
Fast riding through the fallow land
Pursuing closely on a band
Of Saracens, who 'fore him fled
As one whom they most held in dread;   8,960
For, since the time when God created
The earth, no man exterminated
So many Turks or wrought such woe
Among them. Often he would go
To fight the Saracens, and came
Back with their heads, like so much game—
Ten, twenty, thirty, would succumb
Before him, grieving pagandom—
And when he undertook to bring
Back living captives, the brave king   8,970
Would do so. No one man, in brief,

---

[13] Ernoul (p. 290) and the *Eracles* (p. 194) say that Richard was at Acre at the time.

Wrought them so much of death and grief.[14]
And now the messengers, who strive
To bring news to the king, arrive;
They come, and they communicate
The count's greeting, and they relate
The adventure of the marquis, and
How all the people now demand
That he be ruler of the realm.

       . . .   8,980

For great and small with one accord
Have chosen him to be their lord
And to espouse the marchioness.
He will not do these things unless
The king so will, and he thereby
Can best serve Christianity.

RICHARD APPROVES THE ELECTION OF HENRY

The king reflected a long time,
To hear how by so foul a crime
And by such misadventure great
The marquis came to meet his fate.   8,990
But his delight was marvelous
To learn folk were desirous
To give his nephew rank so high
And honor. He thus made reply:
"Lords, sergeants, much do I desire,
Please God, that he be royal sire
When that the land is conquerèd;
The marchioness he should not wed,
Her whom the marquis took away
From her true lord, and with her lay   9,000

[14] The *Itinerarium* (pp. 334–36) inserts four chapters omitted by the *Estoire*. They deal with the ransom of Mashtub and with a detailed account of a series of raids and counter raids engaged in by Franks and Moslems in the country around Gaza, Blanchegarde, and Daron. Richard was personally the hero of two of these incidents, in one of which he slew a great boar and in the other killed four Saracens and captured seven.

Counter to God's and reason's laws.
Such wrongful doing should be cause
Why he this marriage should not make
With her,[15] if he my counsel take;
But let him be the king and rule.

. . .

I give him Acre for his use
And all the seaport's revenues,
Tyre and Jaffa, and command
To govern all the conquered land,   9,010
For 'tis my will he have them. Say
To him that with what speed he may,
He come and join the host's campaign,
Bringing the Frenchmen in his train.
I wish to capture Le Daron
If the Turks dare to wait thereon."
These envoys hearkened to receive
The king's word. Then they took their leave
And set forth to bear full account
Of it to Tyre unto the count,   9,020
Relating to him everything
That had been told them by the king.

ISABELLE MARRIES HENRY AND MAKES HIM KING

What more of this should I relate?
About the count the joy was great
At Tyre when the envoys returned.

---

[15] Richard's opposition to the marriage may well have been due to the fact, commented upon by the eastern writers, though ignored by the western, that Isabelle was at the moment pregnant with a child by Conrad (*Eracles*, p. 193, variant; Ibn al Athir, p. 59; Abu Chamah, pp. 52–53; Bar Hebraeus, p. 339). Or it may have been caused by an unwillingness to have Henry's title dependent on his wife. Richard could not but recall the difficulties which beset Guy, who held his throne through his wife, and may have wished to spare Henry a possible repetition of such troubles. Or again he may have opposed the marriage with the thought that as Isabelle's husband Henry would be too closely involved with baronial families which had not been friendly to Richard. The *Eracles* gives an entirely different account, according to which Henry was reluctant to marry Isabelle, but Richard insisted on it.

Great crowds of lords gathered, concerned
To offer counsel and advice,
And all gave counsel in this wise—
That he should wed the marchioness.
He did not dare do, nonetheless,   9,030
That which the English king had banned.
But she was heiress of the land,
And the count still was covetous
Of her. The thing was managed thus:
The countess, her own self—though some
Essayed to dissuade her therefrom—
Took the keys of the city and
Gave them into the count's own hand.
The French delayed not in the least,
But sent straightway to fetch the priest   9,040
And caused the count to wed the dame.[16]
My soul, I should have done the same,
For she was fair and beautiful,
And, so may God be merciful
To me, the count, unless I err,
Was well disposed to marry her.
Now was there joy and wedding sport:
I think that in my life such sort
I never yet did hear or see.
'Twas settled without jealousy,   9,050
With none contentious or irate.
The land was in a hopeful state:
The count, who held its governance,
Was nephew of the king of France

[16] There is considerable disagreement about the exact date of Henry's marriage to Isabelle. According to Abu Chamah (p. 52) the wedding took place on the very day of Conrad's murder; Ernoul (pp. 290–91) dates the murder on Tuesday and the marriage the following Thursday. Ralph of Diceto (p. 104) says that the marriage took place May 5, which would agree with the statements of the *Estoire* and the *Itinerarium* that it was after the first of May. The earlier date would not allow time for the messages which Ambroise says were sent back and forth; nevertheless, Ernoul's narrative, according to which Richard brought Henry with him and was present, seems in some ways preferable.

And of England's brave king, too. He sent
His word through the whole land's extent,
To Acre and Jaffa and elsewhere,
To seize the strongholds and declare
That homage unto him was due;
He had the summons cried unto   9,060
The host, so that in unison
The lords might move to take Daron.

HENRY IS JOYFULLY RECEIVED IN ACRE

When that the feasts were done, and when
The count had gathered all his men,
By counsel of the baronage
And Frenchmen of his lineage
He planned to go to Acre, and lead
Them there, equip them at their need,
And buy feed and provision
For marching on toward Ascalon.   9,070
He left good guards at Tyre, to spy
And keep their watch from points on high
O'er town and country, far and wide,
Lest evil folk should slip inside.
The count took his wife with him.[17] She
Was white as any gem to see.
Now forth from Tyre the host pursues
Its way. And now to Acre news
Of the count's coming there is sent.
And everyone is so content   9,080
And satisfied that he should reign
O'er them that they can scarce refrain
From making merry day and night.
Ye had seen the streets richly bedight:
In gladsome celebration
Men gathered in procession,
While courts and windows were adorned
With censers in which incense burned.

[17] The *Itinerarium* (p. 349) says with the duke of Burgundy.

And, armed in their accouterment,
The townsfolk forth from Acre went, 9,090
Full sixty thousand, bent to greet him
And to go on till they could meet him,
To show that they as lord revered
Him, and unto his cause adhered.
The clergy to the minster bore him
And holy relics placed before him.
He kissed the Cross, nor failed to bring,
With many more, his offering.
Then to the palace they conveyed him
And very ample welcome made him. 9,100
The count is richly lodged. Ah, would
That I had anything so good!

GUY ACQUIRES CYPRUS

When the count thus became the sire
Of Jaffa, Arsur, Acre, and Tyre,
King Guy was left without a realm,
Who got such strokes upon his helm
And paid the price he had to pay
Only to see it reft away.
He suffered many cruel blows
And many injuries and woes, 9,110
Not for his sins, because no king
Had more good will in everything.
One single fault alone he had:
He did not know what things were bad.
This fault men call simplicity.
'Twas he who with audacity
Besieged the town of Acre when
'Twas captured by the Saracen.
Before his fortunes came to naught
It happened that the Templars bought 9,120
The isle of Cyprus from the king,
Who had won it with his battling.
But then this bargain was undone,

So that King Guy was later on
Made emperor thereof and lord,[18]
And this somewhat his pride restored.

CONTRADICTORY NEWS FROM ENGLAND

While the marquis at Tyre beneath
The thrusts of daggers met his death,
We saw, both then and later on,
On many an occasion,   9,130
How envoys came, who to the king
Of England gave disquieting:
While some brought him anxiety,
Others spoke of security.
Some told him he should come away,
While others counseled him to stay
And serve still for the Lord God's sake.
Thus each one in his own way spake:
Some told him that his land remained
At peace, and that no strife there reigned;   9,140
Others assured him it was rent
Apart by warfare and dissent,
So that what one man would confide
To him, by others was denied,
And 'tis no marvel if he knew
Not what course he would best pursue,
Or if he felt extreme concern
Because of the French king's return.

[18] This title is wrong; Guy was never emperor of Cyprus. He was king of Jerusalem and continued to use the title of "king" after he removed to Cyprus, but he was never officially called king of Cyprus. After his death Aymeri used only the title lord of Cyprus until the royal title was bestowed upon him by the grant of the emperor, Henry VI, in 1197 (*Eracles*, p. 212; Mas Latrie, *Histoire*, I, 126–28). Guy had already purchased the island of Cyprus before the death of Conrad. Richard had sold it to the Templars, but the Knights turned it back after a short and unsuccessful rule. Guy paid the Templars 40,000 besants and pledged 60,000 which were still due to Richard (*Eracles*, p. 191; Mas Latrie, *Histoire*, I, 37–38). The exact chronology is a bit vague; Guy seems to have entered into possession of the island about the same time that Henry became king of Jerusalem.

Who has bad neighbors, so folk say,
Awakens to an evil day.   9,150

RICHARD MARCHES TO LE DARON

During the time while the French folk,
Of whom some time ago I spoke,
At Acre were working to prepare
Their harness and themselves for war
To go lay siege to Le Daron—
Count Henry of these lords was one—
In God's name, Who gives everything
Of good, from Ascalon the king
Set forth. He would not longer stay.
He bade his men load and convey   9,160
Engines to Le Daron by sea;
He armed his goodly soldiery,
And he took sergeants in his hire,
Paying them richly. Through the entire
Countryside he distributed
Them through the fortresses, and said
That they should keep close oversight
On them, and watch them well by night,
Nor let the caravans pass through,
Nor let the Turks their way pursue   9,170
To Le Daron, as they were used
To do. Much harm had this produced
For us. King Richard, brave and good,
Then mounted on his horse, and rode
Forth with his household troops alone;
One Sunday he reached Le Daron.   May 17
Before Le Daron he took stand
With all the barons in his band,
Yet all their numbers were so few
That neither they nor the king knew   9,180
How to attack the stronghold best.
If on all sides they should invest

It and the Turks sallied to assail
Their force, they never could prevail
Against a violent attack,
And they must needs be driven back.
Therefore, they gathered on one side

.   .   .

Skirmished and harassed them anew
And then within the fort withdrew   9,190
And set themselves with utmost care
Their strong defenses to prepare,
Barring their firm and sturdy gate,
In which their confidence was great.

RICHARD SETS UP HIS SIEGE MACHINERY

After the Turks withdrew and barred
Their gate and fortified their guard,
The vessels came upon the scene
And disembarked each war machine,
Carried in sections to the strand.
The valiant king of England's land,   9,200
Himself, with his own men, meseems,
Upon their shoulders bore the beams
Thereof, carrying strut and rod
On foot. With sweaty brows they trod
Upon the sand, nigh a league's course,
Laden like any mare or horse.
Then the machines were set up there
And given to the constables' care.
The king kept one in his own power
Wherewith was stormed the greatest tower.   9,210
The Normans, men of valiant heart,
Also had one for their own part;
I think the soldiers from Poitou
Had one for their own service, too.
Upon the stronghold all three flung
Their stones, causing great fear among

The Turks, who must have confidence
In their full stores and strong defense.
But the king, without let or stay,
Assailed it ever, night and day,   9,220
And with such fierceness on them smote
That they were marvelous distraught.

AND ASSAILS THE WALLS

Seventeen towers and turrets there
Were on Le Daron, strong and fair;
Surpassing all the others' might
Was one great tower of loftier height.
A deep moat girt it all around,
Which masonry on one side bound,
While the other of bare rock was made.
But they grew timid and afraid,   9,230
Seeing no way they could escape.
King Richard had his soldiers sap
Beneath the ground most skilfully
Until they reached the masonry,
The which they shattered from behind;
And next the wall they undermined,
Flinging the earth back from their works.
The engines hurled rocks at the Turks:
A mangonel, set up erect
On their great tower, thereby was wrecked,   9,240
Which caused them sorrow and dismay.
See how in many a different way
Attacks beset the citadel!
The Turks, defending themselves well,
From battlement and loophole cast
Their shafts, that rained down thick and fast
To strike our soldiers on the face;
But when they moved from place to place,
Our crossbowmen upon them spied,
And artfully their weapons plied   9,250
With all the skill that they could wield,

And missiles poured on targe and shield,
And wounded many; scarce they dared
To move, and very ill they fared.
Behold now how the gate is shattered
And burned by fire, and split, and battered
By the king's mighty siege machine!
A fierce attack ye might have seen,
And the defenders sorely pressed,
Discouraged, hemmed in, and distressed;   9,260
For they are harried day and night
And much disheartened by their plight.

RICHARD REFUSES TO GRANT TERMS

King Richard and his lords went on
Thus with their siege of Le Daron.
Nor day nor night did they relax
For three full days their bold attacks.
The fourth day, which on Friday fell,[19]   May 22
The Turks of whom I speak saw well
That they no longer could withstand
The onslaughts which on every hand   9,270
Filled them with terror and dismay;
That all throughout the fortress lay
Men stricken down with many a wound;
That under and above the ground
They were beleaguered and enclosed,
The while the king was all disposed
To capture them with ease. This state
Made them no longer hesitate
To think of how they might survive.
They sent three Saracens to give   9,280
King Richard word they would surrender
If he would grant to each defender
The right to go forth, with his life

[19] That is, Friday, May 22. This is the date given by the *Itinerarium* (p. 355) and Roger of Hoveden (III, 180). Ibn al Athir (p. 60), Beha ed Din (p. 337), and Abu Chamah (p. 54) say May 23.

Protected, and his goods and wife.
The king told them to make an end
Of talk and, if they could, defend
Themselves. They to the fort withdrew.
Just then the master engine threw
A rock, which, striking in its course
A turret, made their state much worse.   9,290
The main tower of the citadel
It struck; by God's will thus it fell.
Beneath the ground it was all sapped,
And all their soldiers had escaped.
Our men armed themselves; round about
They gathered and essayed to rout
The enemy. I think they all
Sought refuge in the great tower's wall,
Then did a deed of cruel wrong;
That is, their horses they hamstrung,   9,300
So that, whatever might betide them,
The Christians might not have nor ride them.

AND FORCES HIS WAY INTO LE DARON

God's folk into the fortress burst;
Here writ are those who entered first.
Seguin Baré was at the start,
And then a squire named Espiart
Was close to Seguin. 'Tis averred
That Peter the Gascon [20] was the third,
And many more there were, no doubt,
Whose titles I could not find out.   9,310
And next there came inside the banners,
Which were of divers kinds and manners.
Stephen de Longchamp's [21] banner went

[20] Seguin Baré, Espiart, and Peter the Gascon are unknown beyond this statement in our text.

[21] Stephen Longchamp, identified by Stubbs as the brother of William, bishop of Ely, is mentioned by the *Gesta* (p. 190) as having been placed in charge of Acre by Richard. He witnesses acts of Richard's with the title "steward" throughout 1189–90. He was lord of Baudemont in the Vexin and was one of the hostages for Richard in 1193 (Landon, *Itinerary*, pp. 8–33, 79, 103).

In first, but it was sorely rent
And not entire, but cut and slit.
There rose directly after it
The count of Leicester's. On a site
Above the wall and at the right
That of Andrew de Chauvigny
Was set; in its vicinity   9,320
Was that of my lord Raymond, too,
The prince's son.[22] On high it flew.
The Pisans and the Genoese
Raised many banners beside these.
Upon the walls thus were unfurled
Our flags; theirs to the earth were hurled.
Ye had seen Turks slaughtered, seen some fall
Down headlong from atop the wall;
Some were made captives; some again
Were beaten, wounded, maimed, or slain.   9,330
Within the fortress there were found
Sixty who lay dead on the ground.
These were the soldiers caught before
They reached the shelter of the tower.

AND CAPTURES THE CITADEL

The Saracens who thus were shut
In the great tower gazed about
Them, saw their fortress capturèd,
Their fellow Turks taken or dead,
And saw how targes were erected
Against the wall, and well directed   9,340
To cut the wall from underneath
While they were up above. . . .
And saw that the emir from whom

[22] Raymond of Tripoli, son of Bohemond III, prince of Antioch. He was given the county of Tripoli by his god-father, Raymond III, but surrendered his title to Tripoli to his younger brother Bohemond in return for recognition as heir to the principality of Antioch. He appears in an act of 1191 (*Regesta*, doc. 689), using the title "son of the prince of Antioch." He died before his father, and the claims of his son Raymond Rupin were contested by Bohemond IV, who seized Antioch as well as Tripoli.

Help was to come had to their doom
Abandoned them—well known to fame
Was he, Caïsac was his name.
And when they realized their plight
And how no succor was in sight,
They yielded themselves up and gave
Themselves to King Richard, the brave,   9,350
Without condition, subjugated,
As slaves and captives, checked and mated.
Of Christian prisoners full two score
There were who gyves and fetters wore.
Their lives were saved: they got surcease
From woe, deliverance and release.
The king had the Turks shut and barred
In the tower under heavy guard,
Where all of Friday night they lay.   9,359
Upon the morn of Saturday,   May 23
The eve of Pentecost, that great
And noble feast we celebrate,
He caused the prisoners to be brought
Down from the tower, and without
Ado he gave command to bind
Them, each man with his hands behind
His back. So tightly were they tied
That piercingly they wailed and cried.[23]
In this way was Le Daron seized;
Its captors would have been displeased   9,370
And downcast, had they not contrived
To take it ere the French arrived,
And would have felt it cause for blame.

RICHARD GIVES LE DARON TO HENRY

Behold, now with Count Henry came
The Frenchmen, spurring on their steeds
And hoping they might share these deeds,

[23] The *Itinerarium* (p. 356) says that there were three hundred prisoners plus a number of women and children.

But they arrived there tardily.
The king went with his company
To welcome his nephew, the count.
What should I lengthily recount? 9,380
Great joy did each one manifest,
And the king, as many can attest,
To the count ceded Le Daron,
Thus giving him what he had won.
We stayed at this place and reposed
All through the day of Pentecost. May 24
On Monday morn our steps were bent May 25
Toward Ascalon; our course, which went
Through Gaza, straight to Herbia drew.
There the king and his retinue 9,390
Halted, and there the night they bode; [24]
To Ascalon the others rode
Without delay or hesitation.
The French there made great celebration.

THEY TAKE THE FIG TREE

Unto the king of England, short
Time after this, came a report
From a spy who had been dispatched
To the Fig Tree, where close he watched
The Saracens. He was aware
That there were a full thousand there 9,400
Or more, he said, with Caïsac,
Preparing to withstand attack
And hold the Christian force at bay.
The brave king, without more delay,
Mounted, and all the army went
With him. Meseems, that night they spent May 27
At the Cannaie des Etourneaux.
The morrow morn was fair, and so
They set forth at the sunrise hour

[24] The *Itinerarium* (pp. 356–57) says they stayed three days and dates it from May 25 to May 27.

And marched until they came before   9,410
The Fig Tree, which the Turks had thought
To hold against them, but did not,
Except for two lone Turks, whom they
Found there and whom they took away.
Before they left, the Turks employed
Greek fire, and thus their gates destroyed,
And then abandoned their château,
Fleeing as fast as they could go
When the host's coming was made known
To them. They thought of Le Daron,   9,420
Knowing 'twas captured by the host
And their companions all were lost,
So they decided to withdraw
From the fort. Our men rode, and saw
How the fort was without defense,
Then climbed upon an eminence
To view the land, in case they might
Find any Turks with whom to fight;
Not one of them was to be found;
Therefore our soldiers turned around   9,430
With all dispatch, returning so
To the Cannaie des Etourneaux.

RICHARD IS DISTRAUGHT BY NEWS OF JOHN'S TREASON

At the Cannaie our men unfold
Their tents, so I have heard it told,
On their return from the Fig Tree;
He who recounts the history
Says that a messenger is come
To the king, a man from his own home:
It was John d'Alençon, a clerk.[25]
He tells the king that treacherous work   9,440
And strife and warfare now divide
The whole of England, far and wide,

---

[25] John d'Alençon has been identified by Stubbs as archdeacon of Lisieux and vice-chancellor. (Meyer's note, G. Maréchal, III, 136–37.)

What with his barons and his brother,
Who, scornful of the queen, his mother,
Would do nothing save his own will.
Matters had gone so very ill
And taken such evil countenance
Through envoys of the king of France,
Who urged his brother to betray
Him and forsake the righteous way　　　　9,450
And make the French king his ally.
The clerk made bold to testify
That if he made not swift return
To his own land, it would be torn
From those to whom he did commit
The power to rule over it.
When he returned 'twas so. The ill
That then arose endureth still,
As doth appear in Normandy,
Laid waste and brought to poverty.　　　　9,460
When the king heard these words, which were
Not good or welcome to his ear,
He was grieved, downcast, lost in thought,
Saying to himself: "If thou dost not
Return, thou hast lost thy domain."
Now is his spirit racked with pain,
Until, deciding, with firm heart
He said that he must needs depart.
When the good folk learned this result,
Know ye that they did not exult.　　　　9,470
Some folk within the army heard
The tidings; others knew no word
Thereof. One said: "The king will go."
Another answered: "Nay, not so."
His enemies would have him leave,
Whereas his friends could only grieve,
For much his honor would be stained
If he departed from the land

At other time than when he should,
Before he did the most of good.   9,480

HOPE SPRINGS ETERNAL

Now did the barons all convene
And held their counsel on the scene—
Frenchmen, Normans, and Poitevins,
English, Manccaux, and Angevins—
Of what to do in this affair.
They said at last that, whatsoe'er
King Richard chose to do or say
Or where he went, together they
Would go on to Jerusalem.
Someone—I know not which of them—   9,490
Slipped out and bore the host these words,
That all the counts and noble lords
Had told the council without fail
Jerusalem they would assail.
Now is rejoicing general
In the host, and in great folk and small
Were such fair hope and gladsomeness,
Such noble zest, such eagerness,
That there was no Christian among
Them, great or small or old or young,   9,500
Who was not filled with ecstasy
Save for the king's own self; while he
In this rejoicing could not share,
But lay down, torn by grief and care
At hearing the distressful news.
But the host's joy was so profuse
That they went not to bed, but danced
Till after midnight, still entranced.

THE HOST MARCHES TOWARD JERUSALEM

'Twas in June, when the sun doth make
The dew to dry away at break   9,510

Of dawn, and all the world is gay,
That the host moved from the Cannaie
Through the plains, where the land doth fall
Toward Ibelin of the Hospital,
By Hebron, where the vale began
Within the which was born Saint Anne,
The mother of that holy Maid,
God's Mother, evermore His aid.
I saw the host there, all delighted
To undertake the labor plighted,   9,520
To move on to Jerusalem
And to lay siege to it, and hem
It in. But there were many men,
Both poor and wealthy, who were fain
To enter there, but never could.
Hear what befell them. They withstood
A very strange affliction,
A direful persecution:
A swarm of little biting flies,
Subtle and tiny, of the size   9,530
Of sparks, into the army came.
We called them "cincinelles" by name.
And as the army moved along
The countryside, they rose and stung
The pilgrims—May Saint Célerin [26]
Sustain me!—biting them on chin
And neck, on hand and throat and face,
So that not a hand's breadth of space
Was free from spots caused by the stings
Of these malignant biting things,   9,540
And young and old all had the look
Of miserable leprous folk.
They made face coverings, to bedeck
And shroud and shelter face and neck.
They had to undergo this ill,

[26] Saint Célerin was especially popular in the Eure district. Paris uses this invocation as one of the arguments to show the Norman origin of the author.

But they derived good comfort still
From their emprise, and were sustained
By the fair hope they entertained.

RICHARD'S INDECISION IS SENSED BY A CHAPLAIN

But the king, pensive and downhearted
At these tidings I have imparted   9,550
To you, thoughtful within his tent
Abode, on naught but thought intent.
One day while quietly the king
Sat in his tent thus pondering,
He saw a chaplain passing, one
From the king's own dominion.
William of Poitiers [27] was he,
Who would have spoken willingly
To the king, had he but dared address
Him, but no thought dared now express,   9,560
For this was not the time or place.
The chaplain grieved: upon his face
Rolled tears that from his eyes did well,
But still he did not dare to tell
The king what blame he had incurred
And what the host said of their lord:
For news from England he now planned
To withdraw from the Holy Land,
Leaving it weak and poor, to retreat
Before his labor was complete.   9,570
King Richard saw and summonèd
The priest. "Tell me the truth," he said,
"By that faith which you owe to me,
Whence comes this infelicity
Which these tears that you shed betray?
Now tell me this, without delay."
The priest stayed not, but made reply
To him at once, with tearful eye

---

[27] William of Poitiers is not known beyond this reference.

And with a voice of gentleness:
"Sire, I shall not speak, unless   9,580
You do assure me that you will
Not be incensed or take it ill."
The king took oath, and reassured
Him, giving him his plighted word,
Pledging that he would never bear
Him any malice anywhere.

WHO EXHORTS HIM

Then said he: "Sire, they speak of you
In blame. The story goes all through
The host of how you would return.
Ah, may we never see the morn   9,590
Dawn of the day when you do such
A deed! May men never reproach
You for it, near or far, elsewhere
Or here! Recall the honors fair
That God so oft has granted you
And which shall e'er be told anew.
For he has given to no king
Of your age less of suffering.
Remember, King, how, as men say,
When you were count of Poitiers   9,600
You had no neighbor skilled and great,
Of lofty and of high estate,
Who e'er made war on you without
Being o'ercome and put to rout.
Remember how you did disperse
The lawless bands of Brabanters,
Whom you defeated frequently
With small strength and small company.
Remember the adventure rich
Of Hautefort,[28] the triumph which   9,610
You won there when you interceded;

---

[28] Hautefort was the castle of Bertrand de Born on the border of the Limousin, which Richard took as the final act of suppressing a revolt of the barons of Aquitaine in 1182–83 (Norgate, *Richard*, pp. 39–56).

The count of Saint-Gilles [29] had proceeded
To lay siege to it, and you came
And drove him forth, to his deep shame.
Remember likewise your own realm
Which, without bearing shield or helm,
You got in amity, as none
Before your time had ever done.

RECALLING HIS PAST PROWESS AND SACRIFICE

Remember your great deeds of might,
The men you conquered in fair fight,   9,620
Messina captured by your arms,
The prowess wrought against the swarms
Of base Greeks whom you overthrew:
'Twas they who sought to capture you.
The Lord God saved you, overcame
Their force, and covered them with shame.
Remember, too, your great success
At Cyprus, where the bounteousness
Of God vouchsafed to you to make
Conquest none else would undertake   9,630
In but a fortnight's time you made
The capture: only through the aid
Of God could you as conqueror
In prison place the emperor.
King, watch that you be not ensnared.
Recall the mighty ship that fared
To Acre, but could not penetrate
Therein, when God willed you to meet
It, and your galleys seized it then,
With full eight hundred well-armed men;   9,640
The serpents that it bore were drowned.
Recall how often you have found
That God His succor did not spare.
Recall the siege of Acre where

[29] Raymond V, count of Toulouse, had joined the league of barons in revolt against
Richard in 1182. The rebels pressed the claims of Prince Henry against Richard and
King Henry II in an attempt to break the power of the king in southern France. The
death of Prince Henry in 1183 broke up the league.

You came in time to take the town,
And God caused you to spend your own
Till it surrendered to your hand.

HE IS GOD'S CHOSEN IMPLEMENT

Good King, did you not understand
Why you survived the malady
That reigned there, called 'léonardie,'   9,650
Whileas no leech's skill could save
The other princes from the grave?
Remember, King, to guard the land
That God has given in your hand
And which depends on you alone
Because the other king has gone.
Remember how you saved the lives
Of Christians, and struck off their gyves
At Le Daron: they were to be
Sent by the Turks to slavery,   9,660
When God sent you in time to bring
Them succor. Now remember, King,
That God has given you bounty great
And raised you to such high estate
That you fear neither king nor baron,
O King! remember well Le Daron,
And how you took the place in four
Days' time, and tarried there no more.
Remember now your parlous plight
Close hemmed in by the paynim's might   9,670
The time that sinfully you slept;
Remember, King, brave and adept,
How God rescued you speedily.
Now we are all condemned to die;
Now it is said by great and small
Who wish your honor, one and all,
How unto Christendom have you
A father been, and brother, too,
And if you leave it without aid,
'Twill surely perish, thus betrayed."   9,680

RICHARD VOWS TO REMAIN UNTIL EASTER

The clerk had done his sermoning
And read his lesson to the king:
All that he had to say was spoken.
The king his silence had not broken,
Nor did the men seated around
Him in the tent utter a sound;
But the king gave thought to the word
And preachment that he had just heard,
And in his mind the light shone clear.
On the next day the host came here   9,690
At hour of nones, coming anon
Before the gates of Ascalon.
The barons and the host without
Exception thought beyond a doubt
That he would order them to pack
Their gear, and start their journey back.
But he had altered his intent
By reason of the message sent
By God first, then by the priest's word,
Whereby his heart was deeply stirred.   9,700
Why should I give more full account?
He said to his nephew, the count,
To the lords, and the duke of Burgundy,
That under no contingency,
Whatever tidings might henceforth
Arrive, for no reason on earth
Would he consent to go away
Or leave the land till Easter Day.
He called Philip, his crier, the man
Whose wont it was to cry his ban,[30]   9,710
And had proclaimed through Ascalon,
In the name of Him by Whom is done
All good, that the king formally
And surely pledged to them that he

---

[30] The *Itinerarium* (p. 365) gives the date: "pridie Nonas Junii, scilicet in hebdo-
mada Sanctae Trinitatis" (June 4).

Would in the Holy Land sojourn
Till Easter, and would not return
To his home. And further he declared
That now they all must be prepared,
With that which God had given them,
To lay siege to Jerusalem.   9,720

HALLELUJAH

When that they heard the crier's voice,
All men in such wise did rejoice
As doth the bird at break of day.
Then they prepared without delay

                    .   .   .

Every man addressed himself
To God high in the firmament,
Saying (may God my worth augment!):
"God, we may thank Thee for Thy grace
And worship Thee and give Thee praise.   9,730
Thy city we shall soon behold,
Which the Turks too long have controlled.
Now blessèd be our long sojourn,
Our long delay, the troubles borne
So constantly by everyone
During our expedition!"
Ye had seen men hurry eagerly
Anxious to don their panoply.
The humble folk of rank obscure
Were filled with gladsomeness so pure   9,740
That each bore on his neck his share
Of food, and each one did declare
That he bore food enough to last
Until a whole month's time were past,
So eager were they to complete
Their task. This only I repeat:
Who serves God, naught can him dismay.

CHAPTER IX

It was just after Whitsunday,   May 30 [June 6]
On Saturday,[1] as I believe,
The army was drawn up to leave   9,750
And to march forth from Ascalon—
A thing which easily was done,
For every man was satisfied
And overjoyed with what he did.
In the forenoon the host began
Its march. I think that never man
Saw army in more fair array
Or nobler. A short march that day
They made, by reason of the heat.
Many a courteous, humble feat   9,760
Of honor and of charity
Was done by the nobility.
For those who had, to serve their needs,
Horses or any other steeds,
Unto the weary pilgrims lent
Them, while young lords and nobles went
Plodding along on foot behind.

---

[1] This date is wrong. The *Itinerarium* (p. 367) says the *octave* of Holy Trinity, which date is confirmed by Beha ed Din (p. 340). This error throws out all the dates of the *Estoire* for some time, as they are all given as so many days after this date. The army left Ascalon for Blanchegarde June 6, went on to Latrun June 9, and from Latrun to Casal Ernaud and Betnuble on June 10.

Ye had seen streaming in the wind
Numerous rich and splendid banners
Most bravely flung in divers manners. 9,770
Ye had seen many sons of mothers,
And many families, nephews, brothers,
And many hauberks, coats of mail,
Men armed in every detail,
With gleaming sword and lance and pike
And spear (one never saw the like
In our grandfathers' day of old),
And many a sturdy sergeant bold!
Ye had seen many a brave man ride,
And horses iron gray or pied, 9,780
And many a mule, and many a good
And valiant knight of fortitude.
I think they might have overthrown
The Turks, though forty to our one.
They moved on, passing as they rode
A stream of water fresh that flowed.
That first night of the march the host
In front of Blanchegarde disposed
Themselves: in God's own care they lay. 9,789
'Twas Sunday; and there died that day   May 31 [June 7]
Within the host a gallant knight
And a brave sergeant by the bite
Or serpents, in a space of ground
So small 'twas less than two ells round.
Their souls be seen and heard by God,
For they died following His road!

THEY CAMP AT BETNUBLE

We dwelt for two days on this spot,
And on the third [2] once more set out   June 2 [June 9]
In closely serried ranks, that had

[2] The *Itinerarium* (p. 368) says the third day; that is, the fifth Ides of June (June 9). This is confirmed by Beha ed Din (p. 341, where it should read 27 Jomada I instead of 27 Rabia I).

The roads all filled with men steel clad.   9,800
Without encounters, stays, or fights
We reached the Toron of the Knights.
A single night we tarried there,
And on the morrow forth did fare,   June 3 [June 10]
But not till after we did eat;
The king gave order to his suite
To set forth; he in person led
The way, and placed him at their head.
He pitched his camp upon the right,
On high, near Casal Ernaud's site.   9,810
Upon the next day thither drew   June 4 [June 11]
The Frenchmen, and the others, too;
Toward Betnuble now they went.
The day was fair, the firmament
Cloudless. The host there tarried on,
Where in the winter had begun
Their march; they tarried to await
Count Henry, as I shall relate.
The king had sent him to convoke
At Acre those misguided folk   9,820
Who would not join the host. Therefore,
During a whole month's time or more
We had to stay in that same place,
Encamped beside the mountain's base,
A spot not far from the high road
Whereon returning palmers trod
When they left that high city blest,
Whereof we have been dispossessed.

THEY FORAGE WITHIN SIGHT OF JERUSALEM

During the sojourn that we made
Within this valley where we stayed,   9,830
There were adventures and alarms
And mishaps, frays, and feats of arms:
We saw them happen, and repressed

Ourselves perforce, and acquiesced.
One day [3] it happened that a spy—
The kind who seek truth to descry—
Came down from the king's vantage height.
I saw him come, filled with delight.
He said that there were Saracens
Upon the mountain's eminence,   9,840
In truth, who there had taken post
To scan the highroads for the host.
Before day the brave king did scale
The height, with him who tells the tale.
Then sought the Turks, to discommode
Them, where Emmaus' water flowed.
At dawn he caught them unaware
And slew a score of them. And there
He took Saladin's crier, the man
Whose wont it was to cry his ban.   9,850
This man he spared, and did not slay.
He took three camels in the fray
And some fine Turcomans likewise.
He also gained, as further prize,
Two very goodly mules, the which
Were laden down with garments rich,
While in their saddlebags they bore
Spices and aloes in fair store.
After the Saracens he flung
Himself, pursuing them among   9,860
The hills. In a vale he came upon
One: from his horse he smote him down,
And, when the evil wretch was slain,
Perceived Jerusalem full plain.
Within Jerusalem such fear
Arose (so we the tale did hear)
That if the army then had been
With the king, so it might be seen,

[3] The *Itinerarium* (p. 369) says: the day after Saint Barnabas, which was Friday (June 12).

Jerusalem would at that hour
Have fallen into Christian power;   9,870
For all the Saracens went out
Of the city, whence they fled in rout;
Thinking the host was moving down
Upon them, none dared hold the town.
Orders and threats could not constrain
Them in the city to remain.[4]
Already saddled and at hand
By Saladin's express command
His finest steed was waiting, for
He dared not stay there any more,   9,880
When there arrived a spy, to say
The great host was not on the way,
Because at this time it pleased not
The Lord such good work should be wrought.

THE SARACENS ATTACK THE CAMP

Upon the same day it befell
(And 'twas known certainly and well)
Whereon the king had struck this blow
Upon their men, and laid them low,
That, swarming down the mountainside,
Two hundred Turks made bold to ride   9,890
Upon the French camp. They attacked
Before we had the time to act
Or to defend us. They had slain,
Close to the army, sergeants twain
(For us it was a shameful thing)
Who had gone forth a-foraging.
The Frenchmen and the Hospital
And Temple hastened to the call
Of the two sergeants in their plight,
And the Turks stood their ground to fight   9,900

[4] Beha ed Din (pp. 348–50) confirms this statement of the great fear felt by the Saracens and of the flight of many emirs from the city. Saladin himself was ready to evacuate it if necessary.

Among the foothills, for their fear
Was great of fighting in the clear.
But there they made a stand anew,
And there one of our knights they slew,
Much to the Frenchmen's blame, 'tis told.
Prowess outvalues balm or gold.

A BRAVE HOSPITALLER IS DISCIPLINED

A Hospitaller with success
Did a brave feat of rare address,
Had he not broken discipline.
His prowess was to blame therein.   9,910
Robert de Bruges [5] was this man's name.
Hearing the outcry, swift he came,
Rode past his brothers, and pressed on
To far beyond the gonfalon,

                . . .[6]

From the host not to separate.
He by his courage was so pressed
That he charged on and left the rest.
He spurred the horse he rode, a marvelous,
Great battle charger vigorous,   9,920
Straight at a Turk whom he had seen
Gay, brightly armored, and serene.
He came upon him at full tilt,
Holding his stout lance by the hilt.
Piercing his yellow coat of mail,
The lance went through him full an ell.
This was the deed he did, and so
The Turkish miscreant was brought low.
His corse was not left there. Straightway

[5] Robert of Bruges, a Hospitaller, is not known aside from this reference. He does not appear on any of the documents in Delaville LeRoulx, *Cartulaire général des Hospitaliers.*

[6] G. Paris notes (p. 438) that the lacuna must be those lines which include the account of the order given to the Hospitallers by their Master not to engage in single combat.

Came on the scene of the affray   9,930
The Master of the Hospital,
Garnier, a courteous knight withal,
Who to the brother spake: "Dismount,
Brother, and list while I recount
How an order is to be obeyed."
On foot the brother thus was made
To walk back to their tent and wait
To learn what was to be his fate,
Until good men of high renown
Prayed of the Master, kneeling down,   9,940
That as a boon he grant them this:
Grace for the brother who remiss
Had been, for his great prowess' sake,
The which had led him on to break
The rule. In mercy he forbore.
"But," said he, "let him err no more." [7]

A CHRISTIAN CARAVAN

Meseems, one Tuesday [8] was the day   June 16
Our caravan was on its way,
Laden with food and fair-disposed
And armored, to rejoin the host.   9,950
Upon that day 'twas to be led,
So I have heard the story said,
By my lord Ferri de Vienne,[9]
Commanding caravan and men
For Count Henry, who should have fared
That day as chief of the rear guard
But who to Acre had been sent.
And therefore my lord Ferri went
And prayed of Baldwin le Caron

---

[7] The *Itinerarium* (p. 372) says the count of Perche, "qui tamen se timide habuit," came to the assistance of the Christians; so did the bishop of Salisbury.

[8] The *Itinerarium* (p. 373) gives Wednesday the fifteenth Kalends of July, St. Botolph's day (June 17).

[9] Ferri de Vienne was a vassal of the count of Champagne (Longnon, *Livre des vassaux*, p. 263, and Arbois de Jubainville, IV, 48).

And Clarembald de Montchablon [10]   9,960
That to their charge he might confide
It, lest men rashly stray aside.
But on that day they rashly strayed,
And for that many of them paid.
There rode Menassier de l'Isle [11]
A charger dappled and gray-steel.
While Richard d'Orques [12] and Thierri [13]
Were there in place of Lord Ferri,
And Philip,[14] and the retinue
Of Lord Baldwin le Caron, too.   9,970
Otto [15] and several squires did play
A part with them in that mêlée,
Their friends and kinsmen, as indeed
They showed that day in hour of need.
Those in the main body marched on,
Having no fear of anyone:
Unburdened, they could lightly tread.
But the rear guard was burdenèd,
So while the others swiftly strode
The rear guard followed on the road   9,980
Like sober folk at sober pace.

[10] Clarembald de Montchablon appears several times in the *Scripta de feodis*, where he is listed as a castellan, as well as holding several military fees.

[11] Menassier de l'Isle (Lille?) is listed by Siedschlag (p. 119, no. 75) as possibly an Englishman. He is unknown save for this reference.

[12] Richard d'Orques is identified by Powicke (*Loss of Normandy*, p. 262) as a follower of Juhel de Mayenne who deserted from John in 1203.

[13] Thierri d'Orques, or de Orca, is also identified by G. Paris as from Maine. He may be the same person whom we find after the crusade, settled in the east, for a Terricus de Orca appears on documents of Henry of Champagne, 1194–95, and Aymeri de Lusignan, 1198–1200 (*Regesta*, docs. 717–24, 743–76). By his marriage with Melissende of Arsur he became lord of that fief, sometime before 1198, when he appears with the title (*Regesta*, doc. 746; *Lignages*, p. 451). He died sometime between 1200, when he last appears on acts, and 1207, at which time Melissende was remarried to John d'Ibelin (the approximate date of her second marriage is determined by the birth dates of her sons).

[14] This Philip is not identifiable.

[15] G. Paris suggests that this might have been Otto of Trasignies, but this seems scarcely possible, as this man was merely a squire.

IS ATTACKED BY THE SARACENS

Suddenly, from a hidden place [16]
Came forth a band of Turks on horse,
And, dashing downhill in full course,
From the high ground they swiftly flung
Themselves on the rear guard. Among
The ranks and cutting through them passed
The Turks, whose steeds were very fast;
They broke the line with their attack
And smote from off his horse's back   9,990
The valiant Baldwin le Caron.
But noble was his heart; o'erthrown,
With his good sword in hand, he spread
Among the foemen fear and dread,
For oft the Turks his mettle felt.
They struck down with the blows they dealt
Both Richard d'Orques and Thierri,
And Baldwin fought on gallantly
Until he was remounted on
A charger that his men had won.   10,000
Brave fighting 'twas: ye had seen men deal
Many a fair stroke, and then wheel
And turn, and many a sword blade flash,
And many a combat fought with dash,
Many a stout and valiant deed,
Many an empty-saddled steed.
Ye had seen the Turks make fierce attack
And ours defend and drive them back.
When the Turks struck one to the ground,
Our men would quickly gather round   10,010
And help him mount. Succor they gave
Each other like good knights and brave
But it was an ill-matched mêlée,
For those on our side in the fray
Were so swamped by the other side

[16] The *Itinerarium* (p. 373) says not far from Ramleh.

That nowise can it be denied
That many nobles to the ground
Were smitten, suffering many a wound,
For the Turks' spears in rapid flight
Had put our horses in sore plight.   10,020
By one of these, so swift impelled,
Baldwin once more to earth was felled;
A sergeant he now made dismount
Who had given already fair account
Of himself. He took his horse away
And later he was heard to say
That he saw presently the head
Of this same sergeant severèd
Who thus had lent to him his horse.
In this way we were blocked perforce.   10,030
They took Philip, companion
Of Baldwin, who great praises won
From all those who were there. And they
Along with Philip took away
By force a stalwart sergeant, too.
Richard's brother [17] they also slew.

AND VALIANTLY DEFENDED

There had ye seen a bitter fight!
In a closed field were hemmed in tight
Baldwin's every companion,
While Clarembald de Montchablon   10,040
Deserting them, had left their side
And fled as fast as he could ride
As soon as he perceived the Turk.
Baldwin kept up his valiant work,
But he was stricken down once more
And by mace blows beaten so sore
Almost he died where he was felled,

---

[17] If this means Thierri d'Orques, the brother of Richard d'Orques, he obviously
cannot be the man who later became lord of Arsur. There is enough ambiguity, however, about this Richard for the possible identification of Thierri to stand.

So that the blood came forth and welled
From out his mouth and out his nose.
His sword was cracked with many blows   10,050
That dulled and breached its edge and broke
It. Then in a loud voice he spoke
To Menassier de l'Isle, through whom
Many a Turk had met his doom:
"Menassier, will you leave me thus?"
My lord Menassier valorous
Went to his aid without delay.
So many Turks then rushed that way
That they were able to unseat
Menassier from his horse. They beat   10,060
Him badly, dealt him blow and slash,
Cut in his leg one mighty gash
That reached the marrow of his bone.
Lost in the crowd and overthrown
Were he and Baldwin. Then God sent
To aid in their predicament
The noble count of Leicester, who
Till then naught of their trouble knew.
Thither the count came speedily.
And, as he reached the battle, he   10,070
Smote down a Turk with such great force
That the Saracen fell from his horse
Over the creature's neck. Thereon
His head was cut off by Ançon,[18]
Stephen de Longchamp's man, who sent
It spinning away incontinent;
My lord Stephen himself did great
Exploits then and at later date.
Our forces, when the news was known,
To such a point of strength were grown   10,080
That the Turks, seeing our numbers swell,
Into the mountains fled pell-mell,

[18] Ançon is identified merely as a companion of Stephen Longchamp (G. Paris, p. 530).

Save those o'ertaken on their way.
And then our wounded men, who lay
There, were on horses' backs disposed
With care, and brought back to the host.
Thus this adventure happened. It
Is such as merits to be writ.[19]

RICHARD RECEIVES A PIECE OF THE TRUE CROSS

'Twas while the host, on the third day   10,089
Before Saint John's,[20] inactive lay,   June 22
That news was brought to it which gave
Unto it consolation grave.
A holy abbot 'twas who brought
The tidings that such comfort wrought,
Abbot of Saint Elias,[21] who fed
On nothing more than roots and bread.
With his great beard that grew untrimmed
A very holy man he seemed.
He told the king he knew a place
Which he had guarded without cease   10,100
A long time, where there lay a cross
Which God had given him to watch close.
It held a part of the true Rood,
Of which are many parts. This good
And pious Christian, who was not
Too aged,[22] had unaided brought
It there, and hid it till the land

---

[19] The *Itinerarium* (p. 376) here inserts a short chapter, telling how the Syrian bishop of St. George brought a piece of the True Cross to the crusaders' camp.

[20] The *Itinerarium* (p. 377) says: "third day before St. John's day, which is St. Alban's day" (June 22).

[21] Although the famous abbey of St. Elias was the Cistercian abbey near Mount Carmel, this abbot was probably a Syrian of another house. Rey (*Colonies*, p. 382) identifies a castle of St. Elie near La Quarantaine in southern Palestine. Roger of Hoveden (III, 182) says that St. Elias was a *chapel* three leagues from Jerusalem. Enlart (*Les Monuments des croisés*, II, 180) mentions a capital of a column from the monastery of St. Elias near Jerusalem and which dates from 1160. It is not mentioned, however, in the *Guide bleu à Syrie-Palestine* (Paris, 1932), which lists three Mar Elias houses, all of them in the Lebanon.

[22] The *Itinerarium* (p. 377), on the other hand, speaks of his "capite cano."

Should be won back by Christian band.
Most dearly had the abbot paid
For this, for Saladin had made 10,110
Demand on him ofttime to yield
It up, yet still he had concealed
It, though they bound him tight and though
He needs must tortures undergo.
They could not, with their pains, compel
Him to surrender it or tell
Where 'twas. He made reply to them
At the capture of Jerusalem
It had been lost. Now when the king
Had learned the truth about this thing, 10,120
He made this holy abbot mount,
Of whom ye heard me now recount.
He mounted, and the barons, too,
And knights in goodly retinue,
They took the road in fair array
And rode along upon the way
After the abbot, coming to
The place whereof I spoke to you,
Wherein the Cross was hid. That day
'Twas raised for worship and display. 10,130
Men rushed to kiss it without cease,
So that one scarcely could appease
Them. To the host straightway 'twas brought
Who therefrom much of comfort got.
Abundantly their tears outpoured,
And greatly was the Rood adored.

RICHARD REFUSES TO BESIEGE JERUSALEM

When that this Cross was raised on high
And much the army cheered thereby,
Some little time it stood, and then
The host's most poor and humble men 10,140
Lifted their voices to inquire,
Saying: "In God's name, fair, sweet sire,

Why stay we here? What now doth stem
Us? Go we to Jerusalem?"
Indeed, so loud did they complain
That the king and the nobles of his train,
Hearing the murmur they did raise,
Counseled, and spoke in divers ways,
Discussing plan and stratagem
If they should go to Jerusalem. 10,150
The Frenchmen, in their counseling,
Several times bespoke the king,
And some said it seemed best to them
That they besiege Jerusalem.
"It cannot be," the king replied,
"And never will you see me guide
Men other than I rightly ought.
Who blames me for it I care not.
Beyond all doubting ye should know
That wheresoe'er our host may go 10,160
Saladin knows our plan, the course
We follow, the number of our force.
We are far distant from the coast.
If he should come down with his host
Of Saracens to Ramleh plain,
And our supplies of food distrain
So that we could not get supplies,
It would not be discreet or wise
For those besieging. Surely they
Would pay for it, and dearly pay. 10,170
The citadel is all immured,
So I am truthfully assured,
With walls that are so thick and strong
That it would take so great a throng

. . .

We could not succor our own host,
Were the Turks minded to assail
It. They would crush it without fail.

BEING UNWILLING TO EXPOSE HIS MEN TO DISASTER

If I should lead the host to lay
Siege to Jerusalem this way   10,180
That ye advise and they should come
To mishap or to martyrdom,
All my life long I should be blamed,
Ever misloved and ever shamed;
And past all doubt I am aware
That there are folk in France and here
Who have desired, and ardently
Do still wish and desire to see
Me make an error of this sort
Which they might turn to ill report.   10,190
We, men of foreign countries, know
Not by what ways and paths to go;
We do not know the roads and traces,
The evil spots, the narrow places . . .
Whereby to vanquish them and quell.
But those who in this country dwell
And who would fain their fiefs regain,
Their counsel we must entertain
And seek advice essential
From Temple and from Hospital.   10,200
And those who have been in the land
Before and learned to understand
It, and who still its ways well know—
To such as these men we must go,
I think, and ask what they advise
Which would be most discreet and wise,
To lay siege here, or to move on
And try to capture Babylon
Or Beirut or Damascus. Thus
Discord shall no more sunder us,   10,210
For never were folk more divided."

A COUNCIL DECIDES TO ATTACK EGYPT

So finally it was decided
They would take Templars four or five,
Who would at some accord arrive
With as many Hospitallers and
As many Syrians of the land
And as many lords of France. No doubt
A score of them were chosen out.[23]
Trusting their loyalty, they then
Would do whate'er these gentlemen   10,220
Decided was the wisest thing.
These men said, after counseling,
That, taking Babylon, they would
Do most for the whole country's good.
And when the Frenchmen heard this, they
Broke faith, refusing to obey,
Saying 'twas their intent to fare
To the siege, nor would they go elsewhere.
When the king learned of this discord,
Which was not ended by the Lord,   10,230
And that 'twas through the men of France,
He said that in this circumstance
Had the French but believed him they
Had gone to Babylon straightway.
"There lies my fleet at Acre moored:
I had prepared to take aboard
All their provisions and supplies,
Their harness, and their panoplies,
Their biscuit and their flour. The host
Would then have marched along the coast.   10,240
Seven hundred knights I would have led,
In God's name, and myself have paid
Them, and two thousand sergeants, too,
Would have been with my retinue.

[23] Beha ed Din (p. 352) says that they elected three hundred men who chose twelve, who chose three, who made the decision.

And let them know that no man leal
In need would have made vain appeal
To the resources of my purse.
But since to this they are adverse,
I am ready to go to the siege,
Save that, by Saint Lambert of Liège,[24]   10,250
I will not lead them, but will be
With them and of their company."
And so a prompt command he sent
To all his men that to the tent
Of the Hospital they should repair,
And there consider and declare
What aid the siege would have from them
When they approached Jerusalem.
They came there, and they sat them down,
And promised richly of their own   10,260
To give, and some folk made great offers
Who had but little in their coffers;
But 'twould have been a grave mistake
At that moment to undertake
The siege, when those of sworn advice
Counseled against the enterprise.

A SPY BRINGS WORD OF A CARAVAN   *et. seq.*

Now while they all were promising
What each man to the siege would bring
And give, behold, Bernard, the spy,
A man in Syria born, drew nigh;   10,270
Of native-born he had two more
With him. Saracen garb they wore.
They were returned from Babylon,
Where they had, for sole mission,
To spy upon the enemy;
I say to you assuredly
That more Saracen seeming folk

---

[24] Saint Lambert of Liège, patron saint of that city, is probably mentioned here merely because of the rhyme. The name is not found in the *Itinerarium*.

I never saw, or men who spoke
More perfectly Saracen speech.
Three hundred marks of silver each   10,280
Of these had from King Richard got
Before the time when they set out.
They came now to the king to say
That he should mount and ride straightway,
He and his men, and they would lead
Them to where caravans proceed—
As they had spied—upon the road
From Babylon, with heavy load.
The king, hearing these men impart
Such news, rejoiced within his heart.   10,290

WHICH RICHARD PREPARES TO ATTACK

He called the duke of Burgundy
To come and join his company
And bring the French with him. They went
Indeed, but e'er they would consent
They said they wished one third the gain
Of all the loot they might obtain.
To this request the king agreed.
Then each one mounted on his steed,
The king, too, and one might have counted
Five hundred knights well armed and mounted   10,300
And a thousand sergeants swift and bold,
Whom the king paid with his own gold;
And he in person led the way.
'Twas evening. Sunday was the day.[25]   June 21
All night by moonlight marched the throng,
Tarrying seldom, never long,
Until they came to Galatie;
There paused the gallant soldiery
All armed for battle. Then they sent

[25] Roger of Hoveden (III, 182) dates it the vigil of St. John's on June 23. Beha ed Din (p. 345) says Tuesday eleventh Jomada II, but here he is off a day, for Tuesday was the tenth. This error is found several places in Beha ed Din. Ibn al Athir (p. 61) says that the Franks started for the attack on the ninth Jomada II (Monday, June 22).

For their supplies' replenishment   10,310
To Ascalon, and there sojourned
Until their squires had returned.
Soon as our men set forth, the king,
And all the troops accompanying,
There was a spy who spied on them
And went straight to Jerusalem
To Saladin, there to recount
How he had witnessed the king mount
To attack his caravans and raid
Them; Saladin nowise delayed.   10,320
Five hundred Turkish troops he chose
Among his best men. They had bows
And light spears for their armament,
And to the caravans he sent
Them, and when they had joined the men
Guarding the caravans, they then
Were full two thousand troops on horse
Besides foot soldiers in some force.

SCOUTS SPY ON THE CARAVAN

Behold a spy came hastening
To Galatie, sought out the king,   10,330
Urged him to let the army stay
Where 'twas, and come without delay
To the Round Cistern, telling him
That gathered round the well-top's brim
There had arrived a caravan.
Whoe'er could plunder it, that man
Would have rich booty to his hand.
This spy was born within the land,
So that the king believed him not
Completely. Therefore he sent out   10,340
A Bedouin and sergeants twain,
Both turcopoles, and brave, skilled men,
To inquire and spy out the ground;
He had the turcopoles swathed round

Exactly like the Bedouin
After the manner Saracen.
They started on their way at night,
First climbing to a hilltop's height.
They climbed and then descended, till
At last they looked down from a hill   10,350
Upon more Saracens than I
Can say. The Bedouin and the spy
Went slowly toward them at a walk,
Telling their comrades not to talk
Lest the Turks should identify
Them. And the Turks were fooled thereby.[26]
They approached them and inquired of them
Their origin and whence they came.
The Bedouin let his tongue run on
Saying they came from Ascalon,   10,360
Where they had gathered goodly prey.
One man made answer in this way:
"You come to do some evil thing
To us; you are with England's king."
The Bedouin replied: "You lie."
Then he was of a mind to fly,
So toward the caravans he fled.
The Turks with bows and light spears sped
Behind, pursuing them apace,
Till, wearied, they gave up the chase.   10,370
These might be their own men, they thought.
The Bedouin then turned about,
For he had learned the truth, and knew
The caravan was there in view.
In this he showed his great good sense.
So quickly he departed thence
And told the king that he was sure
The caravan was in his power.
Now, in Saint George's name, the king
Ordered the steeds' provisioning   10,380

[26] But they seem not to have been fooled completely (M. J. Hubert).

Of barley. The troops ate, and then
They mounted. All night rode our men
Until they reached the place in which
The caravan had chosen to pitch
Its camp. Now our men halted there.

THE CRUSADERS CHARGE THE CARAVAN

'Twas summer and the weather fair.
The king and all his troops did on
Their arms, and each battalion
Was ranged. The French kept watch and ward
In the rear. The king took the vanguard   10,390
And had throughout the army cried
That those whose honor was their pride
Should give no thought to loot or gain
But fight with all their might and main
To batter down the Turks, and deal
Them great blows with their brands of steel.
While they proceeded thus to harry
Of battle ready for the fray,
Another spy rode to the king
At full speed, swiftly galloping,   10,400
To tell him that since break of dawn
They had prepared the caravan
And knew the attack was imminent.
When the king learned of this, he sent
His archers forward in the van
With turcopole and crossbowman
To skirmish with the Turks and strive
To press them till he could arrive.
While they were ranging the array
Them, our soldiers did not tarry   10,410
But quickly to the foe drew nigh.
When the Turks saw we were close by,
They moved their line of battle till
'Twas drawn up backed against a hill,
With their battalions ranged aright,

Though none too eager for the fight.
Into two parts the king decided
That his battalions be divided,
And when his main forces drew nigh
His skirmishers were letting fly   10,420
Their arrows, thick as dew at dawn.
The Turks had stopped their caravan,
And the good king, for a fair start,
Into their forward ranks did dart,
And with such vigor laid about
Him that I tell you beyond doubt
That he and those who with him went
Delivered blows so violent
That every foe whom in their course
They met was flung down from his horse.   10,430
And no Turk could escape their might
Unless he saved himself by flight,
Nor could they form their lines anew,
But, just as the greyhounds pursue
The hare throughout the countryside,
Ye might have seen our soldiers ride
Pursuing them among the hills
And dealing them such griefs and ills
That in confusion they fled,
Scattered, dispersed, discomfited.   10,440
And thus they left the caravan.

AND CAPTURE IT

Our troops, hot for the battle, ran
Pursuing the foe left and right,
And he relates who saw the fight
That the Turks were constrained to flee
So far through the broad *berruie* [27]
That dead of utter thirst did some
Fall down. Those caught were overcome

[27] A "berruie" is defined by G. Paris as uncultivated land, a term found commonly
in Syria.

By knights, who charged and overthrew them,
And after that the sergeants slew them.   10,450
Ye had seen saddles twisted round,
And men with many a cut and wound,
And England's king, noble and brave,
Deal many a fair stroke with his glaive.
But think not that I here shall try
To speak of him in flattery.
His deeds were seen by such a throng
Of folk that I may hold my tongue.
The king pursued the Turks, his brand
Of steel held firmly in his hand;   10,460
He followed closely on the foes
And, when he caught them, dealt such blows
No armor could hold up beneath
His sword, which split them to the teeth.
They scattered headlong in their flight
Like lambs when the wolf comes in sight.
While the first group pursued the chase
Through the hills, following on apace
There came along a hidden path
Some thirty Saracens, in wrath   10,470
And fury, and they suddenly
Fell on Roger de Téoni.
The battle horse he rode they slew
And he was near made prisoner, too,
When a companion, Juquel
De Mayenne,[28] charged the infidel.
He, too, was stricken to the ground
And Roger, with foes all around
Him, went on foot to bear him aid.
Then our folk hastened thither, laid   10,480
About them, striking left and right:
The count of Leicester joined the fight.

[28] Juquel or Juhel de Mayenne, viscount of Ste. Susanne, was an early partisan of Richard's. Later he became one of the important adherents of Philip II (Guillaume le Breton, pp. 227, 294).

Gilbert Malesmains [29] came in haste,
With two men—or with one at least;
And Alexander Arsis,[30] with more
Than fifteen knights—mayhap a score;
And then Stephen de Longchamp flung
Himself amid the pagan throng
Defending Roger with such force
That he could once more mount a horse.   10,490
And now ye might have seen anew
The rout of this unnatural crew;
Seen sword blows which upon them beat
And lopped off hands and heads and feet,
Split eyes and mouths with many a wound,
Seen corpses strewn upon the ground
Like logs, making our soldiers tread
And stumble o'er the piles of dead.
Fair blows were dealt by Poitevins,
Normans, English,[31] and Angevins.   10,500
The noble and most fearless king
Surpassed them all in everything.

THE SPOILS OF THE EGYPTIANS

Never did our ancestors see
Such slaughter or such butchery
Of Turks. They were so beaten down
And broken that it is well known
That a mere stripling boy might then
Have laid low seven of them, or ten.
The drivers of the caravan
Straight to our knights and sergeants ran,   10,510
And as our prisoners they surrendered

[29] Gilbert Malesmains is listed in the *Scripta de feodis* as holding a fief at Gereville and a fief worth £40 at Cheveillie near Rouen. He also held fiefs in Kent, owing guard at Dover castle (S. Painter).

[30] Alexander Arsis, or Arsic, held lands in Oxfordshire for 20 knights' service (Siedschlag, p. 112, no. 8) though he is listed in the *Guillaume le Maréchal* (l. 4719) as a Norman.

[31] The *Itinerarium* (p. 389) says French instead of English.

Themselves. Their great camels they tendered
Us. They brought them in on lead,
With mules, too, laden down indeed
With goods of wealth and nobleness
And great value and preciousness:
Silver and gold, soft tissues and
Rich fabrics from Damascus land,
And Bagdad weaves, stuffs finely wrought,
Greek silks, silks from the Orient brought,   10,520
The coats of mail worn by the Turk,
Coverlets, garments of rich work,
And fine pavilions and fair tents
Wrought with unusual excellence,
Biscuit and barley, grains and flour,
Electuaries, drugs of power,
Basins, chessboards, skins for wine,
Pots, candlesticks of silver fine,
Pepper and cumin, sugar, wax—
To tell them all would overtax   10,530
My tale. So many kinds of spice
There were, so many things of price,
And so much splendid armor, bright
And solid and secure and light,
And so much sumptuousness, that there
Was no one who would not declare
That in that country no campaign
Or war had ever brought such gain.[32]

CAMELS AND CASUALTIES

When these base cattle had been slain
And the caravan with its rich gain   10,540
Was seized, they captured precious loot,
But they were very sorely put

[32] Both Ibn al Athir (pp. 60–61) and Beha ed Din (pp. 342–47) have long accounts of this skirmish. Beha ed Din calls it "a most disgraceful event" and opines "it
was long since Islam had sustained so serious a disaster." He estimated that the Moslem
losses were 500 men, 3,000 horses and 3,000 camels captured, and the chamberlain
Yusuf slain.

To catch those camels of swift stride
Who irritated and defied
The host; they fled at such a course
That when one followed them on horse
God never made a thing could go
So fast—gazelle or stag or doe—
That it could catch them when they sped
Away, if once they got ahead.   10,550
Those who collected them averred
That altogether in the herd
Four thousand seven hundred head
Were gathered and assembled;
And there came mules in such a throng
And asses firmly built and strong
That they could not even be numbered.
Indeed the mass of them encumbered
Us. 'Tis said that in the chase
Were slain, of low or lofty race,   10,560
One thousand seven hundred mounted
Turks on hill and vale. This counted
Not the footmen, who, forced to remain
And flee not, on the spot were slain.

DIVISION OF THE SPOILS

Onward they marched and each day spanned
The march that for that day was planned,
Until they came before Betaffa,[33]
Which is four leagues away from Jaffa,
And there they paused their loot to share;
And when they went away from there   10,570
They went to Ramleh. In a day
They marched that portion of the way.
The host returned from Acre then,
And there Count Henry and his men

[33] We have not been able to find Betaffa on any map, in the *Guide Bleu*, or in Röhricht's "Mittelalterlichen Geographie und Topographie Syriens," *Z.D.P.V.*, Vol. X (1887). G. Paris accepts Clermont Ganneau's identification as a place ten leagues from Jaffa and four from Ascalon.

Came with the host to reunite
The force.[34] Then was there great delight,
Marvel, and admiration
At all the beasts the host had won.
The king gave every knight his share
Of camels—never were beasts more fair: 10,580
Those knights guarding the army got
Them just as did the ones who fought.
And he distributed the prize
Of mules in the same generous wise,
And he bestowed the asses all
Upon the sergeants, great and small.
The host had such a numerous train
Of beasts that it could scarce contain
Them all. The young camels they slew
And ate the meat, for it is true   10,590
They have a white and savory flesh
When larded well and roasted fresh.

DISCONTENT AT FAILURE TO ATTACK JERUSALEM

Now when the beasts were all disposed
Of and divided 'mongst the host,
And many muttered at the price
Of barley that perforce must rise,
Those who were full of discontent
Began once more to make lament,
For there was great desire in them
To lay siege to Jerusalem;   10,600
And they were restless and forlorn.
Now those men who before had sworn
And counseled 'gainst the enterprise
Once more repeated their advice:

[34] The *Estoire* here omits an important line found in the *Itinerarium* (p. 392) to the
effect that after the army had been joined by Henry, they all went back from Ramleh to
Betnuble. Later in this chapter the *Estoire* speaks of the host as having been but four
leagues from Jerusalem and speaks of their march from St. George to Ramleh to Casal
Moyen. This shows that they had not remained at Ramleh, as the text would imply in
this passage.

That should they lay siege and surround
The town, small water would be found
There, not enough for horse or beast
Or man to drink—if it so pleased
The Turks—without great pain and woe.   10,609
'Twas near Saint John's day, when the glow   June 24
Of heat sends forth a blast to dry
All things, such is its quality.
The Saracens, too, had seen fit
To break and to destroy and split
Ruthlessly and without pity
The cisterns all about the city,[35]
So that for two good leagues around—
Wherein no peace or friend were found—
No water could be got without
Great pains—'twas known beyond a doubt—   10,620
Except one small stream which doth drop
Adown the Mount of Olives' slope
To the Vale of Josaphat. This is
Siloë. They did not advise
It as judicious or discreet
During the blaze of summer heat
To try to lay siege to the town.
Now when this news was widely known,
How they could not try to attack
Jerusalem but would turn back,   10,630
Then you could hear men desolate
Heap curses on the lengthy wait
That they had made; with violence
They cursed the pitching of their tents,
Because Jerusalem would not
Be won by them, nor a siege fought.
They asked no more to live, indeed,
If once Jerusalem were freed.

[35] Beha ed Din (p. 346) tells how Saladin ordered all the wells and cisterns around
Jerusalem to be polluted.

LITTLE BITING SONGS

My lords, now be ye not astounded
If God thus troubled and confounded   10,640
Our pilgrims, making their work vain;
Because we saw, oft and again,
When men at eve would pitch their camp,
All wearied from the long day's tramp,
The Frenchmen, it was manifest,
Would move apart from all the rest
And pitch tents on another side,
And in such manner did divide
The host, that neither could endure
The other nation, it is sure.   10,650
One would say, "Thou art such and such."
The other then, "Thou art as much."
And Hugh, the duke of Burgundy,[36]
Added to this antipathy.
He had a song written about
The king, most shamefully to flout
Him; it was all filled to excess
With insolence and wickedness,
And was sung widely through the throng.
What could the king but write a song   10,660
In turn, of those who vilify
Him in their spite and perfidy?
No good song ever shall acclaim
People so false and lost to shame;
Nor shall their efforts please the Lord,
As it had once before occurred,
When Antioch was besieged, and when
By force 'twas entered by our men,
To whom God gave the victory—
'Tis still retold in history—   10,670

[36] The text has "Henri," as does the *Itinerarium*. As it was Hugh, not Henry, who
was on the crusade, we have accepted the correction.

By Bohemond and Tancred, too,
Both pilgrims excellent and true,
Along with Godfrey de Bouillon,
And high princes of great renown,
And other folk who went and served
The Lord and from this task ne'er swerved,
And for this service diligent
God gave reward to their content:
He lifted up their works on high
And oft was pleased to magnify   10,680
Them and the children of their race,
Who still hold great and lofty place.

DISCONSOLATE, THE HOST RETREATS TOWARD JAFFA

In truth some ten days did elapse,
It seems to me—or twelve perhaps—
After they seized the caravan;
Still stayed the host no different than
They were, as told in this my tale.
Seeing that naught would them avail,
Nor all their labor let them go
To the Holy Sepulcher, although   10,690
They were a mere four leagues apart,
Sorrow wrung every pilgrim's heart.
So now they started their return
So downcast, stricken, and forlorn
That never men of good estate
Were more grieved or disconsolate.
Their rear guard they arranged; and they
No sooner set out on their way
Than down the mountainside the pack
Of Saracens rushed to attack   10,700
Them. For one sergeant they accounted;
But our knights, on good horses mounted,
Drove them away incontinent.
Then forward on our road we went
Until we managed to arrive

Between Saint George and Ramleh. Five
Full years ago that day the land $\qquad$ July 4
Was torn by war from out our hand.[37]
The French were on the left. The king
With his men rode on the right wing, $\qquad$ 10,710
And on the morrow's journey changed
Nowise the way they were arranged.
Before Casal Moyen they made
A halt, and there they camped and stayed;
And there were some who thence departed
And on the road to Jaffa started,
Poverty-stricken and forlorn
With all the sorrows they had borne.

SALADIN REASSEMBLES HIS FORCES

When Saladin learned beyond doubt
That we were forced to turn about $\qquad$ 10,720
And go back, since we had no choice
But that, greatly did he rejoice.
He chose swift messengers and wrote
His letters, sending them hotfoot
To tell the Turks who loved him how
The Christians were departing now,
How they were torn apart by strife,
And how discord and wrath were rife
Among them. And he wrote that they
Who wished to serve his cause for pay $\qquad$ 10,730
Should come now to Jerusalem.
He gathered such a crowd of them
That twenty thousand, beyond doubt,
Were there, inside the town and out,
Of Turks all well armed and well mounted,
With footmen more than could be counted
Or numbered easily. Our state
They knew and oft did demonstrate

[37] The *Itinerarium* (p. 397) omits this, but does say that the next day was "pridie nonas Julii" (July 6). The battle of Hattin was on July 4, 1187.

How well they were informed thereof

. . .   10,740

As soon as our men had returned
To that place where our men sojourned.

RICHARD ASKS A TRUCE, WHICH IS REFUSED

Men left the host day after day:
Disheartened, many went away
To Jaffa, broken by distress
And by their life of wretchedness.
And when the king saw them depart
And saw that he had not the art
To lead the host upon the true
Path—what shall I now say to you,   10,750
Save that he sent to Saphadin
That he should speak to Saladin
And give him answer speedily
If he might have the truce that he
Had offered him on Ramleh field [38]
(As this our story hath revealed),
Till he could come back from his land?
He sent the sultan this demand,
Who from the first day had complete
Tidings and news of our retreat,   10,760
And who would not let them induce
Him to accord them such a truce
If Ascalon were not torn down.[39]
Now in the host this news was known
And carried to the king. Indeed

[38] See chapter vii, under heading "Richard opens negotiations with Saladin," and n. 14 to that chapter.

[39] Beha ed Din (pp. 355–60) tells more about these negotiations. The Moslem council urged Saladin to make peace, as both sides were exhausted. The sultan thereupon offered to surrender the Holy Sepulcher, and all cities then occupied by the Christians with the exception of Ascalon, which must be destroyed and left as neutral ground. Richard balked over the destruction of Ascalon which he had refortified at great expense. Saladin offered him Lydda in compensation for his expenses at Ascalon, but Richard refused.

He paid it not the slightest heed,
Nor would he list to their account.

THE HOST RETREATS TO ACRE

At once he gave command to mount
To Templars, Hospitallers, and
Three hundred more knights. His command   10,770
Was that they tear down Le Daron,
And have watch kept on Ascalon,
And never to relax this ward
Through carelessness or disregard.
They went there and destroyed it. They
Then came back to the host straightway.
The host then went to Jaffa, worn
And heavyhearted and forlorn,
And then to Acre their way they made.
But many men at Jaffa stayed   10,780
Behind, many of them sick, some well;
On them great terror later fell.
So now the host, taking the track
On which it marched before, came back
To Acre, one Sunday, mortified.   July 26
This haps to those whom sin doth guide.

CHAPTER X

As soon as ever Saladin
And his blood brother Saphadin
Learned that we had set out again
From Jaffa, as we have made plain,   10,790
And had gone back disconsolate,
As ye have just heard me relate
The tale, he summoned now to come
The proudest ranks of pagandom:
So that the sultan, at that hour
Ruled o'er a host in which were more
Than twenty thousand Turks on horse.
The emir of Byla [1] was of the force,
And the Assassin's son. [2] Of peers
There were one hundred six emirs,   10,800
And mountain footmen in such number
That they did the whole plain encumber.
Leaving Jerusalem, this host

---

[1] G. Paris claims that this emir of Bile is a fictitious person, as Bile is a place found only in the *chansons de geste*. The emir of Byla is, however, listed among the vassals of Saladin in the *Itinerarium* (p. 12). Probably it refers to Biraedjik on the Euphrates, a dependency of Maridin (Rey, *Les Colonies franques en Syrie*, p. 306).

[2] The *Itinerarium* (p. 400) says *filius Arcissi;* the reference seems to be to the son of the Old Man of the Mountain, at this time Sinan.

Came down, and pitched camp, and disposed
Themselves on Ramleh plain; and there
Could be seen many a courser fair.

DESCENDS UPON JAFFA

Upon a Sunday ³—'twas the same   July 26
Day on which we to Acre came—
Down upon Jaffa swept the horde
Of pagan miscreants abhorred.   10,810
On Monday their assault began.   July 27
[Forth from the walls our soldiers ran]
And in the gardens met the attack.
The whole day long they fought them back
And harassed them so much that they
Approached the stronghold not that day;
Nor Tuesday, the next day, nor yet   July 28
The third day. Thursday the onset   July 30
Around the city closely pressed,
And folk within were sore distressed.   10,820
Then Saladin had set upright
Four catapults both strong and light
And two stout mangonels likewise.
Then from the town arose the cries
Of the Christian folk, lamenting sore.
There were five thousand there or more,
Some in good health, while some lay ill,
And their laments rose loud and shrill.
"Ah, king of England," was their cry,
"Why did you go to Acre, ah, why?   10,830
Oh Christendom, how you have failed!"
Ye might have seen these men assailed
With such fierce violence unbounded,
Have seen so many killed and wounded,
Seen them so sturdily defend
Themselves, climb swiftly, then descend

³ The *Itinerarium* (p. 400) says the Sunday before the feast of St. Peter in Chains (July 26).

That, seeing all this, ye could not
But feel great pity for their lot.
Ever the catapults released
Their shots. The mangonels ne'er ceased.   10,840
Within were catapults as well,
But they knew not how to propel
The stones. The Turks pounded the gate
Facing Jerusalem with such weight
That the arches above gave way,
Filling our people with dismay,
Next they broke down the right-hand wall,
Making two perches of it fall.

THEY CAPTURE THE TOWN, BUT THE CITADEL RESISTS

On Friday was this downfall wrought.   July 31
There was a bitter battle fought   10,850
When through the breach the Turkish band
Poured in the city. Hand to hand
They fought. The Turks, whose numbers grew
As their host sent fresh men and new,
Broke our men's strength with their attack
And drove our forces up and back
To the Toron [4] before the tower.
A dreadful sight 'twas, at that hour,
To see the foe come in and slay
The sick who in the houses lay.   10,860
Many achieved there martyrdom,
And many left the rest, to come
In swift flight down toward the sea.
Then came the cruel enemy
Into the houses, seized what gain
They could, carried off all the grain,
And poured out all the wine upon
The ground. Then some stormed the Toron,

---

[4] This toron was the hill of Jaffa, that is, the citadel. The *Itinerarium* (p. 402) says
"turrim castri principatem."

Where the Lord's people fought to hold
Them back with stout defense and bold, 10,870
And others rushed down to the marges
Of the sea, where there were ships and barges,
Which some of our men sought to board
For what refuge they would afford.
There many died, who reached the sea
Too tardily. There Auberi
Of Rheims,[5] who was to guard the fort,
Like a base coward did comport
Himself. For he, thinking to slip
Away to sea, boarded a ship; 10,880
But his good men, with many a shout
Of protest, made him turn about
Back into the town by force.
Then said he: "Since no other course
There is, for God let us die here."
On every side the Turks drew near
The foot of the Toron, on right
And left; so many stormed the height
They knew not what side to defend
Themselves. Now arrows without end 10,890
Fell thicker than hail ever fell.
Men fought on foot, and fought pell-mell.
The fight lasted all day. But our
Men could not have withstood the power
Of their assaults without God's aid,
Who caused the patriarch newly made [6]

---

[5] Auberi of Rheims was in command of the citadel of Jaffa. He was taken prisoner by the Saracens. (Roger of Hoveden, III, p. 183.)

[6] This patriarch is called Ralph by Siccard (Muratori, *Scriptores*, VII, 616), but Röhricht prefers to term him anonymous ("Syria Sacra," in *Z.D.P.V.*, X [1887], 8). Ralph, bishop of Bethlehem, was called patriarch-elect in an act of 1192, according to Mas Latrie ("Les Patriarches latins de Jérusalem," *Rev. Or. Lat.*, I, 18–19), but we can find no such act, nor indeed any Ralph, bishop of Bethlehem, after the famous chancellor bishop who died in 1174. Between the death of Heraclius in 1191 and the accession of Monachus in 1194 there is great confusion, as several prelates were elected, but none ever entered into possession of the see or apparently was even invested.

To stay there. Fear of death could dim
His soul no whit, nor hinder him
From saving those who, while a breath
Of life remained, would fight till death.   10,900

THE DEFENDERS ASK FOR TRUCE, OFFERING TERMS

He sent a word to Saladin,
The brave and generous Saracen,
And asked of Saphadin to pray
That he would grant a truce that day,
Only until the morrow. He
Himself would pledge and guarantee
That if, ere nones, came succor none
From those of Acre, or Ascalon,
Or Richard, king of the English land,
Upon whom he had made demand,   10,910
As hostage he himself would go
With others of rank far from low
And let themselves be bound or chained,
That every Christian who remained
On the Toron still fighting in
The fray should pay to Saladin
Ten golden besants that their lives
Be spared. So with women and wives,
Each would pay besants five, and for
The little children pay three more.[7]   10,920
Hearing the terms of the demand
Thus made, Saladin gave command
To grant them and to cease the attack.
At once the messenger came back.
The truce was settled in this way,
And fighting ended for the day.
Thereon two hostages they sent
The Turks, who with the patriarch went—

[7] Beha ed Din (pp. 363–66) gives a slightly different story. The besieged in Jaffa asked the same terms as those granted Jerusalem before the city was attacked. Saladin refused and stormed the city. The defenders retreated into the citadel and then arranged a truce.

Thibaut de Troyes,[8] and Auberi.[9]
Thibaut, well known for bravery,   10,930
Count Henry's man, had reared and taught
The father of the count and brought
Him up. Others there may have been
Whose names I have not learned nor seen.

RICHARD, AT ACRE, LEARNS THE PLIGHT OF JAFFA

Ye heard me tell the tale, and well
It is such tale as this to tell,
For the great good which therefrom flowed—
How the host back to Acre rode,
Grief-stricken and disconsolate
And discontented with their fate.   10,940
Now all of them supposed that they
Would seek their ships without delay.
Even Richard himself, the king—
With our own eyes we saw this thing
Take place—had taken leave of all
The Temple and the Hospital,
And viewed his galleys to make sure
They were well ordered and secure,
And on the morrow without fail,
So says the book, he was to sail   10,950
For Beirut with his retinue.
He had already sent, 'tis true,
Seven galleys that went on to smite
Those of the fortress, who took flight.
They had not waited there if they
Had seen more galleys come that way.
One eve the king, thus occupied,
Sat in his tent at vespertide,

[8] Thibaut of Troyes was, according to G. Paris, one of the followers of the counts of Champagne.
[9] Auberi of Rheims, the commander of the citadel of Jaffa. See above, p. 401, n. 5. The *Itinerarium* (p. 403) lists, besides the hostages mentioned here, Augustus of London, Osbert Waldin, Henry de St. John, and others. They were all sent as prisoners to Damascus.

When, lo, a vessel swiftly driven
Came sailing into Acre haven.   10,960
And those who disembarked stayed not,
But straightaway the king they sought.
Jaffa was taken, so they told
Him, its men shut in the stronghold
Of the Toron, where they would die
If he his succor should deny,
As I have told you. The good king,
Noble in this and every thing,
Gave up the projects he had made,
Saying: "I go to bear them aid,"   10,970
And he convoked the host at once.
But the French all refused response
To this his summons, and opposed
Him, jealous folk and ill-disposed.
They would not move their feet, they said,
Nor ever follow where he led.
His rule and all rule they forswore,
And so they died. Of them no more.

RICHARD GOES TO THE RELIEF OF JAFFA

However, those who feared God's name,
From whatsoever land they came,   10,980
Templars and Hospitallers, good
Knights numerous of many a blood,
Donned armor and accouterment,
Mounted, and took the road. They went
By land to Cæsarea, while
The brave king of the English isle
Went with the galleys by the sea.[10]
They were all armed so splendidly,
No panoplies could be more fair.
One saw the count of Leicester there,   10,990
Likewise Andrew de Chauvigny,

[10] Beha ed Din (p. 369) says that he brought thirty-five galleys to Jaffa.

And also Roger de Saci [11]
And Jordan des Homez. This last
Knight died before the year was passed.
And also Ralph de Mauléon,[12]
Who has a lion broidered on
His banner. Ançon du Faï [13]—
Many a Saracen smote he—
As well as those of Préaux, who
Were of the royal retinue,   11,000
And many another known to fame
Of whom I have not learned the name.
They went to do God's work. With these
The Pisans and the Genoese,
Who did great deeds when they were needed.
Now hear ye how affairs proceeded.
Those who to Jaffa chose to fare
By land, and thought to go straight there,
Were stopped at Cæsarea, nor
Had they been there much time before   11,010
They were informed that Saladin
Guarded the roads and hemmed them in
So well that they could not go on:
This time 'twas the Assassin's son
Who came 'twixt Cæsarea and
Arsur.[14] Such strong winds smote the band

[11] Roger de Saci subsequently accompanied Berengaria home from Palestine (Landon, *Itinerary*, p. 75). His name appears on Richard's acts from 1190–98, and in 1197 he was one of the guarantors of Richard's treaty with Flanders (*ibid.*, pp. 35–132 *passim*).

[12] Ralph de Mauléon was the father of the poet Savari de Mauléon (Siedschlag, p. 91). He was lord of Châtillon-sur-Saône, an important baron of Bas-Poitou (S. Painter).

[13] Ançon du Faï, from the Calvados. (G. Paris, p. xi.) Can this be the companion of Stephen de Longchamp mentioned above? A Bartholomey de Faï and a William de Faï are mentioned as holding fiefs in the *Scripta de feodis*.

[14] Beha ed Din (p. 366) says that Kaimaz en Najmi had been stationed near Acre to keep watch on the movements of the Christian forces. He reported Richard's departure to Saladin. There is no mention of the Assassins or of any group detached to harass the Christians.

Upon the ships that were to bring
The king's companions and the king
That for three days they had to stay
'Neath Caïphas, and there they lay   11,020
And the king cried: "Mercy, O Lord!
Why do You hold me and retard
Me when I go upon Your quest?"
The Lord God then did manifest
His favor, sending a north wind
That took the fleet and blew behind
It. They reached Jaffa late, when day
Was done, on Friday. Saturday [15]   July 31–Aug. 1
At nones would have ended the truce,
And sorrow, torture and abuse,   11,030
And death had been the certain lot
Of the defenders, had God not,
Through the king, saved them from such fate,
As briefly we shall now relate.

BRUTAL TREACHERY OF THE SARACENS

The good king with his nobles kept
Within the galleys and there slept
During the rest of Friday night;
[Saturday morn they rose, bedight]
Themselves, and did their armor on.
Hear now how the convention   11,040
Was kept, how treacherously respected,
And with what faith the Turks protected
Those of the city who had bought
Safe-conduct for themselves, they thought,
By all the gold besants which they
Had promised. They began to pay
Them, and were paying them that morn.

[15] The *Itinerarium* (p. 405) says Saturday, the feast of St. Peter in Chains (August 1). Beha ed Din (p. 364) says the attack took place on Friday, the eighteenth Rajab, and Richard arrived the next day. Here again Beha ed Din is correct on his day, but not his date: Friday was the nineteenth Rajab.

The Saracens, as each in turn
Came to them with his gold and made
His payment, cut off each one's head.[16]   11,050
They thought this was a noble deed,
But shame be on such swinish creed!
Already seven had been cut down
And in a ditch their bodies thrown,
When from the Toron's walls their fate
Was seen. Those who were there relate
That there was a most piteous sight
Before the tower, on Toron's height;
For, certain they were doomed to die
At once, ye heard men wail and cry   11,060
In dreadful terror and dismay,
And kneel upon the ground, and pray,
Confess their fault, cry out their sin.
And those outside fought to get in
Among the thickest crowd, to try
And be among the last to die;
For all things, when death comes apace,
Ask for a little time and space.
They waited for their martyrdom,
And well may it be said, in sum,   11,070
That many tears that day were wept
Which God with pleasure did accept;
Because they welled forth from distress
Of death and their hearts' deep recess,
Which now to Him they dedicated.

RICHARD HESITATES TO LAND AT JAFFA

While they thuswise their death awaited
And had no expectation save
To go in this way to their grave,
The Turks observed the port, and they

[16] Beha ed Din (p. 368) says that forty-nine men left the citadel, but no more would come out. He does not mention any slaughter and gives the impression that they were spared.

Could see that there the galleys lay.   11,080
Down to the shore at rapid course
They hurried, both on foot and horse,
In such great numbers that the banks
Were crowded with their serried ranks.
They carried with them shields and targes
And sent their missiles at the barges
And at the galleys of the king.
Spirited was the galloping
And charging of their cavalry,
Who flung themselves into the sea,   11,090
Shooting their arrows, to withstand
The purpose of our men to land.
The noble Richard, meseems, chose
To bring his ships together close,
To speak to all his company.
Then said he to his chivalry:
"Fair knights, what shall we do? Now mark
Ye, shall we leave or disembark?
And in what way shall we proceed?"
The question was discussed indeed,   11,100
And some of those knights who replied
As their opinion testified
That 'twas a useless thing, in short,
To try to land or take the port,
Maintaining it was clear and plain
That all the garrison were slain.

HE HEARS THAT THE CITADEL STILL RESISTS

And while they argued thus and sought
To know whether to land or not,
Behold, the king of England spied
A man who leaped into the tide   11,110
From offshore, a mass-singing priest,
Who swam straight toward the king, nor ceased
Till they had taken him aboard.
Then said he: "Fair king, if the Lord

And you aid not the folk who wait
Here for you, death will be their fate."
"Good friend," the king replied, "how say
You? Do they live? And where are they?"
"Yes, sire, they do: before that tower
They wait together for their hour   11,120
Of death." When the king heard him thus,
He stayed no longer to discuss,
But said: "God sent us here, 'tis sure,
To suffer death and to endure;
And, since death needs must be our lot,
Shame be on him who cometh not!"

AND FORCES A LANDING ON THE BEACH

He sent the galleys closer, stripped
The armor from his legs, and leaped
Into the sea, which came waist-high,
By happy chance. So to the dry   11,130
Land he pushed boldly on in front,
Second or first, as was his wont.
Geoffrey du Bois [17] went, too, also
The king's good man, Pierre de Préaux,
And all the rest were not far back;
They came together to attack
The Turks, with whom the shore was filled.
The noble king in person killed
Them with his arbalest. His rude
And sturdy followers pursued   11,140
Them all along the strand. In dread
The Turks before him broke and fled,
Because they did not dare withstand
Him. With his sword of steel in hand,
He charged full tilt upon the foe
And harried them most fiercely, so
That they had no way to defend
Themselves, nor did they dare contend

[17] Geoffrey du Bois, an English knight from Hampshire (Siedschlag, p. 114, no. 28).

Against the stout knights that he had
With him, who smote like men gone mad;   11,150
So fierce their charge and their career
That soon the waterside was clear
Of Turks. They drove them all away,
And after that they seized on stray
Barrels and wooden boards, broad planks,
Old ships and galleys from the banks,
And blocked the shore as a defense
Between them and the Saracens.
The king set knights and sergeants there
And arbalesters, who took care   11,160
To harass well the infidels.
The latter sent forth shrieks and yells
And fled, scattered and impotent.

RICHARD RECAPTURES JAFFA

Up a round stair the king now went,
Which to the Templars' house doth lead:
He was the first one to succeed
In entering the town. He found
Three thousand Saracens all round
The fort engaged in plundering
And carrying off everything.   11,170
King Richard, bravest in the world,
Soon as he topped the wall unfurled
His banners, flinging them on high
And showing them against the sky
To the Christian folk whom he relieved.
And just as soon as they perceived
Them, "Holy Sepulcher!" they cried
In unison; they did not bide
Or stay, but took their arms and armed
Themselves. The pagans were alarmed   11,180
When they saw how our men descended,
What Turkish corpses lay extended
On earth, whom the king's strokes laid low!

No one dared wait to face his blow
But forfeited his life thereby.
And now came down our soldiery
Into the town and through the streets.
And men were wounded, noble feats
Of arms were done, men slashed and slain.
Thus were avenged the wounds and pain   11,190
Of those folk, helpless, sick, and ill,
Whom the Turks had seen fit to kill
When they had found them in the town.
And still our men kept coming down
And still kept dealing shame among
The Saracens.[18] But why prolong
The tale? All those whom they could take
Within the walls, who could not make
Escape most promptly from the city,
Were killed at once and without pity.   11,200
Thus was the city freed, and shame
Was heaped upon their people's name.

SALADIN'S RETREAT

Though he had fought the whole day through,
The king sped after to pursue
The foe. He then had but three steeds.
Not even in Roncevaux were deeds
Performed, by old or youthful men,
By Christian or by Saracen,
In such a way or such a manner;
For, when his foes perceived his banner,   11,210
They quailed before him left and right.
No place for cowards was this fight,
For God never made snow or rain
(Even when in a hurricane

[18] Beha ed Din (pp. 369–71) confirms this in almost every detail, including the incident of the man who swam out to tell Richard that the citadel still held out. He adds that those within the citadel, when they saw that Richard was not landing his forces, felt themselves abandoned and sent envoys asking terms of surrender. The envoys were talking to Saladin when the fighting broke out afresh.

They fall) that drove so thick and fast
But that the darts that there were cast—
And bolts from crossbows that did fill
The air—rained on us thicker still.
Now his men hastened to unfold
The news to Saladin. They told   11,220
Him how his folk were battered thus;
And he, base man and infamous,
More raging than a wolf, was made
To be a-fevered and afraid.
He dared not longer wait there, hence
He gave command to strike his tents
And move pavilions to the plain.
The king, with his brave gallant train,
Kept following upon their tracks
And harrying them with fresh attacks.   11,230
Our arbalesters, too, well skilled
At shooting bolts, their horses killed.
We did so harry and pursue
Them, that two full leagues they withdrew.
The king gave his command to pitch
His tent on the same spot in which
Saladin had not dared to wait;
And there encamped Richard the Great.

A PLOT TO CAPTURE RICHARD

When that day's battle was completed
And the Turks' forces had retreated,   11,240
Their host was mortified with shame
Because foot soldiers overcame
Them, though there were but few of us,
While the Turks' force was numerous.
But God thereto had lent His arm
That His men might not suffer harm.
Saladin gave word to convoke
His Saracens and Turkish folk
Of highest rank and dignity,

And asked them: "Who made you to flee?   11,250
Was it the host of Acre then,
Returned to deal thus with my men?
And were these troops on foot or horse
Who swept down on you with such force?"
A traitor, who knew how the thing
Had happed, and who had seen the king,
Made answer: "Sire, no mount, indeed,
Had they with them, or mule or steed,
Save that the mighty king renowned
In Jaffa three war chargers found;   11,260
And that is all they have, and they
Cannot have more whate'er they pay.
If any dared to undertake
The deed, they very well might make
Him captive, with small trouble spent,
For he sleeps alone within his tent."

THE STENCH OF SLAUGHTER

It happened on a Saturday,   Aug. 1
So says the tale that I convey,
That thus the town was won and freed
Of Saracens and of their breed.   11,270
They had done deeds deliberate
That men shall evermore relate,
For they had captured Jaffa, slain
The Christians sick and racked with pain
Whom they discovered in the town.
And further, of a truth 'tis known,
They set themselves to slaughter all
The pigs inside the city wall,[19]
And this was an infinity.
It is a well-known verity   11,280
That they eat not the flesh of swine,

[19] Ibn Jubair (quoted in G. Le Strange, *Palestine under the Moslems*, p. 332) re-marked concerning Acre under the Christian rule: "It is the meeting place of Moslem and Christian merchants of all lands. The place is full of pigs and crosses."

And therefore kill them by design.
More than aught else on earth they hate
Them, just as they abominate
The Christian faith. They mingled then
The corpses of the swine and men.
But Christian folk, who were devout
To serve God, took the bodies out,
Buried the Christians found among
The heap, and then outside they flung   11,290
Saracens killed on Saturday.
There stinking with the swine they lay,
Such stench as could be borne by none.
Sunday the king had work begun—   Aug. 2
They worked Monday and Tuesday, too—   Aug. 3–4
Repairing Jaffa's walls anew
And making whole each shattered spot,
Till they had built it up somewhat.
Though they had not mortar or lime,
It would protect them in a time   11,300
Of need. The host remained outside
The walls, where it seemed best to bide.

THE PLOT TO TAKE RICHARD

Saladin's mamelukes, the hordes
Drawn from Aleppo, and the Kurds,
And all the swift and mettlesome
Nobles of hated pagandom
Together in a council came;
They all said they were filled with shame
That they fled Jaffa before powers
As small in number as were ours,   11,310
Who had no horses of our own.
They talked the matter up and down
And swore to an agreement, so
That they were pledged by oath to go
And, having seized the king within

His tent, take him to Saladin.
The plan was sworn thus and contrived.

RICHARD LACKS MEN AND HORSES

From Cæsarea now arrived
Count Henry of Champagne. He brought
His company with him by boat.   11,320
At Cæsarea, where first went
The host, they had to stop, being pent
In by the Saracens, whose masses
Guarded the rivers and the passes;
And so the whole company gave
The king no aid nor succor, save
Alone the count his nephew. Thus
He had no force more numerous
To help him pass in safety through
The dangers that were to ensue   11,330
Than a mere fifty knights alone—
Or at most, sixty—of his own,
Sergeants and arbalesters filled
With courage, sturdy men and skilled,
And the Pisans and the Genoese,
Who did the tasks of God. With these
Were some two thousand more, indeed.
And since the day on which they freed
The city they sought steeds, but could
Find only fifteen, bad and good.   11,340
His men so suffered from this dearth
They would have perished from the earth,
Had God not saved them from the works
And from the plottings of the Turks.

DISSENSION AMONG THE CONSPIRATORS

Hear now a marvelous event
That must compel astonishment;
For all our men would have been caught

And seized on Wednesday by that plot   Aug. 5
To take the king which they had hatched,
Had God not stopped and overmatched   11,350
Them. It was matins that night when
Took horse the soldiers Saracen;
They ranged their forces in array
And laced their visors down, and they
Rode forth by moonlight. Then God chose
This as the moment to disclose
The goodness that doth swell His glory,
And it should be retold in story
When He performs His gracious works.
Down through the level land the Turks   11,360
Rode close ranked on their enterprise.
The Lord God made a quarrel rise
Among them, with most bitter words
Between the mamelukes and Kurds,
About whose duty it was then
To dismount and to stop our men
From going back into the fort
And finding safety and support.
Each one said: "You dismount, you must."
"Nay, you!" "Nay, you!" "Nay, you, 'tis just   11,370
That we should have the right to ride."
And so they quarreled and defied
Each other, and the strife among
Them as they rode lasted so long
That they saw morning rise serene
Just as the Lord God had foreseen.
And still the king slept in his tent.

THE CAMP IS WARNED

Hear now the splendid incident
Of one from Genoa. This man
Arose just at the break of dawn   11,380
And went out in the *berruie;*
As he prepared to turn back he

Could hear the Turks come and catch sight
Of helmets gleaming in the light
By lowering his head. His shout
Of danger instantly rang out,
Sending forth warnings and alarms
And calling all our men to arms.
The cry awoke the king; before
That day was done he labored sore.   11,390
He leaped from bed, and as he rose
He quickly put on, I suppose,
A hauberk strong and firm and white,
And gave command that every knight
Should be awakened and should rise.
Small wonder that, with a surprise
Like this which suddenly had come
On them, they found it cumbersome
To clothe and arm themselves with speed.
And I can well affirm, indeed,   11,400
They were so hurried and so pressed,
The king and many of the rest,
That with their legs unarmed and bare,
Covered by naught but sky and air,
They fought that day; some even lacked
Their breeches; when they were attacked
And wounded sorely, this did bring
Them more distress than anything.

THE CRUSADERS ARM THEMSELVES

While our men armed themselves, the crew
Of Saracens still closer drew.   11,410
The king upon his charger mounted.
And at his side there could be counted
No more than ten of mounted knights.
He who relates the story writes
That with his soldiers and his mount
Was Henry of Champagne, the count;
Robert, the count of Leicester, fought

With them that day, as well he ought;
Bartholomew of Mortemer [20]
Rode with them, that I can declare;   11,420
And Raoul de Mauléon, a knight
Who never wearied of a fight;
Likewise Andrew de Chauvigny,
In stirrups a stout man was he;
Gerard de Furneval,[21] who rode
His horse and at the king's side bode;
Roger de Saci, mounted on
A horse wretched and woebegone;
While William de l'Estanc was borne
By a beast worn-out and forlorn;   11,430
And there was brave Hugh de Neville,[22]
A noble sergeant full of zeal;
Henry le Tyois,[23] who that day
Bore the king's banner in the fray.
And now our forces were disposed
To meet the pagans' cruel host,
Drawn up in order, with each band
United under one command.
Along the shore our knights were set
Leftwards, to face the Turkish threat   11,440
Directed toward Saint Nicholas; [24]
A fitting place for them this was,

[20] Bartholomew of Mortemer may have been English or Norman. (Siedschlag, p. 113, no. 14.) G. Paris (p. xii) locates him doubtfully as from the Eure. Mortimer is a common name, both in England and in Normandy.

[21] Gerard de Furneval, a Norman, appears on Richard's acts, 1194–99 (Landon, *Itinerary*). He settled in England after his return from the crusade and was the founder of the house of Furneval. His son Gerard II, who became lord of Sheffield, Yorkshire, went on the fifth crusade. (Siedschlag, p. 91; Round, *E.H.R.*, XVIII, 476; S. Painter.)

[22] Hugh de Neville of Wethersfield, Essex, was one of the sources of information employed by Ralph of Coggeshall (Siedschlag, p. 117, no. 59). He died in 1222 (Round, *op. cit.*, pp. 476–77). His name occurs frequently on the acts of Richard (Landon, *Itinerary*).

[23] Henry le Tyois is known only in this reference. Meyer (*G. Maréchal*, III, 51) notes that "Tiois" meant usually a Hollander, sometimes a German. Round says that he probably settled in England after the crusade.

[24] Saint Nicholas is identified by G. Paris as a church near Jaffa.

For the Turks swarmed there in a crowd,
Beating their drums and shouting loud;
Before their gardens now took station
People of many a different nation.
Pisans were there and Genoese,
Nor can it here be told how these
Men had to suffer, thrusting back
The hated infidels' attack.   11,450

AND DRAW UP IN BATTLE ARRAY

The Turks now set to work to shoot,
To shriek and shout and yell and hoot;
And a fierce onslaught did ensue,
Giving our good folk much to do.
Right down upon the ground they kneeled,
Holding erect target and shield
Before them, each with lance in hand.
The king, who well for battle planned,
Placed 'twixt each pair who held a shield
An arbalester well concealed   11,460
And a man who, at his request,
Would wind for him his arbalest
And give it him when it was needed;
In this manner the host succeeded
In making their defense most stout.
Of course it is beyond all doubt
That those who were in such a pass,
Confronted by such mighty mass
Of Turks, for their heads felt great fear.
But, just as true as you are here,   11,470
The king went 'mong the knights, beseeching
Them, encouraging, and preaching
With gallant words. Jean de Préaux
Went, too, exhorting them also.
And they said: "Now we shall observe
Who well and nobly strives to serve
So long as God his life doth spare:

'Tis our sole business and affair
To sell our lives dear, then succumb,
And thus await our martyrdom,   11,480
Since it is sent to us by God.
Now we are in the rightful road,
Since through His goodness He bestows
The goal that we all sought and chose.
Here lies our rightful recompense."
The ranks were ranged for the defense;
And now the Turkish troops drew nigh.
Our men kept their legs solidly
And firmly fixed, deep in the sand,
Each with his leveled lance in hand,   11,490
All ready for the foe to come.

THE SARACENS ATTACK WITH FURY

The squadrons of base pagandom
Now charged, and with such impetus
And fury hurled themselves at us
That if our men had flinched, 'tis true
That their charge would have broken through;
And in each of the squadrons were
A thousand Turks, unless I err.[25]
When they had got so close that they
Could see our men would not give way,   11,500
They veered their course, and rode along
Our line. Our arbalesters flung
Their bolts. The Turks dared not remain,
For these bolts stretched them on the plain,
Striking and wounding beasts and men;
And then their squadrons charged again,
Rode swiftly over the same ground,
Then stopped and veered and wheeled around.
And they charged several times this way.
When the king's men perceived that they   11,510

[25] The *Itinerarium* (p. 417) gives seven squadrons of 1,000 each.

Would not do more, although their force
Was numerous and all on horse,
With lances leveled our men started
Forward, among the paynim darted,
Breaking their ranks and dealing stroke
On stroke among the miscreant folk.
So fierce the onslaught that the shock
Made the foes' ranks tremble and rock,
And even their third line felt the blow.
When the king looked about him, lo,   11,520
He saw dismounted at the right
The count of Leicester, that bold knight,
Who, well though he had fought, indeed,
Had been unseated from his steed.
When the king rushed to extricate
Him, what a crowd of Turks went straight
To where the lion banner flew!
There was Raoul de Mauléon, too,
Whom the Turks had made prisoner,
When the king saw him and put spur   11,530
Into his battle charger's flanks
And rescued him from out their ranks.

RICHARD'S VALOR AND SAPHADIN'S COURTESY

The king did brave and valiant work
Against the Persian and the Turk,
And no man ever, weak or strong,
In one day fought so hard or long:
Among the Turks full tilt he drove,
Smiting unceasingly, and clove
Them to the teeth. With blows so fierce
And endless did he slash and pierce   11,540
The foe, dealing them stroke on stroke,
That on his hands his own skin broke.
Now came a Saracen who parted
From the other Turks and thither started

On a swift-striding steed: behold,
'Twas Saphadin d'Arcade,[26] the bold,
Who did things like a generous
And noble man and courteous.
As I say, he came rapidly
With two good steeds of Araby   11,550
And to the king of England sent
Them, asking him that he consent—
For the brave deeds that he had done
And all the prowess he had won—
To mount them, with this covenant:
That if it should please God to grant
That he survive the fight that day,
Some fitting guerdon he should pay.
Later a rich reward he reaped.
The king was most glad to accept   11,560
Them, saying he would readily
From his most mortal enemy
Take many more of them, indeed,
If they came in such hour of need.

THE FIGHT SPREADS TO THE TOWN

Now grew the battle more intense:
Never was seen such violence.
The Turkish spears lay all around
So that they covered up the ground:
They gathered them in armfuls. Then
Were seen so many wounded men   11,570
That the galley men, by fear o'ertaken,
Fled to the ships they had forsaken.

[26] The *Itinerarium* (p. 419) says "Saphadinus de Archadia, frater Saladini" which leaves no room for doubt about the identity of this generous knight. G. Paris (p. 530) goes to great lengths to discuss the meaning of the Arcadia which he points out is a legendary country. Stubbs (p. cix) identified a *Baffadinus Archadius* mentioned in the *Itinerarium* (p. 13) as Bohadin or Saphadin of Arka. Ernoul (p. 281) claims that it was Saladin himself who sent the horses to Richard and that Richard refused them. But Ernoul places the incident before the capture of Daron, consequently his authority here is the slightest. The *Eracles* (pp. 196–97) says that Saladin told Saphadin to send horses to Richard when he landed at Jaffa, and Saphadin sent him two.

Who flees now gains disgrace thereby.
Now from the town arose the cry
That all the Turks were drawing near
In full force, seeking front and rear
To catch and hold us in this manner;
The noble king came with his banner
And with him two more of his knights.[27]

· · ·   11,580

When he went in, the first to greet
Him in the middle of a street
Were three Turks mounted sumptuously.
He fell upon them royally,
And with such dash and fury struck
Them that in little time he took
Two horses, and the Turks he slew.
The other Turks by force he threw
Out of the town, then did not wait
But had blocked up at once the gate   11,590
Which they had entered, and took care
That sentries should be stationed there.
And then without delay he sped
To the galleys, where his men had fled
In their great terror and distress.
Richard, the son of nobleness,
Went to encourage them once more:
He got them to come back to shore,
Being able in this way to rally
All of his troops. Thus in each galley   11,600
Were left but five men. Leading the rest,
Back to the host he sped with zest.

THE HEROISM OF RICHARD

They had not rested. Then did he
His charge of great audacity.
Never did man such mighty deed:

[27] The *Itinerarium* (p. 420) gives two knights and two arbalesters.

He charged among the miscreant breed
So deep that he was hid from sight
Of his own men, and hemmed in quite.
And they came near to shattering
Their ranks and following the king.　　11,610
We had been lost indeed had they
Done this. But the king knew his way:
Forward and back he hewed a swath
About him, cutting deadly path
With his good sword, whose might was such
That everything that it could touch,
Or man or horse, was overthrown
And to the earth was battered down.
I think 'twas there he severèd
At one stroke both the arm and head　　11,620
Of an emir, an infidel
Steel-clad, whom he sent straight to hell.
And when the Turks perceived this blow,
They made broad path before him, so
That, thank God, he could come back safe.
But he was covered with such sheaf
Of arrows which the foe shot thick
And fast at him and which did stick
In horse and horsecloth that, in fine,
He looked just like a porcupine.　　11,630
Thus he returned from the mêlée,
Which lasted all the livelong day,
From morning till the fall of night,
So desperate and fierce a fight
That if God had not aided us
It would have been calamitous.
That He was with us well we knew,
Because we lost but one or two
Men in the combat, at the most;
Whereas, the foe, for their part, lost　　11,640
Full fifteen hundred steeds or more,
Who lay dead, scattered widely o'er

The ground. Seven hundred Turks were slain,
And more, whose corpses strewed the plain.
And still, with all their battling,
They did not carry off the king,
Who did before these folk we hate
His deeds of chivalry so great
And such fair prowess as to stun
And to bewilder everyone.   11,650
They marveled, too, at those with him,
Who like him ventured life and limb.

THE SARACENS PRAISE RICHARD

When the Lord God thus graciously
Had succored Christianity
And saved the Christians and their lord
From capture by the paynim horde,
And when the army had retreated,
There came a word that was repeated
How Sultan Saladin requested
News of his Saracens and jested   11,660
With them, making his jesting sting:
"Where are these men who took the king?
Who gives him now into my hand?"
Then a Turk from a far-off land
Made answer to him: "Sire, in sooth,
I shall relate to you the truth.
Never did any man behold
One so clear-sighted or so bold
Or better tried in noble deeds,
Always prepared to meet all needs;   11,670
We strove with him as best we could,
And we dealt stalwart blows and good,
But capture him we never can,
For no one dares confront the man,
Such is his courage and his might."
Lords, 'tis no idle talk I write:
Well the Turks knew his character

And would have made him prisoner
Except for God and his own skill.
For he fought with such dauntless will   11,680
And did such deeds of gallantry,
He and his men of chivalry,
That of a malady they fell
Ill, near the accursed infidel,
Part from the labors they had done,
Part from the stench of carrion.
Such foul corruption filled the town
And their health was so broken down
That they were very near to die,
The king and all his company.   11,690

SICK UNTO DEATH, RICHARD YET DEFIES SALADIN

Just at the time when the king, stricken
Down by this malady, did sicken,
Saladin sent him word, to tell
Him he and his Saracens as well
Would come and fetch him should he dare
To stay and to await them there.
The king to answer was not slow,
Saying he might believe and know
That he would stay there and would face
Him; never at any time or place,   11,700
While he could stand erect on feet
Or crawl on knees, would he retreat
From him one single foot of land.
Thus he accepted warfare, and
God knew well in what state of ease
He uttered valiant words like these.
Then he commanded that the Count
Henry (so doth the tale recount)
Should go to Cæsarea for
The French, who had gone there before,   11,710
And for the others, with command
To come and help defend the land.

He told them of their pledges sworn
And of his own state, sick and worn.
But succor they would not provide:
They spurned him, and he would have died
Unaided, had he not made truce.

.   .   .

But none should call this a mistake,
For the Turks would have come to take   11,720
Him, and he would have undergone
Much anguish, and lost Ascalon
Beyond doubt to the infidel,
And mayhap Tyre and Acre as well.[28]

[28] The *Eracles* (p. 197) relates that Richard returned to Acre after the battle of Jaffa.

CHAPTER XI

RICHARD FEELS THAT HIS CAUSE IS LOST

The king lay sick at Jaffa, spent
And worn, in deep discouragement,
And thus reflecting as he lay
He thought 'twere best to go away,
For the town's weakness and its lack
Of means to fend off an attack.   11,730
He sent then for Count Henry, one
Who was the king's own sister's son,
And for the Templars, and sent call
For those who served the Hospital,
And he spoke to them, to explain
His heart's grief and his body's pain.
He said that some must needs go on
To mount a guard on Ascalon;
Others must stay at Jaffa, where
They were, and guard the town with care;   11,740
And he would go to Acre, where he
Might be cured of his malady.[1]
He said to them that he could do
No more. What shall I say to you,
Save that they one and all excused

---

[1] Richard of Devizes (p. 499) says that Richard recovered his health when he heard
the news of the death of Hugh of Burgundy and the departure of the French.

Themselves, and in plain words refused
To serve without him, in this sort,
As garrison of any fort?
So, without further words, they went.
The king's anger was violent.   11,750
When the king saw all men betray
Him, fail their trust, and disobey—
A thing not loyal, clean, or kind—
He was most troubled in his mind,
All disconcerted and confounded.
My lords, now be ye not astounded
If the king did what in this case
Seemed best, considering time and place.
Who feareth shame and seeketh honor
Of two ills still will choose the minor: 11,760
For it is better to demand
A truce than 'twere to leave the land
In peril, since the rest were starting
To leave him, in their ships departing.

HE ASKS SAPHADIN TO ARRANGE A TRUCE

Then he sent word to Saphadin,
Who was brother of Saladin
And loved him for his knighthood's sake,
Requesting him at once to make
A truce on the best terms he could,
Saying that he for his part would   11,770
Accept them.[2] Saphadin complied,

[2] Richard of Devizes (pp. 448–52) relates that while Richard was sick a truce was
sought by Henry of Champagne and Hubert Walter. When the king recovered, he knew
nothing of the truce and ordered his men to arms, but they refused to fight, so that
Richard was compelled to arrange the peace. The most detailed account of the negotiations is to be found in Beha ed Din (pp. 371–87). The first move was made by Richard,
when on the evening of August 1, the very day on which he recaptured Jaffa, he asked
that Abu Bekr be sent him that they might discuss terms of peace. Saladin offered the
land from Tyre to Cæsarea; Richard demanded Jaffa and Ascalon as well, but offered
to become the vassal of the sultan for these lands. Saladin agreed to the Christian lordship of Jaffa, but insisted on keeping Ascalon for himself, which did not suit Richard.
Hoping for better terms if he could deal with Saphadin, Richard asked for a personal

And so his efforts multiplied
That Saladin now authorized
A truce upon these terms devised:
He asked that Ascalon, whose fort
Did greatly hinder him and thwart
His kingdom's power, should be torn down,
And none should fortify the town
For three years. After that, he who
Could do so might rebuild anew.   11,780
And Jaffa should be fortified
And by the Christians occupied.
All the remainder of the plain
Between the mountains and the main,
Where nobody now dwelt, should be
By honest truce made clear and free;

---

interview with him, but Saphadin was sick and could not grant it. These negotiations had taken place through envoys on August 1 and 2. After the failure of these negotiations there was a renewal of hostilities, during which time Saladin was strengthened by the arrival of reinforcements from Mosul and from Egypt, while Richard was weakened by the illness which was upon him. The king "constantly sent messengers to the sultan for fruit and snow, for all the while he was ill he had a great longing for pears and peaches." The messengers who delivered the fruit took the occasion to spy out carefully the conditions of the Christian camp, so that Saladin was well informed as to the enemy. On August 24 the Moslem council decided to attack Jaffa in force on the morrow. Then, just as the advance scouts were reconnoitering the city, Abu Bekr appeared in the camp with renewed offers from Richard. The king, he reported, would accept compensation for Ascalon (which had been the offer he refused earlier). His one desire was that he should be allowed to save his face and his honor among his own people; Saladin could easily reconquer any lands ceded, but Richard could not return to his own country without a treaty which seemed to give him the victory. Impressed by these words, Saladin dispatched Saphadin to Richard on Friday, August 28, authorizing him to make peace, but only on condition that Richard surrender Ascalon. That same day Bedr ed Din Dolderon reported that an embassy headed by Huat (Hubert Walter) had sought him with offers of peace. They went so far as to relinquish all claims for compensation for the expenses of Ascalon. On Saturday Dolderon was able to report to Saphadin that Richard would agree to the terms previously offered him, although at first he had insisted that he had not authorized the relinquishing of the claims for compensation. The terms were submitted to Saladin on Sunday; the next day (August 31) the sultan held a council and a convention was finally drawn up. The last item to be settled was the status of Ramleh which was at length partitioned. The treaty was signed Wednesday, September 2, and was to be valid for three years; Saphadin signed for his brother while Henry of Champagne and Balian d'Ibelin signed for Richard, who was too sick to affix his own signature.

And those who rightly kept it so
Might safely come and safely go
To seek the Holy Sepulcher;
And goods of every character   11,790
Should pass toll-free throughout the land.[3]
Thus was the truce devised and planned.

RICHARD ACCEPTS TERMS FOR THREE YEARS

Its terms were written as related,
And brought back to the king, and stated.
He, with no succor to invoke
And being so near the hated folk,
Whose host was but two leagues away,
Accepted it. Who would gainsay
Me, or would change or modify
The story—such a man would lie.   11,800
When they had brought the truce to submit
To the king and he accepted it—
Since he could not do otherwise—
He could not then his heart disguise,
But straight to Saladin sent word
(Which many Turks of high rank heard)
For him to note and take good heed
That to this truce he had agreed,
As it was well that he should know,
For three years only:[4] one to go   11,810

[3] The best account of the terms of the Treaty of Jaffa is to be found in Beha ed Din (pp. 381–85), and supplementary details are to be found in Ibn al Athir (p. 66), Ralph of Diceto (p. 105), and the *Eracles* (p. 199). The Christians were to hold the sea coast while the Saracens retained the mountains and the hinterland. Specifically the Christians were to hold: Tyre, Acre, Cæsarea, Arsur, Caïphas, and Jaffa with their dependencies, but they were not to receive Nazareth, Saforia, Ibelin, or Mirabel. Ramleh and Lydda were to be divided equally; Ascalon was to be razed. The Christians were to be allowed freedom of pilgrimage to the Holy City. Antioch, Tripoli, and all the Moslem states were to be considered included in the treaty. Subsequently Saladin restored half of Sidon to its former lord, Renaud.

[4] The date of the *terminus ad quem* of the treaty is variously given. The *Itinerarium* (p. 428) and Roger of Hoveden (III, 184) say three years beginning Easter 1192; Beha ed Din (p. 384) says three years beginning September 2, 1192; Ralph of Diceto (p. 105) says three years, three months, three weeks, three days, and three hours. This

Back to his own country, and then
One to collect and gather men,
One to return and to win back
The land, if he dared wait the attack.
The sultan sent him back reply
Through those who bore the embassy
That by the faith from which he swerved
No whit, and by the God he served,
He so esteemed his bravery,
His great heart, and his gallantry   11,820
That if the land must needs be won
During his life by anyone,
Of all those whom, before or since,
He ever knew, he was the prince
Whom with best will and least remorse
He would see conquer it by force.
This end the king thought to attain
And win the Sepulcher again,
But he knew not, nor could he know,
That which he was to undergo.   11,830

THE FRENCH RETURN HOME WITHOUT SIGHT OF JERUSALEM

When this truce had been ratified
And sworn by those on either side,
Its terms made clear, and its intent
Set forth in chart and document,
The good king had himself borne down,
For cure and healing, to the town
Of Caïphas upon the sea
To take his cure and remedy.
The Frenchmen who did still sojourn
[At Acre] were anxious to return   11,840
To France, but first they said that they
[Would go upon their pilgrims' way].
Yet they had disapproved the truce,

elaborate form was a common usage in medieval treaties—as witness the Treaty of
Jaffa between Frederick II and Egypt in 1229.

Heaping scorn on it and abuse,
And, in great need, refused to bring
Succor to Jaffa or the king.
When the king learned what they desired
And that safe-conduct they required
To make complete their pilgrimage,
He summonèd his embassage,   11,850
And sent request to Saladin
And to the emir Saphadin,
To let no Christian, whether young
Or old, unhindered pass along—
If they wished him to be their debtor—
To Jerusalem without a letter
From him or from Count Henry.[5] They
Were filled with fury and dismay
When they were told of this command;
So with all speed most of the band   11,860
Packed their gear, and in petulance
Took ship and started back to France.

THE PILGRIMS SET OUT FOR THE SEPULCHER

When they had seen fit to depart,
Most of these French, the greater part
Of those folk who had most maligned
The king and hindered him in mind
And deed, in whom no trust at all
He had, the king had cried the call
To go now to the Sepulcher;
And each his offering should bear   11,870
To help build Jaffa's walls anew.
And what more shall I say to you?
They went to the Sepulcher divided
Into three groups: each one was guided
By a constable who took command.

[5] Bar Hebraeus (p. 340) claims that this was done to prevent the pilgrims from being able to fulfill their vows by visiting the Sepulcher and make them willing to return for a renewal of the crusade. Ralph of Diceto (p. 105) says that the interdict was placed on all who visited Jerusalem under Saracen conduct.

One constable, I understand,
Was Sir Andrew de Chauvigny:
Cluny has far worse monks than he;
Another, Ralph Taissons, renowned
For love of music and sweet sound;   11,880
The bishop of Salisbury,[6] the same
Who later archbishop became,
Commanded the third group. I know
Beyond a doubt that this is so.
When these had each his document,
Upon their way the pilgrims went,
Marching in ranks, in close array.
Now hear how sin doth lead astray
Many a man in many a place
Who seeks the rightful path to trace!   11,890
As these folk traveled, they passed by
The plains of Ramleh, which were nigh
At hand. The barons then who guided
The band, took counsel and decided
To send Saladin word of them,
How they draw nigh Jerusalem
To see the Sepulcher, and bring
Safe-conducts from the English king.

THE MESSENGERS ARE NEGLIGENT

The men who bore the message were
Wise men of noble character,   11,900
But either sin or slothfulness
Made their nobility transgress.
One was William des Roches,[7] whose head

---

[6] The *Itinerarium* (p. 432) names him: Hubert (Walter).

[7] William des Roches later became seneschal of Anjou, Maine, and Touraine. He was the son-in-law of Robert de Sablé and a firm partisan of Richard. After Richard's death William championed the cause of young Arthur. Subsequently he served under both John and Philip Augustus, changing his allegiance frequently. He was one of the chief barons in securing the French occupation of Anjou. See Gaston Dubois, "Récherches sur la vie de Guillaume des Roches," *B.E.C.*, Vol. XXX–XXXIV (1869–73). Dubois was ignorant of William's participation in the crusade.

Was well and fairly helmeted;
Girard de Furneval also
Was one. So was Pierre de Préaux.
Down Ramleh plain they rode on horse
Till, following their proper course,
They reached the Toron of the Knights.
There they decided that by rights   11,910
They should pause, and seek out Saphadin
For his safe-conduct to march in
The town. In fact, they went to sleep
And stayed so long in slumber deep
That all the afternoon was spent.
The main body still marching, went
Past the whole plain, and had come close
To where the mountain flanks arose.
And then they saw, my lord André
And those with him, to their dismay,   11,920
Those men whom they had sent to bear
Their word approaching from the rear.
When they were seen and recognized,
The main group halted, much surprised
And shocked. The leaders then declared:
"Lord God, we grievously have fared
If now the Saracens should see
Us! Those who bore our embassy,
Behold them, they but now are come!
Our march is rash and venturesome,   11,930
For see, the vesper hour doth close
Upon us, and our savage foes
Have not quitted their host or gone
Away. If we should march straight on
Without sending them word, no doubt
They would at once attack and rout
Us. We should lose our heads, and so
Would all the folk who with us go,
Who all unarmed and helpless came."
The messengers incurred much blame;   11,940

Nevertheless, men asked and prayed
Them to pursue their embassade,
And greatly urged and hurried them.
They went on toward Jerusalem.

THE PILGRIMS ARE TERRIFIED

More than two thousand Turks they found
Outside the city, camped all round.
They searched till they discoverèd
The emir Saphadin, and said
That our pilgrims were traveling
Thither, with letters from the king.   11,950
They asked him to take every care
That they might have safe-conduct there.
Reproachfully Saphadin spake
To them: it was a mad mistake,
He said, and rash and perilous
To plan to lead the pilgrims thus:
They little loved their lives, indeed,
Who thus would venture to proceed
Without safe-conduct. And while they
Were speaking came the end of day.   11,960
Our group arrived, all unprovided
With arms, and without wisdom guided.
The Saracens, when they had seen
Them, showed such grim and fearsome mien
That—'tis the truth that I impart—
None in the group had such stout heart
But that he felt a keen desire
To be safe back in Acre or Tyre.
They slept beside a wall that night
And, know ye, they were in great fright.   11,970

SALADIN INSURES THEIR SAFE-CONDUCT

The Saracens next morn came in
To address themselves to Saladin.
They came, and at his feet they kneeled,

While thus they urged him and appealed
To him: "Just Sultan, 'twere the right
And fitting moment to requite
The massacre by these folk done
On ours when Acre was overthrown.
Great Sire, let us avenge our fathers,
Our kinsfolk, and our sons and brothers,   11,980
Who by these cruelly were slain.
Each man may vengeance thus obtain."
He answered that—and this was just—
He would consult his men of trust.
This council on the sultan waited
And carefully deliberated.
Great Saracens took part therein,
Mashtub and also Saphadin,
Bedred Din Dolderon [8] likewise.
And they said: "Sire, we shall advise   11,990
What best becomes your noble name:
'Twould be a source of bitter shame
And a reproach to pagandom
If now these Christians, who have come
Here under our authority
With full faith in your loyalty,
Were massacred, to the abuse
Of the agreement and the truce
Made 'twixt the king of England and
Ourselves. How could you e'er hold land   12,000
If you, for whatsoever sake,
Your word and treaty thus should break?
Who would e'er trust us from that day?"
Then Saladin without delay
Asked that his sergeants be sent in
And gave command, through Saphadin,

---

[8] Bedr ed Din Dolderon, lord of Tell Bashir, was one of Saladin's chief emirs. He had commanded a large body of Turcomans at the siege of Acre, was in charge of the advance guard against Richard in June, 1192, and was the chief agent in securing the treaty of Jaffa.

That his safe-conduct be respected
And that the Christians be protected
And kept from harm at every stage
While they performed their pilgrimage.   12,010
From that time till they started back
To Acre no honor did they lack.

AMBROISE VISITS JERUSALEM

When these men started to retrace
Their steps, our group came to the place.
The hour was at the break of day.
The sultan sent his men to stay
And guard the road in loyalty
The while the pilgrim folk marched by,
So that we passed secure from ills.
And then we climbed into the hills   12,020
And soon we reached the Montjoie's [9] height.
Then in our hearts was great delight
To see Jerusalem. We felt
Such joy that on the ground we knelt,
As all who come there ought to do.
We saw the Mount of Olives, too,
The place whence started the procession
When the Lord God went to His passion.
We went next on our pilgrimage
To where God won His heritage,   12,030
The city. Those who rode first were
Allowed to kiss the Sepulcher;
The knights and those men who were mounted,
When they were with our troop, recounted
How Saladin showed and disclosed
That Holy Cross, the Which was lost
During the battle, and saw fit
To have them kiss and worship It.

---

[9] Montjoie was the place about four kilometers from Jerusalem, from which the pilgrims from the western road got their first sight of the Holy City. The abbey of Saint Samuel was built on the spot. (*Guide bleu*, p. 561.)

We others were on foot, and we
Saw all the things that we could see.   12,040
We saw in truth the monument
Wherein God's body evident
Was laid away, when death He suffered.
There a few offerings were offered.
But since the Saracens would take
What offerings we chose to make,
We offered little. But large share
We gave to the poor captives there,
The Franks and Syrians, detained
In wretched bondage and enchained.   12,050
To these our offerings were borne;
They said: "May God grant them return
For this!" They lay in servitude.

AND SEES THE HOLY PLACES

Another holy place we viewed:
Mount Calvary, on the right side,
Where He Who deigned to be born died,
There where the Cross was set, and where
Nails in the Holy Flesh did tear,
For the rock shattered at its base
As far as Golgotha.[10] This place   12,060
We were allowed to see and kiss.
We went to the church, after this,
Upon Mount Sion; all defaced
It lies, and ruined and laid waste.
Leftwards we saw a spot, from whence
The Mother of God's omnipotence
Rose into heaven, to God, Her Father,
That God Who made Her His sweet Mother.
And this spot we kissed tearfully.
From there we went on hurriedly   12,070
To see the Holy Table, at

[10] The *Itinerarium* (p. 436) mentions that here was the split rock in which the Cross had been set in Golgotha.

Which God willingly ate and sat.
We kissed it likewise, but did not
Linger long time upon the spot,
Because the Saracens would steal
Our pilgrims, seize them and conceal
Them in some grotto or some cave,
Here three, here four, which gave us grave
Misgivings. Downward now our course
We took, both those on foot and horse   12,080
To Josaphat, on Siloë.
We were advised to go that way.
And there it was we saw the tomb
Of Her Who bore God in Her womb.
This tomb we kissed with fealty
And warmth of heart and piety,
And then we went, in doubt and fear,
Into that selfsame grotto where
God was when those men seized Him who
His precious earthly body slew.   12,090
We kissed this place at once, with mourning
Hearts all filled with piteous yearning,
And there we shed hot tears in deep
Distress. It was fit place to weep,
For there were stables in the place
For horses of the devil's race,
Who did God's holy spots defile,
Grieving our pilgrims much the while.
We left Jerusalem and bent
Our steps toward Acre, and thither went.   12,100

HUBERT WALTER IS COURTEOUSLY RECEIVED BY SALADIN

The third group, 'neath the bishop's guard—
That bishop who was afterward
The archbishop of Canterbury—
Was next to come. And for his glory,
It is most true, and for the fame
And prowess of his knightly name

Saladin rendered honors great
To him, as I shall now relate;
For he dispatched his men to greet
Him and to urge him and entreat   12,110
That he stay with him as his guest,
At his cost; the bishop expressed
His thanks and told the Saracens
That he came as a pilgrim, hence
He could not have his costs defrayed,
Nor to that end accept such aid.
When he refused this, Saladin
Ordered his household and his kin
To show him and his retinue
Great honors. Many rich gifts, too,   12,120
He gave, and had him led where God
Our Lord with His Own feet had trod.
And then he asked him to come there
And speak with him, to see his air
And mien, the Holy Cross displayed
To him, and in his presence made
Him sit. Together they conferred
Long time, and much they said and heard.
Of England's sovereign he began
To ask, and what manner of man   12,130
He was; and after this he sought
To learn just what our Christians thought
About himself. To which replied
The bishop: "Sire, I say with pride
That my lord is the finest knight
On earth, and the most skilled to fight.
Noble is he and generous.
I count not sins we have in us,[11]
But if one had your qualities
United and conjoined with his,   12,140
We say that there could not be found
In all the world that stretches round

---

[11] The *Itinerarium* (p. 437) says, with less tact, "exceptis peccatis tuis."

Any two princes to outvie
Your every valiant quality."
The sultan heard the bishop through,
And answered: "Well I know 'tis true
That brave and noble is the king,
But with what rashness doth he fling
Himself! Howe'er great prince I be,
I should prefer to have in me   12,150
Reason and measure and largesse
Than courage carried to excess."

SALADIN'S LARGESSE

Saladin thus held long discourse
With the bishop—and he spoke perforce
Through interpreters who did his word
Expound. The bishop gladly heard.
Saladin asked him to suggest
Some gift, whate'er he might request
That lay within his power to give.
That which he asked he would receive.   12,160
The bishop gave him thanks for this
And said: "Upon my faith, here is
A great thing, if one judge it right;
I should prefer to wait. Tonight,
If it so please you, I shall seek
God's will. Then I shall come and speak
Tomorrow." The sultan agreed
And the next day he asked indeed,
And they a great thing did confer:
He asked that at the Sepulcher—   12,170
Wherein God was not served, except
By Syrians who their own way kept—
Each day two of our priests, both Latins,
At evening service and at matins,
Accompanied by deacons twain
To give them aid, should there remain,
Serve with the Syrians, and live

On offerings they might receive.
He asked, too, that at Bethlehem
Be done as at Jerusalem, 12,180
And so at Nazareth. Thereon
The sultan willed it should be done
So long as he should hold the land.
The good bishop then gave command
That priests should come and sing aloud
[The mass]. The bishop might be proud
That he to God had given back
The chanting which till then did lack.

       . . .

Had done what they sought to achieve, 12,190
From Saladin they took their leave.
They left Jerusalem that day
And back to Acre went their way.

THE RETURN OF THE PILGRIMS

Upon the safe return of all
The people, both the great and small,
From the Sepulcher, where they had fared,
And when the ships had been prepared,
The pilgrims boarded them and sailed
As soon as a good wind prevailed.
The ships were soon driven astray, 12,200
Scattered on many a different way;
And some of them were safely driven,
Safely to reach their chosen haven;
Others of them through perils passed
In places far where they were cast,
While some men died at sea, and these
Pilgrims had bitter obsequies.
Bitter? Nay, sweet. The sweet thereof
Shall be theirs in the realm above.
And some fell ill, and nevermore 12,210
Were whole men as they were before;

And some had left their fathers, others
Their cousins-german and their brothers,
Who had died of wounds or illness there,
Giving them grief and black despair.
As we have known martyrs forsake
This world and for God's will partake
Of various sufferings and pain—
In the same way I dare maintain
That they suffered from divers woes   12,220
And had divers adventures, those
Men who this pilgrimage performed.
Yet many people ill-informed
Said in their foolishness that naught
Of good in Syria was wrought,
Since they won not Jerusalem.

THOSE WHO RETURNED NOT

The true facts were not known to them,
But ignorantly they reproved
A task on which their feet ne'er moved.
But we ourselves who went and who   12,230
Were there and saw what happed and knew
And underwent the sufferings,
We must not lie about the things
That others suffered for God's love,
As we with our own eyes did prove.
In pilgrims' hearing I declare
A hundred thousand men died there
Because from women they abstained:
'Twas for God's love that they restrained
Themselves. They had not perished thus,   12,240
Had they not been abstemious.
I dare say, too, with certainty,
By famine and by malady
More than three thousand were struck down [12]

[12] The *Itinerarium* (p. 440) gives 300,000, a more consistent figure. Ibn al Athir (p. 66) reports that Balian d'Ibelin said that there had been 600,000 crusaders, of whom not one in twelve survived.

At the siege of Acre and in the town.
The worthy folks and gentle lords
Who had chaplains and heard the words
Of service, like a bishop, say,
Or a holy archbishop, each day,
And who succumbed to maladies   12,250
While they were living in this wise,
Shall be with God, at His right hand,
In high Jerusalem's heavenly land.
These, through the good deeds done by them
Won that fairer Jerusalem.

FAREWELL TO SYRIA

When in the Holy Land the king
Of England had been sojourning
Till it was time for him to fare
Homewards, he gave word to prepare
His journey. Then his ship was got   12,260
In order, so that it lacked naught—
Food, arms, supplies—that it might need.
He then performed a noble deed,
Like a most loyal man and true:
To get William de Préaux, who
For him fell captive, he gave ten
High ranking nobles Saracen,
Who would have brought much wealth: to save
William all ten of them he gave.[13]
Then he had cried that he would pay   12,270
All debts, without plaint or gainsay,
And he paid every debt and claim.
When he took leave, the people came
And wept to see him go, and made
Tender lament, and for him prayed
With warm words for his bravery,

[13] The *Itinerarium* (p. 440) here contains the amazing statement that the ten Turks who were exchanged would have given much money to keep William. See the article by Edwards in *Historical Essays in Honor of James Tait.*

Valor, and generosity.
They said: "Ah, Syria, you are left
Helpless, and of all aid bereft!
God! If they now should undertake—   12,280
As oft has happed before—to break
The truce, whom could we count upon
For succor, now the king is gone?"
Many were seen to weep. The king,
Who still was ill and suffering,
Took leave and, lingering no more,
Boarded his ship and left the shore,
With sails spread to the wind. That night
He sailed, having the stars for light.[14]
Next morning, at the dawn's bright trace,   12,290
Toward Syria he turned his face
And said, so that his people could
Hear clear, and others understood:
"Ah, Syria, I now commend
You to the Lord God! May He lend
Me time enough, if He so will,
That I may yet relieve your ill!
For still I think to succor you."

JOURNEY'S END

Then the wind far and swiftly blew
His ship. But he knew not the cares,   12,300
The sorrows, mishaps, and despairs
That hung before him as his fate,
Nor the torments that lay in wait,
Through treason plotted in advance
And sent from Syria to France
To the king, about Assassins sent.
This tale caused his imprisonment

---

[14] The *Itinerarium* (p. 441), Roger of Hoveden (III, 135), Ralph of Diceto (II, 106) give the date: October 9, 1192. The queens had already sailed on September 29. The *Eracles* (p. 200) says that he disguised himself as a Templar.

While he was on God's pilgrimage.[15]
Thereby they seized his heritage
And his châteaux in Normandy— 12,310
An act of greedy perfidy.
Much silver did his ransom cost,
Which on his subjects thus imposed
High tax. Crosses and reliquaries
And vessels from the sanctuaries
He took, and gold and silver plate
And coin. And his need was so great
That never saint of God our Lord—
Many and many there are—incurred
For His sake more of suffering, 12,320
Just short of death, than did the king
In Austrian dungeon cell, in which
He lay, and in Germany the rich.
Of all this he knew not a word;
But God, Whom he had served as Lord,
His sense and generosity,
His foresight and his bravery,

.   .   .

.   .   .

Barons with children, who sent these 12,330
To be their sovereign's hostages
Till he won back his heritance
And made war on the king of France.
He strove until he could restore
As much of land, or even more
Than his estates that had been seized.
God works with justice and is pleased
To give reward to him who spends
Service and labor for His ends.

[15] The *Estoire* here unduly simplifies history. Richard was captured by the duke of Austria, who turned him over to Emperor Henry VI, who held him for ransom. John and Philip tried to have him kept in prison, but he purchased his freedom for 250,000 marks.

EXPLICIT

Let all men living, and also   12,340
All who will live in future, know
That here endeth this history,
And telleth of a verity
That the year when, to our great loss,
The Saracens conquered the Cross
Was eleven hundred eighty eight [16]—
So doth the story truly state—
After the Incarnation, when
The Son of God was born 'mong men,
Who dwelleth at His Father's side: 12,350
May He take us with Him to bide.

AMEN [17]

[16] Actually the crucial battles were all fought in 1187.
[17] The numbering of the lines differs from that of G. Paris, who lost a line in his numbering at line 12,190.

APPENDICES

APPENDIX A: CONDENSED GENEALOGIES TO ILLUSTRATE RELATIONSHIPS MENTIONED BY AMBROISE

ABBREVIATED GENEALOGY OF THE PLANTAGENETS AND CAPETIANS

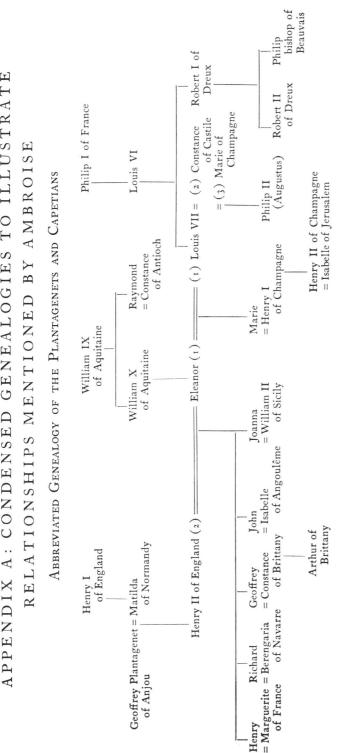

GENEALOGY OF THE KINGS OF JERUSALEM

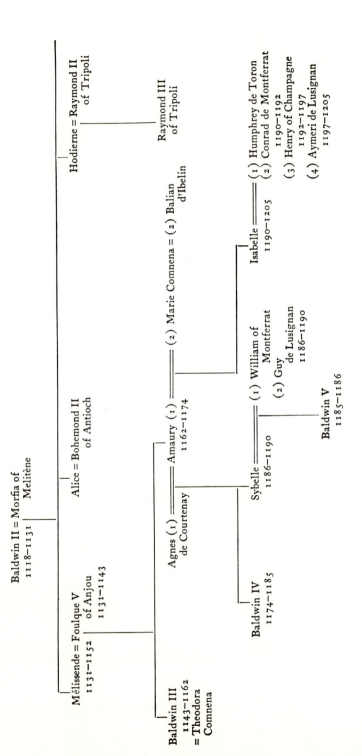

GENEALOGY OF THE KINGS OF SICILY

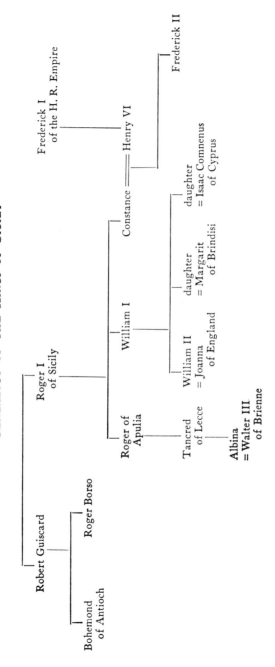

GENEALOGY OF THE COUNTS OF CHAMPAGNE

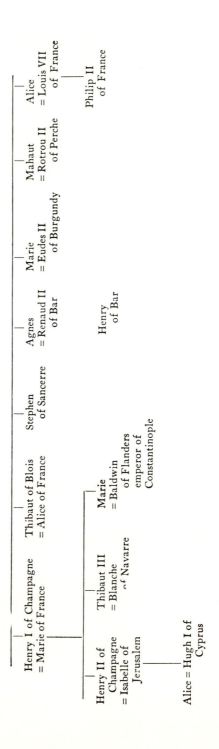

APPENDIX B: RICHARD'S ITINERARY FROM MARSEILLES TO MESSINA AUGUST 7–SEPTEMBER 22, 1190

Hoveden (III, 39–41, 54) and the *Gesta* (II, 113–116) give a day by day itinerary of Richard's voyage from Marseilles to Messina. The fleet seems to have left Marseilles in sections whenever the various ships were loaded and ready. Hoveden says that the king left on August 7; Diceto (84) says that the fleet left August 9; the *Itinerarium* (153) explains that the ships carrying the common soldiers waited three weeks in Marseilles and did not sail until August 16. The following itinerary is for Richard's own galleys.

August 7: They depart from Marseilles.
August 8–12: They coast along the Riviera.
August 13: They arrive at Genoa; Richard visits Philip.
August 14: They sail to Portofino.
August 15–18: They rest at Portofino.
August 19: They sail to Porto Venere (near La Spezia).
August 20: They sail to Pisa.
August 21: They sail past the Island of Gorgona.
August 22: They sail to Baratti, where the king leaves the ship to ride across the cape.
August 23: The king rides across the cape to Piombino, where he rejoins his ship and sails on to Talamone.
August 24–25: They sail past Porto Ercole and Città Vecchia to Ostia, where Richard has an interview with Octavian, cardinal bishop of Ostia.
August 26: The king rides along the coast to Nettuno.
August 27: The king rejoins the ship and sails to the Island of Capri.
August 28: They sail to Naples and land there.
August 29–September 7: They rest at Naples.
September 8: They go from Naples to Salerno.
September 9–12: They rest at Salerno.
September 13: They start south from Salerno.
September 14–17: They go along the coast south towards Scalea.
September 18: They go to Scalea.
September 19: They come to Santa Luchee.
September 20: They go to Santa Euphemia.
September 21: They go to Mileto.
September 22: They cross the Strait to Messina.

The slowness of the journey and the frequent stops along the route were due to the delay necessary so that the slower transports could catch up with the faster galleys. Richard wanted to arrive at Messina in full force.

APPENDIX C: RICHARD'S MARCH FROM ACRE TO JAFFA, AUGUST 22– SEPTEMBER 10, 1191

From chronological indications given in the *Estoire*, the *Itinerarium*, and Beha ed Din it is possible to reconstruct an exact chronology of Richard's march from Acre to Jaffa. This itinerary is substantially the same as those worked out by Landon (*Itinerary*, pp. 53–55) and by Norgate (*Richard*, pp. 176–193), but Norgate follows Ambroise's habit of including the night on which the host reached a given place, in counting the days they camped there.

Thursday, August 22: Richard leaves Acre and goes to the river Belus.

Friday, August 23: Richard crosses the Belus river and waits for the army.

Saturday, August 24: Richard still waits for the army.

Sunday, August 25: The army marches to Caïphas; it is attacked on the way. [This march is broken into two days by most modern historians; we have explained in our notes why we think that this is the correct chronology.]

Monday, August 26: The army camps outside Caïphas.

Tuesday, August 27: They march to Le Destroit (Khirbet Dustrey, Casale of the Narrow Pass). [Landon errs in dating this Aug. 28: the *Itinerarium* p. 252 clearly says "Martis."]

Wednesday, August 28: They rest at Le Destroit.

Thursday, August 29: The army remains at Le Destroit: Richard goes to La Merle.

Friday, August 30: The army joins the king at La Merle.

Saturday, August 31: They march to Cæsarea.

Sunday, September 1: They march to the Dead River: skirmish on the way.

Monday, September 2: They rest at the Dead River.

Tuesday, September 3: They march to the Salt River.

Wednesday, September 4: They rest at the Salt River.

Thursday, September 5: Saphadin confers with Richard and with Humphrey de Toron: the army marches to Rochetaille.

Friday, September 6: They rest at Rochetaille.

Saturday, September 7: They march to Arsur: Battle of Arsur.

Sunday, September 8: They rest at Arsur: burial of Jacques d'Avesnes.

Monday, September 9: They march to the River of Arsur.

Tuesday, September 10: They arrive at Jaffa.

BIBLIOGRAPHY OF WORKS CONSULTED

EDITIONS AND TRANSLATIONS OF THE TEXT
AND WORKS RELATING TO IT

L'Estoire de la Guerre Sainte par Ambroise. Edited by Gaston Paris. Paris, 1871. "Documents inédits sur l'histoire de France."
This is the edition of the text that was used as the basis for our translation.

Itinerarium peregrinorum et gesta regis Ricardi. Edited by William Stubbs: Chronicles and Memorials of the Reign of Richard I, Vol. I. London, 1864. "Chronicles and Memorials of Great Britain and Ireland (Rolls Series)."
Referred to in the notes as *Itinerarium*; the relationship between our text and this work is discussed in our Introduction.

Stone, Edward N., Three Old French Chronicles of the Crusades. Seattle, 1939. "University of Washington Publications in the Social Sciences."
This contains a prose translation of Ambroise, based on the text edited by G. Paris. Dr. Stone's work appeared only after our translation was completed; neither of us had any knowledge of the other's work.

Geoffrey de Vinsauf's Itinerary of Richard I and Others to the Holy Land, in Chronicles of the Crusades. London, 1848. "Bohn's Antiquarian Library," Vol. VI.
A poor translation of the *Itinerarium* based on an inferior text to that edited by Stubbs.

Archer, T. A. The Crusade of Richard I. London, 1900. "English History by Contemporary Writers."
Contains fragmentary translations of selections from the *Estoire*, *Itinerarium*, and other materials relating to the crusade of Richard.

Bovée, Dorothy, The Sources of the Third Crusade.
Manuscript thesis for the degree of M.A. in the Library of the University of Minnesota, Minneapolis.

Edwards, J. G., "The Itinerarium regis Ricardi and the Estoire de la Guerre Sainte," in Historical Essays in Honor of James Tait (Manchester, 1933), 59–78.

Norgate, Kate, "The Itinerarium peregrinorum and the Song of Ambroise," *English Historical Review*, XXV (1910), 523–47.

CONTEMPORARY CHRONICLES AND COLLECTIONS OF DOCUMENTS

Abu Chamah, Le Livre des deux jardins. Paris, 1898–1906. "Recueil des historiens des croisades, Historiens orientaux," IV–V.

Assises de Jérusalem, Les. Paris, 1841–43. "Recueil des historiens des croisades, Lois," I–II.

Bar Hebraeus, The Chronography of Gregory Abu'l Faraj commonly known as Bar Hebraeus. Edited by E. A. Wallis Budge. 2 vols, Oxford, 1932.
All references are to the translation in Vol. I.

Beha ed Din, The Life of Saladin; or, What Befell Sultan Yusuf. Translated into English by C. W. Wilson, with notes by Col. Conder. London, 1897. "Palestine Pilgrims Text Society Publications," XIII.
The Arabic text and a French translation of this work are to be found in the "Recueil des historiens des croisades, Historiens orientaux," III, Paris, 1884. All references in our notes are to the English translation.

Breton, Guillaume le, see Rigord.

Cobham, Claude Delaval, Excerpta Cypri. Cambridge, 1908.

Coggeshall, Ralph, Chronicon Anglicanum. Edited by J. Stevenson. London, 1875. "Rolls Series."

De expugnatione Terre Sanctae per Saladinum libellus. Edited by Stevenson. In Radulphi Coggeshall chronicon Anglicanum. London, 1875. "Rolls Series."

Delaville LeRoulx, J., Cartulaire général de l'Ordre des Hospitaliers de St. Jean de Jérusalem. 4 vols. Paris, 1894–1904.

Devizes, Richard of, De rebus gestis Ricardi Primi. Edited by Howlett. In Chronicles of the Reigns of Stephen, Henry II and Richard. Vol. III. London, 1886. "Rolls Series."

Diceto, Ralph of, The Historical Works of Ralph of Diceto. Edited by W. Stubbs. 2 vols. London, 1876. "Rolls Series."

Eracles, Le Livre d'Eracles Empereur. Paris, 1859. "Recueil des historiens des croisades, Historiens occidentaux," II.

Ernoul and Bernard le Trésorier, Le Chronique d'Ernoul et de Bernard le Trésorier. Edited by L. de Mas Latrie. Paris, 1871. "Société de l'histoire de France."

Gesta regis Ricardi. Edited by W. Stubbs, in Chronicles of Henry II and Richard I, Vol. II. London, 1867. "Rolls Series."

Guillaume le Maréchal, L'Histoire de Guillaume le Maréchal. Edited by P. Meyer. 3 vols. Paris, 1891–1900. "Société de l'histoire de France."

Haymarus, De expugnata Accone liber tetrastichus. Edited by P. Riant.

Paris, 1865. Also edited by W. Stubbs in Chronica Magistri Rogeri de Hovedene, Vol. III. London, 1870. "Rolls Series."
References are to lines of the poem which are the same in both editions.

Histoire des ducs de Normandie. Edited by F. Michel. Paris, 1840. "Société de l'histoire de France."

Hoveden, Roger of, Chronica. Edited by W. Stubbs. 4 vols. London, 1868–71. "Rolls Series."
An English translation by H. T. Riley is in the "Bohn Antiquarian Library," 2 vols., London, 1853.

Ibn al Athir, Kamel Altevarykh. Paris, 1872–87. "Recueil des historiens des croisades, Historiens orientaux," I–II.
All page references are to Vol. II unless specifically cited.

Ibn Kallikan, Biographical Dictionary. Translated by Baron McGuckin de Slane. 4 vols. Paris, 1843–71. "Oriental Translation Fund."

Lignages d'Outremer, Les. Edited by Beugnot. Paris, 1843. "Recueil des historiens des croisades, Lois," II.

Livre des vassaux du comté de Champagne et de Brie. Edited by A. Longnon. In Arbois de Jubainville, Histoire des ducs et des comtes de Champagne, Vol. VII. Paris, 1869.

Müller, Giuseppe, Documenti sulle relazione delle città toscane coll'oriente cristiano e coi Turchi. Florence, 1879. "Documenti degli archivi toscani."

Newburgh, William of, Historia rerum Anglicarum. Edited by R. Howlett. In Chronicles of the Reigns of Stephen, Henry II and Richard I, Vols. I–II. London, 1884–85. "Rolls Series."

Novare, Philip de, The Wars of Frederick II against the Ibelins in Syria and Cyprus. Translated by J. L. LaMonte and M. J. Hubert. New York, 1936. "Records of Civilization."

Rigord, Chronique. Edited by H. F. Delaborde, in Œuvres de Rigord et Guillaume le Breton, 2 vols. Paris, 1882. "Société de l'histoire de France."

Röhricht, Reinhold, Regesta regni Hierosolymitani. Innsbruck, 1898; with Additamentum, 1904.

Salloch, Marianne, Die lateinische Fortsetzung Wilhelms von Tyrus. Greifswald, 1934.

Scripta de feodis ad regem spectantibus. Paris, 1894. "Recueil des historiens des Gaules de la France," XXIII.

William, archbishop of Tyre, Historia rerum in partibus transmarinis gestarum. Paris, 1844. "Recueil des historiens des croisades, Historiens occidentaux," I.

SECONDARY AUTHORITIES

Arbois de Jubainville, H., Histoire des ducs et comtes de Champagne. 7 vols., Paris, 1859–69.

Baldwin, Marshall W., Raymond III of Tripolis. Princeton, 1936.

Bridrey, E., La Condition juridique des croisés. Paris, 1901.

Byrne, Eugene H., Genoese Shipping in the Twelfth Century. Cambridge, Mass., 1930. "Monographs of the Mediaeval Academy of America."

Cartellieri, Alexander, Philipp II August, König von Frankreich: II, Der Kreuzzug. Leipzig, 1906.

———— Richard Löwenherz im Heiligen Lande," *Historische Zeitschrift*, CI (1908), 1–27.

Chalandon, Ferdinand, Histoire de la domination normande en Italie et en Sicile. 2 vols., Paris, 1907.

Comfort, William W., "The Literary Role of the Saracens in the French Epic," PMLA, LV (1940), 628–59.

Delaville LeRoulx, J., Les Hospitaliers en Terre Sainte et à Chypre. Paris, 1904.

Dictionary of National Biography. 63 vols., London.

Dubois, Gaston, "Récherches sur la vie de Guillaume des Roches," Bibliothèque de l'école des chartes, XXX (1869), 377–424; XXXII (1871), 88–145; XXXIV (1873), 502–41.

Dugdale, Sir William, Monasticon Anglicanum . . . 6 vols., London, 1849.

Enlart, Camille, Les Monuments des croisés dans le Royaume de Jérusalem. 4 vols., Paris, 1925–26.

————, Les Villes mortes du moyen âge. Paris, 1920.

Familles d'Outremer de C. D. DuCange, Les. Edited by E. G. Rey. Paris, 1869. "Documents inédits sur l'histoire de France."

Gams, P. B., Series episcoporum. Leipzig, 1931.

Grousset, René, Histoire des croisades et du royaume franc de Jérusalem. 3 vols., Paris, 1934–36.

Guide Bleu à Syrie-Palestine, Iraq-Transjordanie, Le. Paris, 1932.

Hackett, J., History of the Orthodox Church of Cyprus. London, 1901.

Ilgen, T., Markgraf Conrad von Montferrat. Marburg, 1880.

Jeffery, George, Cyprus under an English King. Nicosia, 1926.

King, E. J., The Knights Hospitallers in the Holy Land. London, 1931.

La Monte, John L., Feudal Monarchy in the Latin Kingdom of Jerusalem, 1100–1291. Cambridge, Mass., 1932. "Monographs of the Mediaeval Academy of America."

———— "Jean d'Ibelin, the Old Lord of Beirut," *Byzantion*, XII (1937), 417–48.

———— "The Rise and Decline of a Frankish Seigneury in Syria in the Time of the Crusades," *Revue historique du sud-est européen*, Bucarest, 1938. Vol. for 1938 issues X–XII, 3–25.

———— "Taki ed Din, Prince of Hama," *Moslem World*, XXXI (1941), 149–60.

———— "The Viscounts of Naplouse in the Twelfth Century," *Syria*, XIX (1938), 272–78.

———— "The Vanished Splendour of Famagusta," *Butrava*, IV (1940), 3–7.

Landon, L., Itinerary of Richard I. London, 1935. "Pipe Roll Society."

Lane-Poole, Stanley, Saladin. London, 1898. "Heroes of the Nations."

Le Strange, Guy, Palestine under the Moslems. London, 1890.

Lusignan, Etienne, Les Généalogies de soixante et sept très nobles et très illustres maisons . . . Paris, 1586.

Marchand, Jean, La Légende de Mélusine. Paris, 1927.

Mas Latrie, Louis de, "Généalogie des rois de Chypre," *Archivo Veneto*, XXI (1881), 1–51.

———— Histoire de l'Ile de Chypre sous la domination de la maison de Lusignan. 3 vols., Paris, 1852–61.

———— "Les Patriarches latins de Jérusalem," *Revue de l'orient latin*, I (1893), 16–42.

———— Trésor de chronologie. Paris, 1890.

Mayer, L. A., Saracenic Heraldry. Oxford, 1933.

Norgate, Kate, Richard the Lion Heart. London, 1924.

Orgeval, G. Barrois d', Le Maréchalat en France. 2 vols., Paris, 1932.

Painter, Sidney. The citations to Painter are to a letter which Dr. Painter wrote me helping to identify some of Richard's barons.

Paris, G., "La Traduction de la légende latine du Voyage de Charlemagne à Constantinople," *Romania*, XXI (1892), 263–64.

Potthast, A., Regesta pontificum Romanorum. 2 vols., Berlin, 1874–75.

Powicke, Frederick M., The Loss of Normandy. Manchester, 1913.

Rajna, Pio, "Contributi alla storia dell'epopea," *Romania*, XIV (1885), 398–420.

Rey, E. G., Les Colonies franques en Syrie. Paris, 1882.

Riant, P., Expéditions et pélerinages des Scandinaves en Terre Sainte au temps des croisades. Paris, 1865.

Röhricht, Reinhold, Geschichte des Königreichs Jerusalem. Innsbruck, 1898.

Röhricht, Reinhold, "Mittelalterlichen Geographie und Topographie Syriens," *Zeitschrift der deutsche Palaestina-Vereins*, X (1887), 195–346.

———— "Syria Sacra," *Zeitschrift der deutsche Palaestina-Vereins*, X (1887), 1–53.

Round, J. Horace, "Garnier de Nablus," *Archaeologia*, LVIII (1903), 383–90.

———— "Some English Crusaders of Richard I," *English Historical Review*, XVIII (1903), 475–81.

Schlumberger, Gustave, Renaud de Châtillon. Revised edition. Paris, 1923.

Siedschlag, Beatrice, English Participation in the Crusades 1150–1220. Randolph, Wis., 1939.

Stouff, Louis, Essai sur Mélusine. Dijon, 1930.

INDEX

Abu Bekr, 429n

Abu Chamah, 23

Abu el Fath Ghazi, 270n

Acre, bishop of, 127n, 159n, 230n

Acre: Guy begins siege, 133; siege of, 133-234 *passim*; crusading contingents arrive, 136, 146; Christian casualties at, 142; famine at, 154, 181; incidents of siege, 159-66; Philip arrives, 191; Richard arrives, 193; terms of surrender, 217

Agoland, Saracen king, 10, 11, 15, 48, 180, 324

Aiaz el Mekrani, 289n

Ajello, Richard son of Mathew, 65n, 66n

Aldebrandus, count, 140n

Alem ed Din Kaisar, 272, 353, 354

Alençon, John d', 355

Aleppo, 109n, 270n, 414

Alexandrian fleet, 171

Alice, *see* France; Jerusalem; Sicily

Alopecia, 196n

Alvira, *see* Sicily

Amaury, king of Jerusalem, 120, 332n

Ambrose (Ambroise): reference to in text, 37, 56, 119, 149, 165, 193, 204, 245, 438-40; *Estoire de la guerre sainte*, 3 ff.; a crusader, 3, 4, 19; eyewitness of third crusade, 4; poet or jongleur, 5, 19; origin and education, 5; comparison of work with that of Richard of Holy Trinity, 7 ff.; includes material for which *Itinerarium* has no equivalent, 8; as traveler, 20 f.; passionate devotion to cause of Christendom, 21; historical value of, 22-27; personal account of siege of Acre, 24; story of Richard in Palestine, 24; personal bias, 24; wrote finest account of crusade of Richard, 27; visits Jerusalem, 438-40

Amiens, Dreux d', 192, 225

Amulaine, *see* Caliph

Ançon, 375

Angelos, Theodora, sister of Isaac, 178n

Angevins, 57, 250, 259

Anjou, 39, 323

Anjou, Foulques of, 41n, 120n

Antioch, Bohemond I, prince of, 394

Antioch, Bohemond III, prince of, 94n, 131, 352n

Antioch, Bohemond IV, prince of, 352n

Antioch, Constance, princess of, 131n

Antioch, Raymond, prince of, 94n, 352n

Antioch, 111n, 122n, 131, 181n, 324, 352n, 393, 431n

Apamia, archbishop of, 95n

Apulia, Richard, count of, 140n

Apulia, king of, *see* Sicily

Aquitaine, Eleanor of, *see* Eleanor of Aquitaine

Aquitaine, William X of, 71n

Archbishops, *see* names of sees

Arches, John d', 159n

Arles, (Pierre d'Isnard) archbishop of, 230n

Armenia, king of, *see* Leo

Armenia, 107n

Armenians, 88, 91, 92, 95

Arsis, Alexander, 388

Arsur, lord of, 243, 374

Arsur, Melissende of, 372n

Arsur: battle of, 188n, 248-65, 277n; Jacques d'Avesnes buried at, 266-67; given to Henry, 345; Christians to hold, 431n

Arsur forest, 248

Arsur river, 273, 274

Arthur, legendary king, 180

Arzillières, Walter d', 159n

Ascalon: siege of, 127, 128; crusaders learn of demolition of, 274; Saladin asks that fort be razed, 275, 396n, 430,

Ascalon (*Continued*)
431*n*; he demands that city should not be rebuilt, 290; Christian leaders decide to turn back to, 302; decision to rebuild wall and bastion, 303; host comes to, 305; French are summoned, 308; refortified, 309; towers, 310; Richard assumes costs of refortifying, 311; host marches out, 365; Saladin insists on keeping, **429*n***

Aspremont, Gaubert d', 159*n*

Aspremont, 10

Assassins: kill Conrad, 335-38; son of chief, 398, 405

Assela, Louis d', 159*n*

Assizes of Romanie, 130*n*

Asti, bishop of, 159*n*

Auberive, **46*n***

Auch, Gerard, archbishop of, 66*n*, 95*n*

Augustus of London, 403*n*

Austria, duke of, Richard captured by, 447*n*

Auvergne, count of, 260*n*

Avesnes, Jacques d', 21, arrives at Acre, 136, 137, 138*n*; in battle of Arsur, 251, 259; death, 265, 266; buried at Arsur, 266-67

Ayas al Tawil, death, 245-46

Aymeri de Lusignan, king of Cyprus, 56*n*, 94*n*, 107*n*, 129*n*, 346*n*, 372*n*

Azay-le-Rideau, 43*n*

Babylon (in Egypt), 147, 215, 303, 312, 313; Richard asks tribute from, 290; council plans to take, 379, 380; spies from, 381, 382

Bagdad, caliph of, 125*n*, 215

Bagdad, 389

Baldwin III, king of Jerusalem, 120*n*

Baldwin IV, king of Jerusalem (Baldwin the Leprous), 93, 120, 121*n*, 178, 281*n*

Baldwin V, king of Jerusalem, 121, 122*n*; rumor that Raymond poisoned, 123*n*

Bar, Thibaut, count of, 140*n*

Bardolf, Hugh, 66*n*

Baré, Seguin, 351

Bar Hebraeus, Abulfaraj, 23

Bar-le-Duc, Henry I, count of, 140, 159*n*

Barletta, 48

Barra, William de, 251*n*

Barres, Peter des, 110*n*

Barres, William des, 69*n*, 191, 238, 251, 264

Bayonne, Bernard, bishop of, 66*n*, 95*n*

Beaufort, 135

Beaujeau, 45*n*

Beaumont, 272

Beauvais, Philip de Dreux, bishop of, 100, 139, 140*n*, 251, 259, 334; Conrad secured adherence of, 177*n*; Isabelle and Conrad married by, 178

Beauvoir, 272

Bédier, Joseph, 3

Bedouin, 125*n*, 136, 311, 384

Bedr ed Din Dolderon, 430*n*; in counsel with Saladin, 437

Beha ed Din, chief oriental source for siege of Acre, 23, 24

Beha ed Din Karakush, *see* Karakush

Beirut, 109*n*, 110, 211, 331, 332*n*, 379, 403; Conrad to have lordship of, 331

Beirut, (Eudes?) bishop of, 230*n*

Bellegiminus, emir of Megisimus, 164

Belleme (castle), 192*n*

Belus river, 173*n*

Berengaria, 71, 72, 81, 85, 95, 108, 278

Bernard, count, 140*n*

Bernard, the spy, 381

Bertulf, count, 140*n*

Besançon, Thierry de Montfauçon, archbishop of, 159*n*, 168, 230*n*

Besant, gold: value, 194*n*

Betaffa, 390

Bethlehem, Ralph, bishop of, 401*n*

Bethlehem, Hubert Walter gains permission for priests to sing mass at, 443

Bethsan, Gautier de, 260*n*

Betnuble, 298, 366-67, 391*n*

Blanchegarde: Saladin orders destruction, 272; Richard made foray against, 293*n*, 341*n*; host encamped at, 365*n*, 366

Bloez, William, 201*n*

Blois, bishop of, 159*n*

Blois, Thibaut, count of, 158, 159*n*

Bohemond of Antioch, *see* Antioch

Bois, Ernaut du, 295
Bois, Geoffrey du, 409
Bois Normand, William du, 84
Bois Sainte Marie, 45n
Bombrac, 286
Bonpas (near Avignon), 46n
Bordeaux, archbishop of, 95n
Born, Bertrand de, 360n
Borrel, William, 258n
Borris, William de, 250
Botron, 109, 143n
Boucherie, rue de la, 203
Bouvines, battle of, 191n, 287n
Bove, Robert de, 159n
Bovée, Dorothy, on textual variation of
    Itinerarium and Estoire, 14
Brescia, bishop of, 159n
Bretons, 250, 259
Breuil, Saol du, 295
Brienne, Andrew de, 139; slain at Acre,
    142
Brienne, Erard II, count of, 139, 141
Brienne, John de, 139n
Brienne, Walter III, count of, 139n
Brindisi, 48
Brittany, Arthur of, 34, 37n, 65, 66n,
    434n
Brittany, Constance, wife of Geoffrey of,
    34n
Brittany, Conon of, 34n
Brittany, Geoffrey of, 34, 37n, 65n
Brittany, Peter de Dreux, duke of, 140n
Bruges, castelan of, 140n
Bruges, Robert de, 370
Buffavento castle, 103n, 105
Bures, 39n
Burgundy, Hugh III, duke of, 41, 61, 69n,
    202, 212n, 221, 225, 252, 259n, 268n,
    305, 344n, 363; recorded as Henricus
    or Henri, 14; Philip entrusts his men
    to, 220; returned to Acre after battle
    of Arsur, 277n; disaffection of, 314;
    shame and infamy inflicted upon, 315,
    316; persuaded Conrad to break his
    word, 317; called to join Richard, 382;
    flouts Richard in song, 393; Richard's
    delight at death of, 428n
Byla, emir of, 398

Cæsarea, bishop of, 159n
Cæsarea: given to Geoffrey de Lusignan,
    211n, 278n; fleet comes, 245; Richard
    comes to, 316; crusaders stopped at,
    404, 405; host pent in by Saracens,
    415; French at, 426; Christians to hold,
    429n, 431n
Cafarnäum, 241
Caieux, William de, 287, 330
Caïmont, 332n
Caïphas, Paien or Paganus of, 98, 177n
Caïphas, 147, 173-74, 406; march to, 239-
    41; Christians to hold, 431n; Richard
    returns to, 432
Cairo, 212n, 215n
Caisac, see Alem ed din Kaisar
Calabria, 324
Caliph of Bagdad, see Bagdad
Calvados, 199n, 296n, 405n
Camardoli, 228n
Camel, hill in Crete, 78n
Camels, savory flesh, 391
Camte, lord of, 159n
Camville, Richard de, 42n, 66n, 108n
Cannaie des Etourneaux, 354, 355, 358
Canterbury, Baldwin, archbishop of, 37n,
    159n, 173, 230n; opposed marriage of
    Isabelle and Conrad, 178; see also Wal-
    ter, Hubert
Caravan (Christian), attack on by Sara-
    cens, 371-74
Caravan (Saracen), raided by Crusaders,
    381-90
Caron, Baldwin le, 258, 371, 372, 373,
    374, 375
Casal of the Baths, 293n
Casal Ernaud, 272, 365n, 367
Casal Imbert, 115, 314, 316
Casal Moyen, 284, 287, 391n; Saladin's
    order to raze, 272; host camped before,
    395
Casal of the Narrow Pass, 241, 243
Casal des Plains, 243n, 284, 301, 305;
    Saladin's order to raze, 272
Castigny, Erard de, 159n
Casualties: at Acre, 142, 230n; on cru-
    sade, 444
Catania, blunder in locating, 15

Celles, 43n

Cerines, see Kyrenia

Chalon, William II, count of, 159, 284

Champagne, Henry, count of, 129n, 140n, 146n, 168, 188, 192n, 221, 251, 259, 305, 320n, 330, 333, 334, 339, 344, 346n, 347, 353, 367, 371, 372n, 390, 391n, 403, 415-17, 426, 428, 429, 429n, 430n, 433; brings reinforcements to Acre, 158; selected king of Jerusalem, 158n, 339, 342; and husband of Queen Isabelle, 158n, 342, 343n; transferred to service of Richard, 194n

Champagne, Henry the Liberal, count of, 158n, 159n, 192n

Champagne, genealogy of counts of, 454

Champagne, Blanche of, see Navarre, Blanche of

Champagne, Mahaut of, countess of Perche, 192n

Champagne, Marie of, see France, Marie of

Champagne, Thibaut III of, 71n

Chanson de Roland, 20, 21

Chansons de geste, 3, 10, 21

Chapelle, La, 43n

Chapelle, William de la, 129

Charlemagne, 3, 180, 324-25

Chartres, bishop of, 69n, 73

Châteaudun, Ralph, viscount of, 200

Château Erald, viscount of, 140n

Châtillon, Guy de, 25, 159n

Châtillon, Lovellus de, 159n

Châtillon, Renaud de, 25, 120n, 121n, 122n

Chauvigny, Andrew de, 66n, 201n, 209, 286, 296, 297, 352, 404, 418, 434, 435

Cherbourg, Wigain de, 66n

Chinon, 107n

Cincinelles, 358

Cisterns, polluted, 392n

Clari, Robert de, 21

Classical heroes, 137, 180

Clément, Aubrey, heroic death, 206; armor worn by Turk, 208; grief over death of, 212

Clément, Robert, 206n

Clement, pope, 66n

Clermont, Ralph, count of, 159, 179n, 188

Cluny, 434

Colchester, archdeacon of, 159n

Comnena, Marie, 120n, 177n, 332n

Conrad, see Montferrat

Constance, see Antioch; Brittany; Sicily

Constantinople, 130n, 178

Corbigny, 45n

Corfu, 54n

Cornebu (Tornebu), John de, 199n

Cornebu (Tornebu), Richard de, 199n

Cornebu (Tornebu), Thomas de, 199n

Cornebure, Simon de, 199n

Cornebure, Walter de, 199n

Cornebure, William de, 199n

Courcy, William de, 66n

Courtenay, Agnes de, 120n, 332n

Courtenay, Joscelyn de, 121n, 122n, 281n

Crac of Montreal, 272, 291

Craon, Guy de, 66n

Crete, 78

Crocodiles, pilgrims eaten by, 245

Crocodiles, river of, 245

Cross: borne into battle, 127, 127n, 223, 224, 438, 441, 448; kept by Saladin, 224n, 228n; a piece of given to Richard, 376; adored by host, 377

Cyprus, Aymeri, king of, see Aymeri

Cyprus, Guy, king of, see Guy

Cyprus: Margarit in, 54; traitorous tyrant of, 79, 81; conquest of by Richard, 81-108, 361; Richard left regents in, 108n; pleasure at Richard's conquest, 117; carobs of, 186n; Ibelin, regent of, 332n; acquired by Guy, 345-46; Richard's horse, see Fauvel

Damascus, 112, 125n, 256, 379, 389, 403n

Damietta, 56n

Dampierre, Guy de, 140n, 146

D'Anguillon, 43n

Danish fleet at Acre, 137

Daron, 271, 312, 318; Saladin orders destruction of, 271; reconnoitered, 323n, 341n; Richard's wish to capture, 342, 344; he marches to, 347; assault: great tower wrecked, 349, 350; capture by

Richard, 347-53, 362; Richard forces his way into, 351; given to Henry of Champagne, 353-54; Saracens abandon hope for, 355; prisoners rescued at, 362; ordered destroyed, 397

Dead River, 246

De expugnatione Terrae Sanctae per Saladinum libellus, 6; excerpt, 6*n*

Denmark, nephew of king of, 140*n*

Déquedin, *see* Taki ed Din

Devizes, Richard of, 22, 23

Diceto, Ralph of, 22, 23

Dieudamor, castle, 103*n*, 104, 105*n*

Doc: crusaders advance to, 172; battle of the, 175

Dolderon, Bedr ed Din, *see* Bedr ed Din

Donzay, 43*n*

Dreux, Peter, *see* Brittany

Dreux, Philip, *see* Beauvais

Dreux, Richard and Philip hold parley at, 40

Dreux, Robert II, count of, 140, 251, 259, 266

Duel, 165

Edessa, 125*n*

Edessa, Baldwin of, 102*n*

Edwards, J. G., 10, 13, 17, 18; quoted, 12

Egypt, 125*n*, 430*n*; Saracen fleet arrives at Acre from, 147, 171*n*; raid into, 318; council decides to attack, 380

El Afdal, 124*n*

Eleanor of Aquitaine, 33*n*, 34*n*, 37*n*; arrives at Messina, 71; sent home to rule England, 72

El Malik el Adil Saf ed Din Abu Bekr Mohammed, 109*n*; *see also* Saphadin

El Malik en Nasr Salah ed Din Yusuf ibn Ayyub, 109*n*; *see also* Saladin

Ely, bishop of, *see* William de Longchamp

Emmaus (river), 368

England: Richard's lieutenants expelled from their domain, 326; disquieting news from, 346; divided by strife and warfare, 355; kings of, *see* Henry; John; Richard

English, antipathy for French, 393

Eracles, 23, 24; as source for account of crusade, 22; viewpoint, 25

Ernoul, account of, represents "colonial" viewpoint, 25

Espiart, 351

Estable, Lucas and Alain de l', 282

Estanc, William de l', 275, 418

Esterpen (Esterp), abbot of, 159*n*

Estoire de la guerre sainte (Ambroise), 3-27; a chief source of factual knowledge of crusade of Richard, 3 ff.; importance of poem, 3, 4; source of, and its relation to *Itinerarium Ricardi*, 4-18; a war correspondent's diary, 4; and *Itinerarium* had origin in common source, 5*n*, 10, 13, 17; written to be recited aloud, 13; nature of lost original, 18; literary qualities, 18-21; battle scenes, 20; validity as historical document, 22; finest account of crusade of Richard, 27

Evrard, 238

Evreux, John, bishop of, 66*n*, 95*n*, 199, 284

Evreux, 40

Faï, Ançon du, 405

Faï, Bartholomey de, 405*n*

Faï, William de, 405*n*

Famagusta, 99, 102*n*, 108

Famine: in Acre, 154; relieved, 156; in camp of crusaders, 176; food held for higher prices, 181, 189; ship brings supplies, 189; soldiers eat horse meat, 182, 247

Fano, Monaldus, bishop of, 188

Fauvel, Richard's Cypriot steed, 98, 101, 264, 281, 302

Ferrara, Alberto di Morra, bishop of, 32

Ferrers, William, earl of Derby, 140*n*, 146

Ferrières, Walchelin de, 159*n*, 188, 251

Fiette, Hugh la, 201*n*

Fig Tree, 271; Richard takes, 354

Fitz-Gerold, Garin (Guarin), 66*n*, 200-201, 294

Fitz-Luke, John, 238*n*

Fitz-Neal, Richard, bishop of London, 39*n*

Fitz-Nicholas, Henry, 295

Fitz-Nicholas, Hugh, 201n

Flanders, Baldwin, count of, 107n

Flanders, Philip of Alsace, count of, 41, 63n, 137n, 191, 199, 202, 219n

Flanders, seneschal of, see Wavrin, Helin de

Fleet, Richard's, 42; Philip's, 51n; voyage to Rhodes, 75; vessels scattered or shipwrecked, 83; attacked by Saracens, 113; sails on to Acre, 114; from Babylon, 147; arrives from Tyre and defeats the Saracen fleet, 151; from Alexandria, 171; Richard's detained at Tyre, 196; brings provisions to casal of the Narrow Pass, 243; joins the host, 215; brings provisions and equipment to Jaffa, 275; itinerary of voyage from Marseilles to Messina, 455

Fontanis, Alan de, 159n

Fontenil, Amaury de, 294n

Fontenil, Dreux de (Drogo de Fontenillo Putrellis), 294

Fortz, William de, of Oléron, 42n, 66n

Fosse, Otho de, 140n

Foulques of Anjou, see Anjou

France, kings of, see Louis VII; Louis VIII; Philip II

France, Alice of, 35n, 63n, 68n, 71n

France, Marie of, 158n

Frederick Barbarossa, Holy Roman emperor, 22, 81, 125n, 215n; dolor at death of, 149-50

Frederick II, 203n, 282n, 432n

French: take no part in rioting at Messina, 55; see English flags and banners fly, 59; Richard made loan to pay troops, 222; withdrawal, 268n; decide to rebuild Jaffa, 277; returned to Acre after battle of Arsur, 277n; scattered, 305; summoned to Ascalon, 308; ask their pay, 314; summoned by Conrad, are parted from Richard's command: he grants them escort, 319; refused to stay with host, 320; convoyed to Acre: the escort returns, 323; how they bore themselves at Tyre, 323; prepare to lay siege to Le Daron, 347; hope to share

deeds in Le Daron, 353; Turks ride upon camp of, 369; determined to go to Jerusalem, 380; ask one third of loot, 382; English antipathy for, 393; refuse response to Richard's summons, 404; asked to come to aid of Richard, 426; they spurn him, 427; return home without sight of Jerusalem, 432; refuse to bring succor to Jaffa: start back to France, 433

Furneval, Gerard de, 418, 435

Furneval, Gerard II de, 418n

Galatia, 271; crusaders pause to arm for battle, 382-83

Galilee, sea of, 126

Ganelon, 82, 324

Garlande, Manserius de, 159n

Garlande, William de, 191, 251

Gascons, at Messina, 57

Gaza, 271, 354

Genoese: Richard refused to accept alliance of, 118; at Acre, 151, 155; and Pisans in fierce dissent, 315; Richard brings reconciliation, 316; bravery, 405; aid Richard, 415; soldier warns camp, 416; sufferings, 419

Germans, join Guy at Acre, 133

Gesta—Hoveden, important occidental account of crusade, 22, 23

Gibelet, 109

Gien, Hervé de, 140n

Gisors, conference at, 34; Gilbert de Vascueil's surrender of, 72

Glanville, Ranulf de, 159n

Godfrey de Bouillon, 394

Goez, William, 140n

Golgotha, 439

Graïr, 166

Gray, Henry de, 296

Greek fire, 152, 155, 164, 168, 169, 202, 204, 205, 355; kept in phials, 111

Greeks: at Messina, 50, 52, 57, 64; in Cyprus, 83-91; fight with pilgrims at Limassol, 86; scatter, pursued into hills, 88; seized or slain, 90

"Green Knight," 129n

Gregory VIII, pope, 32

Grenville, Geoffrey de, 140n
Guiscard, Robert, 49
Guiteclin, 180, 324
Gurnay, Hugh de, 159n, 250
Guy de Lusignan, king, 14, 24, 56n, 93n, 94n, 98n, 120, 121, 122, 123, 155, 267, 278, 281n, 293n, 332n, 342n; incompetence, 26; aids Richard in Cyprus, 93, 99, 103, 104; valor, 107; war with Saladin, 124, 125, 126, 127, 128; besieges Acre, 129-30, 131, 132, 133, 141, 143, 144; death of daughters, 171; treaty between Conrad and, 210; upheld by Richard, 211; commanded vanguard, 243n; prepares for battle, 250; Pisans faithful to, 315; barons desert for Conrad, 329; left without a realm, 345; acquired Cyprus, 108n, 346

Hainault, Baldwin V of, 40n, 191n, 219n
Hainault, Isabelle of, 40n
Hainault, Yolande of, 191n
Hattin, battle of, 93n, 125n, 126n, 127n, 129n, 143n, 395n
Hautefort, castle of, 360
Hauterive, Ralph de, 159n
Haymarus, 23, 24
Hebron, bishop of, 230n
Hebron, 358
Henry II, king of England, 33, 34, 36, 38n, 61n, 67n, 71n, 81, 192n, 200n, 361n
Henry VI, emperor, 40n, 54n, 107n, 346n, 447n
Henry, prince, 361n
Herbia, Richard in, 354
Herdecourt, Rodin de, 83, 200
Hereford, Robert, prior of, 326
Herod, 79
Hessedin Jordic of Aleppo, prisoner spared by Richard, 228n
Hessedin, son of Caulior, prisoner spared by Richard, 228n
Historiography, beginnings of, in modern sense, 4
Hodierne, of Jerusalem, countess of Tripoli, 122n
Holy fire, 321

Holy Roman Empire, see Frederick Barbarossa; Frederick II; Henry VI
Homez, Jordan des, constable of Séez, 66n, 199, 405
Homs, 272n
Hospital: marshal of (Wm Borrell), 258n; marshal of (Lambert), 258n; master of, see Naplouse, Garnier de; Moulins, Roger des
Hospital (Hospitallers), 16, 32, 124n, 141, 202, 243n, 267, 337, 369, 379, 380, 381, 397, 403, 404; on march from Caïphas, 241; in rear guard, 250; sore distraught, 254, 257; premature charge, 258; raid near Jerusalem, 293n; oppose advance on Jerusalem, 300, 302; escort French to Acre, 320n, 323n; disciplined, 370; ordered not to engage in single combat, 370n; Richard ill, gives instructions to, 428; they refuse to serve without him, 429
Hoveden, 22, 23, 24
Hungary, Nicholas, count of, 140n, 231

Ibelin, Baldwin d', 122n
Ibelin, Balian d', 98n, 177n, 332, 430n, 444n
Ibelin, Helvis, daughter of Balian d', 332n
Ibelin, John of Beirut, 332n, 372n
Ibelin, John of Jaffa, 98n
Ibelin, Philip, 332n
Ibelin, 305, 431n
Ibelin of the Hospital, 358
Ibn al Athir, 23
Ibn Kallikan, 23
India, 125n
Infré, 109
Innocent III, Pope, 130n
Ionian Islands, 54n
Isaac Comnenus, 21, 54n; seized governance of Cyprus, 82; attempts to capture queens, 83-85; sues for peace, 96; swears fealty to Richard, 97; treacherously flees, 98; pursued by Richard and Guy, 99; mistreatment of pilgrims, 102; daughter captured by King Guy, 103; surrenders, 104; learns of his daughter's capture: begs mercy

of Richard, 105; in silver chains, 106; guarded by King Guy, 107; daughter sent to Berengaria, 107; subsequent career, 107n

Isaac of Cyprus, *see* Isaac Comnenus

Isabelle, queen of Jerusalem, 120n, 122n, 129n, 337, 339; marries Conrad, 98n, 100n, 177, 178n, 179; marries Henry of Champagne, 158n, 342-44

Isle, Menassier de l', 372, 375

Itineraries, Richard's: Tours to Vézelay, 43n; from Vézelay to Lyons, 45n; Lyons to Marseilles, 46n; Marseilles to Messina, 455, Appendix B; Messina to Cyprus, 74-81; Acre to Jaffa, 456, Appendix C

Itinerarium regis Ricardi: a chief source of factual knowledge of crusade of Richard, 3 ff.; relation to *Estoire*, 4-18; once accepted as original work of Richard of Holy Trinity, 6

Jaffa, William Longsword, count of, 93n, 121n

Jaffa, 159n, 211, 283-84, 299, 307, 317, 318, 390, 395, 396, 397, 428, 433; razed by Saladin, 272-74; crusaders march to and fortify, 274-78; given to Geoffrey de Lusignan, 278; host marches out from, 283-84; French return to, 305; given to Count Henry, 342-45; host retreats toward, 394; crusaders forced to go back to, 395, 396; capture and rescue of, 398-414; battle of, 416-25; Christian lordship of, 429n, 431n; chronology of Richard's march from Acre to, 456

Jaffa, treaty of, 429-32, 437

Jerusalem, Alice, daughter of Sybelle of, 171n

Jerusalem, Marie, daughter of Sybelle of, 171n

Jerusalem, Heraclius, patriarch of, 159n, 230

Jerusalem, Monachus, patriarch of, 401n

Jerusalem, patriarch of, 401-402

Jerusalem: dynasty of, 120; conquered, 127 f.; Saladin's order to raze, 272;

crusaders advance on, 299; opposed, 300, 302; Richard dissuaded from his proposed march, 303n; Conrad to have lordship, 331; Richard's barons decide to go on to, 357; Richard bids host prepare to lay siege, 364; crusaders forage within sight of, 367; fear in, 368; Richard refuses to besiege, 377; discontent at failure to attack, 391; wells and cisterns polluted around, 392n; Christians allowed freedom of pilgrimage to, 431n; French return home without sight of, 432; Ambroise visits, 438; pilgrims leave, 440; Hubert Walter asks that priests be allowed to hold services at, 443; kings of, genealogy, 452; *see also* Amaury; Brienne, John de; Guy de Lusignan; Isabelle; Melissende; Sybelle

Jews, massacres of, throughout England, 37n

Jezira, 125n

Joanna Plantagenet, queen of Sicily, 40n, 49, 107n; dower claimed by Richard, 61; brought back to Richard, 67-68; sent forth in ship with Berengaria, 72-73; Greeks' attempts to capture, 83, 85; brought to Jaffa, 278; marriage to Saphadin proposed, 290n, 331n

Johan, dragoman of Isaac, 92

John Lackland, 34, 37, 59n, 65n, 200n, 372n, 434n; seized castles and revenues in England, 327n; Richard distraught by news of his treason, 355; tried to have Richard kept in prison, 447n

Joinville, 3, 4

Jordan river, 290n

Josaphat, 392, 440

Joscelyn, count, 140n

Kahedin, prisoner spared by Richard, 228n

Kaimaz el Adeli, 264n

Kaimaz en Najmi, 405n

Kantara, Isaac Comnenus' château, 102, 105

Karakush, 138n, 212, 213n, 214n, 218n, 221, 222n, 228n

Kerak, 109n

Kharruba, 136n

Kurds, filled with shame that they fled Jaffa, 412, 414; quarrel with Mamelukes, 416

Kyrenia (Cerines), capture of, 103, 104n, 105n

Lancellis, Geoffrey de, 201n

Laodicea, 54n, 82n

Latrun, see Toron of the Knights

Lazarus, 312

Lebanon, 376n

Lecce, Constance of, see Sicily, Constance of

Lecce, Tancred of, see Tancred of Lecce

Lecce, Walter of, see Brienne, Walter of

Leicester, Robert, earl of, 16, 200, 209, 225n, 250, 259, 287, 288, 293, 297, 352, 375, 387, 404, 417, 421

LeMans, 71n

Leo, of Armenia, 94n, 130n

Leogria, John, count of, 140n

Léonardie, 196, 362

Libellus, 6, 23, 24

Lighush, 264n

Limassol, 80n, 81n, 84n, 85, 93, 95, 97, 107

Limousin, 360n

Lions, king's feast at, 39

Lisbon, 42n, 137n

Longchamp, Stephen de, 351, 375; in attack on caravan, 388, 405n

Longchamp, William de, bishop of Ely and chancellor, 39n, 326n, 327, 351n

Longobards, 52, 54, 55, 56, 58, 64

Loreora, Chotard de, 201n

Loriol, 46n

Louis VII of France, 71n, 206n

Louis VIII of France, 219n, 294n

Lusignan, Aymeri de, of Cyprus, see Aymeri de Lusignan

Lusignan, Geoffrey de, 94n, 131-32, 136, 141n, 142n, 144, 176, 197, 275, 278n, 301, 318n; given Ascalon and Jaffa, 211

Lusignan, Guy de, of Jerusalem, see Guy de Lusignan

Lusignan, Hugh I of, 94n

Lusignan, Hugh II of, 94n

Lusignan, Hugh VIII of, 56n, 232n

Lusignan, Hugh le Brun, IX lord of, and count of La Marche, 56, 66n, 94n, 201n, 209, 233

Lusignan, house of, 94n

Lydda, bishop of, see St. George

Lydda, offered to Richard, 396n; divided, 431n

Lyons, 45n, 46n; collapse of Rhone bridge at, 14, 21, 47; pilgrims' arrival at, 45

Magna Villa, Ernauld de, 201n

Mahomerie, 141

Mailly, Jacques de, 124

Maine, 323

Male Cousine, 201

Malesmains (Malmains, Malleman), Gilbert, 159n, 388

Malet, William, 201n

Male Voisine, 201

Malus Catulus, Roger, 83n

Mamelukes: filled with shame that they fled Jaffa, 412, 414; quarrel among Kurds and, 416

Manceaux, 57, 259

Manche, La, 199n

Mare, Hugh de la, 90

Mare, Robert de la, 201n

Mare, William de la, 201n

Marescallie, 127

Margarit of Brindisi, count of Malta and Cephalonia, 51n, 54, 55; participation in third crusade, 82n

Margat, 82n, 106n, 109

Mariduc, 166

Maron, 281n

Maron, Renier de, 281

Maron, Walter de, 281

Marone, Peter de, 282n

Marquis, the, see Montferrat, Conrad

Marranus, Pontius, 282n

Marseilles, 26, 42n, 48, 147; itinerary of Richard's voyage from, to Messina, 455

Marsile, 325

Martel, William, 201n

Martigue, 46n

Martin, Sanchez, 129n

Mary, Virgin, tomb, 440

Mashtub, 212, 213n, 214n, 218n, 228n, 341n, 437

Mategrifon, built by Richard, 64

Mauléon, Raoul de, 201n, 405, 418, 421

Mauléon, Savari de, 405n

Mayenne, Juquel de, 387

Meisières, Guy de, 159n

Melissende of Jerusalem, 120n, 122n

Melitène, Gabriel of, 102n

Mello (Merle), Dreux de, 69n, 100, 251

Mello, William de (G. de), 69n, 192, 251

Melloc, William and Henry de, 295

Merle, 243

Mesnil, Thoril de, 157

Messina, Richard, archbishop of, 55n, 66n

Messina, Lighthouse, Beacon, or Pharos of, 48, 71, 74; Philip's arrival at, 50; Richard's arrival at and capture of, 51-73; itinerary of Richard's voyage from Marseilles to, 455

Milly, Henry de, 257n

Milly, Philip de, 281n

Milly, Stéphanie de, 121n

Mirabel, 272, 302, 317, 431n

Monreale, William, archbishop of, 55n, 66, 230n

Montbéliard, Eudes de, 130n

Montchablon, Clarembald de, 372, 374

Montdragon, 46n

Mont Escot, 45n

Montferrat, Conrad, marquis of, 14, 21, 24, 25, 93n, 98n, 100n, 115n, 121n, 129n, 132, 139n, 143, 158n, 212n, 277n, 282n, 287n, 332n, 335n, 338n, 342n, 343n, 346n; vassalage to Saladin, 27; refusal to surrender Tyre, 132; despite him many join Guy, 132; at Acre, 143; seeking the crown, marries Isabelle, 177; wives, 178, 179; Saracens raid wedding feast, 179; returns to Tyre, 180; crusaders vituperate the marquis, 182-87; treaty between Guy and, 210; upheld by Philip, 211; given Beirut, Sidon, and Tyre, 211; truculence, 224; refuses to join host, 225, 313; led to yield his hostages, 226;

hostages slaughtered by Christians, 227; Saladin negotiating for separate peace with, 291n; Genoese stood by, 315; sows dissension, 316; summons French, 319; barons ask that he be made king, 329; always with the French, 329; barons sent to fetch him and the French back, 330; earlier negotiations with Saladin, 330; terms of peace with Saladin, 331; receives news of his election, preparations for coronation, 333; assassination, 334; despair at his death, 336

Montferrat, William III, marquis of, 93n, 121n, 132n; son of, see Jaffa, William Longsword, count of

Montfort, Amaury de, 66n

Montgibel, 74n

Montjoie, 438

Montoire, Sir Joscelyn de, 188

Montmiral, John de, 159n

Montmorency, Mathew de, 69n

Montreal, Aurelin de, 140n

Montreal, Crac of, see Crac of Montreal

Montrichard, 43n

Mont Saint Angelo (county), 61n

Mordrensis (?), bishop of, 159n

Mortemer, Bartholomew of, 418

Mosul, 429n

Motte de Galure, 46n

Moulins, Roger des, 124n

Moulins-Engelbert, 45n

Mount Calvary, 439

Mount Musart, 115n, 138

Mount of Olives, pilgrimage to, 392, 438

Mount Sion, 439

Museh, Kurdish emir, 264n

Naples, 54n

Naplouse, Garnier de, 10, 15, 257, 371; confusion in references to, in Itinerarium, 12

Naplouse, 122n, 281n, 332n

Navarre, Berengaria of, see Berengaria

Navarre, Blanche of, 71n

Navarre, Sancho VI of, 71

Nazareth, 431n; battle of, 124n; Hubert Walter gains permission for priests to sing mass at, 443

Nazareth, bishop of, 159n
Nazereth (Letard?), archbishop of, 230n
Néel, Robert, 294
Neubourg, Henry de, earl of Warwick, 199n
Nevers, count of, 69n
Neville, Hugh de, 418
Newbroke, Robert de, 66n, 199, 295
Nicholas, chaplain, 95n
Nicosia, 91n, 96, 101, 102, 103, 104
Norgate, Kate, 11, 12, 18; quoted, 8 ff.; on Ambroise and Richard of Holy Trinity, 9
Normans, 250, 261; at Messina, 57
Novare, Philip de, 130n
Noyers, Clarembald de, 159n

Old Man of the Mountain, head of religious sect of the Assassins, 335, 336; blamed for assassination of Conrad, 338n, Sinan, 398n
Oliver, 198
Olives, Mount of, 438
Orange, 46n
Orontes river, watermills on, 149n
Orques, Richard d', 372, 373, 374n
Orques, Thierri d', 372, 373, 374n
Orsini, 54n
Ostia, bishop of, 159n
Otto, a squire, 372

Palermo, 49, 57, 62
Paleys, 46n
Paris, son of Priam, 180
Paris, Gaston, 18; his edition of Estoire first brought MS to light, 4; facts deduced about Ambroise, 5; conclusions regarding poem and its relation to Itinerarium regis Ricardi, 6; belief that Richard of Holy Trinity was plagiarist, 7; on Ambroise, 19
Passelari, constable of Concon, prisoner spared by Richard, 228n
Patriarch of Jerusalem, see Jerusalem
Pepin, 180
Perche, Rotrou II, count of, 192, 371n
Persians, 421
Peter the Gascon, 351

Philip, 372, 374
Philip II, king of France, 5, 6, 33, 34n, 40-41, 41n, 46, 55n, 59-63nn, 68, 69, 70, 73n, 80, 81n, 93, 93n, 100, 100n, 116, 140n, 156n, 191, 191n, 192n, 193, 199n, 200n, 206n, 212n, 218n, 219, 219n, 221, 268n, 338n, 387n, 434n; meeting at Vézelay, 43; agree to division of conquests, 44; uncourtly arrival at Messina, 50; arrival at Acre, 51n, 80, 191; at Messina, 55, 56, 58, 60, 64; perfidy, 63; conservative financially, 194n; moves to the attack, 196; taken sick, 196n, 198, 201; wall is breached by, 205; granted truce to Mashtub and Karakush, 213n; plans to quit the crusade, 218; haste to return home the result of his sickness, 219; Richard plotted the death of, 219n; entrusts his men to duke of Burgundy, 220; swears to keep peace in the West, 220-21; disposition of hostages, 221; discord and severance from Richard's host, 319, 324; warned to guard against Assassins, 338; envoys of, urged John to betray Richard, 356; tried to have Richard kept in prison, 447n
Philip de Dreux, bishop of Beauvais, see Beauvais, bishop of
Pin, Jourdain du, 51n, 54, 55
Pisa, archbishop of, 55n
Pisa, Alberic, archbishop of, 178n
Pisans, Richard allied with, 118; join Guy, 133; valiant stand at Acre, 138, 141, 151; punished for profiteering, 190; badly timed attack by, 210; and Genoese in fierce dissent, 315; Richard brings reconciliation, 316; bravery, 405; aid Richard, 415; sufferings, 419
Plantagenets, abbreviated genealogy, 451; see Henry; Joanna; John; Richard
Plebanus, the Pisan, 143n
Plunder, 92, 106; host fall upon rich, 318; spoils of the Egyptian caravan, 388
Poitevins, 57, 259
Poitiers, Raymond of, 131n
Poitiers, William of, 359-61
Ponthieu, John, count of, 159n

Préaux, John de, *66n*, *200n*, 405, 419

Préaux, Pierre (Peter) de, *188n*, *200n*, 224, 296, 405, 409, 435

Préaux, William de, 10, *200n*, 281-82, 405; ransom of, 445

Prices, high, 181; drop, 190

Pulani, 16

Quahadin, *see* Taki ed Din

Quarantaine, La, *376n*

Quincy, Robert de, 225

Ram, made by crusaders, 168; burned, 170

Ramleh, Saladin's order to raze, 272; Turkish host at, 284-85; crusaders encamp at, 292, 390; town wrecked, 292; Richard returns to, 305; partitioned, *430n*, *431n*

Rançon, Geoffrey de, *66n*, *201n*

Raymond Rupin, *129n*, *352n*

Recordane, 174

Reggio, William, archbishop of, 66

Reggio, 71

Rheims, Auberi of, 401, 403

Rhodes, voyage to, 75-80

Rhone, crossing of, 46; collapse of bridge, 14, 21, 47

Ribole, Hugh de, 284

Richard, king, knowledge gained during campaigns in Palestine, 27; coronation, 37; preparations for the crusade, 38; meeting at Vézelay, 43; agrees to division of conquests, 44; arrival at Messina, 51; attacks Messina, 57-60; Joanna's dower claimed by, 61; builds Mategrifon, 63; freed of his obligation to marry Alice of France, *63n*, *68n*; lordship of Gisors surrendered, *63n*; offered concessions by Tancred, 64; sister brought back to him, 67; peace with Tancred restored, 68; generosity, 68, 193; met by his mother accompanying Berengaria, 71; leaves Messina, 73; finds his sister and his bride in Cyprus, 81; vessels scattered or shipwrecked, 83; marries Berengaria, 95; captures Cyprus, 84-107; arrival at Acre, 116, 192; accepts alliance of Pisans, but refuses that of Genoese, 118; malady

causes delay, 194, 196, 201, 203; though ill, directs attack on Acre, 207; refused truce to Mashtub and Karakush, *213n*; plotted death of Philip, *219n*; refuses to give up prisoners or to give hostages, *227n*; decision to slay Saracens, 228; plans to move southward, 228; suffers a slight wound, 246; conference with Saphadin, *248n*; Saracens repulsed anew with great loss at Arsur, 264; Saracens pay tribute to his valor, 270; advises against allowing destruction of Ascalon, 276; goes back to Acre to rally his men, 278; falls into an ambush, 280; spurns counsels of caution: marches out from Jaffa, 283; imperious demands upon Saracens, 290; terms upon which Saladin will meet demands, 290; rejected, 291; advised not to lay siege to Jerusalem, 300; dissuaded from his proposed march on Jerusalem, *303n*; reunites the host, 308; assumes costs of refortifying Ascalon, 311; effort to persuade French to stay with him, 320; ill tidings from England, 326; slandered, 337; blamed for assassination of Conrad, *338n*; hears news of Henry's election, 340; approves election of Henry: opposes his marriage, 341; envoys bring disquieting news from England, 346; marches to Le Daron, 347; gives Le Daron to Henry, 353; takes the Fig Tree, 354; decides that he must depart, 356; accused by host of planning to withdraw from Holy Land, 359, 360; vows to remain until Easter, 363; receives a piece of the True Cross, 376; refuses to besiege Jerusalem, 377; flouted in song, writes one of those who vilify him, 393; asks a truce, which is refused, 396; goes to the relief, 404; forces a landing on beach, 409; heroism, 408, 410, 421, 423, 425; recaptures Jaffa, 410; plot to capture him, 412, 414; sick unto death, defies Saladin, 426; feels that cause is lost, 428; asks Saphadin to arrange a truce, 429; land from Tyre to Cæsarea and lordship of

Jaffa given to, 429n; desire to save his face and honor among his people, 430n; Treaty of Jaffa, 431; ill and suffering, leaves Syria, 446; journey's end, 446; in Austrian dungeon cell and in Germany, 447; itinerary from Marseilles to Messina, 455; march from Acre to Jaffa, 456

Richard of Holy Trinity, *Itinerarium regis Ricardi*, 6; comparison of his work and that of Ambroise, 7 ff.; Paris's belief that he was a plagiarist, 7; quoted, 11; reference to auditor, 13

Richard de Templo, *see* Richard of Holy Trinity

Ridefort, Girard de, Master of the Temple, 124n, 143n

Rigord, 22

Roche Guillaume, 135n

Roches, William des, 201n, 434

River Rochetaillée, 249

Roger II, king of Sicily, 40n

Roland, 198

Romans, 46n

Rome, 32, 79, 323

Rouen, Walter of Coutances, archbishop of, 66n, 67, 72

Round Cistern, caravan with rich booty reported at, 383

Rovroi, Ralph de, 58

Sablé, Robert de, 42n, 61, 66n, 434n

Saci, Roger de, 405, 418

Sacrilege, reward of, 164

Saforie, 126, 431n

St. Abacuc, 278

St. Anne, 358

St. Celerin, 358

St. Denis, 41

St. Edmund's Bury monastery, 91n

St. Elias, abbot of, given watch over the True Cross, 376

St. George, Syrian bishop of, 376n

St. George of Lydda, bishop of, 127n, 230n

St.-George of Lydda, 272, 323n, 391n, 395; battle with Turks at, 293-95

St.-Gilles, count of, 361; *see also* Toulouse

St. Hilarion castle, *see* Dieudamor

St. James the Apostle, 266

St. John, Henry de, 403n

St. Lambert of Liège, 381

St. Leonard, 313

Ste.-Marie, Sir Ralph de, 295

St. Nicholas church (near Acre), 134n

St. Nicholas church (near Jaffa), 418

St. Omer, Walter de, 129n

St. Paul en Provence, 46n

St. Pol, Hugh IV, count of, 191n, 247, 287, 288, 293n

St. Pol, Yolande of Hainault, countess of, 191n

St. Samuel abbey, 438n

St. Valery, Bernard de, 159n

Saladin, vassalage of Conrad to, 27; alliance with Isaac Comnenus, 82; alliance with Raymond of Tripoli, 122; invades Syria, 124; summons men from his nine realms, 125; domains, 125n; overwhelms army at Hattin, 126; overruns the land, 127; fortifies and defends Acre, 134, 135; pledged to make such a peace as Saracens demand, 213; Saracens plead with, for aid, 213; promises succor, 215; which he is unable to send, 216; agreed to surrender, 216; let hostages perish, 224; refused to return the Cross, 224n; fails to redeem Conrad's hostages, 226; failure to come to appointed meeting with Richard, 226; returned captives to previous owners, kept money and Cross, 228n; army of, 256; jeers at his men, 269; answered by his son, 270; orders destruction of fortresses of Ascalon, 271; Richard opens negotiations with, 289; terms upon which he meets Richard's demands, 290; Richard rejects terms, 291; negotiating for separate peace with Conrad, 291n; repairs to Jerusalem, 298; sent Christian captives, 312; death, 322; terms of peace with Conrad, 331; blamed for assassination of Conrad, 338n; Richard asks a truce, which is refused, 396; demands that Ascalon be destroyed and left as neutral ground, 396n; host of, 398;

Saladin (*continued*)
    descends upon Jaffa, 399; makes jesting
    with his Saracens sting, 425; terms of
    peace with Richard, 429*n;* declares
    Richard the prince whom with least re-
    morse he would see conquer the land,
    432; insures safe-conduct of pilgrims,
    436; Hubert Walter courteously re-
    ceived by, 440; offers bishop any gift
    within his power to give, 442
Salisbury, bishop of, *see* Hubert Walter
Salisbury, Patrick, earl of, 93*n*
Salloch, Marianne, *Die lateinische Fort-
    setzung Wilhelms von Tyrus,* 5*n*
Salon, 46*n*
Salt river, Richard encamped on, 247
Sancerre, Stephen, count of, 159
Sanguin d'Aleppo, tribute to Richard, 270
San Severino, William de, 65*n*
Saphadin, 27, 109, 115, 205, 238*n*, 248*n*,
    271, 290, 291, 396, 398, 421, 433, 435,
    436, 437; Richard knighted son of,
    318*n*; refused consent to pact between
    Saladin and Conrad, 331; proposed
    marriage of Joanna to, 49*n*, 290*n*,
    331*n*; asked to intercede for a truce at
    Jaffa, 402; offers steeds of Araby to
    Richard, 422; Richard asks him to ar-
    range a truce, 429; authorized to make
    peace, 430*n*
Satalie, gulf of, 80
Satya, Roger de, 201*n*
Sauçoi, Maheu de, 57
Scalons, abbot of, 159*n*
Scandalion, Agnes de, 282*n*
Scandalion, 115, 134
Scurvy, attacks the host, 183
Scylla and Charybdis, 48*n*
Seis, John, count of, 140*n*
Senas, 46*n*
Senlis, Guy de, 178*n*, 179
Sepulcher: pilgrims set out for, 32, 36,
    150, 299, 300, 321, 394, 396*n*, 410,
    431, 433; Hubert Walter asks that
    priests be allowed to hold services at,
    442
Serpents, 242; stowed in Saracen ship, 111
Shipwreck, 83

Shirkuh, 109*n*, 212*n*
Sicily, Constance of, 40*n*
Sicily: participation in third crusade, 48,
    50, 53, 82*n*, 147; Richard sojourns in,
    48-73; genealogy of kings of, 453;
    kings of, *see* Tancred; William II
Sidon, Renaud of, 135*n*, 177*n*, 332, 431*n*
Sidon, (Eudes) bishop of, 230*n*
Sidon, 431*n*; Conrad to have lordship of,
    211, 331
Siege machinery, at Acre, 148; batters
    walls of Acre, 201; set up by Richard,
    348
Siloë, 392
Sinan, *see* Old Man of the Mountain
Sion, Mount, 439
Sorgues, 46*n*
Spartevento, cape, 74*n*
Stinging worms, 242
Storm: at sea, 74; delays arrival of sup-
    plies, 306
Stubbs, William, editor of *Itinerarium,* 6
Stuteville, N. de, 201*n*
Sybelle, queen, 93*n*, 120*n*, 121*n*; crowned,
    122*n*; death of, and her daughters, 170-
    71

Tabarie, 126
Tabarie brothers, 129; join Guy, 133; *see
    also* Tiberias
Taissons, Ralph de, 200, 434
Taki ed Din Omar, lord of Hama, 115*n*,
    205*n*, 262*n*
Talbot, Gilbert (Gerard), 14, 66*n*, 200
Tancarville, William II, chamberlain of,
    66*n*, 200
Tancred of Lecce, king of Sicily, 14, 40*n*,
    49, 54*n*, 55*n*; interview with King
    Richard, 15; Richard sends envoys to,
    60; Richard requires of him Joanna's
    dower, 61; replies with fair words, 62;
    Philip swears aid to, 63; offers conces-
    sions to Richard, 64; daughters of (Al-
    vira, Constance, Sybelle), 65*n*; offers
    his daughter to Arthur of Brittany, 65;
    which Richard accepts, 66; peace with
    Richard restored, 67, 68
Tantourah, 243*n*

Tarantulas, 242

Temple (Templars), 16, 32, 124, 143, 175, 218n, 227n, 267, 287, 369, 379, 380, 397, 403, 404, 410; at Acre, 141, 202; advance to the Doc, 175; on march from Caïphas, 241; take care of rear guard, 243, 247, 273; man vanguard, 250; guard foraging party, 285; attacked by Saracens, 286; raid near Jerusalem, 293n; oppose advance on Jerusalem, 300, 302; escort French to Acre, 320n, 323n; bought isle of Cyprus, 345, 346n; Richard ill, gives instructions to, 428; they refuse to serve without him, 429

Temple, Master of the, died at Acre, 143

Temple, Masters of, see Sablé, Robert de; Ridefort, Girard de

Teoni, Roger de, 251; at Acre, 199; Saracens fall on, 387, 388

Testudo, 203, 204, 207

Teutonic Knights, investiture of Maron granted to, 282n

Thuringia, Louis II, landgrave of, 139, 141, 155

Tiberias, Eschive of, 122n, 129n, 130n

Tiberias, Hugh of, 129, 130n, 133

Tiberias, Oste of, 129, 130n, 133

Tiberias, Ralph of, 129, 130n, 133

Tiberias, William of, 129, 130n, 133

Tiberias, bishop of, 230n

Tillières, Gilbert de, 159n

Tireproie, Peter, 57

Torel, Aymeri, 66n

Toron (near Acre), 134, 135, 136, 138, 141, 147

Toron (near Jaffa), 400, 401, 402, 403, 407

Toron of the Knights, 15, 367, 435; Saladin's flight to, 272, 292, 296, 365n, 367, 435; towers of, torn down, 298

Toron, Humphrey de, the constable, 121n

Toron, Humphrey IV de, 94n, 100n, 120, 121n, 122n, 178n, 332n; Isabelle's divorce from, 177

Tortosa, 109, 128

Toucy, Narjot de, 140n

Toulon, bishop of, 159n

Toulon, 45n

Toulouse, Raymond V, count of, 361n

Toulouse, Raymond VI of, 49n, 107n

Tours, 42, 43n

Tower of Flies, 167

Tower Maudite, 201, 202, 206

Tower of the Patriarch, 115n

Towers: built by crusaders, 155; burned, 156; of Ascalon, 310

Tozelais, 200

Trasignies, Otto of, 287, 330, 372n

Trie, conference between Gisors and, 34

Tripoli, Raymond III, count of, 25, 93n, 120n, 121n, 126, 129n, 143n, 177n, 332n, 352; charges against, 123; treason of, 122; described, 125; death, 124n, 128

Tripoli, 54n, 82n, 109, 129, 130, 131, 132, 352n; included in treaty of Jaffa, 431n

Tristan, 180

Troyes, Thibaut de, 403

Trussebot, Robert, 159n, 188

Turcomans, captured by Richard, 125n, 368, 437n

Turcoples, 101, 383, 385

Turenne, viscount of, 140n

Turnham, Robert de, 72n, 108n

Turnham, Stephen de, 83n, 108n, 290n, 293n, 332

Tyois, Henry de, 418

Tyre, Joscius, archbishop of, 35

Tyre: defense of, 26; Richard's fleet before, 115; siege of, 129; barred to King Guy, 132; food detained at, 177; French return, 305; French summoned to, 319; Isabelle charged to guard, 337; lords of France contrive to seize, 339; given to Count Henry, 342, 345; Christians to hold, 431n

Valence, 46n

Vascueil, Gilbert de, 66n, 72

Venetians, 126

Verdun, Bertrand de, 66n, 200

Vernon, Richard de, 159n

Verona, Adelardo Cattaneo, bishop of, 140n, 146, 188

Vézelay, Richard and Philip arrange to meet at, 41; meeting, 43, 44, 45n

Viaires, 74

Vienne, Ferri de, 371, 372

Vienne, Ingelremmus de, 140n

Villefranche, 45n

Villehardouin, 3, 4, 18

Vipont, Ivo de, 159n

Waldin, Osbert, 403n

Walter, Hubert, bishop of Salisbury and archbishop of Canterbury, 39n, 159n, 187, 189, 209, 224, 371n, 434; generosity, 191; truce sought by, 429n; received by Saladin, 440; he praises Richard and the Sultan, 441; offered any gift within Saladin's power, 442; he asks that priests be allowed to hold services at the Sepulcher, 442; and at Bethlehem and Nazareth, 443

Wavrin, Helin de, 139

Wells, polluted, 392n

Welshman, duel with Turk, 166

William II, king of Sicily, 40, 49, 54n, 61n, 62, 82, 131n

William of Tyre, first book of the *Itinerarium* derived from Latin Continuator of, 5n, 22

Williams, H. M., quoted, 196n

Winchester, Geoffrey de Lucy, bishop of, 39n

Windmill, first in Syria, 149

Women, remain in Acre, 233; at Jaffa, 277

York, Geoffrey, archbishop of, 39n

Yusuf, chamberlain, 389n